Penguin Nature Library
GENERAL EDITOR: EDWARD HOAGLAND
NORTH AMERICAN INDIANS

GEORGE CATLIN was born at Wilkes-Barre, Pennsylvania, in 1796, the fifth of fourteen children. He was educated as a lawyer and practiced in Philadelphia for two years before abandoning the bar in 1823 for a career as a portrait painter. Catlin had been interested in Indian life since his boyhood, and in 1831 he began a series of visits to various tribes, chiefly in the plains. He spent several years living among the Indians of North America, acquiring their languages, studying their habits, customs and mode of life, and making copious notes and numerous sketches for paintings. In 1837, he gathered together his huge collection of pictures and artifacts and repaired to Albany, New York, to prepare what he called "Catlin's Indian Gallery"—310 oil paintings and 200 oils of other subjects, as well as a large number of ornamental shirts, robes, drums, headdresses and other articles. The show was exhibited around the United States and in Europe to great acclaim. His journals, *The Manners, Customs and Condition of the North American Indian*, were published in Philadelphia in 1841. In his late fifties, Catlin traveled extensively throughout South America and the Pacific coast of North America—a journey described in his *Last Rambles Amongst the Indians of the Rocky Mountains and the Andes* (1867). He died in Jersey City, New Jersey on December 22, 1872.

PETER MATTHIESSEN was born in New York City in 1927 and had already begun his writing career by the time he graduated from Yale University in 1950. A founder of *The Paris Review*, Matthiessen is the author of five novels, a collection of short stories, and numerous works of nonfiction, including *In the Spirit of Crazy Horse*, *Indian Country* and *The Snow Leopard*, which won the National Book Award in 1978.

PENGUIN NATURE LIBRARY

Beautiful Swimmers by William W. Warner
(Introduction by John Barth)

Cape Cod by Henry David Thoreau
(Introduction by Paul Theroux)

Driftwood Valley by Theodora C. Stanwell-Fletcher
(Introduction by Wendell Berry)

The Exploration of the Colorado River by John Wesley Powell
(Introduction by Wallace Stegner)

The Journals of Lewis and Clark
(Edited and with an Introduction by Frank Bergon)

The Land of Little Rain by Mary Austin
(Introduction by Edward Abbey)

North American Indians by George Catlin
(Edited and with an Introduction by Peter Matthiessen)

The Maine Woods by Henry David Thoreau
(Introduction by Edward Hoagland)

Mountaineering in the Sierra Nevada by Clarence King
(Introduction by William Howarth)

My First Summer in the Sierra by John Muir
(Introduction by Gretel Ehrlich)

The Naturalist on the River Amazons by Henry Walter Bates
(Introduction by Alex Shoumatoff)

Nature's Diary by Mikhail Prishvin
(Introduction by John Updike)

The Outermost House by Henry Beston
(Introduction by Robert Finch)

Songs of the North by Sigurd Olson
(Edited and with an Introduction by Howard Frank Mosher)

This Incomperable Lande: A Book of American Nature Writing
Edited by Thomas J. Lyon

Travels by William Bartram
(Introduction by James Dickey)

Wild Animals I Have Known by Ernest Thompson Seton
(Introduction by Noel Perrin)

North American Indians

GEORGE CATLIN

EDITED AND WITH
AN INTRODUCTION BY

Peter Matthiessen

PENGUIN BOOKS

PENGUIN BOOKS
Published by the Penguin Group
Viking Penguin, a division of Penguin Books USA Inc.,
375 Hudson Street, New York, New York 10014, U.S.A.
Penguin Books Ltd, 27 Wrights Lane,
London W8 5TZ, England
Penguin Books Australia Ltd, Ringwood,
Victoria, Australia
Penguin Books Canada Ltd, 10 Alcorn Avenue, Suite 300,
Toronto, Ontario, Canada M4V 3B2
Penguin Books (N.Z.) Ltd, 182–190 Wairau Road,
Auckland 10, New Zealand

Penguin Books Ltd, Registered Offices:
Harmondsworth, Middlesex, England

This edition first published in simultaneous hardcover and paperback
editions by Viking Penguin, a division of Penguin Books USA Inc. 1989

5   7   9   10   8   6   4

Introduction copyright © Peter Matthiessen, 1989
All rights reserved

Artwork courtesy of the National Museum of American Art, Smithsonian
Institution, Gift of Mrs. Joseph Harrison, Jr.

LIBRARY OF CONGRESS CATALOGING IN PUBLICATION DATA
Catlin, George, 1796–1872.
North American Indians/by George Catlin; edited and with an
introduction by Peter Matthiessen.
p.   cm.—(Penguin nature library)
ISBN 0 14 017.014 6
1. Indians of North America.   2. Indians of North America—West
(U.S.)   I. Matthiessen, Peter.   II. Title.   III. Series.
E77.C415   1989
978′.00497—dc19   88–40484

Printed in the United States of America

Set in Bulmer
Designed by Ann Gold

PENGUIN NATURE LIBRARY

Nature is our widest home. It includes the oceans that provide our rain, the trees that give us air to breathe, the ancestral habitats we shared with countless kinds of animals that now exist only by our sufferance or under our heel.

Until quite recently, indeed (as such things go), the whole world was a wilderness in which mankind lived as cannily as deer, overmastering with spears or snares even their woodsmanship and that of other creatures, finding a path wherever wildlife could go. Nature was the central theater of life for everybody's ancestors, not a hideaway where people went to rest and recharge after a hard stint in an urban or suburban arena, and many of us still do swim, hike, fish, birdwatch, sleep on the ground or paddle a boat on vacation, and will loll like a lizard in the sun any other chance we have. We can't help grinning for at least a moment at the sight of surf, or sunlight on a river meadow, as if remembering in our mind's eye paleolithic pleasures in a home before memories officially began.

It is a thoughtless grin because nature predates "thought." Aristotle was a naturalist, and nearer to our own time, Darwin and Thoreau made of the close observation of bits of nature a lever to examine life in many ways on a large scale. Yet nature writing, despite its basis in science, usually rings with rhapsody as well—a belief that nature is an expression of God.

In this series we are presenting some nature writers of the past century or so, though leaving out great novelists like Turgenev, Melville, Conrad and Faulkner, who were masters of natural description, and poets such as Homer (who was perhaps the first nature writer, once his words had been transcribed). Nature writing now combines rhapsody with science and connects science with rhapsody. For that reason it is a very special and a nourishing genre.

—Edward Hoagland

INTRODUCTION

◄——————————————►

*E*arly fire in the leaves brightens the ravines of high, bare hills across the canyon. A cool autumnal wind wanders this lookout high above the great Snake River, which not far south of this Wyoming peak bends westward through the Tetons into its high hawk-shadowed canyons in south Idaho. This is spare country of great space and light, of thin air and faraway echoes. Even the pine forests seem spare, and the wind in the pine boughs deepens the silence, with its faint seeping melancholy of mortality.

From this high prospect on a clear Indian Summer day, I can gaze up the broad river valley all the way north to the Absarokas. The Snake is born there in the Absarokas, east of Yellowstone, and this pine slope seems an auspicious spot to take first notes for an homage to George Catlin, for it is here in our northern Rocky Mountain ranges, with their national parks and forests, that one faintly discerns the great western America that Catlin saw one hundred and fifty years ago.

Indeed it was Catlin who first recommended the creation of a "nation's Park" for the great bison herds in the northern plains at the confluence of the Yellowstone River with the upper Missouri:

> And in future what a splendid contemplation . . . when one . . . imagines them as they *might* be seen, by some great protecting policy of government preserved in their pristine beauty and wildness, in a *magnificent park*, where the world could see for ages to come, the native Indian in his classic attire, galloping his wild horse, with sinewy bow, and shield and lance, amid the fleeting herds of elks and buffaloes. . . . A *nation's Park*, containing man and beast, in all the wild and freshness of their nature's beauty!

Forty years would pass before a very different park of mountains, lakes, and forest would eventually be created at the Yellowstone's headwaters, not far north of this mountainside where I now write.

In his great study of the Plains tribes, Catlin called the Shoshone "the Snake Indians," the name provided to the westering white men by the tribe's Lakota enemies—themselves called "Sioux," or "Adders," by their Ojibwa enemies to the east. The Snake River below is named accordingly. The Shoshone and the Absaroka (called "the Crow") departed the upper Yellowstone with the founding of the Park in 1872, and the Indians are gone from this part of Wyoming, though some Arapaho and eastern Shoshone subsist on the Wind River reservation, to the east.

Even today, moose, elk, and bear prevail in this rough country. Drifting the Snake in the burning September light, casting along the gravel bars for cutthroat trout, one may see Lewis's woodpecker or Clark's nutcracker carry the sun across the sparkling river to the spruce and aspens. On yesterday's trip across the ridges to the east, five mule deer stood in silhouette in the silver ripples of a daybreak creek. Where the mountains descended to the Plains I saw antelope and sandhill cranes, a golden eagle, a great company of migrant hawks, a darting mink in the rocks of the Green River.

If Meriwether Lewis and William Clark were the first white Americans to explore the west half of the continent, from the Mississippi at St. Louis to the northwest Pacific coast, George Catlin traveled at least as many miles on his journeys by canoe and horse from Minnesota and the Montana border south to eastern Texas, as well as forays to the Gulf states and South Carolina, seeking to record the Indians in paintings and journals. Taken together, Catlin's works constitute the first, last, and only "complete" record of the Plains Indians ever made at the height of their splendid culture, so soon destroyed by traders' liquor and disease, rapine, and bayonets.

Even while he immortalized the western horse tribes, he anticipated and deplored the certain doom of these honest and innocent peoples, outgunned and outnumbered, who stood in the way of the westward course of empire. "The tribes of the red men of North America, as a nation of human beings, are on their wane," as he concludes in his first letter; "(to use their own very beautiful figure), 'they are fast travelling to the shades of their fathers, towards the setting sun.'"

North American Indians (more properly, *Letters and Notes on the Manners, Customs and Conditions of the North American Indians Written During Eight Years' Travel (1832–1839) Amongst the Wildest Tribes of Indians of North America*) is the second of three classic accounts of the Indians and landscapes and wild creatures of the American West written in the first half of the nineteenth century. The first was the *Journal of Captain Meriwether Lewis* (concerning his westward journey of discovery with William Clark in 1803–6), which sets forth the majesty and silence of an unknown country of wild peoples; the third was Francis Parkman's *The California and Oregon Trail*, published in 1849—less than a half century later—in which Catlin's dire prophecies about the future of the Indians are already coming to pass. These epochal works are supported by more particular accounts by writers, naturalists, and others (Prince Maximilian de Wied, Thomas Say, Thomas Nuttall, James Fenimore Cooper, Washington Irving, John James Audubon, for example), some of whom accompanied government exploring surveys of the new Territories.

Meanwhile, such contemporary artists as Titian Peale and Karl Bodmer (who accompanied Prince Maximilian)—and later Albert Bierstadt, Thomas Moran, and many others, all of them formally trained as George Catlin was not—imposed the romantic and melancholy grandeur of the Hudson River School on western landscapes. Mostly these artists failed to capture the broad light of the Plains and the dry grit and feel of Indian country. Bodmer's work was frequently superb, yet he seemed more struck by Indian finery than by the strong quirks of countenance in the untamed men and women that are so affecting in Catlin's portraits. In the field Catlin made sketches in brown ink as well as formal studies, which seem to anticipate the studio portraits by the photographer Edward Curtis. (Like many nineteenth-century oil portraitists, he would paint the backgrounds in his spare time, and the figures later.)

Because Catlin perceived his colorful subjects as individual human beings, worthy of criticism and gentle ridicule as well as profound admiration (by Parkman's time, a racist contempt for

Indians was already the murderous fashion), his people are unromanticized and never stereotyped, neither in his paintings nor in his prose. His painting was vital and his narrative gift exceptional—one has only to read the story of the Dog (pp. 240–247).

Catlin's painting was occasionally belittled as self-taught and "primitive," lacking sophistication in perspective as well as anatomy, and it is true that he lacked the fine technique of his contemporaries in the Hudson River School, or of Bierstadt and Bodmer, for that matter. His one wish was faithfully to record American Indians before their "native dignity and beauty and independence" were destroyed. This noble ambition, which seized George Catlin early in his career, has put us forever in his debt.

My own interest in George Catlin began in the 1950s with the preparation of *Wildlife in America,* an account of the rare, threatened, and extinct species of North American vertebrates, and an early text on modern conservation. That book was based on library research, correspondence with biologists, and field trips, which took me to most of the game preserves, parks, and fish and wildlife refuges in the West. In the course of this research, I came upon George Catlin. Four of his animal paintings— "Hunting Antelope," "Buffalo Hunting in Winter," "Prairie Dog Town," "Buffalo Hunting with Wolf Skins"—together with a page of sketches of symbols and totems were used as endpapers and illustrations for that book.

Catlin's wonderful accounts of American Indians are everywhere infused with celebrations of the bountiful North American plains game, at that time unmatched anywhere on earth excepting Africa, and also the myriad fish, birds, and furred animals which supported the abundant culture of the horse tribes. The utter diminishment of these wild creatures—the bison and wolf, golden eagle, and grizzly in particular—deepens our feeling of great loss that such a wild and splendid spectacle is gone forever. Yet these striking creatures may still be found in remote corners of these Rocky Mountain foothills and northern plains. In my travels for *Wildlife in America,* I saw an astonishing congregation of thirty-seven grizzlies at the Trout Creek dump back in the sage plains of Yellowstone Park, and elk and bison as abundant as in Catlin's day on the grassy hills just across the Wyoming border, in Montana.

In fact the only animal that seems to have disappeared is the black-footed ferret, an elegant nocturnal predator of the prairie dog towns, which was first scientifically described in 1849 (by John James Audubon and John Bachman, from a specimen sent by a British trader from "the Plains of the Platte River, in Nebraska") thirteen years after Catlin's journeys in the region, and has been deemed extinct on several occasions since. I once spent a night here in Wyoming, in prairie dog range east of Meteetse, hunting in vain for this elusive mustelid, which that same summer (1985) was reduced by epidemic in its only known habitat from 128 animals to none—its most recent presumed extinction in the wild.

George Catlin, fifth of Putnam and Polly Catlin's fourteen children, began a dramatic and near-tragic life in 1796 in the Wyoming Valley of Pennsylvania, where his mother had been taken captive in an Indian massacre only eighteen years before. In his childhood the family moved up the Susquehanna Valley to a riverbank house in New York State, where Catlin acquired the expertise with canoes, firearms, and fishing rods that would later sustain him on the western rivers. At twenty-one, he studied law in Litchfield, Connecticut, and two years later he was practicing in Lucerne, Pennsylvania, but already he was teaching himself to sketch and draw. In 1823, with the boldness that would mark his whole career, he sold his law books, disposed of almost everything but his rifle and fishing tackle, and moved to the country's cultural seat at Philadelphia, where he established himself quickly as a portrait painter and was speedily elected to the Philadelphia Academy of Art. One of his subjects was Governor DeWitt Clinton, in magisterial robes, bearing a scroll, at New York City Hall.

Catlin's work with Indians was contemporaneous with the dark period of Indian Removal, when most of the great eastern tribes were banished to the West. The western tribes were still intact, and in this period, Catlin observed in Philadelphia a delegation of undomesticated Indians from the Great Plains on their way through to Washington, D.C. Catlin realized at once where his work lay. "Nothing," he wrote, "short of the loss of my life shall prevent me from visiting their country and becoming their historian."

Catlin had already executed his first known portrait of an Indian, a strong and enigmatic portrait of the Seneca orator Red Jacket done in 1826, three years before the portrait of Governor Clinton, but these Six Nations people of northern New York, already acculturated, could scarcely be compared with the "wild" Indians seen in Philadelphia. Once again, this impetuous man—in an early self-portrait, at least, he is handsome, a slender, large-eyed, and open-faced young fellow, with dark wavy hair—abandoned his hard-earned security, surmounted the protests of friends and family ("I broke from them all—from my wife and my aged parents—myself my only adviser and protector"), and committed himself to the creation of an "Indian Gallery," to be based on his own fieldwork in the West.

It was Lewis's associate, General William Clark, now Superintendent of Indian Affairs for the western tribes, who in the spring of 1831 welcomed George Catlin to St. Louis. That summer Clark escorted Catlin up the Mississippi to Prairie du Chien, in present-day Wisconsin, where the Sioux, Iowa, Missouri, and Sauk and Fox were holding council. Back in St. Louis, he painted the Sauk and Fox chief Black Hawk, vanquished leader of the so-called Black Hawk's War, who was being sent "to be gazed at" in the eastern cities (and would remind President Andrew Jackson, instigator of the Indian Removal Act, "You are a man; I am another"). Early the next year he went up the Missouri and the Platte in what is now Nebraska to see the Oto and Omaha, the Missouri and Pawnee. Wherever he went, he set out a little sign: "G. Catlin, Artist."

Then, in the spring of 1832, on the maiden voyage of the American Fur Company steamboat *Yellow Stone,* he journeyed two thousand miles up the wide Missouri, stopping to paint some Lakota or "Teton Sioux" at the fur-trading post at Fort Pierre (now Pierre, South Dakota), and arriving eventually at Fort Union at the mouth of the Yellowstone, on the present-day North Dakota–Montana border. Here he celebrated his first impressions of Blackfoot and Assiniboin, Ojibwa, Crow, and "Knisteneaux" (Plains Cree). It was on this voyage that Catlin executed his first live scenes, not only riverscapes but Indian ceremonies, buffalo hunts, symbols or totems, animal studies. At the same time he wrote copious notes and open "letters" as correspondent for the *Spectator,* the *Daily Commercial Advertiser,* and other New York City publications. His eight "letters" from "the Mouth of the Yellow Stone" and the thirteen from a "Mandan Village," on the return journey, are by far the most extensive in all his accounts, constituting together nearly half of the whole journal; the exhilarated notes and paintings from this upper Missouri region are the very heart of Catlin's work.

At the end of that summer of 1832, Catlin descended from Fort Union by canoe with two trapper-guides, sending his paintings and huge artifact collection back downriver on the steamboat. On the way, he recorded the Pawnee (rather vaguely rendered by Titian Peale on the Platte River in 1820) and other buffalo hunters of the region, as well as the semi-civilized eastern peoples, mostly agriculturalists, who had been "removed" to the Plains. Meanwhile he stopped over at Fort Clark, the trading post nearest to the Mandan villages, where his paintings included a portrait of a beautiful young Mandan woman, "Mint," as well as the four-day "torture ceremony," a variation on the sun dance of the Plains tribes.

Captain Lewis wrote about the Mandans, with whom his expedition overwintered in 1804–5, but by comparison with those of Catlin, his observations had little insight into the culture of these curious and exceptionally interesting people, who would disappear forever as a tribe within a few years of Catlin's visit. In appendices to his second volume, Catlin vividly describes the sudden, appalling extinction of the Mandans by smallpox and suicide, and presents his evidence for a theory that this light-skinned, often light-haired people of peculiar customs were descended from an expedition of Welshmen in ten ships who were thought to have entered the Mississippi early in the fourteenth century, and that they came to the Missouri from the region of the Midwest that we associate today with the lost culture of the Mound-Builders. Whatever the validity of these ideas, Catlin's observations on these fascinating people are the best we have.

Farther south, Catlin visited some displaced eastern tribes—Shawnee, Delaware, Kickapoo, Kaskaskia—which had gathered disconsolately around Fort Leavenworth. He arrived back in St. Louis in the autumn and returned to his family in the East.

In 1834, Catlin painted the Osages around Fort Gibson, on the Arkansas River, and also the great displaced peoples of the Southeast, the Creek, Cherokee, and Choctaw, still in the throes of removal west of the Mississippi to "Indian Territory" in what would later be called Oklahoma. From there he travelled west into present-day Texas, on a very dangerous foray of mounted dragoons to "wild and untried regions of hostile Camanchees." (One of the dragoons, and a friend of Catlin, was young Jeff Davis, later President of the Confederacy.) In the winters of his arduous journeys, Catlin would travel with his wife, Clara, to the Gulf coast, taking notes on Indian peoples all the way.

The following spring (1835), he headed up the Mississippi from New Orleans to the woodland tribes around Fort Snelling in present-day Wisconsin, and from there in a birch-bark canoe to Iowa, where he portrayed the Sauk and Fox chief Keokuk. He went north again in 1836, recording Winnebagos and Menominees, and taking time for an expedition to the ancient quarry in southwest Minnesota that produces the brick-red stone named catlinite used by all the northern tribes for sacred pipes. (Catlin first observed such a pipe in the hand of the Blackfoot chief Buffalo's Back Fat, at Fort Union.) The pipestone quarry lay in the domain of hostile eastern Sioux, who tried to stop him. In a dangerous argument, Catlin advised them, "We have started to go and see it, and we cannot think of being stopped." Without this bold attitude, Catlin's great work would never have come into being.

In 1837, Catlin visited the Yuchis and "Seminoles"—Muskogee and Miccosukee Creeks—who were prisoners of war held at Fort Moultrie, near Charleston, South Carolina. Among the most moving passages in his letters is his account of the dying Muskogee war chief Osceola, whose astonishing likeness, with its grief-stricken eyes and enigmatic smile, is as fine as any portrait ever done by his academic contemporaries. (Among those who testified to Catlin's accuracy was the assistant surgeon at Fort Moultrie, Dr. Weedon, who subsequently—or so it is related—severed Osceola's head and used it to scare and discipline his children.)

> . . . he is a most extraordinary man, and one entitled to a better fate. In stature he is about at mediocrity, with an elastic and graceful movement; in his face he is good looking, with rather an effeminate smile; but of so peculiar a character, that the world may be ransacked over without finding another just like it. In his manners, and all his movements in company, he is polite and gentlemanly, though all his conversation is entirely in his own tongue; and his general appearance and actions, those of a full-blooded and wild Indian.

That Osceola was painted and described at the very end of Catlin's early travels suggests how surely his talents as painter and writer were maturing.

George Catlin is scarcely irreproachable. In the casual manner of his period, he blithely loots graves for the skulls of chiefs and empties his gun into a nuisance grizzly as he drifts away from the riverbank, simply to punish it. His plans for a "nation's Park" displaying hunting Indians for the white men's edification are as racist and delusory as they are well meant, and his conclusions about Indian cruelty in the Seminole wars (see p. 450) reflect the European prejudice that he condemns throughout his work. (Compare the letters of Lt. Ethan Allen Hitchcock, who was on the scene.) But only an honest and courageous man could adventure so bravely, survive near calamities, and write with Catlin's clear passion for his task, which carried him to the last days of his life. We trust him at once; the historical and ethnographic value of his work was recognized by informed people from the very start.

Later in 1837, having gathered together his huge collection of pictures and artifacts, Catlin repaired to Albany, New York, to prepare what he called "Catlin's Indian Gallery"—310 oil portraits and 200 oils of other subjects, according to the artist, as well as a large number of drawings, decorated shirts and moccasins, buffalo robes, drums, feather headdresses, and other articles, including a Crow tepee of buffalo hide tanned white. This show was presented to great acclaim in Philadelphia, Washington, Boston, and New York, and his journals were published in Philadelphia in 1841.

Soon after, Catlin travelled to Europe, where he was received by Queen Victoria and invited by King Louis-Philippe to exhibit at the Louvre. His "Letters" on the North American Indians, published in London in 1844, were illustrated by simple drawings or linecuts of the originals. Meanwhile he brought some Iowa and Ojibwa to Europe, and continued painting.

But Catlin's wife and son would die in Europe, and his three daughters were raised in America by his wife's family. Expenses mounted, the Gallery in England closed, and the artist struggled to locate a permanent home for his collection. In this quest he was aided by high praise from his friends Baron Alexander von Humboldt and Prince Maximilian de Wied (whose splendid *Voyage dans l'Intérieur de l'Amérique du Nord,* 1832–34, has recently become available in English), as well as by congressional endorsements from Henry Clay and Daniel Webster promoting the purchase of Catlin's Indian Gallery by the Smithsonian ("I look upon it as a thing more important to us than the ascertaining of the South Pole, or anything that can be discovered in the Dead Sea or the River Jordan," Webster told the Senate in 1849).

The Secretary of War, the Commissioner, and the Superintendent of Indian Affairs (General Clark), a number of Indian agents, and others directly acquainted with his Indian subjects had long since provided admiring testimonials to Catlin's accuracy, yet the Smithsonian purchase was fought hard. Karl Bodmer's admirers dismissed Catlin's paintings as crude and exaggerated (though Catlin's admirer Prince de Wied had been Bodmer's patron and the owner of all his expedition paintings). Henry Schoolcraft, Indian Agent for the Western Territories, to whom the artist had refused permission to use the paintings to illustrate Schoolcraft's own work, cast similar aspersions on his rival's text. Then Senator Jefferson Davis of Kentucky, though he still liked Catlin from their days together on the desperate expedition of the First Dragoons in 1834, and praised his work, voted against him in the 1852–53 Congress for political reasons—his Southern Democratic Party was "anti-Indian." The Smithsonian purchase was defeated by that single vote.

By 1852, Catlin had become penniless as well as deaf, and a creditor named Joseph Harrison, by paying the artist's debts, acquired the entire Gallery, which was stored in the basement of his boilerworks in Philadelphia and inhabited for decades by mice and insects. After a fire in the building, and an ensuing flood of water, the Gallery was all but ruined.

The dauntless Catlin re-created many of these works from sketchbooks and fond memory, after which, in his late fifties, he departed for South America and the Pacific coast of North America, sketching and painting all the way. The journey is described in his *Last Rambles Amongst the Indians of the Rocky Mountains and the Andes*—"Oh, how I love a people," he cries, "who don't live for the love of money!" This rather incoherent book appeared in 1868, the same year Catlin's photograph, taken in Brussels, revealed a haggard though still resolute man with heavy bags under his eyes, weak hands clasped on a cane.

In 1870, he returned to New York with his new collection, which included such typical works as "Chasing the Wild Horse," done on the Pampas in 1857 (and reminiscent in its fleet Indian horses of "Prairie Fire," 1832), but also strange, wild jungle paintings unlike anything he had done before. This collection was stored by the American Museum of Natural History, where it gathered dust for almost one hundred years. Toward the end of his life, the artist was invited to exhibit at the Smithsonian, and he continued to reside and paint at the Smithsonian until his death in 1872, in Jersey City.

Despite that late homage, George Catlin died with his longing to see his work installed in a proper setting still unsatisfied. In 1874, after Harrison's death, the moldering Gallery artifacts were virtually shoveled from the gutted building to be buried in the yard, but some 445 sadly damaged oils were presented and shipped by freight car to the Smithsonian, which staged a desultory exhibit in 1883. They were then returned to storage for another half century. After a travelling exhibition put together by a government agency in the mid-fifties, most were cleaned and restored, and a collection of twenty-seven was hung in the White House in 1961.

Four years later, the Gallery paintings, at long last, were properly exhibited in a Smithsonian exhibition.*

In mid-October of 1988, on a journey to the scene of the great Rocky Mountain fires, I visited the Fort Union site at "the Mouth of the Yellow Stone," where that river joins the diminished Missouri. Old Fort Union is gone, and the Montana–North Dakota border country all around seems vast and empty. The only large town in two hundred miles is Minot, North Dakota, and well beyond that radius, in any direction, there is not much, either. After years of drought, the northern plains looked like endless flat dust-brown plateaus, with only faint stains of green in the dry bottoms. Even there, the scarce, sere trees looked barren, and the birds were gone, all but the magpies noted here at the Yellowstone-Missouri confluence by Clark and Lewis. "The immence numbers of antelope . . . the beavers in every bend," the elk and deer, bighorn sheep and bison, wolves and grizzly they recorded in these "wide and fertile vallies" were represented by two scraggy bison hugging a barbed-wire fence, not far from a road-killed porcupine and a squashed badger.

In Catlin's time, Fort Union had little trouble with the Indians, but by midcentury, the warrior Lakota, driven north and west by the white men's incursions, had made life at the trading post so precarious that the dilapidated fort was taken over by the U.S. Army. Its strong palisades were dismantled to construct Fort Buford, two miles to the east, which aimed to make this country safe for farmers. Here Chief Joseph of the Nez Percé was held prisoner in 1877, and here Chief Sitting Bull surrendered.

"The Mouth of the Yellow Stone" on the far side of the Missouri is perhaps best seen about a mile below Fort Buford. Even today,

*By 1894, thirty-five oils had been acquired by the Chicago Natural History Museum from General Clark's niece Emily O'Fallon, and a number of works have been assembled since by the Gilcrease Institute in Tulsa and other institutions (New-York Historical Society; Newberry Library, Chicago; University of Pennsylvania; National Museum of American Art, Washington, D.C.). The 351 paintings of the second collection, stored at the American Museum of Natural History, were bought by Paul Mellon and presented to the National Gallery in Washington. In 1980, $280,000—the record sale price for a Catlin work—was paid for "Battle Between Sioux and Sauk & Fox," a 26- by 32-inch oil.

amid stunted horizons of dust and smoke, slow oil pumps, gas flares, power lines, and scarring roads, the quiet harmony of rivers under these high plains of the northwest Missouri River is a beautiful blue, sparkling in the autumn gold of willow and cottonwood under the pale bluffs and lonesome buttes of the Dakota Badlands. But the bountiful grasslands where Catlin envisioned his "nation's Park" have been sadly eroded by a century and a half of white dominion, and the magnificent Plains hunters reduced to despairing remnants on bleak reservations.

Fort Union's old foundations, reduced to humble mounds in the plains grass, were located in 1966. The old trading post is now in the process of reconstruction by the National Park Service, whose pamphlet on the place, ignoring Catlin, is illustrated by Karl Bodmer's works. The house of the Bourgeois (the fur company superintendent), reconstructed from foundations as well as early paintings, is already rebuilt. This two-story white frame building, very large and handsome by frontier standards, has a tall flagpole at its front door as in the Bodmer painting, and a river prospect across the upper Missouri into Montana.

After decades of hard drought, wind, and blizzards, there is new talk of replacing the marginal ranching in the "Big Open" of eastern Montana with the sort of great game park for bison, antelope, and elk that Catlin foresaw, and it is suggested that the park would be managed by Indians—a far wiser use of this uncompromising country than ranchers and farmers have found for it so far.

We cannot know what Catlin's stature as an artist might have been had he not been confined by his own ambitions for his Indian Gallery, yet surely our culture has benefited more from his bold work than from the art of another Bodmer, Peale, or Bierstadt. "We have started to go and see it," he said, "and we cannot think of being stopped." Nor was he. George Catlin has earned an immortal place as a chronicler of that wild West that still stirs us today as echo and meditation.

—Peter Matthiessen

SUGGESTIONS
FOR FURTHER READING

◄─────────────────────────────►

Works by George Catlin

Episodes from *Life Among the Indians* and *Last Rambles*. Edited by
    Marvin C. Ross. The University of Oklahoma Press (Norman,
    Oklahoma: 1980).
*Letters and Notes on the Manners, Customs and Conditions of the North
    American Indians*. With an Introduction by Marjorie Halpin.
    Repr. of 1844 edition, in two volumes. Dover Publications, Inc.
    (New York: 1973).

Works about George Catlin

Ewers, John C. "George Catlin, Painter of Indians and the West," in
    Smithsonian Institution Report (1956), pp. 483–528.
_____. *Indian Art in Pipestone: George Catlin's Portfolio in the Brit-
    ish Museum*. Smithsonian Institution Press (Washington, D.C.:
    1979).
Halpin, Marjorie. *Catlin's Indian Gallery: The George Catlin Paint-
    ings in the United States National Museum*. Smithsonian Institu-
    tion Press (Washington, D.C.: 1965).
Hassrick, Royal. *George Catlin Book of American Indians*. Watson-
    Guptill Publications (New York: 1977).
McCracken, Harold. *George Catlin and the Old Frontier*. The Dial
    Press (New York: 1959).
Quimby, George I. *Indians of the Western Frontier: Paintings of George
    Catlin*. Chicago Natural History Museum (Chicago: 1954).
Ross, Marvin C. *George Catlin*. The University of Oklahoma Press.
    (Norman, Oklahoma: 1959).

Truettner, William H. *The Natural Man Observed: A Study of Catlin's Indian Gallery.* The Smithsonian Institution Press (Washington, D.C.: 1979).

EDITOR'S NOTE

◄——————————►

George Catlin's splendid "Letters and Notes" on the North American Indians have always been overshadowed by the paintings, and this undue neglect has certainly been worsened by the nineteenth century rhetoric and repetitions with which he encumbered his otherwise excellent prose. Together with the extended descriptions of each painting and some appendix matter, this expendable stuff has mostly been removed.

The author's decision to commence his "Letters" at the farthest point of his journey up the Missouri River, then introduce his upstream notes on the way down, invited considerable repetition and confusion. In the interests of clarity as well as continuity, certain paragraphs have been relocated here and there so that related observations on the same topic or tribe may be in the same place. (For example, some errant material on the Crow, originally in Letter 24, appears with the rest of the Crow accounts in Letters 7 and 8.)

It is my hope that this edition will bring George Catlin's admirable accounts to the wide readership that they deserve.

—Editor

CONTENTS

◄─────────►

LETTER—NO. 1.

Wyöming, birth-place of the Author, p. 1.—His former Profession— First cause of his Travels to the Indian Country—Delegation of Indians in Philadelphia—First start to the Far West, in 1832 p. 1.—Probable extinction of the Indians, p. 3.—Former and present numbers of— The proper mode of approaching them, and estimating their character, pp. 3–8.

LETTER—NO. 2.

MOUTH OF YELLOW STONE, UPPER MISSOURI, 1832.

Mouth of Yellow Stone, p. 9.—Distance from St. Louis—Difficulties of the Missouri—Politeness of Mr. Chouteau and Major Sanford—Fur Company's Fort—Indian Epicures—New and true School for the Arts—Beautiful Models, pp. 9–11.

LETTER—NO. 3.

MOUTH OF YELLOW STONE, UPPER MISSOURI.

Character of Missouri River, p. 12, Illus. 1.—Beautiful prairie shores, p. 14.—Picturesque clay bluffs, p. 15.—First appearance of a steamer at the Yellow Stone, and curious conjectures of the Indians about it, p. 16.—Fur Company's Establishment at the mouth of Yellow Stone— M'Kenzie—His table and politeness, p. 17.—Indian tribes in this vicinity, p. 17.

LETTER—NO. 4.

MOUTH OF YELLOW STONE, UPPER MISSOURI.

Upper Missouri Indians—General character, p. 18.—Buffaloes—Description of, p. 19.—Modes of killing them—Buffalo-hunt, p. 19.

LETTER—NO. 5.
MOUTH OF YELLOW STONE, UPPER MISSOURI.

LETTER—NO. 6.
MOUTH OF YELLOW STONE, UPPER MISSOURI.

LETTER—NO. 7.
MOUTH OF YELLOW STONE, UPPER MISSOURI.

LETTER—NO. 8.
MOUTH OF YELLOW STONE, UPPER MISSOURI.

LETTER—NO. 9.
MOUTH OF YELLOW STONE, UPPER MISSOURI.

LETTER—NO. 10.
MANDAN VILLAGE, UPPER MISSOURI.

G. Catlin

A BRIEF CHRONOLOGY OF CATLIN'S TRAVELS

1. SUMMER 1831. St. Louis north up Mississippi to Prairie du Chien (present-day Iowa–Nebraska border).   2. EARLY SPRING 1832. Northwest on Missouri and Platte rivers (Nebraska).
3. SPRING–SUMMER 1832. Ascent of Missouri to Ft. Union (North Dakota–Montana border) with sojourn at Ft. Pierre (South Dakota).   4. SUMMER–EARLY FALL 1832. Descent of Missouri, with sojourn at Ft. Clark near Mandan villages (North Dakota) to Ft. Leavenworth (Kansas) and St. Louis.   5. SPRING 1834. Descent of Mississippi and ascent of Arkansas River to Fort

Gibson (Oklahoma). 6. SUMMER 1834. Overland journey from Ft. Gibson to Comanche territory (Texas). 7. WINTER 1834–1835. Down Mississippi to Gulf Coast, and east to Florida. 8. SPRING 1835. New Orleans up Mississippi and Wisconsin River to Ft. Snelling (Wisconsin). 9. SPRING 1836. St. Louis up Mississippi to Wisconsin Territory and Pipe Stone Quarry (Minnesota). 10. 1837. Visit to Seminole prisoners at Ft. Moultrie, near Charleston, South Carolina.

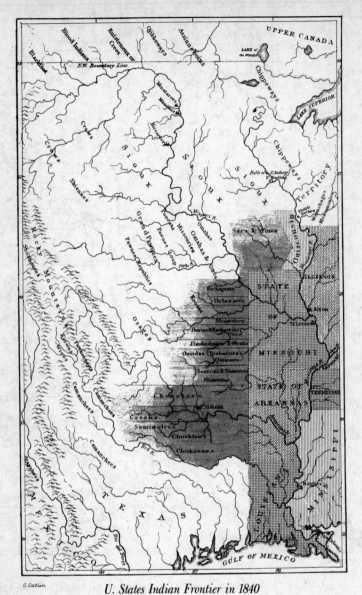

G. Catlin

U. States Indian Frontier in 1840

Shewing the Positions of the Tribes that have been removed west of the Missisippi.

NORTH AMERICAN
INDIANS

◄─────────────────────►

LETTER—NO. 1.

As the following pages have been hastily compiled, at the urgent request of a number of friends, from a series of Letters and Notes written by myself during several years' residence and travel amongst a number of the wildest and most remote tribes of the North American Indians, I have thought it best to make this page the beginning of my book; dispensing with Preface, and even with Dedication, other than that which I hereby make of it, with all my heart, to those who will take the pains to read it . . .

Leaving my readers, therefore, to find out what is in the book, without promising them anything, I proceed to say—of *myself*, that I was born in Wyöming,* in North America, some thirty or forty years since, of parents who entered that beautiful and famed valley soon after the close of the revolutionary war, and the disastrous event of the "Indian massacre."

The early part of my life was whiled away, apparently, somewhat in vain, with books reluctantly held in one hand, and a rifle or fishing-pole firmly and affectionately grasped in the other.

At the urgent request of my father, who was a practising lawyer, I was prevailed upon to abandon these favourite themes, and also my occasional dabblings with the brush, which had secured already a corner in my affections; and I commenced reading the law for a profession, under the direction of Reeve and Gould, of Connecticut. I attended the lectures of these learned judges for two years—was admitted to the bar—and practised the law . . . in my native land, for the term of two or three years; when I very deliberately sold my

*The Wyöming Valley in Pennsylvania—ed.

law library and all (save my rifle and fishing-tackle), and converting their proceeds into brushes and paint pots, I commenced the art of painting in Philadelphia, without teacher or adviser.

I there closely applied my hand to the labours of the art for several years; during which time my mind was continually reaching for some branch or enterprise of the art, on which to devote a whole life-time of enthusiasm; when a delegation of some ten or fifteen noble and dignified-looking Indians, from the wilds of the "Far West," suddenly arrived in the city, arrayed and equipped in all their classic beauty,—with shield and helmet,—with tunic and manteau,—tinted and tasselled off, exactly for the painter's palette!

In silent and stoic dignity, these lords of the forest strutted about the city for a few days, wrapped in their pictured robes, with their brows plumed with the quills of the war-eagle, attracting the gaze and admiration of all who beheld them. After this, they took their leave for Washington City, and I was left to reflect and regret, which I did long and deeply, until I came to the following deductions and conclusions.

Black and blue cloth and civilization are destined, not only to veil, but to obliterate the grace and beauty of Nature. Man, in the simplicity and loftiness of his nature, unrestrained and unfettered by the disguises of art, is surely the most beautiful model for the painter,—and the country from which he hails is unquestionably the best study or school of the arts in the world: such I am sure, from the models I have seen, is the wilderness of North America. And the history and customs of such a people, preserved by pictorial illustrations, are themes worthy the life-time of one man, and nothing short of the loss of my life, shall prevent me from visiting their country, and of becoming their historian.

There was something inexpressibly delightful in the above resolve, which was to bring me amidst such living models for my brush; and at the same time, to place in my hands again, for my living and protection, the objects of my heart above-named; which had long been laid by to rust and decay in the city, without the remotest prospect of again contributing to my amusement.

I had fully resolved—I opened my views to my friends and relations, but got not one advocate or abettor. I tried fairly and faithfully, but it was in vain to reason with those whose anxieties were ready to fabricate every difficulty and danger that could be imagined, without being able to understand or appreciate the extent or importance of my designs, and I broke from them all,—from my wife and my aged parents,—myself my only adviser and protector.

With these views firmly fixed—armed, equipped, and supplied, I started out in the year 1832, and penetrated the vast and pathless wilds which are familiarly denominated the great "Far West" of the North American Continent, with a light heart, inspired with an enthusiastic hope and reliance that I could meet and overcome all the hazards and privations of a life devoted to the production of a literal and graphic delineation of the living manners, customs, and character of an interesting race of people, who are rapidly passing away from the face of the earth—lending a hand to a dying nation, who have no historians or biographers of their own to portray with fidelity their native looks and history; thus snatching from a hasty oblivion what could be saved for the benefit of posterity, and perpetuating it, as a fair and just monument, to the memory of a truly lofty and noble race . . .

The Indians (as I shall call them), the savages or red men of the forests and prairies of North America, are at this time a subject of great interest and some importance to the civilized world; rendered more particularly so in this age, from their relative position to, and their rapid declension from, the civilized nations of the earth. A numerous nation of human beings, whose origin is beyond the reach of human investigation,—whose early history is lost—whose term of national existence is nearly expired—three-fourths of whose country has fallen into the possession of civilized man within the short space of 250 years—twelve millions of whose bodies have fattened the soil in the mean time; who have fallen victims to whiskey, the small-pox, and the bayonet; leaving at this time but a meagre proportion to live a short time longer, in the certain apprehension of soon sharing a similar fate . . .

The Indians of North America . . . with long black hair, black eyes, tall, straight, and elastic forms—are less than two millions in number—were originally the undisputed owners of the soil, and got their title to their lands from the Great Spirit who created them on it,—were once a happy and flourishing people, enjoying all the comforts and luxuries of life which they knew of, and consequently cared for:—were sixteen millions in numbers, and sent that number of daily prayers to the Almighty, and thanks for his goodness and protection. Their country was entered by white men, but a few hundred years since; and thirty millions of these are now scuffling for the goods and luxuries of life, over the bones and ashes of twelve millions of red men; six millions of whom have fallen victims to the small-pox, and the remainder to the sword, the bayonet, and whiskey; all of which means of their death and destruction have been introduced and visited upon them by acquisitive white men; and by white men, also, whose forefathers were welcomed and embraced in the land where the poor Indian met and fed them with "ears of green corn and with pemican." Of the two millions remaining alive at this time, about 1,400,000, are already the miserable living victims and dupes of white man's cupidity, degraded, discouraged and lost in the bewildering maze that is produced by the use of whiskey and its concomitant vices; and the remaining number are yet unroused and unenticed from their wild haunts or their primitive modes, by the dread or love of the white man and his allurements.

It has been with these, mostly, that I have spent my time, and of these, chiefly, and their customs, that the following Letters treat. Their habits (and their's alone) as we can see them transacted, are native, and such as I have wished to fix and preserve for future ages . . .

The reader, then, to understand me rightly, and draw from these Letters the information which they are intended to give, must follow me a vast way from the civilized world; he must needs wend his way from the city of New York, over the Alleghany, and far beyond the mighty Missouri, and even to the base and summit of the Rocky Mountains, some two or three thousand miles from the Atlantic coast. He should forget many theories he has read in the books of Indian barbarities, of wanton butcheries and murders; and divest himself, as far as possible of the deadly prejudices which he has carried from his childhood, against this most unfortunate and most abused part of the race of his fellow-man.

He should consider, that if he has seen the savages of North America without making such a tour, he has fixed his eyes upon and drawn his conclusions (in all probability) only from those who inhabit the frontier; whose habits have been changed—whose pride has been cut down—whose country has been ransacked—whose wives and daughters have been shamefully abused—whose lands have been wrested from them—whose limbs have become enervated and naked by the excessive use of whiskey—whose friends and relations have been prematurely thrown into their graves—whose native pride and dignity have at last given way to the unnatural vices which civilized cupidity has engrafted upon them, to be silently nurtured and magnified by a burning sense of injury and injustice, and ready for that cruel vengeance which often falls from the hand that is palsied by refined abuses, and yet unrestrained by the glorious influences of refined and moral cultivation.—That if he has laid up what he considers well-founded knowledge of these people, from books which he has read, and from newspapers only, he should pause at least, and withhold his sentence before he passes it upon the character of a people, who are dying at the hands of their enemies, without the means of recording their own annals—struggling in their nakedness with their simple weapons, against guns and gunpowder—against whiskey and steel, and disease, and mailed warriors who are continually trampling them to the earth, and at last exultingly promulgating from the very soil which they have wrested from the poor savage, the history of his cruelties and barbarities, whilst his bones are quietly resting under the very furrows which their ploughs are turning.

So great and unfortunate are the disparities between savage and civil, in numbers—in weapons and defences—in enterprise, in craft, and in education, that the former is almost universally the sufferer either in peace or in war; and not less so after his pipe and his tomahawk have retired to the grave with him, and his character is left to be entered upon the pages of history, and that justice done to his memory from necessity, he has entrusted to his enemy.

Amongst the numerous historians, however, of these strange people, they have had some friends who have done them justice; yet as a part of all systems of justice whenever it is meted to the poor Indian, it comes invariably too late, or is administered at an ineffectual distance; and that too when his enemies are continually about him, and effectually applying the means of his destruction.

Some writers, I have been grieved to see, have written down the character of the North American Indian, as dark, relentless, cruel and murderous in the last degree; with scarce a quality to stamp their existence of a higher order than that of the brutes:—whilst others have given them a high rank, as I feel myself authorized to do, as honourable and highly-intellectual beings; and others, both friends and foes to the red men, have spoken of them as an "anomaly in nature!"

In this place I have no time or inclination to reply to so unaccountable an assertion as this; contenting myself with the belief, that the term would be far more correctly applied to that part of the human family who have strayed farthest from nature, than it could be to those who are simply moving in, and filling the sphere for which they were designed by the Great Spirit who made them.

From what I have seen of these people I feel authorized to say, that there is nothing very strange or unaccountable in their character; but that it is a simple one, and easy to be learned and understood, if the right means be taken to familiarize ourselves with it. Although it has its dark spots, yet there is much in it to be applauded, and much to recommend it to the admiration of the enlightened world. And I trust that the reader, who looks through these volumes with care, will be disposed to join me in the conclusion that the North American Indian in his native state, is an honest, hospitable, faithful, brave, warlike, cruel, revengeful, relentless,—yet honourable, contemplative and religious being . . .

I am fully convinced, from a long familiarity with these people, that the Indian's misfortune has consisted chiefly in our ignorance of their true native character and disposition, which has always held us at a distrustful distance from them; inducing us to look upon them in no other light than that of a hostile foe, and worthy only of that system of continued warfare and abuse that has been for ever waged against them . . .

The very use of the word savage, as it is applied in its general sense, I am inclined to believe is an abuse of the word, and the people to whom it is applied. The word, in its true definition, means no more than *wild*, or *wild man;* and a wild man may have been endowed by his Maker with all the humane and noble traits that inhabit the heart of a tame man. Our ignorance and dread or fear of these people, therefore, have given a new definition to the adjective; and nearly the whole civilized world apply the word *savage,* as expressive of the most ferocious, cruel, and murderous character that can be described . . .

I have roamed about from time to time during seven or eight years, visiting and associating with, some three or four hundred thousand of these people, under an almost infinite variety of circumstances; and from the very many and decided voluntary acts of their hospitality and kindness, I feel bound to pronounce them, by nature, a kind and hospitable people. I have been welcomed generally in their country, and treated to the best that they could give me, without any charges made for my board; they have often escorted me through their enemies' country at some hazard to their own lives, and aided me in passing mountains and rivers with my awkward baggage; and under all of these circumstances of exposure, no Indian ever betrayed me, struck me a blow, or stole from me a shilling's worth of my property that I am aware of.

This is saying a great deal, (and proving it too, if the reader will believe me) in favour of the virtues of these people; when it is borne in mind, as it should be, that there is no law in their land to punish a man for theft—that locks and keys are not known in their country—that the commandments have never been divulged amongst them; nor can any human retribution fall upon the head of a thief, save the disgrace which attaches as a stigma to his character, in the eyes of his people about him.

And thus, in these little communities, strange as it may seem, in the absence of all systems of jurisprudence, I have often beheld peace and happiness, and quiet, reigning supreme, for which even kings and emperors might envy them. I have seen rights and virtue protected, and wrongs redressed; and I have seen conjugal, filial and paternal affection in the simplicity and contentedness of nature. I have unavoidably, formed warm and enduring attachments to some of these men which I do not wish to forget—who have brought me near to their hearts, and in our final separation have embraced me in their arms, and commended me and my affairs to the keeping of the Great Spirit.

For the above reasons, the reader will be disposed to forgive me for dwelling so long and so strong on the justness of the claims of these people; and for my occasional expressions of sadness, when my heart bleeds for the fate that awaits the remainder of their unlucky race; which is long to be outlived by the rocks, by the beasts, and even birds and reptiles of the country they live in;—set upon by their fellow-man, whose cupidity, it is feared, will fix no bounds to the Indian's earthly calamity, short of the grave.

I cannot help but repeat, before I close this Letter, that the tribes of the red men of North America, as a nation of human beings, are on their wane; that (to use their own very beautiful figure) "they are fast travelling to the shades of their fathers, towards the setting sun;" and that the traveler who would see these people in their native simplicity and beauty, must needs be hastily on his way to the prairies and Rocky Mountains, or he will see them only as they are now seen on the frontiers, as a basket of *dead game*,—harassed, chased, bleeding and dead; with their plumage and colours despoiled; to be gazed amongst in vain for some system or moral, or for some scale by which to estimate their true native character, other than that which has too often recorded them but a dark and unintelligible mass of cruelty and barbarity.

Without further comments I close this Letter, introducing my readers at once to the heart of the Indian country, only asking their forgiveness for having made it so long, and their patience whilst travelling through the following pages (as I journeyed through those remote realms) in search of information and rational amusement; in tracing out the true character of that *"strange anomaly"* of man in the simple elements of his nature, undissolved or compounded into the mysteries of enlightened and fashionable life.

LETTER—NO. 2.

◆—————————————————▶

Mouth of Yellow Stone, Upper Missouri, 1832.*

I arrived at this place yesterday in the steamer "Yellow Stone," after a voyage of nearly three months from St. Louis, a distance of two thousand miles, the greater part of which has never before been navigated by steam; and the almost insurmountable difficulties which continually oppose the *voyageur* on this turbid stream, have been by degrees overcome by the indefatigable zeal of Mr. Chouteau, a gentleman of great perseverance, and part proprietor of the boat. To the politeness of this gentleman I am indebted for my passage from St. Louis to this place, and I had also the pleasure of his *company*, with that of Major Sanford, the government agent for the Missouri Indians.

The American Fur Company have erected here, for their protection against the savages, a very substantial Fort, 300 feet square, with bastions armed with ordnance; and our approach to it under the continued roar of cannon for half an hour, and the shrill yells of the half-affrighted savages who lined the shores, presented a scene of the most thrilling and picturesque appearance. A voyage so full of incident, and furnishing so many novel scenes of the picturesque and romantic, as we have passed the numerous villages of the "astonished natives," saluting them with the puffing of steam and the thunder of artillery, would afford subject for many epistles; and I

*The Upper Missouri chapters ("Mouth of Yellow Stone" and "Mandan Village") directly followed Catlin's introductory letter. Earlier notes made on his way upriver were intermingled with his downstream journals (see p. 208).

cannot deny myself the pleasure of occasionally giving you some little sketches of scenes that I have witnessed, and *am witnessing*; and of the singular feelings that are excited in the breast of the stranger travelling through this interesting country. Interesting (as I have said) and *luxurious*, for this is truly the land of Epicures; we are invited by the savages to feasts of *dog's meat*, as the most honourable food that can be presented to a stranger, and glutted with the more delicious food of beavers' tails, and buffaloes' tongues.

You will, no doubt, be somewhat surprised on the receipt of a Letter from me, so far strayed into the Western World; and still more startled, when I tell you that I am here in the full enthusiasm and practice of my art. That enthusiasm alone has brought me into this remote region, 3500 miles from my native soil; the last 2000 of which have furnished me with almost unlimited models, both in landscape and the human figure, exactly suited to my feelings . . . This feeling, together with the desire to study my art, independently of the embarrassments which the ridiculous fashions of civilized society have thrown in its way, has led me to the wilderness for a while, as the true school of the arts . . .

No man's imagination, with all the aids of description that can be given to it, can ever picture the beauty and wildness of scenes that may be daily witnessed in this romantic country; of hundreds of these graceful youths, without a care to wrinkle, or a fear to disturb the full expression of pleasure and enjoyment that beams upon their faces—their long black hair mingling with their horses' tails, floating in the wind, while they are flying over the carpeted prairie, and dealing death with their spears and arrows, to a band of infuriated buffaloes; or their splendid procession in a war-parade, arrayed in all their gorgeous colours and trappings, moving with most exquisite grace and manly beauty, added to that bold defiance which man carries on his front, who acknowledges no superior on earth, and who is amenable to no laws except the laws of God and honour.

In addition to the knowledge of human nature and of my art, which I hope to acquire by this toilsome and expensive undertaking, I have another in view, which, if it should not be of equal service to me, will be of no less interest and value to posterity. I have, for many years past, contemplated the noble races of red men who are now spread over these trackless forests and boundless prairies, melting away at the approach of civilization. Their rights invaded, their morals corrupted, their lands wrested from them, their customs changed, and therefore lost to the world; and they at last sunk into the earth, and the ploughshare turning the sod over their graves, and I have flown to their rescue—not of their lives or of their race (for they are *"doomed"* and must perish), but to the rescue of their looks and their modes, at which the acquisitive world may hurl their poison and every besom of destruction, and trample them down and crush them to death; yet, phœnix-like, they may rise from the "stain on a painter's palette," and live again upon canvass, and stand forth for centuries yet to come, the living monuments of a noble race. For this purpose, I have designed to visit every tribe of Indians on the Continent, if my life should be spared; for the purpose of procuring portraits of distinguished Indians, of both sexes in each tribe, painted in their native costume; accompanied with pictures of their villages, domestic habits, games, mysteries, religious ceremonies, &c. with anecdotes, traditions, and history of their respective nations.

If I should live to accomplish my design, the result of my labours will doubtless be interesting to future ages; who will have little else left from which to judge of the original inhabitants of this simple race of beings, who require but a few years more of the march of civilization and death, to deprive them of all their native customs and character. I have been kindly supplied by the Commander-in-Chief of the Army and the Secretary of War, with letters to the commander of every military post, and every Indian agent on the Western Frontier, with instructions to render me all the facilities in their power, which will be of great service to me in so arduous an undertaking . . .

LETTER—NO. 3.

◄———————————►

Mouth of Yellow Stone, Upper Missouri.

*T*he Missouri is, perhaps, different in appearance and charac-
. . . ter from all other rivers in the world; there is a terror in its
manner which is sensibly felt, the moment we enter its muddy
waters from the Mississippi. From the mouth of the Yellow Stone
River, which is the place from whence I am now writing, to its
junction with the Mississippi, a distance of 2000 miles, the Missouri,
with its boiling, turbid waters, sweeps off, in one unceasing current;
and in the whole distance there is scarcely an eddy or resting-
place for a canoe. Owing to the continual falling in of its rich
alluvial banks, its water is always . . . muddy and yellow, and
from its boiling and wild character and uncommon colour, a
stranger would think, even in its lowest state, that there was a
freshet upon it.

For the distance of 1000 miles above St. Louis, the shores of this
river (and, in many places, the whole bed of the stream) are filled
with snags and raft, formed of trees of the largest size, which have
been undermined by the falling banks and cast into the stream; their
roots becoming fastened in the bottom of the river, with their tops
floating on the surface of the water, and pointing down the stream,
forming the most frightful and discouraging prospect for the adventurous voyageur. Almost every island and sand-bar is covered with
huge piles of these floating trees, and when the river is flooded, its
surface is almost literally covered with floating raft and drift wood
which bid positive defiance to keel-boats and steamers, on their way
up the river.

*Illustration 1. View of the Missouri about 600 miles above St. Louis,
filled with snags and rafts—the River of Sticks.*

With what propriety this "Hell of Waters" might be denominated the "River Styx," I will not undertake to decide; but nothing could be more appropriate or innocent than to call it the River *of Sticks*.

The scene is not, however, all so dreary; there is a redeeming beauty in the green and carpeted shores, which hem in this huge and terrible deformity of waters. There is much of the way though, where the mighty forests of stately cotton wood stand, and frown in horrid dark and coolness over the filthy abyss below; into which they are ready to plunge headlong, when the mud and soil in which they were germed and reared have been washed out from underneath them, and with the rolling current are mixed, and on their way to the ocean.

The greater part of the shores of this river, however, are without timber, where the eye is delightfully relieved by wandering over the beautiful prairies; most of the way gracefully sloping down to the water's edge, carpeted with the deepest green, and, in distance, softening into velvet of the richest hues, entirely beyond the reach of the artist's pencil. Such is the character of the upper part of the river especially; and as one advances towards its source, and through its upper half, it becomes more pleasing to the eye, for snags and raft are no longer to be seen; yet the current holds its stiff and onward turbid character.

It has been, heretofore, very erroneously represented to the world, that the scenery on this river was monotonous, and wanting in picturesque beauty. This intelligence is surely incorrect ... One thousand miles or more of the upper part of the river, was, to my eye, like fairy-land; and during our transit through that part of our voyage, I was most of the time rivetted to the deck of the boat, indulging my eyes in the boundless and tireless pleasure of roaming over the thousand hills, and bluffs, and dales, and ravines; where the astonished herds of buffaloes, of elks, and antelopes, and sneaking wolves, and mountain-goats, were to be seen bounding up and down and over the green fields; each one and each tribe, band, and gang, taking their own way, and using their own means to the greatest advantage possible, to leave the sight and sound of the puffing of our boat; which was, for the first time, saluting the green and wild shores of the Missouri with the din of mighty steam.

From St. Louis to the falls of the Missouri, a distance of 2600 miles, is one continued prairie; with the exception of a few of the bottoms formed along the bank of the river, and the streams which are falling into it, which are often covered with the most luxuriant growth of forest timber.

The summit level of the great prairies stretching off to the west and the east from the river, to an almost boundless extent, is from two to three hundred feet above the level of the river; which has formed a bed or valley for its course, varying in width from two to twenty miles. This channel or valley has been evidently produced by the force of the current, which has gradually excavated, in its floods and gorges, this immense space, and sent its débris into the ocean. By the continual overflowing of the river, its deposits have been lodged and left with a horizontal surface, spreading the deepest and richest alluvion over the surface of its meadows on either side; through which the river winds its serpentine course, alternately running from one bluff to the other, which present themselves to its shores in all the most picturesque and beautiful shapes and colours imaginable—some with their green sides gracefully slope down in the most lovely groups to the water's edge; whilst others, divested of their verdure, present themselves in immense masses of clay of different colours, which arrest the eye of the traveller, with the most curious views in the world.

These strange and picturesque appearances have been produced by the rains and frosts, which are continually changing the dimensions, and varying the thousand shapes of these denuded hills, by washing down their sides and carrying them into the river . . . It is amidst these wild and quiet haunts that the mountain-sheep, and the fleet-bounding antelope sport and live in herds, secure from their enemies, to whom the sides and slopes of these bluffs (around which they fearlessly bound) are nearly inaccessible.

The grizzly bear also has chosen these places for his abode; he sullenly sneaks through the gulphs and chasms, and ravines, and frowns away the lurking Indian; whilst the mountain-sheep and antelope are bounding over and around the hill tops, safe and free from harm of man and beast.

. . . If anything did ever literally and completely "astonish (and astound) the natives," it was the appearance of our steamer, puffing and blowing, and paddling and rushing by their villages which were on the banks of the river. These poor and ignorant people for the distance of 2000 miles, had never before seen or heard of a steam-boat, and in some places they seemed at a loss to know what to do, or how to act; they could not, as the Dutch did at Newburgh, on the Hudson River, take it to be a *"floating saw-mill"*—and they had no name for it—so it was, like every thing else (with them), which is mysterious and unaccountable, called *medicine* (mystery). We had on board one twelve-pound cannon and three or four eight-pound swivels, which we are taking up to arm the Fur Company's Fort at the mouth of Yellow Stone; and at the approach to every village they were all discharged several times in rapid succession, which threw the inhabitants into utter confusion and amazement—some of them laid their faces to the ground, and cried to the Great Spirit—some shot their horses and dogs, and sacrificed them to appease the Great Spirit, whom they conceived was offended—some deserted their villages and ran to the tops of the bluffs some miles distant; and others, in some places, as the boat landed in front of their villages, came with great caution, and peeped over the bank of the river to see the fate of their chiefs, whose duty it was (from the nature of their office) to approach us, whether friends or foes, and to go on board. Sometimes, in this plight, they were instantly thrown 'neck and heels' over each other's heads and shoulders—men, women and children, and dogs—sage, sachem, old and young—all in a mass, at the frightful discharge of the steam from the escape-pipe, which the captain of the boat let loose upon them for his own fun and amusement.

There were many curious conjectures amongst their wise men, with regard to the nature and powers of the steam-boat. Amongst the Mandans, some called it the "big thunder canoe;" for when in distance below the village, they 'saw the lightning flash from its sides, and heard the thunder come from it;' others called it the "big medicine canoe with eyes;" it was *medicine* (mystery) because they could not understand it; and it must have eyes, for said they, "it sees its own way, and takes the deep water in the middle of the channel" . . .

The Fort in which I am residing was built by Mr. M'Kenzie, who now occupies it. It is the largest and best-built establishment of the kind on the river, being the great or principal head-quarters and depôt of the Fur Company's business in this region. A vast stock of goods is kept on hand at this place; and at certain times of the year the numerous out-posts concentrate here with the returns of their season's trade, and refit out with a fresh supply of goods to trade with the Indians.

The site for the Fort is well selected, being a beautiful prairie on the bank near the junction of the Missouri with the Yellow Stone rivers; and its inmates and its stores well protected from Indian assaults . . .

This post is the general rendezvous of a great number of Indian tribes in these regions, who are continually concentrating here for the purpose of trade; sometimes coming, the whole tribe together, in a mass. There are now here, and encamped about the Fort, a great many, and I am continually at work with my brush; we have found us at this time the Knisteneaux, Crows, Assinneboins and Blackfeet, and in a few days are to have large accessions.

The first specimens of Indians on the Continent are in these regions; and before I leave these parts, I shall make excursions into their respective countries, to their own native fire-sides; and there study their looks and peculiar customs . . . The tribes which I shall be enabled to see and study by my visit to this region, are the Ojibbeways, the Assinneboins, Knisteneaux [Plains Cree], Blackfeet, Crows, Shiennes [Cheyennes], Grosventres, Mandans, and others; of whom and their customs, their history, traditions, costumes, &c., I shall in due season, give you further and minute accounts.

LETTER—NO. 4.

◄——————————————————————►

Mouth of Yellow Stone, Upper Missouri.

The several tribes of Indians inhabiting the regions of the Upper Missouri, . . . are undoubtedly the finest looking, best equipped, and most beautifully costumed of any on the Continent. They live in a country well-stocked with buffaloes and wild horses, which furnish them an excellent and easy living; their atmosphere is pure, which produces good health and long life; and they are the most independent and the happiest races of Indians I have met with: they are all entirely in a state of primitive wildness, and consequently are picturesque and handsome, almost beyond description. Nothing in the world, of its kind, can possibly surpass in beauty and grace, some of their games and amusements—their gambols and parades, of which I shall speak and paint hereafter.

As far as my travels have yet led me into the Indian country, I have more than realized my former predictions that those Indians who could be found most entirely in a state of nature, with the least knowledge of civilized society, would be found to be the most cleanly in their persons, elegant in their dress and manners, and enjoying life to the greatest perfection. Of such tribes, perhaps the Crows and Blackfeet stand first; and no one would be able to appreciate the richness and elegance (and even taste too), with which some of these people dress, without seeing them in their own country. I will do all I can, however, to make their looks as well as customs known to the world; I will paint with my brush and scribble with my pen, and bring their plumes and plumage, dresses, weapons, &c., and every thing but the Indian himself, to prove to the world the assertions which I have made above.

Every one of these red sons of the forest (or rather of the prairie) is a knight and lord—his squaws are his slaves; the only things which he deems worthy of his exertions are to mount his snorting steed, with his bow and quiver slung, his arrow-shield upon his arm, and his long lance glistening in the war-parade; or, divested of all his plumes and trappings, armed with a simple bow and quiver, to plunge his steed amongst the flying herds of buffaloes, and with his sinewy bow, which he seldom bends in vain, to drive deep to life's fountain the whizzing arrow.

The buffalo herds, which graze in almost countless numbers on these beautiful prairies, afford them an abundance of meat; and so much is it preferred to all other, that the deer, the elk, and the antelope sport upon the prairies in herds in the greatest security; as the Indians seldom kill them, unless they want their skins for a dress. The buffalo (or more correctly speaking bison) is a noble animal, that roams over the vast prairies, from the borders of Mexico on the south, to Hudson's Bay on the north. Their size is somewhat above that of our common bullock, and their flesh of a delicious flavour, resembling and equalling that of fat beef. Their flesh which is easily procured, furnishes the savages of these vast regions the means of a wholesome and good subsistence, and they live almost exclusively upon it—converting the skins, horns, hoofs and bones, to the construction of dresses, shields, bows, &c. The buffalo bull is one of the most formidable and frightful looking animals in the world when excited to resistance; his long shaggy mane hangs in great profusion over his neck and shoulders, and often extends quite down to the ground. The cow is less in stature, and less ferocious; though not much less wild and frightful in her appearance.

The mode in which these Indians kill this noble animal is spirited and thrilling in the extreme . . . They are all (or nearly so) killed with arrows and the lance, while at full speed; and the reader may easily imagine, that these scenes afford the most spirited and picturesque views of the sporting kind that can possibly be seen . . .

LETTER—NO. 5.

◄————————————►

Mouth of Yellow Stone, Upper Missouri.

*I*n my former epistle I told you there were encamped about the
Fort a host of wild, incongruous spirits—chiefs and sachems—
warriors, braves, and women and children of different tribes—of
Crows and Blackfeet—Ojibbeways—Assinneboins—and Crees or
Knisteneaux. Amongst and in the midst of them am I, with my paint
pots and canvass, snugly ensconced in one of the bastions of the
Fort, which I occupy as a painting-room. My easel stands before me,
and the cool breech of a twelve-pounder makes me a comfortable
seat, whilst her muzzle is looking out at one of the port-holes. The
operations of my brush are *mysteries* of the highest order to these red
sons of the prairie, and my room the earliest and latest place of
concentration of these wild and jealous spirits, who all meet here to
be amused and pay me signal honours; but gaze upon each other,
sending their sidelong looks of deep-rooted hatred and revenge
around the group. However, whilst in the Fort, their weapons are
placed within the arsenal, and naught but looks and thoughts can be
breathed here; but death and grim destruction will visit back those
looks upon each other, when these wild spirits again are loose and
free to breathe and act upon the plains.

I have this day been painting a portrait of the head chief of the
Blackfoot nation; he is a good-looking and dignified Indian, about
fifty years of age, and superbly dressed (Illustration 2); whilst sitting
for his picture he has been surrounded by his own braves and
warriors, and also gazed at by his enemies, the Crows and the
Knisteneaux, Assinneboins and Ojibbeways; a number of distin-

guished personages of each of which tribes, have laid all day around the sides of my room; reciting to each other the battles they have fought, and pointing to the scalp-locks, worn as proofs of their victories, and attached to the seams of their shirts and leggings. This is a curious scene to witness, when one sits in the midst of such inflammable and combustible materials, brought together, unarmed, for the first time in their lives; peaceably and calmly recounting over the deeds of their lives, and smoking their pipes upon it, when a few weeks or days will bring them on the plains again, where the war-cry will be raised, and their deadly bows will again be drawn on each other.

The name of this dignitary, of whom I have just spoken, is Stu-mick-o-sucks (the buffalo's back fat), *i.e.* the "hump" or "fleece," the most delicious part of the buffalo's flesh. I have also painted, of the Blackfeet, Pe-toh-pee-kiss (the eagle ribs), and Mix-ke-mote-skin-na (the iron horn), and Wun-nes-tou (the white buffalo), and Tcha-aes-sa-ko-mah-pee (the bear's child), and In-ne-o-cose (the buffalo's child), and half-a-dozen others, and all in rich and costly dresses.

There is no tribe, perhaps, on the Continent, who dress more comfortably, and more gaudily, than the Blackfeet, unless it be the tribe of Crows. There is no great difference, however, in the costliness or elegance of their costumes; nor in the materials of which they are formed; though there is a distinctive mode in each tribe, of stitching or ornamenting with the porcupine quills, which constitute one of the principal ornaments to all their fine dresses; and which can be easily recognized, by any one a little familiar with their modes, as belonging to such or such a tribe. The dress, for instance, of the chief . . . whose portrait I have just painted, consists of a shirt or tunic, made of two deer skins finely dressed, and so placed together with the necks of the skins downwards, and the skins of the hind legs stitched together, the seams running down on each arm, from the neck to the knuckles of the hand; the seam is covered with a band of two inches in width, of very beautiful embroidery of porcupine quills, and suspended from the under edge of this, from the shoulders to the hands, is a fringe of the locks of black hair, which he had taken from the heads of victims slain by his own hand in

*Illustration 2. Stu-mick-o-sucks, Buffalo's Back Fat,
head chief of the Blackfoot nation.*

battle. The leggings are also of the same material; and down the outer side of the leg, from the hip to the feet, extends also a similar band or belt of the same width; and wrought in the same manner, with porcupine quills, and fringed with scalp locks. These locks of hair are procured from scalps, and worn as trophies.

The wife (or squaw) of this dignitary Eeh-nis-kin (the crystal stone), I have also placed upon my canvas (Illustration 3); her countenance is rather pleasing, which is an uncommon thing amongst the Blackfeet—her dress is made of skins, and being the youngest of a bevy of six or eight, and the last one taken under his guardianship, was smiled upon with great satisfaction, whilst he exempted her from the drudgeries of the camp; and keeping her continually in the halo of his own person, watched and guarded her as the apple of his eye. The grandson also of this sachem, a boy of six years of age, and too young as yet to have acquired a name, has stood forth like a tried warrior; and I have painted him at full length (Illustration 4), with his bow and quiver slung, and his robe made of a racoon skin. The history of this child is somewhat curious and interesting; his father is dead, and in case of the death of the chief, of whom I have spoken, he becomes hereditary chief of the tribe. This boy has been twice stolen away by the Crows by ingenious stratagems, and twice re-captured by the Blackfeet, at considerable sacrifice of life, and at present he is lodged with Mr. M'Kenzie, for safe keeping and protection, until he shall arrive at the proper age to take the office to which he is to succeed, and able to protect himself.

The scalp of which I spoke above, is procured by cutting out a piece of the skin of the head, the size of the palm of the hand or less, containing the very centre or crown of the head, the place where the hair radiates from a point, and exactly over what the phrenologists call self-esteem. This patch then is kept and dried with great care, as proof positive of the death of an enemy, and evidence of a man's claims as a warrior: and after having been formally "danced," as the saying is, (i.e. after it has been stuck up upon a pole or held up by an "old woman," and the warriors have danced around it for two or three weeks at intervals,) it is fastened to the handle of a lance, or the end of a war-club, or divided into a great many small locks and used to fringe and ornament the victor's dress. When these dresses are

Illustration 3. Eeh-nis-kin, Crystal Stone, wife of Stu-mick-o-sucks.

Illustration 4. The chief's grandson.

seen bearing such trophies, it is of course a difficult matter to purchase them of the Indian, for they often hold them above all price . . .

In the chief's dress, which I am describing, there are his moccasins, made also of buckskin, and ornamented in a corresponding manner. And over all, his robe, made of the skin of a young buffalo bull, with the hair remaining on; and on the inner or flesh side, beautifully garnished with porcupine quills, and the battles of his life very ingeniously, though rudely, pourtrayed in pictorial representations. In his hand he holds a very beautiful pipe, the stem of which is four or five feet long, and two inches wide, curiously wound with braids of the porcupine quills of various colours; and the bowl of the pipe ingeniously carved by himself from a piece of red steatite of an interesting character, and which they all tell me is procured somewhere between this place and the Falls of St. Anthony, on the head waters of the Mississippi.

This curious stone has many peculiar qualities, and has, undoubtedly, but one origin in this country, and perhaps in the world. It is found but in the hands of the savage, and every tribe, and nearly every individual in the tribe has his pipe made of it. I consider this stone a subject of great interest, and curiosity to the world; and I shall most assuredly make it a point, during my Indian rambles, to visit the place from whence it is brought. I have already got a number of most remarkable traditions and stories relating to the "sacred quarry;" of pilgrimages performed there to procure the stone, and of curious transactions that have taken place on that ground. It seems, from all I can learn, that all the tribes in these regions, and also of the Mississippi and the Lakes, have been in the habit of going to that place, and meeting their enemies there, whom they are obliged to treat as friends, under an injunction of the Great Spirit.

So then is this sachem (the buffalo's back fat) dressed; and in a very similar manner, and almost the same, is each of the others above named; and all are armed with bow and quiver, lance and shield. These north western tribes are all armed with the bow and lance, and protected with the shield or arrow fender, which is carried outside of the left arm, exactly as the Roman and Grecian shield was carried, and for the same purpose.

There is an appearance purely classic in the plight and equipment of these warriors and "knights of the lance." They are almost literally always on their horses' backs, and they wield these weapons with desperate effect upon the open plains; where they kill their game while at full speed, and contend in like manner in battles with their enemy. There is one prevailing custom in these respects, amongst all the tribes who inhabit the great plains or prairies of these western regions. These plains afford them an abundance of wild and fleet horses, which are easily procured; and on their backs at full speed, they can come alongside of any animal, which they easily destroy.

The bow with which they are armed is small, and apparently an insignificant weapon, though one of great and almost incredible power in the hands of its owner, whose sinews have been from childhood habituated to its use and service. The length of these bows is generally about three feet, and sometimes not more than two and a half. They have, no doubt, studied to get the requisite power in the smallest compass possible, as it is more easily and handily used on horseback than one of the greater length. The greater number of these bows are made of ash, or of "bois d'arc" (as the French call it), and lined on the back with layers of buffalo or deer's sinews, which are inseparably attached to them, and give them great elasticity. There are very many also (amongst the Blackfeet and the Crows) which are made of bone, and others of the horn of the mountain-sheep. Those made of bone are decidedly the most valuable, and cannot in this country be procured of a good quality short of the price of one or two horses. About these there is a mystery yet to be solved, and I advance my opinion against all theories that I have heard in the country where they are used and made. I have procured several very fine specimens, and when purchasing them have inquired of the Indians, what bone they were made of? And in every instance, the answer was, "That's medicine," meaning that it was a mystery to them, or that they did not wish to be questioned about them. The bone of which they are made is certainly not the bone of any animal now grazing on the prairies, or in the mountains between this place and the Pacific Ocean; for some of these bows are three feet in length, of a solid piece of bone, and that as close-grained—as hard—as white, and as highly polished as any ivory; it cannot, therefore be made from the elks' horn (as some have supposed), which is of a dark colour and porous: nor can it come from the buffalo. It is in my opinion, therefore, that the Indians on the Pacific coast procure the bone from the jaw of the sperm whale, which is often stranded on the coast, and bringing the bone into the mountains, trade it to the Blackfeet and Crows, who manufacture it into these bows without knowing any more than we do, from what source it has been procured.

One of these little bows in the hands of an Indian, on a fleet and well-trained horse, with a quiver of arrows slung on his back, is a most effective and powerful weapon in the open plains. No one can easily credit the force with which these missiles are thrown, and the sanguinary effects produced by their wounds, until he has rode by the side of a party of Indians in chase of a herd of buffaloes, and witnessed the apparent ease and grace with which their supple arms have drawn the bow, and seen these huge animals tumbling down the gushing out their hearts' blood from their mouths and nostrils.

Their bows are often made of bone and sinews, and their arrows headed with flints or with bones, of their own construction, or with steel, as they are now chiefly furnished by the Fur Traders quite to the Rocky Mountains. The quiver, which is uniformly carried on the back, and made of the panther or otter skins is a magazine of these deadly weapons, and generally contains two varieties. The one to be drawn upon an enemy, generally poisoned, and with long flukes or barbs, which are designed to hang the blade in the wound after the shaft is withdrawn, in which they are but slightly glued;—the other to be used for their game, with the blade firmly fastened to the shaft, and the flukes inverted; that it may easily be drawn from the wound, and used on a future occasion.

Such is the training of men and horses in this country, that this work of death and slaughter is simple and easy. The horse is trained to approach the animals on the *right* side, enabling its rider to throw his arrows to the left; it runs and approaches without the use of the halter, which is hanging loose upon its neck bringing the rider within three or four paces of the animal, when the arrow is thrown with great ease and certainty to the heart; and instances sometimes occur, where the arrow passes entirely through the animal's body.

An Indian, therefore, mounted on a fleet and well-trained horse, with his bow in his hand, and his quiver slung on his back, containing an hundred arrows, of which he can throw fifteen or twenty in a minute, is a formidable and dangerous enemy. Many of them also ride with a lance of twelve or fourteen feet in length, with a blade of polished steel; and all of them (as a protection for their vital parts), with a shield or arrow-fender made of the skin of the buffalo's neck, which has been smoked, and hardened with glue extracted from the hoofs. These shields are arrow-proof, and will glance off a rifle shot with perfect effect by being turned obliquely, which they do with great skill.

This shield or arrow-fender is, in my opinion, made of similar materials, and used in the same way, and for the same purpose, as was the clypeus or small shield in the Roman and Grecian cavalry . . .

In this wise then, are all for these wild red knights of the prairie, armed and equipped,—and while nothing can possibly be more picturesque and thrilling than a troop or war-party of these fellows, galloping over these green and endless prairies; there can be no set of mounted men of equal numbers, so effective and so invincible in this country as they would be, could they be inspired with confidence of their own powers and their own superiority; yet this never can be done;—for the Indian, as far as the name of white man has travelled, and long before he had to try his strength with him, is trembling with fright and fear of his approach; he heard of white man's arts and artifice—his tricks and cunning, and his hundred instruments of death and destruction—he dreads his approach, shrinks from him with fear and trembling—his heart sickens, and his pride and courage wither, at the thoughts of contending with an enemy, whom he thinks may war and destroy with weapons of *medicine* or mystery.

Of the Blackfeet . . . whose portraits are standing in my room, there is another of whom I must say a few words: Pe-toh-pee-kiss, the eagle ribs (Illustration 5). This man is one of the extraordinary men of the Blackfoot tribe; though not a chief, he stands here in the Fort, and deliberately boasts of eight scalps, which he says he has taken from the heads of trappers and traders with his own hand. His

Illustration 5. Pe-toh-pee-kiss, Eagle Ribs.

Illustration 6. Wun-nes-tou, White Buffalo, a medicine man.

dress is really superb, almost literally covered with scalp-locks, of savage and civil.

I have painted him at full length, with a head-dress made entirely of ermine skins and horns of the buffalo. This custom of wearing horns beautifully polished and surmounting the head-dress, is a very curious one, being worn only by the bravest of the brave; by the most extraordinary men in the nation . . .

Besides the chiefs and warriors above-named, I have also transferred to my canvass the "looks and very resemblance" of an aged chief, who combines with his high office, the envied title of mystery or medicine-man, *i.e.* doctor—magician—prophet—soothsayer—jongleur—and high priest, all combined in one person, who necessarily is looked upon as "Sir Oracle" of the nation. The name of this distinguished functionary is Wun-nes-tou, the white buffalo (Illustration 6); and on his left arm he presents his mystery-drum or tambour, in which are concealed the hidden and sacred mysteries of his healing art . . .

LETTER—NO. 6.

◄————————►

Mouth of Yellow Stone, Upper Missouri.

Now for medicines or mysteries—for doctors, high-priests, for hocus pocus, witchcraft, and animal magnetism! . . .

I must needs stop here—my painting and every thing else, until I can explain the word *"medicine,"* and *"medicine-bag;"* and also some *medicine operations,* which I have seen transacted at this place within a few days past. "Medicine" is a great word in this country; and it is very necessary that one should know the meaning of it . . .

The Fur Traders in this country, are nearly all French; and in their language, a doctor or physician, is called *"Medecin."* The Indian country is full of doctors; and as they are all magicians, and skilled, or profess to be skilled, in many mysteries, the word "medecin" has become habitually applied to every thing mysterious or unaccountable; and the English and Americans, who are also trading and passing through this country . . . have denominated these personages "medicine-men," which means something more than merely a doctor or physician. These physicians, however, are all *medicine-men,* as they are all supposed to deal more or less in mysteries and charms, which are aids and handmaids in their practice . . . There were many personages amongst them, and also amongst the white men who visit the country, who could deal in mysteries, though not skilled in the application of drugs and medicines . . . For instance, I am a "medicine-man" of the highest order amongst these superstitious people, on account of the art which I practice; which is a strange and unaccountable thing to them, and of course, called the greatest of "medicine." My gun and pistols, which have percussion-locks, are great medicine; and no Indian can be prevailed to fire them off, for they say they have nothing to do with white man's medicine.

The Indians do not use the word medicine, however; but in each tribe they have a word of their own construction, synonimous with mystery or mystery-man.

The "medicine-bag" then, is a mystery-bag; and its meaning and importance necessary to be understood, as it may be said to be the key to Indian life and Indian character. These bags are constructed of the skins of animals, of birds, or of reptiles, and ornamented and preserved in a thousand different ways, as suits the taste or freak of the person who constructs them. These skins are generally attached to some part of the clothing of the Indian, or carried in his hand—they are oftentimes decorated in such a manner as to be exceedingly ornamental to his person, and always are stuffed with grass, or moss, or something of the kind; and generally without drugs or medicines within them, as they are religiously closed and sealed, and seldom, if ever, to be opened. I find that every Indian in his primitive state, carries his medicine-bag in some form or other, to which he pays the greatest homage, and to which he looks for safety and protection through life ... Feasts are often made, and dogs and horses sacrificed, to a man's medicine; and days, and even weeks, of fasting and penance of various kinds are often suffered, to appease his medicine, which he imagines he has in some way offended ... Every male in the tribe carries this, his supernatural charm or guardian, to which he looks for the preservation of his life, in battle or in other danger; at which times it would be considered ominous of bad luck and an ill fate to be without it.

The manner in which this curious and important article is instituted is this: a boy, at the age of fourteen or fifteen years, is said to be making or "forming his medicine," when he wanders away from is father's lodge, and absents himself for the space of two or three, and sometimes even four or five, days; lying on the ground in some remote or secluded spot, crying to the Great Spirit, and fasting the whole time. During this period of peril and abstinence, when he falls asleep, the first animal, bird, or reptile, of which he dreams (or pretends to have dreamed, perhaps), he considers the Great Spirit has designated for his mysterious protector through life. He then returns home to his father's lodge, and relates his success; and after allaying his thirst, and satiating his appetite, he sallies forth with weapons or traps, until he can procure the animal or bird, the skin of which he preserves entire, and ornaments it according to his own fancy, and carries it with him through life, for "good luck" (as he calls it); as his strength in battle—and in death his guardian *Spirit*, that is buried with him, and which is to conduct him safe to the beautiful hunting grounds, which he contemplates in the world to come.

The value of the medicine-bag to the Indian is beyond all price; for to sell it, or give it away, would subject him to such signal disgrace in his tribe, that he could never rise above it; and again, his superstition would stand in the way of any such disposition of it, for he considers it the gift of the Great Spirit. An Indian carries his *medicine-bag* into battle, and trusts to it for his protection; and if he loses it thus, when fighting ever so bravely for his country, he suffers a disgrace scarcely less than that which occurs in case he sells or gives it away; his enemy carries it off and displays it to his own people as a trophy; whilst the loser is cut short of the respect that is due to other young men of his tribe, and for ever subjected to the degrading epithet of "a man without medicine," or "he who has lost his medicine," until he can replace it again; which can only be done, by rushing into battle and plundering one from an enemy whom he slays with his own hand. This done, his medicine is restored, and he is reinstated again in the estimation of his tribe; and even higher than before, for such is called the best of medicine, or *"medicine honourable."*

It is a singular fact, that a man can institute his mystery or medicine, but once in his life; and equally singular that he can reinstate himself by the adoption of the medicine of his enemy; both of which regulations are strong and violent inducements for him to fight bravely in battle: the first, that he may protect and preserve his medicine; and the second, in case he has been so unlucky as to lose it, that he may restore it, and his reputation also, while he is desperately contending for the protection of his community . . .

Such then is the medicine-bag—such its meaning and importance; and when its owner dies, it is placed in his grave and decays with his body . . .

The Knisteneaux or Crees are a very numerous tribe, extending from this place as high north as the shores of Lake Winnepeg; and even much further in a north-westerly direction, towards, and even through, a great part of the Rocky Mountains . . . Their customs may properly be said to be primitive, as no inroads of civilized habits have been as yet successfully made amongst them. Like the other tribes in these regions, they dress in skins, and gain their food, and conduct their wars in a very similar manner. They are a very daring and most adventurous tribe; roaming vast distances over the prairies and carrying war into their enemy's country. With the numerous tribe of Blackfeet, they are always waging an uncompromising warfare; and though fewer in numbers and less in stature, they have shewn themselves equal in sinew, and not less successful in mortal combats . . .

Not many weeks since, a party of Knisteneaux came here from the north, for the purpose of making their summer's trade with the Fur Company; and, whilst here, a party of Blackfeet, their natural enemies (the same who are here now), came from the west, also to trade. These two belligerent tribes encamped on different sides of the Fort, and had spent some weeks here in the Fort and about it, in apparently good feeling and fellowship; unable in fact to act otherwise, for, according to a regulation of the Fort, their arms and weapons were all locked up by M'Kenzie in his "arsenal," for the purpose of preserving the peace amongst these fighting-cocks.

The Knisteneaux had completed their trade, and loitered about the premises, until all, both Indians and white men, were getting tired of their company, wishing them quietly off. When they were ready to start, with their goods packed upon their backs, their arms were given them, and they started; bidding everybody, both friends and foes, a hearty farewell. They went out of the Fort, and though the party gradually moved off, one of them undiscovered, loitered about the Fort, until he got an opportunity to poke the muzzle of his gun through between the piquets; when he fired it at one of the chiefs of the Blackfeet, who stood within a few paces, talking with

Mr. M'Kenzie, and shot him with two musket bullets through the centre of his body! The Blackfoot fell, and rolled about upon the ground in the agonies of death. The Blackfeet who were in the Fort seized their weapons and ran in a mass out of the Fort, in pursuit of the Knisteneaux, who were rapidly retreating to the bluffs. The Frenchmen in the Fort, also, at so flagrant and cowardly an insult, seized their guns and ran out, joining the Blackfeet in the pursuit. I, at that moment, ran to my painting-room in one of the bastions overlooking the plain, where I had a fair view of the affair; many shots were exchanged back and forward, and a skirmish ensued which lasted half an hour; the parties, however, were so far apart that little effect was produced; the Knisteneaux were driven off over the bluffs, having lost one man and had several others wounded. The Blackfeet and Frenchmen returned into the Fort, and then, I saw what I never saw before in my life—I saw a *"medicine-man"* performing his mysteries over a dying man. The man who had been shot was still living, though two bullets had passed through the centre of his body, about two inches apart from each other; he was lying on the ground in the agonies of death, and no one could indulge the slightest hope of his recovery; yet the *medicine-man* must needs be called (for such a personage they had in their party), and hocus pocus applied to the dying man, as the dernier resort, when all drugs and all specifics were useless, and after all possibility of recovery was extinct!

I have mentioned that all tribes have their physicians, who are also medicine (or mystery) men. These professional gentlemen are worthies of the highest order in all tribes. They are regularly called and paid as physicians, to prescribe for the sick; and many of them acquire great skill in the medicinal world, and gain much celebrity in their nation. Their first prescriptions are roots and herbs, of which they have a great variety of species; and when these have all failed, their last resort is to *"medicine"* or mystery; and for this purpose, each one of them has a strange and unaccountable dress, conjured up and constructed during a life-time of practice, in the wildest fancy imaginable, in which he arrays himself, and makes his last visit to his dying patient,—dancing over him, shaking his frightful rattles, and singing songs of incantation, in hopes to cure him by a charm. There are some instances, of course, where the exhausted patient unaccountably recovers, under the application of these absurd forms;

and in such cases, this ingenious son of *Indian* Esculapius will be seen for several days after, on the top of a wigwam, with his right arm extended and waving over the gaping multitude, to whom he is vaunting forth, without modesty, the surprising skill he has acquired in his art, and the undoubted efficacy of his medicine or mystery. But if, on the contrary, the patient dies, he soon changes his dress, and joins in doleful lamentations with the mourners; and easily, with his craft, and the ignorance and superstition of his people, protects his reputation and maintains his influence over them; by assuring them, that it was the will of the Great Spirit that his patient should die, and when sent for, his feeble efforts must cease.

Such was the case, and such the extraordinary means resorted to in the instance I am now relating. Several hundred spectators, including Indians and traders, were assembled around the dying man, when it was announced that the *"medicine-man"* was coming; we were required to "form a ring," leaving a space of some thirty or forty feet in diameter around the dying man, in which the doctor could perform his wonderful operations; and a space was also opened to allow him free room to pass through the crowd without touching any one. This being done, in a few moments his arrival was announced by the death-like "hush——sh——" through the crowd; and nothing was to be heard, save the light and casual tinkling of the rattles upon his dress, which was scarcely perceptible to the ear, as he cautiously and slowly moved through the avenue left for him; which at length brought him into the ring, in view of the pitiable object over whom his mysteries were to be performed . . .

His entrée and his garb were somewhat thus:—he approached the ring with his body in a crouching position (Illustration 7), with a slow and tilting step—his body and head were entirely covered with the skin of a yellow bear, the head of which (his own head being inside of it) served as a mask; the huge claws of which also, were dangling on his wrists and ankles; in one hand he shook a frightful rattle, and in the other brandished his medicine-spear or magic wand; to the rattling din and discord of all of which, he added the wild and startling jumps and yelps of the Indian, and the horrid and appalling grunts, and snarls, and growls of the grizzly bear, in ejaculatory and guttural incantations to the Good and Bad Spirits, in

Illustration 7. Medicine man, performing his mysteries over a dying man.

behalf of his patient; who was rolling and groaning in the agonies of death, whilst he was dancing around him, jumping over him, and pawing him about, and rolling him in every direction.

In this wise, this strange operation proceeded for half an hour, to the surprise of a numerous and death-like silent audience, until the man died; and the medicine-man danced off to his quarters, and packed up, and tied and secured from the sight of the world, his mystery dress and equipments . . .

Such is a medicine-man or a physician, and such is one of his wild and ridiculous manœuvres, which I have just witnessed in this strange country . . . In all councils of war and peace, they have a seat with the chiefs—are regularly consulted before any public step is taken, and the greatest deference and respect is paid to their opinions.

LETTER—NO. 7.

◄——————►

Mouth of Yellow Stone, Upper Missouri.

My painting-room has become so great a lounge, and I so
...great a "medicine-man," that all other amusements are left,
and all other topics of conversation and gossip are postponed for
future consideration. The chiefs have had to place "soldiers" (as they
are called) at my door, with spears in hand to protect me from the
throng, who otherwise would press upon me; and none but the
worthies are allowed to come into my medicine apartments, and
none to be painted, except such as are decided by the chiefs to be
worthy of so high an honour.

The Crows and Blackfeet who are here together, are enemies of
the most deadly kind while out on the plains; but here they sit and
smoke quietly together, yet with a studied and dignified reserve.

The Blackfeet are, perhaps, one of the most (if not entirely the
most) numerous and warlike tribes on the Continent. They occupy
the whole of the country about the sources of the Missouri, from this
place to the Rocky Mountains; and their numbers, from the best
computations, are something like forty or fifty thousand—they are
(like all other tribes whose numbers are sufficiently large to give
them boldness) warlike and ferocious, *i.e.* they are predatory, are
roaming fearlessly about the country, even into and through every
part of the Rocky Mountains, and carrying war amongst their enemies,
who are, of course, every tribe who inhabit the country about them.

The Crows who live on the head waters of Yellow Stone, and
extend from this neighbourhood also to the base of the Rocky
Mountains, are similar in the above respects to the Blackfeet; roam-

ing about a great part of the year—and seeking enemies wherever they can find them.

They are a much smaller tribe than the Blackfeet, with whom they are always at war, and from whose great numbers they suffer prodigiously in battle; and probably will be in a few years entirely destroyed by them.

The Crows have not, perhaps, more than 7000 in their nation, and probably not more than eight hundred warriors or fighting men. Amongst the more powerful tribes, like the Sioux and Blackfeet, who have been enabled to preserve their warriors, it is a fair calculation to count one in five as warriors; but among the Crows and Minatarees, and Poncas, and several other small but warlike tribes, this proportion cannot exist; as in some of these I have found two or three women to a man in the nation; in consequence of the continual losses sustained amongst their men in war, and also whilst pursuing the buffaloes on the plains for food, where their lives are exceedingly exposed.

The Blackfeet and the Crows, like the Sioux and Assinneboins, have nearly the same mode of constructing their wigwam or lodge; in which tribes it is made of buffalo skins sewed together, after being dressed, and made into the form of a tent; supported within by some twenty or thirty pine poles of twenty-five feet in height, with an apex or aperture at the top, through which the smoke escapes and the light is admitted. These lodges, or tents, are taken down in a few minutes by the squaws, when they wish to change their location, and easily transported to any part of the country where they wish to encamp; and they generally move some six or eight times in the course of the summer; following the immense herds of buffaloes, as they range over these vast plains, from east to west, and north to south. The objects for which they do this are two-fold,—to procure and dress their skins, which are brought in, in the fall and winter, and sold to the Fur Company, for white man's luxury; and also for the purpose of killing and drying buffalo meat, which they bring in from their hunts, packed on their horses' backs, in great quantities; making pemican, and preserving the marrow-fat for their winter quarters; which are generally taken up in some heavy-timbered bottom, on the banks of some stream, deep imbedded within the surrounding bluffs, which break off the winds, and make their long and tedious winter tolerable and supportable. They then sometimes erect their skin lodges amongst the timber, and dwell in them during the winter months; but more frequently cut logs and make a miserable and rude sort of log cabin, in which they can live much warmer and better protected from the assaults of their enemies, in case they are attacked; in which case a log cabin is a tolerable fort against Indian weapons.

The Crows, of all the tribes in this region, or on the Continent, make the most beautiful lodge ... They construct them as the Sioux do, and make them of the same material; yet they oftentimes dress the skins of which they are composed almost as white as linen, and beautifully garnish them with porcupine quills, and paint and ornament them in such a variety of ways, as renders them exceedingly picturesque and agreeable to the eye ...

The manner in which an encampment of Indians strike their tents and transport them is curious, and ... a very ... unexpected sight ... Whilst ascending the river to this place, I saw an encampment of Sioux, consisting of six hundred of these lodges, struck, and all things packed and on the move in a very few minutes. The chief sends his runners or criers ... through the village, a few hours before they are to start; announcing his determination to move, and the hour fixed upon, and the necessary preparations are in the meantime making; and at the time announced, the lodge of the chief is seen flapping in the wind, a part of the poles having been taken out from under it; this is the signal, and in one minute, six hundred of them (on a level and beautiful prairie), which before had been strained tight and fixed, were seen waving and flapping in the wind, and in one minute more all were flat upon the ground. Their horses and dogs, of which they had a vast number, had all been secured upon the spot, in readiness; and each one was speedily loaded with the burthen allotted to it, and ready to fall into the grand procession.

For this strange cavalcade, preparation is made in the following manner: the poles of a lodge are divided into two bunches, and the little ends of each bunch fastened upon the shoulders or withers of a horse, leaving the butt ends to drag behind on the ground on either side. Just behind the horse, a brace or pole is tied across, which keeps the poles in their respective places; and then upon that and the poles behind the horse, is placed the lodge or tent, which is rolled up, and also numerous other articles of household and domestic furniture, and on the top of all, two, three, and even (sometimes) four women and children! Each one of these horses has a conductress, who sometimes walks before and leads it, with a tremendous pack upon her own back; and at others she sits astride of its back, with a child, perhaps, at her breast, and another astride of the horse's back behind her, clinging to her waist with one arm, while it affectionately embraces a sneaking dog-pup in the other.

In this way five or six hundred wigwams, with all their furniture (Illustration 8), may be seen drawn out for miles, creeping over the grass-covered plains of this country; and three times that number of men, on good horses, strolling along in front or on the flank; and, in some tribes, in the rear of this heterogeneous caravan, at least five times that number of dogs, which fall into the rank, and follow in the train and company of the women, and every cur of them, who is large enough, and not too cunning to be enslaved, is encumbered with a car or sled (or whatever it may be better called), on which he patiently drags his load—a part of the household goods and furniture of the lodge to which he belongs. Two poles, about fifteen feet long, are placed upon the dog's shoulder, in the same manner as the lodge poles are attached to the horses, leaving the larger ends to drag upon the ground behind him; on which is placed a bundle or wallet which is allotted to him to carry, and with which he trots off amid the throng of dogs and squaws . . .

The Crows, like the Blackfeet, are beautifully costumed, and perhaps with somewhat more of taste and elegance; inasmuch as the skins of which their dresses are made are more delicately and whitely dressed. The art of dressing skins belongs to the Indians in all countries; and the Crows surpass the civilized world in the beauty of their skin-dressing . . .

The usual mode of dressing the buffalo, and other skins, is by immersing them for a few days under a lye from ashes and water, until the hair can be removed; when they are strained upon a frame or upon the ground, with stakes or pins driven through the edges into the earth; where they remain for several days, with the brains of

Illustration 8. Band of Sioux moving camp.

the buffalo or elk spread upon and over them; and at last finished by "graining," as it is termed, by the squaws; who use a sharpened bone, the shoulder-blade or other large bone of the animal, sharpened at the edge, somewhat like an adze; with the edge of which they scrape the fleshy side of the skin; bearing on it with the weight of their bodies, thereby drying and softening the skin, and fitting it for use.

The greater part of these skins, however, go through still another operation afterwards, which gives them a greater value, and renders them much more serviceable—that is, the process of smoking. For this, a small hole is dug in the ground, and a fire is built in it with rotten wood, which will produce a great quantity of smoke without much blaze; and several small poles of the proper length stuck in the ground around it, and drawn and fastened together at the top, around which a skin is wrapped in form of a tent, and generally sewed together at the edges to secure the smoke within it; within this the skins to be smoked are placed, and in this condition the tent will stand a day or so, enclosing the heated smoke; and by some chemical process or other, which I do not understand, the skins thus acquire a quality which enables them, after being ever so many times wet, to dry soft and pliant as they were before, which secret I have never yet seen practised in my own country; and for the lack of which, all of our dressed skins when once wet, are, I think, chiefly ruined.

An Indian's dress of deer skins, which is wet a hundred times upon his back, dries soft; and his lodge also, which stands in the rains, and even through the severity of winter, is taken down as soft and as clean as when it was first put up.

A Crow is known wherever he is met by his beautiful white dress, and his tall and elegant figure; the greater part of the men being six feet high. The Blackfeet on the other hand, are more of the Herculean make—about middling stature, with broad shoulders, and great expansion of chest; and the skins of which their dresses are made, are chiefly dressed black, or of a dark brown colour; from which circumstance, in all probability, they having black leggings or mocassins, have got the name of Blackfeet.

The Crows are very handsome and gentlemanly Indians in their personal appearance: and have been always reputed, since the first acquaintance made with them, very civil and friendly . . .

In profile, the *semi-lunar* outline of the face ... strongly characterizes them as distinct from any relationship or resemblance to, the Blackfeet, Shiennies, Knisteneaux, Mandans, or other tribes now existing in these regions. The peculiar character of which I am speaking, like all other national characteristics, is of course met by many exceptions in the tribe, though the greater part of the men are thus strongly marked with a bold and prominent anti-angular nose, with a clear and rounded arch, and a low and receding forehead; the frontal bone oftentimes appearing to have been compressed by some effort of art, in a certain degree approaching to the horrid distortion thus produced amongst the Flatheads beyond the Rocky Mountains. I learned however from repeated inquiries, that no such custom is practiced amongst them, but their heads, such as they are, are the results of a natural growth, and therefore may well be offered as the basis of a national or tribal *character* ...

These people to be sure, have in some instances plundered and robbed trappers and travellers in their country; and for that I have sometimes heard them called rascals and thieves, and rogues of the first order, &c.; yet they do not consider themselves such; for thieving in their estimation is a high crime, and considered the most disgraceful act that a man can possibly do. They call this *capturing*, where they sometimes run off a Trader's horses, and make their boast of it; considering it a kind of retaliation or summary justice, which they think it right and honourable and that they should administer. And why not? For the unlicensed trespass committed through their country from one end to the other, by mercenary white men, who are destroying the game, and catching all the beaver and other rich and valuable furs out of their country, without paying them an equivalent, or, in fact, anything at all, for it; and this too, when they have been warned time and again of the danger they would be in, if they longer persisted in the practice.

Reader, I look upon the Indian as the most honest and honourable race of people that I ever lived amongst in my life; and in their native state, I pledge you my honour they are the last of all the human family to pilfer or to steal, if you trust to their honour; and for this never-ending and boundless system of theft and plunder, and debauchery, that is practiced off upon these rightful owners of

the soil, by acquisitive white men, I consider the infliction, or
retaliation, by driving off and appropriating a few horses, but a
lenient punishment, which those persons at least should expect; and
which, in fact, none but a very honourable and high-minded people
could inflict, instead of a much severer one; which they could easily
practice upon the few white men in their country, without rendering
themselves amenable to any law . . .

I have conversed often and much with Messrs. Sublette and
Campbell, two gentlemen of the highest respectability, who have
traded with the Crows for several years, and they tell me they are one
of the most honourable, honest, and high-minded races of people on
earth; and with Mr. Tullock, also, a man of the strictest veracity,
who is now here with a party of them; and, he says, they never
steal,—have a high sense of honour,—and being fearless and proud,
are quick to punish or retaliate . . .

No part of the human race could present a more picturesque
and thrilling appearance on horseback than a party of Crows rigged
out in all their plumes and trappings—galloping about and yelping,
in what they call a war-parade, *i.e.* in a sort of tournament or
sham-fight, passing rapidly through the evolutions of battle, and
vaunting forth the wonderful character of their military exploits.
This is an amusement, of which they are excessively fond; and great
preparations are invariably made for these occasional shows. No tribe
of Indians on the Continent are better able to produce a pleasing
and thrilling effect in these scenes, nor any more vain, and consequently better prepared to draw pleasure and satisfaction from them,
than the Crows.

LETTER—NO. 8

◆————————————▶

Mouth of Yellow Stone, Upper Missouri.

I have just been painting a number of the Crows, fine looking
... and noble gentlemen. They are really as handsome and
well-formed a set of men as can be seen in any part of the world.
There is a sort of ease and grace added to their dignity of manners,
which gives them the air of gentlemen at once. I observed the other
day, that most of them were over six feet high, and very many of
these have cultivated their natural hair to such an almost incredible
length, that it sweeps the ground as they walk; there are frequent
instances of this kind amongst them, and in some cases, a foot or
more of it will drag on the grass as they walk, giving exceeding grace
and beauty to their movements . . .

This extraordinary length of hair amongst the Crows is confined
to the men alone; for the women, though all of them with glossy and
beautiful hair, and a great profusion of it, are unable to cultivate it to
so great a length; or else they are not allowed to compete with their
lords in a fashion so ornamental (and on which the men so highly
pride themselves), and are obliged in many cases to cut it short off.

The fashion of long hair amongst the men, prevails throughout all
the Western and North Western tribes, after passing the Sacs and
Foxes; and the Pawnees of the Platte, who, with two or three other
tribes only, are in the habit of shaving nearly the whole head.

The present chief of the Crows . . . is called "Long-hair," and has
received his name as well as his office from the circumstance of
having the longest hair of any man in the nation . . . On ordinary
occasions it is wound with a broad leather strap, from his head to its

extreme end, and then folded up into a budget or block, of some ten or twelve inches in length, and of some pounds weight; which when he walks is carried under his arm, or placed in his bosom, within the folds of his robe; but on any great parade or similar occasion, his pride is to unfold it, oil it with bear's grease and let it drag behind him, some three or four feet of it spread out upon the grass, and black and shining like a raven's wing . . .

The Crow women (and Blackfeet also) are not handsome, and I shall at present say but little of them. They are, like all other Indian women, the slaves of their husbands: being obliged to perform all the domestic duties and drudgeries of the tribe, and not allowed to join in their religious rites or ceremonies, nor in the dance or other amusements.

The women in all these upper and western tribes are decently dressed, and many of them with great beauty and taste; their dresses are all of deer or goat skins, extending from their chins quite down to the feet; these dresses are in many instances trimmed with ermine, and ornamented with porcupine quills and beads with exceeding ingenuity.

The Crow and Blackfeet women, like all others I ever saw in any Indian tribe, divide the hair on the forehead, and paint the separation or crease with vermilion or red earth. For what purpose this little, but universal, custom is observed, I never have been able to learn . . .

These two tribes, whom I have spoken of connectedly, speak two distinct and entirely dissimilar languages; and the language of each is different, and radically so, from that of all other tribes about them. As these people are always at war, and have been, time out of mind, they do not intermarry or hold converse with each other, by which any knowledge of each other's language could be acquired. It would be the work of a man's life-time to collect the languages of all the different tribes which I am visiting; and I shall, from necessity, leave this subject chiefly for others, who have the time to devote to them, to explain them to the world . . .

The Blackfeet are, perhaps, the most powerful tribe of Indians on the Continent; and being sensible of their strength, have stubbornly resisted the Traders in their country, who have been gradually forming an acquaintance with them, and endeavouring to establish a permanent and profitable system of trade. Their country abounds in beaver and buffalo, and most of the fur-bearing animals of North America; and the American Fur Company, with an unconquerable spirit of trade and enterprize, has pushed its establishments into their country; and the numerous parties of trappers are tracing up their streams and rivers, rapidly destroying the beavers which dwell in them. The Blackfeet have repeatedly informed the Traders of the Company, that if their men persisted in trapping beavers in their country, they should kill them whenever they met them. They have executed their threats in many instances, and the Company lose some fifteen or twenty men annually, who fall by the hands of these people, in defence of what they deem their property and their rights. Trinkets and whiskey, however, will soon spread their charms amongst these, as they have amongst other tribes; and white man's voracity will sweep the prairies and the streams of their wealth, to the Rocky Mountains and the Pacific Ocean; leaving the Indians to inhabit, and at last to starve upon, a dreary and solitary waste.

The Blackfeet, therefore, having been less traded with, and less seen by white people than most of the other tribes, are more imperfectly understood; and it yet remains a question to be solved— whether there are twenty, or forty or fifty thousand of them? for no one, as yet, can correctly estimate their real strength. From all I can learn, however, which is the best information that can be got from the Traders, there are not far from 40,000 Indians (altogether), who range under the general domination of Blackfeet.

From our slight and imperfect knowledge of them, and other tribes occupying the country about the sources of the Missouri, there is no doubt in my mind, that we are in the habit of bringing more Indians into the computation, than are entitled justly to the appellation of "Blackfeet" . . . The Blackfeet proper are divided into four bands or families, as follow:—the "Pe-a-gans," of 500 lodges; the "Blackfoot" band, of 450 lodges; the "Blood" band, of 450 lodges; and the "Small Robes," of 250 lodges. These four bands constituting about 1650 lodges, averaging ten to the lodge, amount to about 16,500 souls . . .

There is in this region a rich and interesting field for the linguist or the antiquarian; and stubborn facts, I think, if they could be well procured, that would do away the idea which many learned gentlemen entertain, that the Indian languages of North America can all be traced to two or three roots. The language of the Dahcotas is entirely and radically distinct from that of the Mandans, and theirs equally so from the Blackfoot and the Crows. And from the lips of Mr. Brazeau, a gentleman of education and strict observation, who has lived several years with the Blackfeet and Shiennes, and who speaks the language of tribes on either side of them, assures me that these languages are radically distinct and dissimilar, as I have above stated; and also, that although he has been several years amongst those tribes, he has not been able to trace the slightest resemblance between the . . . Blackfoot, and Shienne, and Crow, and Mandan tongues; and from a great deal of corroborating information, which I have got from other persons acquainted with these tribes, I am fully convinced of the correctness of his statements.

Besides the Blackfeet and Crows, whom I told you were assembled at this place, are also the Knisteneaux (or Crees, as they are commonly called), a very pretty and pleasing tribe of Indians, of about 3000 in number, living on the north of this, and also the Assinneboins and Ojibbeways [Ojibwa, or Anishinasi]; both of which tribes also inhabit the country to the north and north-east of the mouth of Yellow Stone.

The chief of that part of the Ojibbeway tribe who in habit these northern regions (Illustration 9), and whose name is Sha-co-pay (the Six), is a man of huge size; with dignity of manner, and pride and vanity, just about in proportion to his bulk. He sat for his portrait in a most beautiful dress, fringed with scalp locks in profusion; which he had snatched, in his early life from his enemies' heads, and now wears as proud trophies and proofs of what his arm has accomplished in battles with his enemies. His shirt of buckskin is beautifully embroidered and painted in curious hieroglyphics, the history of his battles and charts of his life. This, and also each and every article of his varied dress, had been manufactured by his wives, of which he had several; and one, though not the most agreeable (Illustration 10), is seen represented by his side.

The Assinneboins of seven thousand, and the Ojibbeways of six thousand, occupy a vast extent of country, in a north-eastern direction from this; extending also into the British possessions as high north as Lake Winnepeg; and trading principally with the British

Illustration 9. Sha-co-pay, The Six, chief of the Ojibbeways.

Illustration 10. Wife of Sha-co-pay.

Company. These three tribes are in a state of nature, living as neighbours, and are also on terms of friendship with each other. This friendship, however, is probably but a temporary arrangement, brought about by the Traders amongst them; and which, like most Indian peace establishments, will be of short duration.

The Assinneboins are a part of the Dahcotas, or Sioux, undoubtedly; for their personal appearance as well as their language is very similar. The Ojibbeways are, undoubtedly, a part of the tribe of Chippeways, with whom we are more familiarly acquainted, and who inhabit the south-west shore of Lake Superior. Their language is the same, though they are separated several hundred miles from any of them, and seem to have no knowledge of them, or traditions of the manner in which, or of the time when, they became severed from each other.

At what time, or in what manner, these two parts of a nation got strayed away from each other is a mystery; yet such cases have often occurred, of which I shall say more in future. Large parties who are, straying off in pursuit of game, or in the occupation of war, are oftentimes intercepted by their enemy; and being prevented from returning, are run off to a distant region, where they take up their residence and establish themselves as a nation . . .

The Assinneboins, or stone boilers, are a fine and noble looking race of Indians; bearing, both in their looks and customs, a striking resemblance to the Dahcotas or Sioux, from whom they have undoubtedly sprung. The men are tall, and graceful in their movements; and wear their pictured robes of the buffalo hide with great skill and pleasing effect. They are good hunters, and tolerably supplied with horses; and living in a country abounding with buffaloes, are well supplied with the necessaries of Indian life, and may be said to live well. Their games and amusements are many, of which the most valued one is the ball-play; and in addition to which, they have the game of the moccasin, horse-racing, and dancing; some one of which, they seem to be almost continually practicing, and of all of which I shall hereafter give the reader (as well as of many others of their amusements) a minute account . . .

I have painted the portrait of a very distinguished young man, and son of the chief (Illustration 11); his dress is a very handsome one,

Illustration 11. Wi-jun-jon, Pigeon's Egg Head.

Illustration 12. Chin-cha-pee, Fire Bug That Creeps, wife of Pigeon's Egg Head.

and in every respect answers well to the descriptions I have given above. The name of this man is Wi-jun-jon (the Pigeon's Egg Head), and by the side of him (Illustration 12) will be seen the portrait of his wife, Chin-cha-pee (the Fire Bug That Creeps), a fine looking squaw, in a handsome dress of the mountain-sheep skin, holding in her hand a stick curiously carved, with which every woman in this country is supplied; for the purpose of digging up the "Pomme Blanche," or prairie turnip, which is found in great quantities in these northern prairies, and furnishes the Indians with an abundant and nourishing food. The women collect these turnips by striking the end of the stick into the ground, and prying them out; after which they are dried and preserved in their wigwams for use during the season.

I have just had the satisfaction of seeing this travelled-gentleman (Wi-jun-jon) meet his tribe, his wife and his little children; after an absence of a year or more, on his journey of 6000 miles to Washington City, and back again (in company with Major Sanford, the Indian agent); where he has been spending the winter amongst the fashionables in the polished circles of civilized society . . .

On his way home from St. Louis to this place, a distance of 2000 miles, I travelled with this gentleman, on the steamer Yellow-Stone; and saw him step ashore (on a beautiful prairie, where several thousands of his people were encamped), with a complete suit *en militaire,* a colonel's uniform of blue, presented to him by the President of the United States, with a beaver hat and feather, with epaulettes of gold—with sash and belt, and broad sword; with high-heeled boots—with a keg of whiskey under his arm, and a blue umbrella in his hand. In this plight and metamorphose, he took his position on the bank, amongst his friends—his wife and other relations; not one of whom exhibited, for an half-hour or more, the least symptoms of recognition, although they knew well who was before them. He also gazed upon them—upon his wife and parents, and little children, who were about, as if they were foreign to him, and he had not a feeling or thought to interchange with them. Thus the mutual gazings upon and from this would-be-stranger, lasted for full half an hour; when a gradual, but cold and exceedingly formal recognition began to take place, and an acquaintance ensued, which ultimately and smoothly resolved itself, without the least apparent emotion, into its former state; and the mutual kindred intercourse seemed to flow on exactly where it had been broken off, as if it had been but for a moment, and nothing had transpired in the interim to check or change its character or expression.

Such is one of the stoic instances of a custom which belongs to all the North American Indians, forming one of the most striking features in their character; valued, cherished and practised, like many others of their strange notions, for reasons which are difficult to be learned or understood; and which probably will never be justly appreciated by others than themselves.

This man, at this time, is creating a wonderful sensation amongst his tribe, who are daily and nightly gathered in gaping and listless crowds around him, whilst he is descanting upon what he has seen in the fashionable world; and which to them is unintelligible and beyond their comprehension; for which I find they are already setting him down as a liar and impostor.

What may be the final results of his travels and initiation into the fashionable world, and to what disasters his incredible narrations may yet subject the poor fellow in this strange land, time will only develop.

He is now in disgrace, and spurned by the leading men of the tribe, and rather to be pitied than envied, for the advantages which one might have supposed would have flown from his fashionable tour . . .

LETTER—NO. 9.

◆―――――――▶

Mouth of Yellow Stone, Upper Missouri.

Since the dates of my other Letters from this place, I have been taking some wild rambles about this beautiful country of green fields; jolted and tossed about, on horseback and on foot, where pen, ink, and paper never thought of going; and of course the most that I saw and have learned, and would tell to the world, is yet to be written. It is not probable, however, that I shall again date a letter at this place, as I commence, in a few days, my voyage down the river in a canoe; but yet I may give you many a retrospective glance at this fairy land and its amusements.

A traveller on his tour through such a country as this, has no time to write, and scarcely time enough to moralize . . . Impressions, however, of the most vivid kind, are rapidly and indelibly made by the fleeting incidents of savage life . . . It is but to paint the splendid panorama of a world entirely different from anything seen or painted before; with its thousands of miles, and tens of thousands of grassy hills and dales, where nought but silence reigns, and where the soul of a contemplative mould is seemingly lifted up to its Creator. What man in the world, I would ask, ever ascended to the pinnacle of one of Missouri's green-carpeted bluffs, a thousand miles severed from his own familiar land, and giddily gazed over the interminable and boundless ocean of grass-covered hills and valleys which lie beneath him, where the gloom *silence* is complete—where not even the voice of the sparrow or cricket is heard—without feeling a sweet melancholy come over him, which seemed to drown his sense of everything beneath and on a level with him? . . .

In traversing the immense regions of the *classic* West, the mind of a philanthropist is filled to the brim with feelings of admiration; but to reach this country, one is obliged to descend from the light and glow of civilized atmosphere, through the different grades of civilization, which gradually sink to the most deplorable condition along the extreme frontier; thence through the most pitiable misery and wretchedness of savage degradation; where the genius of natural liberty and independence have been blasted and destroyed by the contaminating vices and dissipations introduced by the immoral part of *civilized* society. Through this dark and sunken vale of wretchedness one hurries, as through a pestilence, until he gradually rises again into the proud and chivalrous pale of savage society, in its state of original nature, beyond the reach of civilized contamination; here he finds much to fix his enthusiasm upon, and much to admire. Even here, the predominant passions of the savage breast, of ferocity and cruelty, are often found; yet *restrained*, and frequently *subdued*, by the noblest traits of honour and magnanimity,—a race of men who live and enjoy life and its luxuries, and practice its virtues, very far beyond the usual estimation of the world, who are apt to judge the savage and his virtues from the poor, degraded, and humbled specimens which alone can be seen along our frontiers. From the first settlements of our Atlantic coast to the present day, the bane of this *blasting frontier* has regularly crowded upon them, from the northern to the southern extremities of our country; and, like the fire in a prairie, which destroys everything where it passes, it has blasted and sunk them, all but their names, into oblivion, wherever it has travelled. It is to this tainted class alone that the epithet of "poor, naked, and drunken savage," can be, with propriety, applied; for all those numerous tribes which I have visited, and are yet uncorrupted by the vices of civilized acquaintance, are well clad, in many instances cleanly, and in the full enjoyment of life and its luxuries. It is for the character and preservation of these noble fellows that I am an enthusiast; and it is for these uncontaminated people that I would be willing to devote the energies of my life. It is a sad and melancholy truth to contemplate, that all the numerous tribes who inhabited our vast Atlantic States *have not* "fled to the West;"—that they are not to be found here—that they have been blasted by the fire which has passed over them—have sunk into their graves, and everything but their names travelled into oblivion.

The distinctive character of all these Western Indians, as well as their traditions relative to their ancient locations, prove beyond a doubt, that they have been for a very long time located on the soil which they now possess; and in most respects, distinct and unlike those nations who formerly inhabited the Atlantic coast, and who (according to the erroneous opinion of a great part of the world), have fled to the West.

It is for these inoffensive and unoffending people, yet unvisited by the vices of civilized society, that I would proclaim to the world, that it is time, for the honour of our country—for the honour of every citizen of the republic—and for the sake of humanity, that our government should raise her strong arm to save the remainder of them from the pestilence which is rapidly advancing upon them. We have gotten from them territory enough, and the country which they now inhabit is most of it too barren of timber for the use of civilized man; it affords them, however, the means and luxuries of savage life; and it is to be hoped that our government will not acquiesce in the continued wilful destruction of these happy people.

My heart has sometimes almost bled with pity for them, while amongst them, and witnessing their innocent amusements, as I have contemplated the inevitable bane that was rapidly advancing upon them; without that check from the protecting arm of government, and which alone could shield them from destruction . . .

LETTER—NO. 10.

◄————————————————►

Mandan Village, Upper Missouri.

W e launched off one fine morning, taking our leave of the
  . . . Fort, and the friends within it; and also, for ever, of the
beautiful green fields, and hills, and dales, and prairie bluffs, that
encompass the enchanting shores of the Yellow Stone.

Our canoe, which was made of green timber, was heavy and
awkward; but our course being with the current, promised us a fair
and successful voyage. Ammunition was laid in in abundance—a
good stock of dried buffalo tongues—a dozen or two of beavers'
tails—and a good supply of pemican. Bogard and Ba'tiste [Catlin's
stalwart trapper guide-companions] occupied the middle and bow,
with their paddles in their hands; and I took my seat in the stern of
the boat, at the steering oar. Our larder was as I have said; and
added to that, some few pounds of fresh buffalo meat.

Besides which, and ourselves, our little craft carried several packs
of Indian dresses and other articles, which I had purchased of the
Indians; and also my canvass and easel, and our culinary articles,
which were few and simple; consisting of three tin cups, a coffee-pot—
one plate—a frying-pan—and a tin kettle.

Thus fitted out and embarked, we swept off at a rapid rate under
the shouts of the savages, and the cheers of our friends, who lined the
banks as we gradually lost sight of them, and turned our eyes towards
St. Louis, which was 2000 miles below us, with nought intervening, save
the widespread and wild regions, inhabited by the roaming savage.

At the end of our first day's journey, we found ourselves handily
encamping with several thousand Assinneboins, who had pitched

their tents upon the bank of the river, and received us with every mark of esteem and friendship.

In the midst of this group, was my friend Wi-jun-jon (the pigeon's egg head), still lecturing on the manners and customs of the "pale faces." Continuing to relate without any appearance of exhaustion, the marvellous scenes which he had witnessed amongst the white people, on his tour to Washington City.

Many were the gazers who seemed to be the whole time crowding around him, to hear his recitals; and the plight which he was in rendered his appearance quite ridiculous. His beautiful military dress, of which I before spoke, had been so shockingly tattered and metamorphosed, that his appearence was truly laughable.

His keg of whiskey had dealt out to his friends all its charms—his frock-coat, which his wife had thought was of no earthly use below the waist, had been cut off at that place, and the nether half of it supplied her with a beautiful pair of leggings; and his silver-laced hat-band had been converted into a splendid pair of garters for the same. His umbrella the poor fellow still affectionately held on to, and kept spread at all times. As I before said, his theme seemed to be exhaustless, and he, in the estimation of his tribe, to be an unexampled liar.

Of the village of Assinneboins we took leave on the following morning, and rapidly made our way down the river. The rate of the current being four or five miles per hour, through one continued series of picturesque grass-covered bluffs and knolls, which everywhere had the appearance of an old and highly-cultivated country, with houses and fences removed.

There is, much of the way, on one side or the other, a bold and abrupt precipice of three or four hundred feet in elevation, presenting itself in an exceedingly rough and picturesque from, to the shore of the river; sloping down from the summit level of the prairies above, which sweep off from the brink of the precipice, almost level, to an unknown distance.

It is along the rugged and wild fronts of these cliffs, whose sides are generally formed of hard clay, that the mountain-sheep dwell, and are often discovered in great numbers. Their habits are much like those of the goat; and in every respect they are like that animal, except in the horns, which resemble those of the ram; sometimes making two entire circles in their coil; and at the roots, each horn is, in some instances, from five to six inches in breadth.

On the second day of our voyage we discovered a number of these animals skipping along the sides of the precipice, always keeping about equi-distant between the top and bottom of the ledge; leaping and vaulting in the most extraordinary manner from point to point, and seeming to cling actually, to the sides of the wall, where neither man nor beast could possibly follow them . . .

Being on shore, and our canoe landed secure, we whiled away the greater part of this day amongst the wild and ragged cliffs, into which we had entered; and a part of our labours were vainly spent in the pursuit of a war-eagle [juvenile golden eagle or "spotted eagle"]. This noble bird is the one which the Indians in these regions, value so highly for their tail feathers, which are used as the most valued plumes for decorating the heads and dresses of their warriors. It is a beautiful bird, and, the Indians tell me, conquers all other varieties of eagles in the country; from which circumstance, the Indians respect the bird, and hold it in the highest esteem, and value its quills . . . This bird has often been called the calumet eagle and war-eagle; the last of which appellations I have already accounted for; and the other has arisen from the fact, that the Indians almost invariably ornament their calumets or pipes of peace with its quills.

Our day's loitering brought us through many a wild scene; occasionally across the tracks of the grizzly bear, and, in sight merely of a band of buffaloes; "which got the wind of us," and were out of the way, leaving us to return to our canoe at night, with a mere speck of good luck. Just before we reached the river, I heard the crack of a rifle, and in a few moments Bogard came in sight, and threw down from his shoulders a fine antelope; which added to our larder, and we were ready to proceed. We embarked and travelled until nightfall, when we encamped on a beautiful little prairie at the base of a series of grass-covered bluffs; and the next morning cooked our breakfast and ate it, and rowed on until late in the afternoon; when we stopped at the base of some huge clay bluffs, forming one of the most curious and romantic scenes imaginable. At this spot the river expands itself into the appearence somewhat of a beautiful lake; and in the midst of it, and on and about its sand-bars, floated and stood, hundreds and thousands of white swans and pelicans.

Though the scene in front of our encampment at this place was placid and beautiful; with its flowing water—its wild fowl—and its almost endless variety of gracefully sloping hills and green prairies in the distance; yet it was not less wild and picturesque in our rear, where the rugged and various coloured bluffs were grouped in all the wildest fancies and rudeness of Nature's accidental varieties.

The whole country behind us seemed to have been dug and thrown up into huge piles, as if some giant mason had been there mixing his mortar and paints, and throwing together his rude models for some sublime structure of a colossal city;—with its walls—its domes—its ramparts—its huge porticos and galleries—its castles—its fosses and ditches;—and in the midst of his progress, he had abandoned his works to the destroying hand of time, which had already done much to tumble them down, and deface their noble structure; by jostling them together, with all their vivid colours, into an unsystematic and unintelligible mass of sublime ruins . . .

In the morning, and before sunrise, as usual, Bogard (who was a Yankee, and a "wide-awake-fellow," just retiring from a ten years' siege of hunting and trapping in the Rocky Mountains,) thrust his head out from under the robe, rubbing his eyes open, and exclaiming as he grasped for his gun, "By darn, look at old Cale! will you!" Ba'tiste, who was more fond of his dreams, snored away, muttering something that I could not understand, when Bogard seized him with a grip, that instantly shook off his iron slumbers. I rose at the same time, and all eyes were turned at once upon *Caleb* (as the grizzly bear is familiarly called by the trappers in the Rocky Mountains—or more often "Cale," for brevity's sake), who was sitting up in the dignity and fury of her sex, within a few rods, and gazing upon us, with her two little cubs at her side! . . . I turned my eyes to the canoe which had been fastened at the shore a few paces from us; and saw that everything had been pawed out of it, and all eatables had been without ceremony devoured. My packages of dresses and Indian curiosities had been drawn out upon the bank, and deliberately opened and inspected. Every thing had been scraped and pawed out, to the bottom of the boat; and even the rawhide thong, with which it was tied to a stake, had been chewed, and no doubt swallowed, as there was no trace of it remaining. Nor was this peep into the secrets of our luggage enough for her insatiable curiosity—we saw by the prints of her huge paws, that were left in the ground, that she had been perambulating our humble mattresses, smelling at our toes and our noses, without choosing to molest us . . . It is a well-known fact, that man and beast, upon their feet, are sure to be attacked when they cross the path of this grizzly and grim monster, which is the terror of all this country; often growing to the enormous size of eight hundred or one thousand pounds.

Well—whilst we sat in the dilemma which I have just described, each one was hastily preparing his weapons for defence, when I proposed the mode of attack; by which means I was in hopes of destroying her—capture her young ones, and bring her skin home as a trophy. My plans, however, entirely failed, though we were well armed; for Bogard and Ba'tiste both remonstrated with a vehemence that was irresistible; saying that the standing rule in the mountains was "never to fight Caleb, except in self-defense" . . . Bogard added, "these darned animals are too much for us, and we had better be off;" at which my courage cooled, and we packed up and re-embarked as fast as possible.

The scenery of this day's travel, as I have before said, was exceedingly beautiful; and our canoe was often run to the shore, upon which we stepped to admire the endless variety of wild flowers, "wasting their sweetness on the desert air," and the abundance of delicious fruits that were about us. Whilst wandering through the high grass, the wild sun-flowers and voluptuous lilies were constantly taunting us by striking our faces; whilst here and there, in every direction, there were little copses and clusters of plum trees and gooseberries, and wild currants, loaded down with their fruit; and amongst these, to sweeten the atmosphere and add a charm to the effect, the wild rose bushes seemed planted in beds and in hedges, and everywhere were decked out in all the glory of their delicate tints, and shedding sweet aroma to every breath of the air that passed over them.

In addition to these, we had the luxury of service-berries, without stint; and the buffalo bushes, which are peculiar to these northern regions, lined the banks of the river and defiles in the bluffs, sometimes for miles together; forming almost impassable hedges, so loaded with the weight of their fruit, that their boughs were everywhere gracefully bending down and resting on the ground . . .

On the morning of the next day, and not long after we had stopped and taken our breakfast, and while our canoe was swiftly gliding along under the shore of a beautiful prairie, I saw in the grass, on the bank above me, what I supposed to be the back of a fine elk, busy at his grazing. I let our craft float silently by for a little distance, when I communicated the intelligence to my men, and slily ran in, to the shore. I pricked the priming of my fire-lock, and taking a bullet or two in my mouth, stepped ashore, and trailing my rifle in my hand, went back under the bank, carefully crawling up in a little ravine, quite sure of my game; when, to my utter surprise and violent alarm, I found the elk to be no more nor less than an Indian pony, getting his breakfast! and a little beyond him, a number of others grazing; and nearer to me, on the left, a war-party reclining around a little fire; and yet nearer, and within twenty paces of the muzzle of my gun, the naked shoulders of a brawny Indian, who seemed busily engaged in cleaning his gun. From this critical dilemma, the reader can easily imagine that I vanished with all the suddenness and secrecy that was possible, bending my course towards my canoe. Bogard and Ba'tiste correctly construing the expression on my face, and the agitation of my hurried retreat, prematurely unmoored from the shore; and the force of the current carrying them around a huge pile of drift wood, threw me back for some distance upon my own resources; though they finally got in, near the shore, and I into the boat, with the steering oar in my hand; when we plied our sinews with effect and in silence, till we were wafted far from the ground which we deemed critical and dangerous to our lives; for we had been daily in dread of meeting a war-party of the revengeful Riccarees, which we had been told was on the river, in search of the Mandans. From and after this exciting occurrence, the entries in my journal for the rest of the voyage to the village of the Mandans, were as follow:—

Saturday, fifth day of our voyage from the mouth of Yellow Stone, at eleven o'clock.—Landed our canoe in the Grand Détour (or Big

Bend) as it is called, at the base of a stately clay mound, and ascended, all hands, to the summit level, to take a glance at the picturesque and magnificent works of Nature that were about us. Spent the remainder of the day in painting a view of this grand scene; for which purpose Ba'tiste and Bogard carried my easel and canvass to the top of a huge mound, where they left me at my work; and I painted my picture (Illustration 13), whilst they amused themselves with their rifles, decoying a flock of antelopes, of which they killed several, and abundantly added to the stock of our provisions . . .

The antelope of this country, I believe to be different from all other known varieties, and forms one of the most pleasing, living ornaments to this western world. They are seen in some places in great numbers sporting and playing about the hills and dales; and often, in flocks of fifty or a hundred, will follow the boat of the descending voyageur, or the travelling caravan, for hours together; keeping off at a safe distance, on the right or left, galloping up and down hills, snuffing their noses and stamping their feet; as if they were endeavouring to remind the traveller of the wicked trespass he was making on their own hallowed ground.

This little animal seems to be endowed, like many other gentle and sweet-breathing creatures, with an undue share of curiosity, which often leads them to destruction; and the hunter who wishes to entrap them, saves himself the trouble of travelling after them. When he has been discovered, he has only to elevate above the tops of the grass, his red or yellow handkerchief on the end of his gun-rod, which he sticks in the ground, and to which they are sure to advance, though with great coyness and caution; whilst he lies close, at a little distance, with his rifle in hand; when it is quite an easy matter to make sure of two or three at a shot, which he gets in range of his eye, to be pierced with one bullet.

On Sunday, departed from our encampment in the Grand Détour; and having passed for many miles, through a series of winding and ever-varying bluffs and fancied ruins, like such as have already been described, our attention was more than usually excited by the stupendous scene (Illustration 14), called by the voyageurs "the Grand Dome," which was lying in full view before us.

Illustration 13. Big Bend on the Upper Missouri, 1900 miles above St. Louis.

Illustration 14. "The Grand Dome."

Our canoe was here hauled ashore, and a day whiled away again, amongst these clay built ruins.

We clambered to their summits and enjoyed the distant view of the Missouri for many miles below, wending its way through the countless groups of clay and grass-covered hills; and we wandered back on the plains, in a toilsome and unsuccessful pursuit of a herd of buffaloes, which we discovered at some distance. Though we were disappointed in the results of the chase; yet we were in a measure repaid in amusements, which we found in paying a visit to an extensive village of prairie dogs, and of which I should render some account . . .

The prairie dog of the American Prairies is undoubtedly a variety of the marmot; and probably not unlike those which inhabit the vast Steppes of Asia. It bears no resemblance to any variety of dogs, except in the sound of its voice, when excited by the approach of danger, which is something like that of a very small dog, and still much more resembling the barking of a gray squirrel.

The size of these curious little animals is not far from that of a very large rat, and they are not unlike in their appearance. As I have said, their burrows, are uniformly built in a lonely desert; and away, both from the proximity of timber and water. Each individual, or each family, dig their hole in the prairie to the depth of eight or ten feet, throwing up the dirt from each excavation, in a little pile, in the form of a cone, which forms the only elevation for them to ascend; where they sit, to bark and chatter when an enemy is approaching their village. These villages are sometimes of several miles in extent; containing (I would almost say) myriads of their excavations and little dirt hillocks, and to the ears of their visitors, the din of their barkings is too confused and too peculiar to be described . . . These curious little animals belong to almost every latitude in the vast plains of prairie in North America; and their villages, which I have sometimes encountered in my travels, have compelled my party to ride several miles out of our way to get by them; for the burrows are generally within a few feet of each other, and dangerous to the feet and the limbs of our horses . . .

On this day, just before night, we landed our little boat in front of the Mandan village . . .

LETTER—NO. 11.

◄—————————————►

Mandan Village, Upper Missouri.

I said that I was here in the midst of a strange people, which is literally true; and I find myself surrounded by subjects and scenes worthy the pens of Irving or Cooper—of the pencils of Raphael or Hogarth; rich in legends and romances, which would require no aid of the imagination for a book or a picture.

The Mandans (or See-pohs-kah-nu-mah-kah-kee, "people of the pheasants," as they call themselves), are perhaps one of the most ancient tribes of Indians in our country. Their origin, like that of all the other tribes is from necessity, involved in mystery and obscurity. Their traditions and peculiarities I shall casually recite in this or future epistles; which when understood, will at once, I think, denominate them a peculiar and distinct race. They take great pride in relating their traditions, with regard to their origin; contending that they were the *first* people created on earth. Their existence in these regions has not been from a very ancient period; and, from what I could learn of their traditions, they have, at a former period, been a very numerous and powerful nation; but by the continual wars which have existed between them and their neighbours, they have been reduced to their present numbers.

This tribe is at present located on the west bank of the Missouri, about 1800 miles above St. Louis, and 200 below the Mouth of Yellow Stone River. They have two villages only, which are about two miles distant from each other; and number in all (as near as I can learn), about 2000 souls. Their present villages are beautifully located, and judiciously also, for defence against the assaults of their enemies.

The site of the lower (or principal) town, in particular, is one of the most beautiful and pleasing that can be seen in the world, and even more beautiful than imagination could ever create. In the very midst of an extensive valley (embraced within a thousand graceful swells and parapets or mounds of interminable green, changing to blue, as they vanish in distance) is built the city, or principal town of the Mandans. On an extensive plain (which is covered with a green turf, as well as the hills and dales, as far as the eye can possibly range, without tree or bush to be seen) are to be seen rising from the ground, and towards the heavens, domes—(not "of gold," but) of dirt—and the thousand spears (not "spires") and scalp-poles, &c. &c., of the semi-subterraneous village of the hospitable and gentlemanly Mandans.

These people formerly (and within the recollection of many of their oldest men) lived fifteen or twenty miles farther down the river, in ten contiguous villages; the marks or ruins of which are yet plain to be seen. At that period, it is evident, as well from the number of lodges which their villages contained, as from their traditions, that their numbers were much greater than at the present day. There are other, and very interesting, traditions and historical facts relative to a still prior location and condition of these people, of which I shall speak more fully on a future occasion . . .

The ground on which the Mandan village is at present built, was admirably selected for defence; being on a bank forty or fifty feet above the bed of the river. The greater part of this bank is nearly perpendicular, and of solid rock. The river, suddenly changing its course to a right-angle, protects two sides of the village, which is built upon this promontory or angle; they have therefore but one side to protect, which is effectually done by a strong piquet, and a ditch inside of it, of three or four feet in depth. The piquet is composed of timbers of a foot or more in diameter, and eighteen feet high, set firmly in the ground at sufficient distances from each other to admit of guns and other missiles to be fired between them. The ditch (unlike that of civilized modes of fortification) is inside of the piquet, in which their warriors screen their bodies from the view and weapons of their enemies, whilst they are reloading and discharging their weapons through the piquets.

The Mandans are undoubtedly secure in their villages, from the attacks of any Indian nation, and have nothing to fear, except when they meet their enemy on the prairie. Their village has a most novel appearance to the eye of a stranger; their lodges are closely grouped together, leaving but just room enough for walking and riding between them; and appear from without, to be built entirely of dirt; but one is surprised when he enters them, to see the neatness, comfort, and spacious dimensions of these earth-covered dwellings. They all have a circular form, and are from forty to sixty feet in diameter. Their foundations are prepared by digging some two feet in the ground, and forming the floor of earth, by levelling the requisite size for the lodge. These floors or foundations are all perfectly circular, and varying in size in proportion to the number of inmates, or of the quality or standing of the families which are to occupy them. The superstructure is then produced, by arranging, inside of this circular excavation, firmly fixed in the ground and resting against the bank, a barrier or wall of timbers, some eight or nine inches in diameter, of equal height (about six feet) placed on end, and resting against each other, supported by a formidable embankment of earth raised against them outside; then, resting upon the tops of these timbers or piles, are others of equal size and equal in numbers, of twenty or twenty-five feet in length, resting firmly against each other, and sending their upper or smaller ends towards the centre and top of the lodge; rising at an angle of forty-five degrees to the apex or sky-light, which is about three or four feet in diameter, answering as a chimney and a sky-light at the same time. The roof of the lodge being thus formed, is supported by beams passing around the inner part of the lodge about the middle of these poles or timbers, and themselves upheld by four or five large posts passing down to the floor of the lodge. On the top of, and over the poles forming the roof, is placed a complete mat of willow-boughs, of half a foot or more in thickness, which protects the timbers from the dampness of the earth, with which the lodge is covered from bottom to top, to the depth of two or three feet; and then with a hard or tough clay, which is impervious to water, and which with long use becomes quite hard, and a lounging place for the whole family in pleasant weather—for sage—for wooing lovers—for dogs and all; an airing place—a lookout— a place for gossip and mirth—a seat for the solitary gaze and medi- tations of the stern warrior, who sits and contemplates the peaceful mirth and happiness that is breathed beneath him, fruits of his hard-fought battles, on fields of desperate combat with bristling Red Men.

The floors of these dwellings are of earth, but so hardened by use, and swept so clean, and tracked by bare and moccassined feet, that they have almost a polish, and would scarcely soil the whitest linen. In the centre, and immediately under the sky-light is the fire-place—a hole of four or five feet in diameter, of a circular form, sunk a foot or more below the surface, and curbed around with stone. Over the fire-place, and suspended from the apex of diverging props or poles, is generally seen the pot or kettle, filled with buffalo meat; and around it are the family, reclining in all the most pictur-esque attitudes and groups, resting on their buffalo-robes and beau-tiful mats of rushes. These cabins are so spacious, that they hold from twenty to forty persons—a family and all their connexions. They all sleep on bedsteads similar in form to ours, but generally not quite so high; made of round poles rudely lashed together with thongs. A buffalo skin, fresh stripped from the animal, is stretched across the bottom poles, and about two feet from the floor; which, when it dries, becomes much contracted, and forms a perfect sacking-bottom. The fur side of this skin is placed uppermost, on which they lie with great comfort, with a buffalo-robe folded up for a pillow, and others drawn over them instead of blankets. These beds, as far as I have seen them (and I have visited almost every lodge in the village), are uniformly screened with a covering of buffalo or elk skins, oftentimes beautifully dressed and placed over the upright poles or frame, like a suit of curtains; leaving a hole in front, sufficiently spacious for the occupant to pass in and out, to and from his or her bed. Some of these coverings or curtains are exceedingly beautiful, being cut tastefully into fringe, and handsomely ornamented with porcupine's quills and picture writings or hieroglyphics.

From the great number of inmates in these lodges, they are necessarily very spacious, and the number of beds considerable. It is no uncommon thing to see these lodges fifty feet in diameter inside (which is an immense room), with a row of these curtained beds extending quite around their sides, being some ten or twelve of them, placed four or five feet apart, and the space between them occupied by a large post, fixed quite firm in the ground, and six or seven feet high, with large wooden pegs or bolts in it, on which are hung and grouped, with a wild and startling taste, the arms and armour of the respective proprietor; consisting of his whitened shield, embossed and emblazoned with the figure of his protecting *medicine* (or mystery), his bow and quiver, his war-club or battle-axe, his dart or javelin—his tobacco pouch and pipe—his medicine-bag—and his eagle—ermine or raven headdress; and over all, and on the top of the post (as if placed by some conjuror or Indian magician, to guard and protect the spell of wildness that reigns in this strange place), stands forth and in full relief the head and horns of a buffalo, which is, by a village regulation, owned and possessed by every man in the nation, and hung at the head of his bed, which he uses as a mask when called upon by the chiefs, to join in the buffalo-dance, of which I shall say more in a future epistle.

This arrangement of beds, of arms, &c., combining the most vivid display and arrangement of colours, of furs, of trinkets—of barbed and glistening points and steel—of mysteries and hocus pocus, together with the sombre and smoked colour of the roof and sides of the lodge; and the wild, and rude and red—the graceful (though uncivil) conversational, garrulous, story-telling and happy, though ignorant and untutored groups, that are smoking their pipes—wooing their sweethearts, and embracing their little ones about their peaceful and endeared fire-sides; together with their pots and kettles, spoons, and other culinary articles of their own manufacture, around them; present altogether, one of the most picturesque scenes to the eye of a stranger, that can be possibly seen; and far more wild and vivid than could ever be imagined.

. . . There is no subject that I know of, within the scope and reach of human wisdom, on which the civilized world in this enlightened age are more incorrectly informed, than upon that of the true manners and customs, and moral condition, rights and abuses, of the North American Indians; and that, as I have also before remarked, chiefly on account of the difficulty of our cultivating a fair and honourable acquaintance with them, and doing them the justice, and ourselves the credit, of a fair and impartial investigation of their true character . . .

. . . And amongst them all, there is none more common, nor more entirely erroneous, nor more easily refuted, than the current one, that "the Indian is a sour, morose, reserved and taciturn man." I have heard this opinion advanced a thousand times and I believed it; but such certainly, is not uniformly nor generally the case . . . No one can look into the wigwams of these people, or into any little momentary group of them, without being at once struck with the conviction that small-talk, gossip, garrulity, and story-telling, are the leading passions with them, who have little else to do in the world, but to while away their lives in the innocent and endless amusement of the exercise of those talents with which Nature has liberally endowed them, for their mirth and enjoyment.

One has but to walk or ride about this little town and its environs for a few hours in a pleasant day, and overlook the numerous games and gambols, where their notes and yelps of exultation are unceasingly vibrating in the atmosphere; or peep into their wigwams (and watch the glistening fun that's beaming from the noses, cheeks, and chins, of the crouching, cross-legged, and prostrate groups around the fire; where the pipe is passed, and jokes and anecdote, and laughter are excessive) to become convinced that it is natural to laugh and be merry . . . They live in a country and in communities, where it is not customary to look forward into the future with concern, for they live without incurring the expenses of life, which are absolutely necessary and unavoidable in the enlightened world; and of course their inclinations and faculties are solely directed to the enjoyment of the present day, without the sober reflections on the past or apprehensions of the future.

With minds thus unexpanded and uninfluenced by the thousand passions and ambitions of civilized life, it is easy and natural to concentrate their thoughts and their conversation upon the little and trifling occurrences of their lives. They are fond of fun and good cheer, and can laugh easily and heartily at a slight joke, of which their peculiar modes of life furnish them an inexhaustible fund, and enable them to cheer their little circle about the wigwam fire-side with endless laughter and garrulity.

. . . For the world who enquire for correct and just information, they must take my words for the truth, or else come to this country and look for themselves, into these grotesque circles of never-ending laughter and fun, instead of going to Washington City to gaze on the

poor embarrassed Indian who is called there by his "Great Father,"
to contend with the sophistry of the learned and acquisitive world, in
bartering away his lands with the graves and the hunting grounds of
his ancestors. There is not the proper place to study the Indian
character; yet it is the place where the sycophant and the scribbler go
to gaze and frown upon him—to learn his character, and write his
history! and because he does not speak, and quaffs the delicious
beverage which he receives from white mens' hands, "he's a speech-
less brute and a drunkard." An Indian is a beggar in Washington
City, and a white man is almost equally so in the Mandan village. An
Indian in Washington is mute, is dumb and embarrassed; and so is a
white man (and for the very same reasons) in this place—he has
nobody to talk to.

A wild Indian, to reach the civilized world, must needs travel
some thousands of miles in vehicles of conveyance, to which he is
unaccustomed—through latitudes and longitudes which are new to
him—living on food that he is unused to—stared and gazed at by
the thousands and tens of thousands whom he cannot talk to—his
heart grieving and his body sickening at the exhibition of white
men's wealth and luxuries, which are enjoyed on the land, and over
the bones of his ancestors. And at the end of his journey he stands
(like a caged animal) to be scanned—to be criticised—to be pitied—
and heralded to the world as a mute—as a brute, and a beggar.

A white man, to reach this village, must travel by steam-boat—by
canoes—on horseback and on foot; swim rivers—wade quagmires—
fight mosquitoes—patch his moccasins, and patch them again and
again, and his breeches; live on meat alone—sleep on the ground the
whole way, and think and dream of his friends he has left behind;
and when he gets here, half-starved, and half-naked, and more than
half sick, he finds himself a beggar for a place to sleep, and for
something to eat; a mute amongst thousands who flock about him, to
look and to criticise, and to laugh at him for his jaded appearance,
and to speak of him as they do of all white men (without distinction)
as liars. These people are in the habit of seeing no white men in their
country but Traders, and know of no other; deeming us all alike, and
receiving us all under the presumption that we come to trade or barter;
applying to us all, indiscriminately, the epithet of "liars" or Traders . . .

LETTER—NO. 12.

◄—————————————►

Mandan Village, Upper Missouri.

. . . I have this morning, perched myself upon the top of one of the earth-covered lodges, which I have before described, and having the whole village beneath and about me (Illustration 15), with its sachems—its warriors—its dogs—and its horses in motion—its medicines (or mysteries) and scalp-poles waving over my head—its piquets—its green fields and prairies, and river in full view, with the din and bustle of the thrilling panorama that is about me . . . There is really a newness and rudeness in every thing that is to be seen. There are several hundred houses or dwellings about me, and they are purely unique—they are all covered with dirt—the people are all red, and yet distinct from all other red folks I have seen. The horses are wild—every dog is a wolf—the whole moving mass are strangers to me: the living, in everything, carry an air of intractable wildness about them . . .

The groups of lodges around me present a very curious and pleasing appearance, resembling in shape (more nearly than anything else I can compare them to) so many potash-kettles inverted. On the tops of these are to be seen groups standing and reclining, whose wild and picturesque appearance it would be difficult to describe. Stern warriors, like statues, standing in dignified groups, wrapped in their painted robes, with their heads decked and plumed with quills of the war-eagle; extending their long arms to the east or the west, the scenes of their battles, which they are recounting over to each other. In another direction, the wooing lover, softening the heart of his fair Taih-nah-tai-a with the notes of his simple lute. On other lodges, and beyond these, groups are engaged in games of the

Illustration 15. Bird's-eye view of the principal Mandan village.

"moccasin," or the "platter." Some are to be seen manufacturing robes and dresses, and others, fatigued with amusements or occupations, have stretched their limbs to enjoy the luxury of sleep, whilst basking in the sun. With all this wild and varied medley of living beings are mixed their dogs, which seem to be so near an Indian's heart, as almost to constitute a material link of his existence.

In the centre of the village is an open space, or public area, of 150 feet in diameter, and circular in form, which is used for all public games and festivals, shews and exhibitions; and also for their "annual religious ceremonies," which are soon to take place, and of which I shall hereafter give some account. The lodges around this open space front in, with their doors towards the centre; and in the middle of this circle stands an object of great religious veneration, as I am told, on account of the importance it has in the condition of those annual religious rites.

This object is in form of a large hogshead, some eight or ten feet high, made of planks and hoops, containing within it some of their choicest medicines or mysteries, and religiously preserved unhacked or scratched, as a symbol of the "Big Canoe," as they call it.

One of the lodges fronting on this circular area, and facing this strange object of their superstition, is called the "Medicine Lodge," or council house. It is in this sacred building that these wonderful ceremonies, in commemoration of the flood, take place. I am told by the Traders that the cruelties of these scenes are frightful and abhorrent in the extreme; and that this huge wigwam, which is now closed, has been built exclusively for this grand celebration. I am every day reminded of the near approach of the season for this strange affair . . .

In ranging the eye over the village from where I am writing, there is presented to the view the strangest mixture and medley of unintelligible trash (independent of the living beings that are in motion), that can possibly be imagined. On the roofs of the lodges, besides the groups of living, are buffaloes' skulls, skin canoes, pots and pottery; sleds and sledges—and suspended on poles, erected some twenty feet above the doors of their wigwams, are displayed on a pleasant day, the scalps of warriors, preserved as trophies; and thus proudly exposed as evidence of their warlike deeds. In other parts are raised on poles the warriors' pure and whitened shields and quivers, with medicine-bags attached; and here and there a sacrifice of red cloth, or other costly stuff, offered up to the Great Spirit, over the door of some benignant chief, in humble gratitude for the blessings which he is enjoying . . . Amidst the blue streams of smoke that are rising from the tops of these hundred "coal-pits," can be seen in distance, the green and boundless, treeless, bushless prairie; and on it, and contiguous to the piquet which encloses the village, a hundred scaffolds, on which their "dead live," as they term it.

These people never bury the dead, but place the bodies on slight scaffolds just above the reach of human hands, and out of the way of wolves and dogs; and they are there left to moulder and decay. This cemetery, or place of deposite for the dead, is just back of the village, on a level prairie; and with all its appearances, history, forms, ceremonies, &c. is one of the strangest and most interesting objects to be described in the vicinity of this peculiar race.

Whenever a person dies in the Mandan village, and the customary honours and condolence are paid to his remains, and the body dressed in its best attire, painted, oiled, feasted, and supplied with bow and quiver, shield, pipe and tobacco—knife, flint and steel, and provisions enough to last him a few days on the journey which he is to perform; a fresh buffalo's skin, just taken from the animal's back, is wrapped around the body, and tightly bound and wound with thongs of raw hide from head to foot. Then other robes are soaked in water, till they are quite soft and elastic, which are also bandaged around the body in the same manner, and tied fast with thongs, which are wound with great care and exactness, so as to exclude the action of the air from all parts of the body.

There is then a separate scaffold erected for it, constructed of four up-right posts, a little higher than human hands can reach; and on the tops of these are small poles passing around from one post to the others; across which a number of willow-rods just strong enough to support the body, which is laid upon them on its back, with its feet carefully presented towards the rising sun.

There are a great number of these bodies resting exactly in a similar way; excepting in some instances where a chief, or medicine-man, may be seen with a few yards of scarlet or blue cloth spread over his remains, as a mark of public respect and esteem. Some hundreds of these bodies may be seen reposing in this manner in this curious place, which the Indians call, "the village of the dead" ... Fathers, mothers, wives, and children, may be seen lying under these scaffolds, prostrated upon the ground, with their faces in the dirt, howling forth incessantly the most piteous and heart-broken cries and lamentations for the misfortunes of their kindred; tearing their hair—cutting their flesh with their knives, and doing other penance to appease the spirits of the dead, whose misfortunes they attribute to some sin or omission of their own, for which they sometimes inflict the most excruciating self-torture.

When the scaffolds on which the bodies rest, decay and fall to the ground, the nearest relations having buried the rest of the bones, take the skulls, which are perfectly bleached and purified, and place them in circles of an hundred or more on the prairie—placed at equal distances apart (some eight or nine inches from each other), with the faces all looking to the centre; where they are religiously protected and preserved in their precise positions from year to year, as objects of religious and affectionate veneration (Illustration 16).

There are several of these "Golgothas" or circles of twenty or thirty feet in diameter, and in the centre of each ring or circle is a little mound of three feet high, on which uniformly rest two buffalo skulls (a male and female); and in the centre of the little mound is erected a "medicine pole," about twenty feet high, supporting many curious articles of mystery and superstition, which they suppose have the power of guarding and protecting this sacred arrangement. Here then, to this strange place do these people again resort, to evince their further affections for the dead—not in groans and lamentations however, for several years have cured the anguish; but fond affections and endearments are here renewed, and conversations are here held and cherished with the dead.

Each one of these skulls is placed upon a bunch of wild sage, which has been pulled and placed under it. The wife knows (by some mark or resemblance) the skull of her husband or her child, which lies in this group; and there seldom passes a day that she does not visit it, with a dish of the best cooked food that her wigwam affords, which she sets before the skull at night, and returns for the

Illustration 16. Back view of Mandan village, showing the cemetery.

dish in the morning. As soon as it is discovered that the sage on which the skull rests is beginning to decay, the woman cuts a fresh bunch, and places the skull carefully upon it, removing that which was under it.

Independent of the above-named duties, which draw the women to this spot, they visit it from inclination, and linger upon it to hold converse and company with the dead. There is scarcely an hour in a pleasant day, but more or less of these women may be seen sitting or laying by the skull of their child or husband—talking to it in the most pleasant and endearing language that they can use (as they were wont to do in former days) and seemingly getting an answer back. It is not unfrequently the case, that the woman brings her needle-work with her, spending the greater part of the day, sitting by the side of the skull of her child, chatting incessantly with it, while she is embroidering or garnishing a pair of moccasins; and perhaps, overcome with fatigue, falls asleep, with her arms encircled around it, forgetting herself for hours; after which she gathers up her things and returns to the village . . .

◄——————————————►

Mandan Village, Upper Missouri.

*H*a-na-tah-nu-mauh, the wolf chief (Illustration 17) . . . is . . . head-chief of the nation . . . a haughty, austere, and overbearing man, respected and feared by his people rather than loved. The tenure by which this man holds his office, is that by which the head-chiefs of most of the tribes claim, that of inheritance. It is a general, though not an infallible rule amongst the numerous tribes of North American Indians, that the office of chief belongs to the eldest son of a chief; provided he shews himself, by his conduct, to be equally worthy of it as any other in the nation; making it hereditary on a very proper condition—in default of which requisites, or others which may happen, the office is elective.

The dress of this chief was one of great extravagance, and some beauty; manufactured of skins, and a great number of quills of the raven, forming his stylish head-dress.

The next and second chief of the tribe, is Mah-to-toh-pa (the four bears). This extraordinary man, though second in office is undoubtedly the first and most popular man in the nation. Free, generous, elegant and gentlemanly in his deportment—handsome, brave and valiant; wearing a robe on his back, with the history of his battles emblazoned on it . . .

The Mandans are certainly a very interesting and pleasing people in their personal appearance and manners; differing in many respects, both in looks and customs, from all other tribes which I have seen. They are not a warlike people; for they seldom, if ever, carry war into their enemies' country; but when invaded, shew their valour and courage to be equal to that of any people on earth. Being a small

Illustration 17. Ha-na-tah-nu-mauh, Wolf Chief.

tribe, and unable to contend on the wild prairies with the Sioux and other roaming tribes, who are ten times more numerous; they have very judiciously located themselves in a permanent village, which is strongly fortified, and ensures their preservation. By this means they have advanced further in the arts of manufacture; have supplied their lodges more abundantly with the comforts, and even luxuries of life, than any Indian nation I know of. The consequence of this is, that this tribe have taken many steps ahead of other tribes in manners and refinements (if I may be allowed to apply the word refinement to Indian life); and are therefore familiarly (and correctly) denominated, by the Traders and others, who have been amongst them, "the polite and friendly Mandans."

There is certainly great justice in the remark; and so forcibly have I been struck with the peculiar ease and elegance of these people, together with the diversity of complexions, the various colours of their hair and eyes; the singularity of their language, and their peculiar and unaccountable customs, that I am fully convinced that they have sprung from some other origin than that of the other North American tribes, or that they are an amalgam of natives with some civilized race . . . . Their *personal appearance* alone, independent of their modes and customs, pronounces them at once, as more or less, than savage.

A stranger in the Mandan village is first struck with the different shades of complexion, and various colours of hair which he sees in a crowd about him; and is at once almost disposed to exclaim that "these are not Indians."

There are a great many of these people whose complexions appear as light as half breeds; and amongst the women particularly, there are many whose skins are almost white, with the most pleasing symmetry and proportion of features; with hazel, with grey, and with blue eyes,—with mildness and sweetness of expression, and excessive modesty of demeanour, which render them exceedingly pleasing and beautiful.

Why this diversity of complexion I cannot tell, nor can they themselves account for it. Their traditions, so far as I have yet learned them, afford us no information of their having had any knowledge of white men before the visit of Lewis and Clarke, made to their village thirty-three years ago. Since that time there have been but very few visits from white men to this place, and surely not enough to have changed the complexions and the customs of a nation. And I recollect perfectly well that Governor Clarke told me, before I started for this place, that I would find the Mandans a strange people and half white.

The diversity in the colour of hair is also equally as great as that in the complexion; for in a numerous group of these people (and more particularly amongst the females, who never take pains to change its natural colour, as the men often do), there may be seen every shade and colour of hair that can be seen in our own country, with the exception of red or auburn, which is not to be found.

And there is yet one more strange and unaccountable peculiarity, which can probably be seen nowhere else on earth; nor on any rational grounds accounted for,—other than it is a freak or order of Nature, for which she has not seen fit to assign a reason. There are very many, of both sexes, and of every age, from infancy to manhood and old age, with hair of a bright silvery grey; and in some instances almost perfectly white.

This singular and eccentric appearance is much oftener seen among the women than it is with the men; for many of the latter who have it, seem ashamed of it, and artfully conceal it, by filling their hair with glue and black and red earth. The women, on the other hand, seem proud of it, and display it often in an almost incredible profusion, which spreads over their shoulders and falls as low as the knee. I have ascertained, on a careful enquiry, that about one in ten or twelve of the whole tribe are what the French call "cheveux gris," or greyhairs; and that this strange and unaccountable phenomenon is not the result of disease or habit; but that it is unquestionably a hereditary character which runs in families, and indicates no inequality in disposition or intellect. And by passing his hair through my hands, as I often have, I have found it uniformly to be as coarse and harsh as a horse's mane; differing materially from the hair of other colours, which amongst the Mandans, is generally as fine and as soft as silk.

The reader will at once see, by the above facts, that there is enough upon the faces and heads of these people to stand them peculiar,—when he meets them in the heart of his almost boundless wilderness, presenting such diversities of colour in the complexion and hair; when he knows from what he has seen, and what he has read, that all other primitive tribes known in America, are dark copper-coloured, with jet black hair.

From these few facts alone, the reader will see that I am amongst a strange and interesting people, and know how to pardon me, if I lead them through a maze of novelty and mysteries to the knowledge of a strange, yet kind and hospitable, people, whose fate, like that of all their race is sealed;—whose doom is fixed, to live just long enough to be imperfectly known, and then to fall before the fell disease or sword of civilizing devastation.

The stature of the Mandans is rather below the ordinary size of man, with beautiful symmetry of form and proportion, and wonderful suppleness and elasticity; they are pleasingly erect and graceful, both in their walk and their attitudes; and the hair of the men, which generally spreads over their backs, falling down to the hams, and sometimes to the ground, is divided into plaits or slabs of two inches in width, and filled with a profusion of glue and red earth or vermillion, at intervals of an inch or two, which becoming very hard, remains in and unchanged from year to year.

This mode of dressing the hair is curious, and gives to the Mandans the most singular appearance. The hair of the men is uniformly all laid over from the forehead backwards; carefully kept above and resting on the ear, and thence falling down over the back, in the flattened bunches, and painted red, extending oftentimes quite on to the calf of the leg, and sometimes in such profusion as almost to conceal the whole figure from the person walking behind them. In the portrait of San-ja-ka-ko-kah (the deceiving wolf, Illustration 18), where he is represented at full length, with several others of his family around him in a group, there will be seen a fair illustration of these and other customs of these people.

The hair of the women is also worn as long as they can possibly cultivate it, oiled very often, which preserves on it a beautiful gloss and shows its natural colour. They often braid it in two large plaits, one falling down just back of the ear, on each side of the head; and on any occasion which requires them to "put on their best looks,"

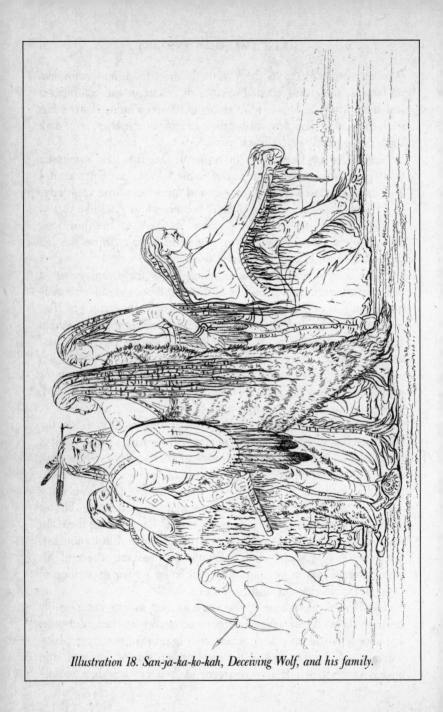

Illustration 18. San-ja-ka-ko-kah, Deceiving Wolf, and his family.

they pass their fingers through it, drawing it out of braid, and spreading it over their shoulders. The Mandan women observe strictly the same custom, which I observed amongst the Crows and Blackfeet (and, in fact, all other tribes I have seen, without a single exception), of parting the hair on the forehead, and always keeping the crease or separation filled with vermillion or other red paint. This is one of the very few little (and apparently trivial) customs which I have found amongst the Indians, without being able to assign any cause for it, other than that "they are Indians," and that this is an Indian fashion . . .

. . . Among them and most other tribes, as with the enlightened world, there are different grades of society—those who care but little for their personal appearance, and those who take great pains to please themselves and their friends. Amongst this class of personages, such as chiefs and braves, or warriors of distinction, and their families, and dandies or exquisites (a class of beings of whom I shall take due time to speak in a future Letter), the strictest regard to decency, and cleanliness and elegance of dress is observed; and there are few people, perhaps, who take more pains to keep their persons neat and cleanly than they do.

At the distance of half a mile or so above the village, is the customary place where the women and girls resort every morning in the summer months, to bathe in the river. To this spot they repair by hundreds, every morning at sunrise, where, on a beautiful beach, they can be seen running and glistening in the sun, whilst they are playing their innocent gambols and leaping into the stream. They all learn to swim well, and the poorest swimmer amongst them will dash fearlessly into the boiling, and eddying current of the Missouri, and cross it with perfect ease. At the distance of a quarter of a mile back from the river, extends a terrace or elevated prairie, running north from the village, and forming a kind of semicircle around this bathing-place; and on this terrace, which is some twenty or thirty feet higher than the meadow between it and the river, are stationed every morning several sentinels, with their bows and arrows in hand, to guard and protect this sacred ground from the approach of boys or men from any directions.

At a little distance below the village, also, is the place where the men and boys go to bathe and learn to swim. After this morning ablution, they return to their village, wipe their limbs dry, and use a profusion of bear's grease through their hair and over their bodies.

The art of swimming is known to all the American Indians; and perhaps no people on earth have taken more pains to learn it, nor any who turn it to better account. There certainly are no people whose avocations of life more often call for the use of their limbs in this way; as many of the tribes spend their lives on the shores of our vast lakes and rivers, paddling about from their childhood in their fragile bark canoes, which are liable to continual accidents, which often throw the Indian upon his natural resources for the preservation of his life.

There are many times also, when out upon their long marches in the prosecution of their almost continued warfare, when it becomes necessary to plunge into and swim across the wildest streams and rivers, at times when they have no canoes or craft in which to cross them. I have as yet seen no tribe where this art is neglected. It is learned at a very early age by both sexes, and enables the strong and hardy muscles of the squaws to take their child upon the back, and successfully to pass any river that lies in their way.

The mode of swimming among the Mandans, as well as amongst most of the other tribes, is quite different from that practised in those parts of the civilized world, which I have had the pleasure yet to visit. The Indian, instead of parting his hands simultaneously under the chin, and making the stroke outward, in a horizontal direction, causing thereby a serious strain upon the chest, throws his body alternately upon the left and the right side, raising one arm entirely above the water and reaching as far forward as he can, to dip it, whilst his whole weight and force are spent upon the one that is passing under him, and like a paddle propelling him along; whilst this arm is making a half circle, and is being raised out of the water behind him, the opposite arm is describing a similar arch in the air over his head, to be dipped in the water as far as he can reach before him, with the hand turned under, forming a sort of bucket, to act most effectively as it passes in its turn underneath him . . .

In addition to the modes of bathing which I have above described, the Mandans have another, which is a much greater luxury, and often resorted to by the sick, but far more often by the well and sound, as a matter of luxury only, or perhaps for the purpose of hardening their limbs and preparing them for the thousand exposures and vicissitudes of life to which they are continually liable. I allude to their vapour baths, or *sudatories* [sweat lodges], of which each village has several, and which seem to be a kind of public property—accessible to all, and resorted to by all, male and female, old and young, sick and well.

In every Mandan lodge is to be seen a crib or basket, much in the shape of a bathing-tub, curiously woven with willow boughs, and sufficiently large to receive any person of the family in a reclining or recumbent posture; which, when any one is to take a bath, is carried by the squaw to the sudatory for the purpose, and brought back to the wigwam again after it has been used.

These sudatories are always near the village, above or below it, on the bank of the river. They are generally built of boughs (in form of a Crow or Sioux lodge which I have before described), covered with buffalo skins sewed tight together, with a kind of furnace in the centre; or in other words, in the centre of the lodge are two walls of stone about six feet long and two and a half apart, and about three feet high; across and over this space, between the two walls, are laid a number of round sticks, on which the bathing crib is placed. Contiguous to the lodge, and outside of it, is a little furnace something similar, in the side of the bank, where the woman kindles a hot fire, and heats to a red heat a number of large stones, which are kept at these places for this particular purpose; and having them all in readiness, she goes home or sends word to inform her husband or other one who is waiting, that all is ready; when he makes his appearance entirely naked, though with a large buffalo robe wrapped around him. He then enters the lodge and places himself in the crib or basket, either on his back or in a sitting posture (the latter of which is generally preferred), with his back towards the door of the lodge; when the squaw brings in a large stone red hot, between two sticks (lashed together somewhat in the form of a pair of tongs) and, placing it under him, throws cold water upon it, which raises a profusion of vapour about him. He is at once enveloped in a cloud of steam, and a woman or child will sit at a little distance and continue to dash water upon the stone, whilst the matron of the lodge is out, and preparing to make her appearance with another heated stone: or he will sit and dip from a wooden bowl, with a ladle made of the mountain-sheep's horn, and throw upon the heated stones, with his own hands, the water which he is drawing through his lungs and pores, in the next moment, in the most delectable and exhilarating vapours, as it distils through the mat of wild sage and other medicinal and aromatic herbs, which he has strewed over the bottom of his basket, and on which he reclines.

During all this time the lodge is shut perfectly tight, and he quaffs this delicious and renovating draught to his lungs with deep drawn sighs, and with extended nostrils, until he is drenched in the most profuse degree of perspiration that can be produced; when he makes a kind of strangled signal, at which the lodge is opened, and he darts forth with the speed of a frightened deer, and plunges headlong into the river, from which he instantly escapes again, wraps his robe around him and "leans" as fast as possible for home. Here his limbs are wiped dry, and wrapped close and tight within the fur of the buffalo robes, in which he takes his nap, with his feet to the fire; then oils his limbs and hair with bear's grease, dresses and plumes himself for a visit—a feast—a parade, or a council; or slicks down his long hair, and rubs his oiled limbs to a polish, with a piece of soft buckskin, prepared to join in games of ball or Tchung-kee.

Such is the sudatory or the vapour bath of the Mandans, and, as I before observed, it is resorted to both as an every-day luxury by those who have the time and energy or industry to indulge in it; and also used by the sick as a remedy for nearly all the diseases which are known amongst them. Fevers are very rare, and in fact almost unknown among these people: but in the few cases of fever which have been known, this treatment has been applied, and without the fatal consequences which we would naturally predict. The greater part of their diseases are inflammatory rheumatisms, and other chronic diseases; and for these, this mode of treatment, with their modes of life, does admirably well. This custom is similar amongst nearly all of these Missouri Indians, and amongst the Pawnees, Omahas, and Punchas and other tribes, who have suffered with the small-pox (the dread destroyer of the Indian race), this mode was practised by the poor creatures, who fled by hundreds to the river's edge, and by hundreds died before they could escape from the waves, into which they had plunged in the heat and rage of a burning fever. Such will yet be the scourge, and such the misery of these poor unthinking people, and each tribe to the Rocky Mountains, as it has been with every tribe between here and the Atlantic Ocean. White men—whiskey—tomahawks—scalping knives—guns, powder and ball—small-pox—debauchery—extermination.

Mandan Village, Upper Missouri.

. . . *A*mongst so many different and distinct nations, always at war with each other, and knowing nothing at all of each other's languages; and amongst whom, fashions in dress seldom if ever change; it may seem somewhat strange that we should find these people so nearly following, or imitating each other, in the forms and modes of their dress and ornaments. This must however, be admitted, and I think may be accounted for in a manner, without raising the least argument in favour of the theory of their having all sprung from one stock or one family; for in their continual warfare, when chiefs or warriors fall, their clothes and weapons usually fall into possession of the victors, who wear them; and the rest of the tribe would naturally more or less often copy from or imitate them; and so also in their repeated councils or treaties of peace, such articles of dress and other manufactures are customarily exchanged, which are equally adopted by the other tribe; and consequently, eventually lead to the similarity which we find amongst the modes of dress, &c. of the different tribes.

The tunic or shirt of the Mandan men is very similar in shape to that of the Blackfeet—made of two skins of deer or mountain-sheep, strung with scalp-locks, beads, and ermine. The leggings, like those of the other tribes, of whom I have spoken, are made of deer skins, and shaped to fit the leg, embroidered with porcupine quills, and fringed with scalps from their enemies heads. Their moccasins are made of buckskin, and neatly ornamented with porcupine quills—over their shoulders (or in other words, over one shoulder and passing under the other), they very gracefully wear a robe from the young buffalo's back, oftentimes cut down to about half its original size, to make it handy and easy or use. Many of these are also fringed on one side with scalp-locks; and the flesh side of the skin curiously ornamented with pictured representations of the creditable events and battles of their lives.

Their head-dresses are of various sorts, and many of them exceedingly picturesque and handsome; generally made of war-eagles' or ravens quills and ermine. These are the most costly part of an Indian's dress in all this country, owing to the difficulty of procuring the quills and the fur. The war-eagle being the *"rara avis,"* and the ermine the rarest animal that is found in the country. The tail of a war-eagle in this village, provided it is a perfect one, containing some six or eight quills, which are denominated first-rate plumes, and suitable to arrange in a head-dress, will purchase a tolerable good horse (horses, however, are much cheaper here than they are in most other countries) . . .

There is occasionally, a chief or a warrior of so extraordinary renown, that he is allowed to wear horns on his head-dress, which give to his aspect a strange and majestic effect. These are made of about a third part of the horn of a buffalo bull; the horn having been split from end to end, and a third part of it taken and shaved thin and light, and highly polished. These are attached to the top of the head-dress on each side, in the same place that they rise and stand on the head of a buffalo; rising out of a mat of ermine skins and tails, which hang over the top of the head-dress, somewhat in the form that the large and profuse locks of hair hang and fall over the head of a buffalo bull . . .

The same custom I have found observed amongst the Sioux,—the Crows—the Blackfeet and Assinneboins, and it is one of so striking a character as needs a few more words of observation. There is a peculiar meaning or importance (in their estimation) to this and many other curious and unaccountable appearances in the habits of Indians, upon which the world generally look as things that are absurd and ridiculous, merely because they are beyond the world's comprehension, or because we do not stop to enquire or learn their uses or meaning.

I find that the principal cause why we underrate and despise the savage, is generally because we do not understand him; and the reason why we are ignorant of him and his modes, is that we do not stop to investigate—the world having been too much in the habit of looking upon him as altogether inferior—as a beast, a brute; and unworthy of more than a passing notice. If they stop long enough to form an acquaintance, it is but to take advantage of his ignorance and credulities—to rob him of the wealth and resources of his country;—to make him drunk with whiskey, and visit him with abuses which in his ignorance he never thought of. By this method his first visitors entirely overlook and never understand the meaning of his thousand interesting and characteristic customs; and at the same time, by changing his native modes and habits of life, blot them out from the view of the enquiring world for ever . . .

An Indian looks among the civilized world, no doubt, with equal, if not much greater, astonishment, at our apparently, as well as *really*, ridiculous customs and fashions; but he laughs not, nor ridicules, nor questions,—for his natural good sense and good manners forbid him—until he is reclining about the fire-side of his wigwam companions, when he vents forth his just criticisms upon the learned world, who are a rich and just theme for Indian criticism and Indian gossip.

An Indian will not ask a white man the reason why he does not oil his skin with bears' grease, or why he does not paint his body—or why he wears a hat on his head, or why he has buttons on the back part of his coat, where they can never be used—or why he wears whiskers, and a shirt collar up to his eyes . . . A wild Indian thrown into the civilized atmosphere will see a man occasionally moving in society, wearing a cocked hat; and another with a laced coat and gold or silver epaulettes upon his shoulders, without knowing or enquiring the meaning of them, or the objects for which they are worn. Just so a white man travels amongst a wild and untaught tribe of Indians, and sees occasionally one of them parading about their village, with a head-dress of eagles' quills and ermine, and elevated above it a pair of beautifully polished buffalo horns; and just as ignorant is he also, of their meaning or importance; and more so, for the first will admit the presumption that epaulettes and cocked hats amongst the civilized world, are made for some important purpose,—but the latter will presume that horns on an Indian's head are nothing more nor

Illustration 19. Mah-to-toh-pa, Four Bears.

less (nor can they be in their estimation), than Indian nonsense and stupidity . . .

This custom then, which I have before observed belongs to all the northwestern tribes, is one no doubt of very ancient origin, having a purely classic meaning. No one wears the head-dress surmounted with horns except the dignitaries who are very high in authority, and whose exceeding valour, worth, and power is admitted by all the nation . . .

This head-dress with horns is used only on certain occasions, and they are very seldom. When foreign chiefs, Indian agents, or other important personages visit a tribe; or at war parades, at the celebration of a victory, at public festivals, &c. they are worn . . . This, reader, is a remarkable instance (like hundreds of others), for its striking similarity to *Jewish customs*, to the kerns (or keren, in Hebrew), the horns worn by the Abysinian chiefs and Hebrews, as a *symbol of power* and command; worn at great parades and celebrations of victories . . .

The reader will see this custom exemplified in the portrait of Mah-to-toh-pa (Illustration 19). This man, although the second chief, was the only man in the nation who was allowed to wear the horns; and all, I found, looked upon him as the leader, who had the power to lead all the warriors in time of war; and that, in consequence of the extraordinary battles which he had fought.

LETTER—NO. 15.

◄——————————————►

Mandan Village, Upper Missouri.

A week or more has elapsed since the date of my last Letter, and nothing as yet of the great and curious event—or the *Mandan religious ceremony*. There is evidently much preparation making for it, however; and from what I can learn, no one in the nation, save the *medicine-men*, have any knowledge of the exact day on which it is to commence. I am informed by the chiefs, that it takes place as soon as the willow-tree is in full leaf; for, say they, "the twig which the bird brought in was a willow bough, and had full-grown leaves on it." So it seems that this celebration has some relation to the Flood.

This great occasion is close at hand, and will, undoubtedly, commence in a few days; in the meantime I will give a few notes and memorandums, which I have made since my last . . .

Perhaps nothing ever more completely astonished these people than the operations of my *brush*. The art of portrait-painting was a subject entirely new to them, and of course, unthought of; and my appearance here has commenced a new era in the arcana of *medicine* or mystery. Soon after arriving here, I commenced and finished the portraits of the two principal chiefs. This was done without having awakened the curiosity of the villagers, as they had heard nothing of what was going on, and even the chiefs themselves seemed to be ignorant of my designs, until the pictures were completed. No one else was admitted into my lodge during the operation; and when finished, it was exceedingly amusing to see them mutually recognizing each other's likeness, and assuring each other of the striking resemblance which they bore to the originals. Both of these pressed their hand over their mouths awhile in dead silence (a custom amongst most tribes, when anything surprises them very much); looking attentively upon the portraits and myself, and upon the palette and colours with which these unaccountable effects had been produced.

They then walked up to me in the most gentle manner, taking me in turn by the hand, with a firm grip; with head and eyes inclined downwards, and in a tone a little above a whisper—pronounced the words "te-ho-pe-nee Wash-ee!" and walked off . . . Te-ho-pe-nee Wash-ee (or medicine white man) is the name I now go by, and it will prove to me, no doubt, of more value than gold, for I have been called upon and feasted by the doctors, who are all mystery-men; and it has been an easy and successful passport already to many strange and mysterious places; and has put me in possession of a vast deal of curious and interesting information, which I am sure I never should have otherwise learned . . .

After I had finished the portraits of the two chiefs, and they had returned to their wigwams, and deliberately seated themselves by their respective fire-sides, and silently smoked a pipe or two (according to an universal custom), they gradually began to tell what had taken place; and at length crowds of gaping listeners, with mouths wide open, thronged their lodges; and a throng of women and girls were about my house, and through every crack and crevice I could see their glistening eyes, which were piercing my hut in a hundred places, from a natural and restless propensity, a curiosity to see what was going on within. An hour or more passed in this way, and the soft and silken throng continually increased, until some hundreds of them were clung, and piled about my wigwam like a swarm of bees hanging on the front and sides of their hive.

During this time, not a man made his appearance about the premises—after awhile, however, they could be seen, folded in their robes, gradually *siding* up towards the lodge, with a silly look upon their faces, which confessed at once that curiosity was leading them reluctantly, where their pride checked and forbade them to go. The rush soon after became general, and the chiefs and medicine-men took possession of my room, placing *soldiers* (braves with spears in their hands) at the door, admitting no one, but such as were allowed by the chiefs, to come in.

Monsr. Kipp (the agent of the Fur Company, who has lived here eight years, and to whom, for his politeness and hospitality, I am much indebted), at this time took a seat with the chiefs, and, speaking their language fluently, he explained to them my views and the objects for which I was painting these portraits; and also expounded to them the manner in which they were made,—at which they seemed all to be very much pleased. The necessity at this time of exposing the portraits to the view of the crowds who were assembled around the house, became imperative, and they were held up together over the door, so that the whole village had a chance to see and recognize their chiefs. The effect upon so mixed a multitude, who as yet had heard no way of accounting for them, was novel and really laughable. The likenesses were instantly recognized, and many of the gaping multitude commenced yelping; some were stamping off in the jarring dance—others were singing, and others again were crying—hundreds covered their mouths with their hands and were mute; others, indignant, drove their spears frightfully into the ground, and some threw a reddened arrow at the sun, and went home to their wigwams.

The pictures seen,—the next curiosity was to see the man who made them . . . I stepped forth, and was instantly hemmed in in the throng. Women were gaping and gazing—and warriors and braves were offering me their hands,—whilst little boys and girls, by dozens, were struggling through the crowd to touch me with the ends of their fingers; and whilst I was engaged, from the waist upwards, in fending off the throng and shaking hands, my legs were assailed (not unlike the nibbling of little fish, when I have been standing in deep water) by children, who were creeping between the legs of the bystanders for the curiosity or honour of touching me with the end of their finger. The eager curiosity and expression of astonishment with which they gazed upon me, plainly shewed that they looked upon me as some strange and unaccountable being. They pronounced me the greatest *medicine-man* in the world; for they said I had made *living beings*,—they said they could see their chiefs alive, in two places—those that I had made a *little* alive—they could see their eyes move—could see them smile and laugh, and that if they could laugh they could certainly speak, if they should try, and they must therefore have *some life* in them.

The squaws generally agreed, that they had discovered life enough in them to render my *medicine* too great for the Mandans; saying that such an operation could not be performed without taking away from the original something of his existence, which I put in the picture, and they could see it move, could see it stir.

This curtailing of the natural existence, for the purpose of instilling life into the secondary one, they decided to be an useless and destructive operation, and one which was calculated to do great mischief in their happy community; and they commenced a mournful and doleful chaunt against me, crying and weeping bitterly through the village, proclaiming me a most "dangerous man; one who could make living persons by looking at them; and at the same time, could, as a matter of course, destroy life in the same way, if I chose. That my medicine was dangerous to their lives, and that I must leave the village immediately. That bad luck would happen to those whom I painted—that I was to take a part of the existence of those whom I painted, and carry it home with me amongst the white people, and that when they died they would never sleep quiet in their graves."

In this way the women and some old quack medicine-men together, had succeeded in raising an opposition against me; and the reasons they assigned were so plausible and so exactly suited for their superstitious feelings, that they completely succeeded in exciting fears and a general panic in the minds of a number of chiefs, who had agreed to sit for their portraits, and my operations were, of course, for several days completely at a stand. A grave council was held on the subject from day to day, and there seemed great difficulty in deciding what was to be done with me and the dangerous art which I was practising; and which had far exceeded their original expectations. I finally got admittance to their sacred conclave, and assured them that I was but a man like themselves,—that my art had no *medicine* or mystery about it, but could be learned by any of them if they would practice it as long as I had—that my intentions towards them were of the most friendly kind, and that in the country where I lived, brave men never allowed their squaws to frighten them with their foolish whims and stories. They all immediately arose, shook me by the hand, and dressed themselves for their pictures . . .

Since this signal success and good fortune in my operations, things have gone on very pleasantly, and I have had a great deal of amusement. Some altercation has taken place, however, amongst the chiefs and braves, with regard to standing or rank, of which they are exceedingly jealous; and they must sit (if at all) in regular order, according to that rank; the trouble is all settled at last, however, and I have had no want of subjects, though a great many have become again alarmed, and are unwilling to sit, for fear, as some say, that they will die prematurely if painted; and as others say, that if they are painted, the picture will live after they are dead, and they cannot sleep quiet in their graves.

I have had several most remarkable occurrences in my painting-room, of this kind, which have made me some everlasting enemies here; though the minds and feelings of the chiefs and medicine-men have not been affected by them. There has been three or four instances where proud and aspiring young men have been in my lodge, and after gazing at the portraits of the head chief across the room (which sits looking them in the eyes), have raised their hands before their faces and walked around to the side of the lodge, on the right or left, from whence to take a long and fair side-look at the chief, instead of staring him full in the face (which is a most unpardonable offence in all Indian tribes); and after having got in that position, and cast their eyes again upon the portrait which was yet looking them full in the face, have thrown their robes over their heads and bolted out of the wigwam, filled equally with astonishment and indignation; averring, as they always will in a sullen mood, that they "saw the eyes move,"—that as they walked around the room "the eyes of the portrait followed them." With these unfortunate gentlemen, repeated efforts have been made by the Traders, and also by the chiefs and doctors, who understand the illusion, to convince them of their error, by explaining the mystery; but they will not hear to any explanation whatever; saying, that "what they see with their eyes is always evidence enough for them;" that they always "believe their own eyes sooner than a hundred tongues," and all efforts to get them a second time to my room, or into my company in any place, have proved entirely unsuccessful.

I had trouble brewing also the other day from another source; one of the *"medicines"* commenced howling and haranguing around my domicil, amongst the throng that was outside, proclaiming that all who were inside and being painted were fools and would soon die;

and very materially affecting thereby my popularity. I however sent for him and called him in the next morning, when I was alone, having only the interpreter with me; telling him that I had had my eye upon him for several days, and had been so well pleased with his looks, that I had taken great pains to find out his history, which had been explained by all as one of a most extraordinary kind, and his character and standing in his tribe as worthy of my particular notice; and that I had several days since resolved that as soon as I had practised my hand long enough upon the others, to get the stiffness out of it (after paddling my canoe so far as I had) and make it to work easily and successfully, I would begin on his portrait, which I was then prepared to commence on that day, and that I felt as if I could do him justice. He shook me by the hand, giving me the "Doctor's grip," and beckoned me to sit down, which I did, and we smoked a pipe together . . . "I know you are a good man (said he), I know you will do no harm to anyone, your medicine is great and you are a great 'medicine-man,' . . . I will go to my wigwam and eat, and in a little while I will come, and you may go to work;"—another pipe was lit and smoked, and he got up and went off. I prepared my canvass and palette, and whistled away the time until twelve o'clock, before he made his appearance; having used the whole of the fore-part of the day at his toilette, arranging his dress and ornamenting his body for his picture.

At that hour then, bedaubed and streaked with paints of various colours, with bear's grease and charcoal, with medicine-pipes in his hands and foxes tails attached to his heels, entered Mah-to-he-hah (the old bear, Illustration 20), with a train of his own profession . . . He took his position in the middle of the room, waving his eagle calumets in each hand, and singing his medicine-song which he sings over his dying patient, looking me full in the face until I completed his picture, which I painted at full length. His vanity has been completely gratified in the operation; he lies for hours together, day after day, in my room, in front of his picture, gazing intensely upon it; lights my pipe for me while I am painting—shakes hands with me a dozen times on each day, and talks of me, and enlarges upon my *medicine* virtues and my talents, wherever he goes; so that this new difficulty is now removed, and instead of preaching against me, he is one of my strongest and most enthusiastic friends and aids in the country . . .

Illustration 20. Mah-to-he-hah, Old Bear, a medicine man.

◄─────────────────►

Mandan Village, Upper Missouri.

Besides chiefs, and braves and doctors, of whom I have heretofore spoken, there is yet another character of whom I must say
a few words before I proceed to other topics. The person I allude to,
is the one mentioned at the close of the last Letter, and familiarly
known and countenanced in every tribe as an Indian *beau* or *dandy*.
Such personages may be seen on every pleasant day, strutting and
parading around the villages in the most beautiful and unsoiled
dresses, without the honourable trophies however of scalp locks and
claws of the grizzly bear, attached to their costume, for with such
things they deal not. They are not peculiarly anxious to hazard their
lives in equal and honourable combat with the one, or disposed to
cross the path of the other; but generally remain about the village, to
take care of the women, and attire themselves in the skins of such
animals as they can easily kill, without seeking the rugged cliffs for
the war-eagle, or visiting the haunts of the grizzly bear. They plume
themselves with swan's-down and quills of ducks, with braids and
plaits of sweet-scented grass and other harmless and unmeaning
ornaments, which have no other merit than they themselves have,
that of looking pretty and ornamental.

These clean and elegant gentlemen, who are very few in each
tribe, are held in very little estimation by the chiefs and braves;
inasmuch as it is known by all, that they have a most horrible
aversion to arms, and are denominated "faint hearts" or "old women"
by the whole tribe, and are therefore but little respected. They seem,
however, to be tolerably well contented with the appellation, together
with the celebrity they have acquired amongst the women and

children for the beauty and elegance of their personal appearance; and most of them seem to take and enjoy their share of the world's pleasures, although they are looked upon as drones in society.

These gay and tinselled bucks may be seen in a pleasant day in all their plumes, astride of their pied or dappled ponies, with a fan in the right hand, made of a turkey's tail—with whip and a fly-brush attached to the wrist of the same hand, and underneath them a white and beautiful and soft pleasure-saddle, ornamented with porcupine quills and ermine, parading through and lounging about the village for an hour or so, when they will cautiously bend their course to the suburbs of the town, where they will sit or recline upon their horses for an hour or two, overlooking the beautiful games where the braves and the young aspirants are contending in manly and athletic amusements;—when they are fatigued with this severe effort, they wend their way back again, lift off their fine white saddle of doe's-skin, which is wadded with buffalo's hair, turn out their pony—take a little refreshment, smoke a pipe, fan themselves to sleep, and doze away the rest of the day.

Whilst I have been painting, from day to day, there have been two or three of these fops continually strutting and taking their attitudes in front of my door; decked out in all their finery, without receiving other benefit or other information, than such as they could discover through the cracks and seams of my cabin. The chiefs, I observed, passed them by without notice, and of course, without inviting them in; and they seemed to figure about my door from day to day in their best dresses and best attitudes, as if in hopes that I would select them as models, for my canvass. It was natural that I should do so, for their costume and personal appearance was entirely more beautiful than anything else to be seen in the village. My plans were laid, and one day when I had got through with all of the head men, who were willing to sit to be painted, and there were two or three of the chiefs lounging in my room, I stepped to the door and tapped one of these fellows on the shoulder, who took the hint, and stepped in, well-pleased and delighted with the signal and honourable notice I had at length taken of him and his beautiful dress. Readers, you cannot imagine what was the expression of gratitude which beamed forth in this poor fellow's face, and how high his heart beat with joy and pride at the idea of my selecting him to be immortal, alongside of the chiefs and worthies whose portraits he saw arranged around the room; and by which honour he, undoubtedly, considered himself well paid for two or three weeks of regular painting, and greasing, and dressing, and standing alternately on one leg and the other at the door of my premises.

Well, I placed him before me, and a canvass on my easel, and "chalked him out" at full length. He was truly a beautiful subject for the brush, and I was filled with enthusiasm—his dress from head to foot was of the skins of the mountain-goat, and dressed so neatly, that they were almost as soft and as white as Canton crape—around the bottom and the sides it was trimmed with ermine, and porcupine quills of beautiful dyes garnished it in a hundred parts;—his hair which was long, and spread over his back and shoulders, extending nearly to the ground, was all combed back and parted on his forehead like that of a woman. He was a tall and fine figure, with ease and grace in his movements, that were well worthy of a man of better caste. In his left hand he held a beautiful pipe—and in his right hand he plied his fan, and on his wrist was still attached his whip of elk's horn, and his fly-brush, made of the buffalo's tail. There was nought about him of the terrible, and nought to shock the finest, chastest intellect.

I had thus far progressed, with high-wrought feelings of pleasure, when the two or three chiefs, who had been seated around the lodge, and whose portraits I had before painted, arose suddenly, and wrapping themselves tightly in their robes, crossed my room with a quick and heavy step, and took an informal leave of my cabin. I was apprehensive of their displeasure, though I continued my work; and in a few moments the interpreter came furiously into my room, addressing me thus:—"My God, Sir! this never will do; you have given great offence to the chiefs—they have made complaint of your conduct to me—they tell me this is a worthless fellow—a man of no account in the nation, and if you paint his picture, you must instantly destroy theirs; you have no alternative, my dear Sir—and the quicker this chap is out of your lodge the better."

The same matter was explained to my sitter by the interpreter, when he picked up his robe, wrapped himself in it, plied his fan nimbly about his face, and walked out of the lodge in silence, but with quite a consequential smile, taking his old position in front of the door for a while, after which he drew himself quietly off without further exhibition . . .

I spoke in a former Letter of Mah-to-toh-pa (the four bears), the second chief of the nation, and the most popular man of the Mandans—a high-minded and gallant warrior . . .

About a week since, this noble fellow stepped into my painting-room about twelve o'clock in the day, in full and splendid dress, and passing his arm through mine, pointed the way, and led me in the most gentlemanly manner, through the village and into his own lodge, where a feast was prepared in a careful manner and waiting our arrival. The lodge in which he dwelt was a room of immense size, some forty or fifty feet in diameter, in a circular form, and about twenty feet high—with a sunken curb of stone in the centre, of five or six feet in diameter and one foot deep, which contained the fire over which the pot was boiling. I was led near the edge of this curb, and seated on a very handsome robe, most ingeniously garnished and painted with hieroglyphics; and he seated himself gracefully on another one at a little distance from me; with the feast prepared in several dishes, resting on a beautiful rush mat, which was placed between us.

The simple feast which was spread before us consisted of three dishes only, two of which were served in wooden bowls, and the third in an earthen vessel of their own manufacture, somewhat in shape of a bread-tray in our own country. This last contained a quantity of *pem-i-can* and *marrow-fat;* and one of the former held a fine brace of buffalo ribs, delightfully roasted; and the other was filled with a kind of paste or pudding, made of the flour of the "*pomme blanche,*" as the French call it, a delicious turnip of the prairie, finely flavoured with the buffalo berries, which are collected in great quantities in this country, and used with divers dishes in cooking, as we in civilized countries use dried currants, which they very much resemble.

A handsome pipe and a tobacco-pouch made of the otter skin, filled with k'nick-k'neck (Indian tobacco), laid by the side of the feast; and when we were seated, mine host took up his pipe, and deliberately filled it; and instead of lighting it by the fire, which he could easily have done, he drew from his pouch his flint and steel, and raised a spark with which he kindled it. He drew a few strong whiffs through it, and presented the stem of it to my mouth, through which I drew a whiff or two while he held the stem in his hands. This done, he laid down the pipe, and drawing his knife from his belt, cut off a very small piece of the meat from the ribs, and pronouncing the word "Ho-pe-ne-chee wa-pa-shee" (meaning a *medicine* sacrifice), threw it into the fire.

He then (by signals) requested me to eat, and I commenced, after drawing out from my belt my knife (which it is supposed that every man in this country carries about him, for at an Indian feast a knife is never offered to a guest). Reader, be not astonished that I sat and ate my dinner *alone,* for such is the custom of this strange land. In all tribes in these western regions it is an invariable rule that a chief never eats with his guests invited to a feast; but while they eat, he sits by, at their service, and ready to wait upon them; deliberately charging and lighting the pipe which is to be passed around after the feast is over. Such was the case in the present instance, and while I was eating, Mah-to-toh-pa sat cross-legged before me, cleaning his pipe and preparing it for a cheerful smoke when I had finished my meal. For this ceremony I observed he was making unusual preparation, and I observed as I ate, that after he had taken enough of the k'nick-k'neck or bark of the red willow, from his pouch, he rolled out of it also a piece of the *"castor,"* which it is customary amongst these folks to carry in their tobacco-sack to give it a flavour; and, shaving off a small quantity of it, mixed it with the bark, with which he charged his pipe. This done, he drew also from his sack a small parcel containing a fine powder, which was made of dried buffalo dung, a little of which he spread over the top, (according also to custom), which was like tinder, having no other effect than that of lighting the pipe with ease and satisfaction. My appetite satiated, I straightened up, and with a whiff the pipe was lit, and we enjoyed together for a quarter of an hour the most delightful exchange of good feelings, amid clouds of smoke and pantomimic signs and gesticulations.

The dish of "pemican and marrow-fat," of which I spoke, was thus:—The first, an article of food used throughout this country, as familiarly as we use bread in the civilized world. It is made of buffalo meat dried very hard, and afterwards pounded in a large wooden mortar until it is made nearly as fine as sawdust, then packed in this dry state in bladders or sacks of skin, and is easily carried to any part of the world in good order. "Marrow-fat" is collected by the Indians from the buffalo bones which they break to pieces, yielding a prodigious quantity of marrow, which is boiled out and put into buffalo bladders which have been distended; and after it cools, becomes quite hard like tallow, and has the appearance, and very nearly the flavour, of the richest yellow butter. At a feast, chunks of this marrow-fat are cut off and placed in a tray or bowl, with the pemican, and eaten together . . . In this dish laid a spoon made of the buffalo's horn, which was black as jet, and beautifully polished; in one of the others there was another of still more ingenious and beautiful workmanship, made of the horn of the mountain-sheep, or "Gros corn," as the French trappers call them; it was large enough to hold of itself two or three pints, and was almost entirely transparent.

I spoke also of the earthen dishes or bowls in which these viands were served out; they are a familiar part of the culinary furniture of every Mandan lodge, and are manufactured by the women of this tribe in great quantities, and modelled into a thousand forms and tastes. They are made by the hands of the women, from a tough black clay, and baked in kilns which are made for the purpose, and are nearly equal in hardness to our own manufacture of pottery; though they have not yet got the art of glazing, which would be to them a most valuable secret. They make them so strong and service-able, however, that they hang them over the fire as we do our iron pots, and boil their meat in them with perfect success. I have seen some few specimens of such manufacture, which have been dug up in Indian mounds and tombs in the southern and middle states, placed in our Eastern Museums and looked upon as a great wonder, when here this novelty is at once done away with, and the whole mystery; where women can be seen handling and using them by hundreds, and they can be seen every day in the summer also, moulding them into many fanciful forms, and passing them through the kiln where they are hardened.

Whilst sitting at this feast the wigwam was as silent as death, although we were not alone in it. This chief, like most others, had a plurality of wives, and all of them (some six or seven) were seated around the sides of the lodge, upon robes or mats placed upon the ground, and not allowed to speak, though they were in readiness to obey his orders or commands, which were uniformly given by signs-manual, and executed in the neatest and most silent manner.

When I arose to return, the pipe through which we had smoked was presented to me; and the robe on which I had sat, he gracefully raised by the corners and tendered it to me, explaining by signs that the paintings which were on it were the representations of the battles of his life, where he had fought and killed with his own hand fourteen of his enemies; that he had been two weeks engaged in painting it for me, and that he had invited me here on this occasion to present it to me . . .

The following was, perhaps, one of the most extraordinary exploits of this remarkable man's life, and is well attested by Mr. Kipp, and several white men, who were living in the Mandan village at the time of its occurrence. In a skirmish, near the Mandan village, when they were set upon by their enemies, the Riccarees, the brother of Mah-to-toh-pa was missing for several days, when Mah-to-toh-pa found the body shockingly mangled, and a handsome spear left piercing the body through the heart. The spear was by him brought into the Mandan village, where it was recognized by many as a famous weapon belonging to a noted brave of the Riccarees, by the name of Won-ga-tap. This spear was brandished through the Mandan village by Mah-to-toh-pa (with the blood of his brother dried on its blade), crying most piteously, and swearing that he would some day revenge the death of his brother with the same weapon.

It is almost an incredible fact, that he kept this spear with great care in his wigwam for the space of four years, in the fruitless expectation of an opportunity to use it upon the breast of its owner; when his indignant soul, impatient of further delay, burst forth in the most uncontroulable frenzy and fury; he again brandished it through the village, and said, that the blood of his brother's heart which was seen on its blade was yet fresh, and called loudly for revenge. "Let every Mandan (said he) be silent, and let no one sound

the name of Mah-to-toh-pa—let no one ask for him, nor where he
has gone, until you hear him sound the war-cry in front of the
village, when he will enter it and shew you the blood of Won-ga-tap.
The blade of this lance shall drink the heart's blood of Won-ga-tap,
or Mah-to-toh-pa mingles his shadow with that of his brother."

With this he sallied forth from the village, and over the plains,
with the lance in his hand; his direction was towards the Riccaree
village, and all eyes were upon him, though none dared to speak till
he disappeared over the distant grassy bluffs. He travelled the distance of two hundred miles entirely alone, with a little parched corn
in his pouch, making his marches by night, and laying secreted by
days, until he reached the Riccaree village; where (being acquainted
with its shapes and its habits, and knowing the position of the
wigwam of his doomed enemy) he loitered about in disguise, mingling himself in the obscure throng; and at last, silently and alone,
observed through the rents of the wigwam, the last motions and
movements of his victim, as he retired to bed with his wife: he saw
him light his last pipe and smoke it "to its end"—he saw the last
whiff, and saw the last curl of blue smoke that faintly steeped from
its bowl—he saw the village awhile in darkness and silence, and the
embers that were covered in the middle of the wigwam gone nearly
out, and the last flickering light which had been gently playing over
them; when he walked softly, but not slyly, into the wigwam and
seated himself by the fire, over which was hanging a large pot, with a
quantity of cooked meat remaining in it; and by the side of the fire,
the pipe and tobacco-pouch which had just been used; and knowing
that the twilight of the wigwam was not sufficient to disclose the
features of his face to his enemy, he very deliberately turned to the
pot and completely satiated the desperate appetite, which he had got
in a journey of six or seven days, with little or nothing to eat; and
then, as deliberately, charged and lighted the pipe, and sent (no
doubt, in every whiff that he drew through its stem) a prayer to the
Great Spirit for a moment longer for the consummation of his
design. Whilst eating and smoking, the wife of his victim, while
laying in bed, several times enquired of her husband, what man it
was who was eating in their lodge? to which, he as many times
replied, "It's no matter; let him eat, for he is probably hungry."

Mah-to-toh-pa knew full well that his appearance would cause no other reply than this, from the dignitary of the nation; for, from an invariable custom amongst these Northern Indians, any one who is hungry is allowed to walk into any man's lodge and eat. Whilst smoking his last gentle and tremulous whiffs on the pipe, Mah-to-toh-pa (leaning back, and turning gradually on his side, to get a better view of the position of his enemy, and to see a little more distinctly the shapes of things) stirred the embers with his toes (readers, I had every word of this from his own lips, and every attitude and gesture acted out with his own limbs), until he saw his way was clear; at which moment, with his lance in his hands, he rose and drove it through the body of his enemy, and snatching the scalp from his head, he darted from the lodge—and quick as lightning, with the lance in one hand, and the scalp in the other, made his way to the prairie! The village was in an uproar, but he was off, and no one knew the enemy who had struck the blow. Mah-to-toh-pa ran all night, and lay close during the days; thanking the Great Spirit for strengthening his heart and his arm to this noble revenge; and prayed fervently for a continuance of his aid and protection till he should get back to his own village. His prayers were heard; and on the sixth morning, at sunrise, Mah-to-toh-pa descended the bluffs, and entered the village amidst deafening shouts of applause, while he brandished and shewed to his people the blade of his lance, with the blood of his victim dried upon it, over that of his brother; and the scalp of Won-ga-tap suspended from its handle . . .

A party of about 150 Shienne warriors had made an assault upon the Mandan village at an early hour in the morning, and driven off a considerable number of horses, and taken one scalp. Mah-to-toh-pa, who was then a young man, but famed as one of the most valiant of the Mandans, took the lead of a party of fifty warriors, all he could at that time muster, and went in pursuit of the enemy; about noon of the second day, they came in sight of the Shiennes; and the Mandans seeing their enemy much more numerous than they had expected, were generally disposed to turn about and return without attacking them. They started to go back, when Mah-to-toh-pa galloped out in front upon the prairie, and plunged his lance into the ground; the blade was driven into the earth to its hilt—he made another circuit around, and in that circuit tore from his breast his reddened sash, which he hung upon its handle as a flag, calling out to the Mandans, "What! have we come to this? we have dogged our enemy two days, and now when we have found them, are we to turn about and go back like cowards? Mah-to-toh-pa's lance, which is red with the blood of brave men, has led you to the sight of your enemy, and you have followed it; it now stands firm in the ground, where the earth will drink the blood of Mah-to-toh-pa! you may all go back, and Mah-to-toh-pa will fight them alone!"

During this manœuvre, the Shiennes, who had discovered the Mandans behind them, had turned about and were gradually approaching, in order to give them battle; the chief of the Shienne war-party seeing and understanding the difficulty, and admiring the gallant conduct of Mah-to-toh-pa, galloped his horse forward within hailing distance, in front of the Mandans, and called out to know "who he was who had stuck down his lance and defied the whole enemy alone?"

"I am Mah-to-toh-pa, second in command of the brave and valiant Mandans."

"I have heard often of Mah-to-toh-pa, he is a great warrior— dares Mah-to-toh-pa to come forward and fight this battle with me alone, and our warriors will look on?"

"Is he a chief who speaks to Mah-to-toh-pa?"

"My scalps you see hanging to my horse's bits, and here is my lance with the ermine skins and the war-eagle's tail!"

"You have said enough."

The Shienne chief made a circuit or two at full gallop on a beautiful white horse, when he struck his lance into the ground, and left it standing by the side of the lance of Mah-to-toh-pa, both of which were waving together their little red flags, tokens of blood and defiance.

The two parties then drew nearer, on a beautiful prairie, and the two full-plumed chiefs, at full speed, drove furiously upon each other! both firing their guns at the same moment. They passed each other a little distance and wheeled, when Mah-to-toh-pa drew off his powder-horn, and by holding it up, shewed his adversary that the bullet had shattered it to pieces and destroyed his ammunition; he then threw it from him, and his gun also—drew his bow from his quiver, and an arrow, and his shield upon his left arm! The Shienne instantly did the same; *his* horn was thrown off, and his gun was thrown into the air—his shield was balanced on his arm—his bow drawn, and quick as lightning, they were both on the wing for a deadly combat! Like two soaring eagles in the open air, they made their circuits around, and the twangs of their sinewy bows were heard, and the war-whoop, as they dashed by each other, parrying off the whizzing arrows with their shields! Some lodged in their legs and others in their arms; but both protected their *bodies* with their bucklers of bull's hide. Deadly and many were the shafts that fled from their murderous bows. At length the horse of Mah-to-toh-pa fell to the ground with an arrow in his heart: his rider sprang upon his feet prepared to renew the combat; but the Shienne, seeing his adversary dismounted, sprang from his horse, and driving him back, presented the face of his shield towards his enemy, inviting him to come on!—a few shots more were exchanged thus, when the Shienne, having discharged all his arrows, held up his empty quiver and dashing it furiously to the ground, with his bow and his shield; drew and brandished his naked knife!

"Yes!" said Mah-to-toh-pa, as he threw *his* shield and quiver to the earth, and was rushing up—*he* grasped for his knife, but his belt had it not; he had left it at home! his bow was in his hand, with which he parried his antagonist's blow and felled him to the ground! A desperate struggle now ensued for the knife—the blade of it was several times drawn through the right hand of Mah-to-toh-pa, inflicting the most frightful wounds, while he was severely wounded in several parts of the body. He at length succeeded however, in wresting it from his adversary's hand, and plunged it to his heart.

By this time the two parties had drawn up in close view of each other, and at the close of the battle, Mah-to-toh-pa held up, and claimed in deadly silence, the knife and scalp of the noble Shienne chief.

LETTER—NO. 17.

◄——————►

Mandan Village, Upper Missouri.

Polygamy is countenanced amongst all of the North American Indians, so far as I have visited them; and it is no uncommon thing to find a chief with six, eight, or ten, and some with twelve or fourteen wives in his lodge. Such is an ancient custom, and in their estimation is right as well as necessary. Women in a savage state, I believe, are always held in a rank inferior to that of the men, in relation to whom in many respects they stand rather in the light of menials and slaves than otherwise; and as they are the "hewers of wood and drawers of water," it becomes a matter of necessity for a chief (who must be liberal, keep open doors, and entertain, for the support of his popularity) to have in his wigwam a sufficient number of such handmaids or menials to perform the numerous duties and drudgeries of so large and expensive an establishment.

There are two other reasons for this custom which operate with equal, if not with greater force than the one above assigned. In the first place, these people, though far behind the civilized world in acquisitiveness, have still more or less passion for the accumulation of wealth, or, in other words, for the luxuries of life; and a chief, excited by a desire of this kind, together with a wish to be able to furnish his lodge with something more than ordinary for the entertainment of his own people, as well as strangers who fall upon his hospitality, sees fit to marry a number of wives, who are kept at hard labour during most of the year; and the avails of that labour enable him to procure those luxuries, and give to his lodge the appearance of respectability which is not ordinarily seen. Amongst those tribes who trade with the Fur Companies, this system is carried out to a great extent, and the women are kept for the greater part of the year, dressing buffalo robes and other skins for the market; and the brave or chief, who has the greatest number of wives, is considered the most affluent and envied man in the tribe; for his table is most bountifully supplied, and his lodge the most abundantly furnished with the luxuries of civilized manufacture, who has at the year's end the greatest number of robes to vend to the Fur Company.

The manual labour amongst savages is all done by the women; and as there are no daily labourers or persons who will *"hire out"* to labour for another, it becomes necessary for him who requires more than the labour or services of one, to add to the number by legalizing and compromising by the ceremony of marriage, his stock of labourers; who can thus, and thus alone, be easily enslaved, and the results of their labour turned to good account . . .

There are other and very rational grounds on which the propriety of such a custom may be urged, one of which is as follows:—as all nations of Indians in their natural condition are unceasingly at war with the tribes that are about them, for the adjustment of ancient and never-ending feuds, as well as from a love of glory, to which in Indian life the battle-field is almost the only road, their warriors are killed off to that extent, that in many instances two and sometimes three women to a man are found in a tribe. In such instances I have found that the custom of polygamy has kindly helped the community to an evident relief from a cruel and prodigious calamity . . .

There are very few instances indeed, to be seen in these regions, where a poor or ordinary citizen has more than one wife; but amongst chiefs and braves of great reputation, and doctors, it is common to see some six or eight living under one roof, and all apparently quiet and contented; seemingly harmonizing, and enjoying the modes of life and treatment that falls to their lot.

Wives in this country are mostly treated for with the father, as in all instances they are regularly bought and sold. In many cases the bargain is made with the father alone, without ever consulting the inclinations of the girl, and seems to be conducted on his part as a mercenary contract entirely, where he stands out for the highest price he can possibly command for her. There are other instances to be sure, where the parties approach each other, and from the expression of a mutual fondness, make their own arrangements, and pass their own mutual vows, which are quite as sacred and inviolable as similar assurances when made in the civilized world. Yet even in such cases, the marriage is never consummated without the necessary form of making presents to the father of the girl.

It becomes a matter of policy and almost of absolute necessity, for the white men who are Traders in these regions to connect themselves in this way, to one or more of the most influential families in the tribe, which in a measure identifies their interest with that of the nation, and enables them, with the influence of their new family connexions, to carry on successfully their business transactions with them. The young women of the best families only can aspire to such an elevation; and the most of them are exceedingly ambitious for such a connexion, inasmuch as they are certain of a delightful exemption from the slavish duties that devolve upon them when married under other circumstances; and expect to be, as they generally are, allowed to lead a life of ease and idleness, covered with mantles of blue and scarlet cloth—with beads and trinkets, and ribbons, in which they flounce and flirt about, the envied and tinselled belles of every tribe . . .

From the enslaved and degraded condition in which the women are held in the Indian country, the world would naturally think that theirs must be a community formed of incongruous and unharmonizing materials; and consequently destitute of the fine, reciprocal feelings and attachments which flow from the domestic relations in the civilized world; yet it would be untrue, and doing injustice to the Indians, to say that they were in the least behind us in conjugal, in filial, and in paternal affection. There is no trait in the human character which is more universal than the attachments which flow from these relations, and there is no part of the human species who have a stronger affection and a higher regard for them than the North American Indians . . .

Such, then, are the Mandans—their women are beautiful and modest,—and amongst the respectable families, virtue is as highly cherished and as inapproachable, as in any society whatever; yet at the same time a chief may marry a dozen wives if he pleases, and so may a white man; and if either wishes to marry the most beautiful and modest girl in the tribe, she is valued only equal, perhaps, to two horses, a gun with powder and ball for a year, five or six pounds of beads, a couple of gallons of whiskey, and a handful of awls.

The girls of this tribe, like those of most of these north-western tribes, marry at the age of twelve or fourteen, and some at the age of eleven years; and their beauty, from this fact, as well as from the slavish life they lead, soon after marriage vanishes. Their occupations are almost continual, and they seem to go industriously at them, as if from choice or inclination, without a murmur.

The principal occupations of the women in this village, consist in procuring wood and water, in cooking, dressing robes and other skins, in drying meat and wild fruit, and raising corn (maize). The Mandans are somewhat of agriculturists, as they raise a great deal of corn and some pumpkins and squashes. This is all done by the women, who make their hoes of the shoulder-blade of the buffalo or the elk, and dig the ground over instead of ploughing it, which is consequently done with a vast deal of labour. They raise a very small sort of corn, the ears of which are not longer than a man's thumb. This variety is well adapted to their climate, as it ripens sooner than other varieties, which would not mature in so cold a latitude. The green corn season is one of great festivity with them, and one of much importance. The greater part of their crop is eaten during these festivals, and the remainder is gathered and dried on the cob, before it has ripened, and packed away in "*caches*" (as the French call them), holes dug in the ground, some six or seven feet deep, the insides of which are somewhat in the form of a jug, and tightly closed at the top. The corn, and even dried meat and pemican, are placed in these *caches*, being packed tight around the sides, with prairie grass, and effectually preserved through the severest winters.

Corn and dried meat are generally laid in in the fall, in sufficient quantities to support them through the winter. These are the principal articles of food during that long and inclement season; and in addition to them, they oftentimes have in store great quantities of dried squashes and dried "*pommes blanches*," a kind of turnip which grows in great abundance in these regions . . . These are dried in great quantities, and pounded into a sort of meal, and cooked with the dried meat and corn. Great quantities also of wild fruit of different kinds are dried and laid away in store for the winter season, such as buffalo berries, service berries, strawberries, and wild plums.

The buffalo meat, however, is the great staple and "staff of life" in this country, and seldom (if ever) fails to afford them an abundant and wholesome means of subsistence. There are, from a fair computation, something like 250,000 Indians in these western regions, who live almost exclusively on the flesh of these animals, through every part of the year. During the summer and fall months they use the meat fresh, and cook it in a great variety of ways, by roasting, broiling, boiling, stewing, smoking, &c.; and by boiling the ribs and joints with the marrow in them, make a delicious soup, which is universally used, and in vast quantities. The Mandans, I find, have no regular or stated times for their meals, but generally eat about twice in the twenty-four hours. The pot is always boiling over the fire, and any one who is hungry (either of the household or from any other part of the village) has a right to order it taken off, and to fall to eating as he pleases. Such is an unvarying custom amongst the North American Indians, and I very much doubt, whether the civilized world have in their institutions any system which can properly be called more humane and charitable. Every man, woman, or child in Indian communities is allowed to enter any one's lodge, and even that of the chief of the nation, and eat when they are hungry, provided misfortune or necessity has driven them to it. Even so can the poorest and most worthless drone of the nation; if he is too lazy to hunt or to supply himself, he can walk into any lodge and everyone will share with him as long as there is anything to eat. He, however, who thus begs when he is able to hunt, pays dear for his meat, for he is stigmatized with the disgraceful epithet of a poltroon and a beggar.

The Mandans, like all other tribes, sit at their meals cross-legged, or rather with their ancles crossed in front of them, and both feet drawn close under their bodies; or, which is very often the case also, take their meals in a reclining posture, with the legs thrown out, and the body resting on one elbow and fore-arm, which are under them. The dishes from which they eat are invariably on the ground or floor of the lodge, and the group resting on buffalo robes or mats of various structure and manufacture.

The position in which the women sit at their meals and on other occasions is different from that of the men, and one which they take and rise from again, with great ease and much grace, by merely bending the knees both together, inclining the body back and the head and shoulders quite forward, they squat entirely down to the ground, inclining both feet either to the right or the left. In this position they always rest while eating, and it is both modest and graceful, for they seem, with apparent ease, to assume the position and rise out of it, without using their hands in any way to assist them.

These women, however, although graceful and civil, and ever so beautiful or ever so hungry, are not allowed to sit in the same group with the men while at their meals. So far as I have yet travelled in the Indian country, I never have seen an Indian woman eating with her husband. Men form the first group at the banquet, and women, and children and dogs all come together at the next, and these gormandize and glut themselves to an enormous extent, though the men very seldom do.

. . . It is everywhere asserted, and almost universally believed, that the Indians are "enormous eaters;" but comparatively speaking, I assure my readers that this is an error. I venture to say that there are no persons on earth who practice greater prudence and self-denial, than the men do (amongst the wild Indians), who are constantly in war and in the chase, or in their athletic sports and exercises; for all of which they are excited by the highest ideas of pride and honour, and every kind of excess is studiously avoided; and for a very great part of their lives, the most painful abstinence is enforced upon themselves, for the purpose of preparing their bodies and their limbs for these extravagant exertions. Many a man who has been a few weeks along the frontier, amongst the drunken, naked and beggared part of the Indian race, and run home and written a book on Indians, has, no doubt, often seen them eat to beastly excess; and he has seen them also guzzle whiskey (and perhaps *sold* it to them) till he has seen them glutted and besotted, without will or energy to move; and many and thousands of such things can always be seen, where white people have made beggars of them, and they have nothing to do but lie under a fence and beg a whole week to get meat and whiskey enough for one feast and one carouse; but amongst the wild Indians in this country there are no beggars—no drunkards—and every man, from a beautiful natural precept, studies to keep his body and mind in such a healthy shape and condition as will at all times enable him to use his weapons in self-defence, or struggle for the prize in their manly games . . .

Their mode of curing and preserving the buffalo meat is somewhat curious, and in fact it is almost incredible also; for it is all cured or dried in the sun, without the aid of salt or smoke! The method of doing this is the same amongst all the tribes, from this to the Mexican Provinces, and is as follows:—The choicest parts of the flesh from the buffalo are cut out by the squaws, and carried home on their backs or on horses, and there cut *"across the grain,"* in such a manner as will take alternately the layers of lean and fat; and having prepared it all in this way, in strips about half an inch in thickness, it is hung up by hundreds and thousands of pounds on poles resting on crotches, out of the reach of dogs or wolves, and exposed to the rays of the sun for several days, when it becomes so effectually dried, that it can be carried to any part of the world without damage. This seems almost an unaccountable thing, and the more so, as it is done in the hottest months of the year, and also in all the different latitudes of an Indian country.

So singular a fact as this can only be accounted for, I consider, on the ground of the extraordinary rarity and purity of the air which we meet with in these vast tracts of country, which are now properly denominated "the great buffalo plains," a series of exceedingly elevated plateaus of *steppes* or *prairies*, lying at and near the base of the Rocky Mountains.

It is a fact then, which I presume will be new to most of the world, that meat can be cured in the sun without the aid of smoke or salt; and it is a fact equally true and equally surprising also, that none of these tribes use salt in any way, although their country abounds in salt springs; and in many places, in the frequent walks of the Indian, the prairie may be seen, for miles together, covered with an incrustation of salt as white as the drifted snow . . .

LETTER—NO. 18.

◄─────────────►

Mandan Village, Upper Missouri.

*T*he Mandans, like all other tribes, lead lives of idleness and leisure; and of course, devote a great deal of time to their sports and amusements, of which they have a great variety. Of these, dancing is one of the principal, and may be seen in a variety of forms: such as the buffalo dance, the boasting dance, the begging dance, the scalp dance, and a dozen other kinds of dances, all of which have their peculiar characters and meanings or objects.

These exercises are exceedingly grotesque in their appearance, and to the eye of a traveller who knows not their meaning or importance, they are an uncouth and frightful display of starts, and jumps, and yelps, and jarring gutturals, which are sometime truly terrifying. But when one gives them a little attention, and has been lucky enough to be initiated into their mysterious meaning, they become a subject of the most intense and exciting interest. Every dance has its peculiar step, and every step has its meaning; every dance also has its peculiar song, and that is so intricate and mysterious oftentimes, that not one in ten of the young men who are dancing and singing it, know the meaning of the song which they are chanting over. None but the medicine-men are allowed to understand them; and even they are generally only initiated into these secret arcana, on the payment of a liberal stipend for their tuition, which requires much application and study. There is evidently a set song and sentiment for every dance, for the songs are perfectly measured, and sung in exact time with the beat of the drum; and always with an uniform and invariable set of sounds and expressions, which clearly indicate certain sentiments, which are expressed by the voice, though sometimes not given in any known language whatever.

They have other dances and songs which are not so mystified, but which are sung and understood by every person in the tribe, being sung in their own language, with much poetry in them, and perfectly metred, but without rhyme . . .

My ears have been almost continually ringing since I came here, with the din of yelping and beating of the drums; but I have for several days past been peculiarly engrossed, and my senses almost confounded with the stamping, and grunting, and bellowing of the *buffalo dance*, which closed a few days since at sunrise (thank Heaven), and which I must needs describe to you.

Buffaloes, it is known, are a sort of roaming creatures, congregating occasionally in huge masses, and strolling away about the country from east to west, or from north to south, or just where their whims or strange fancies may lead them; and the Mandans are sometimes, by this means, most unceremoniously left without any thing to eat; and being a small tribe, and more powerful enemies, are oftentimes left almost in a state of starvation. In any emergency of this kind, every man musters and brings out of his lodge his mask (the skin of a buffalo's head with the horns on), which he is obliged to keep in readiness for this occasion; and then commences the buffalo dance, of which I have above spoken, which is held for the purpose of making "buffalo come" (as they term it), of inducing the buffalo herds to change the direction of their wanderings, and bend their course towards the Mandan village, and graze about on the beautiful hills and bluffs in its vicinity, where the Mandans can shoot them down and cook them as they want them for food.

For the most part of the year, the young warriors and hunters, by riding out a mile or two from the village, can kill meat in abundance; and sometimes large herds of these animals may be seen grazing in full view of the village. There are other seasons also when the young men have ranged about the country as far as they are willing to risk their lives, on account of their enemies, without finding meat. This sad intelligence is brought back to the chiefs and doctors, who sit in solemn council, and consult on the most expedient measures to be taken, until they are sure to decide upon the old and only expedient which "never has failed."

The chief issues his order to his runners or criers, who proclaim it through the village—and in a few minutes the dance begins. The place where this strange operation is carried on is in the public area in the centre of the village, and in front of the great medicine or mystery lodge. About ten or fifteen Mandans at a time join in the dance, each one with the skin of the buffalo's head (or mask) with the horns on, placed over his head, and in his hand his favourite bow or lance, with which he is used to slay the buffalo.

I mentioned that this dance always had the desired effect, that it never fails, nor can it, for it cannot be stopped (but is going incessantly day and night) until "buffalo come." Drums are beating and rattles are shaken, and songs and yells incessantly are shouted, and lookers-on stand ready with masks on their heads, and weapons in hand, to take the place of each one as he becomes fatigued, and jumps out of the ring.

During this time of general excitement, spies or "*lookers*" are kept on the hills in the neighbourhood of the village, who, when they discover buffaloes in sight, give the appropriate signal, by "throwing their robes," which is instantly seen in the village, and understood by the whole tribe. At this joyful intelligence there is a shout of thanks to the Great Spirit, and more especially to the mystery-man, and the dancers, who *have been the immediate cause of their success!* There is then a brisk preparation for the chase—a grand hunt takes place. The choicest pieces of the victims are sacrificed to the Great Spirit, and then a surfeit and a carouse.

These dances have sometimes been continued in this village two and three weeks without stopping an instant, until the joyful moment when buffaloes made their appearance. So they *never fail;* and they think they have been the means of bringing them in . . .

. . . The signal was given into the village on that morning from the top of a distant bluff, that a band of buffaloes were in sight, though at a considerable distance off, and every heart beat with joy, and every eye watered and glistened with gladness.

The dance had lasted some three or four days, and now, instead of the doleful tap of the drum and the begging chaunts of the dancers, the stamping of horses was heard as they were led and galloped through the village—young men were throwing off their robes and their shirts,—were seen snatching a handful of arrows from their quivers, and stringing their sinewy bow, glancing their eyes and their smiles at their sweethearts, and mounting their ponies.   *   *   *

    *   *   A few minutes there had been of bustle and boasting, whilst bows were twanging and spears were polishing by running their blades into the ground—every face and every eye was filled with joy and gladness—horses were pawing and snuffing in fury for the outset, when Louison Frénié, an interpreter of the Fur Company, galloped through the village with his rifle in his hand and his powder-horn at his side; his head and waist were bandaged with handkerchiefs, and his shirt sleeves rolled up to his shoulders—the hunter's yell issued from his lips and was repeated through the village; he flew to the bluffs, and behind him and over the graceful swells of the prairie, galloped the emulous youths, whose hearts were beating high and quick for the onset.

In the village, where hunger had reigned, and starvation was almost ready to look them in the face, all was instantly turned to joy and gladness. The chiefs and doctors who had been for some days dealing out minimum rations to the community from the public crib, now spread before their subjects the contents of their own private *caches*, and the last of every thing that could be mustered, that they might eat a thanksgiving to the Great Spirit for his goodness in sending them a supply of buffalo meat. A general carouse of banqueting ensued, which occupied the greater part of the day; and their hidden stores which might have fed an emergency for several weeks, were pretty nearly used up on the occasion—bones were half picked, and dishes half emptied and then handed to the dogs. *I* was not forgotten neither, in the general surfeit; several large and generous wooden bowls of pemican and other palatable food were sent to my painting-room, and I received them in this time of scarcity with great pleasure.

After this general indulgence was over, and the dogs had licked the dishes, their usual games and amusements ensued—and hilarity and mirth, and joy took possession of, and reigned in, every nook

and corner of the village; and in the midst of this, screams and
shrieks were heard! and echoed everywhere. Women and children
scrambled to the tops of their wigwams, with their eyes and their
hands stretched in agonizing earnestness to the prairie, whilst blackened warriors ran furiously through every winding maze of the
village, and issuing their jarring gutturals of vengeance, as they
snatched their deadly weapons from their lodges, and struck the
reddened post as they furiously passed it by! Two of their hunters
were bending their course down the sides of the bluff toward the
village, and another broke suddenly out of a deep ravine, and yet
another was seen dashing over and down the green hills, and all
were goading on their horses at full speed! and then came another,
and another, and all entered the village amid shouts and groans of
the villagers who crowded around them; the story was told in their
looks, for one was bleeding, and the blood that flowed from his
naked breast had crimsoned his milk white steed as it had dripped
over him; another grasped in his left hand a scalp that was reeking in
blood—and in the other his whip—another grasped nothing, save
the reins in one hand and the mane of the horse in the other, having
thrown his bow and his arrows away, and trusted to the fleetness of
his horse for his safety; yet the story was audibly told, and the fatal
tragedy recited in irregular and almost suffocating ejaculations—the
names of the dead were in turns pronounced and screams and
shrieks burst forth at their recital—murmurs and groans ran through
the village, and this happy little community were in a moment
smitten with sorrow and distraction.

Their proud band of hunters who had started full of glee and
mirth in the morning, had been surrounded by their enemy, the
Sioux, and eight of them killed. The Sioux, who had probably
reconnoitred their village during the night, and ascertained that they
were dancing for buffaloes, laid a stratagem to entrap them in the
following manner:—Some six or eight of them appeared the next
morning (on a distant bluff, in sight of their sentinel) under the
skins of buffaloes, imitating the movements of those animals whilst
grazing; and being discovered by the sentinel, the intelligence was
telegraphed to the village, which brought out their hunters as I have
described. The masked buffaloes were seen grazing on the top of a high

bluff, and when the hunters had approached within half a mile or so of them, they suddenly disappeared over the hill. Louison Frénié, who was leading the little band of hunters, became at that moment suspicious of so strange a movement, and came to a halt * * * * "Look"! (said a Mandan, pointing to a little ravine to the right, and at the foot of the hill, from which suddenly broke some forty or fifty furious Sioux, on fleet horses and under full whip, who were rushing upon them); they wheeled, and in front of them came another band more furious from the other side of the hill! they started for home (poor fellows), and strained every nerve; but the Sioux were too fleet for them; and every now and then, the whizzing arrow and the lance were heard to rip the flesh of their naked backs, and a grunt and a groan, as they tumbled from their horses. Several miles were run in this desperate race; and Frénié got home, and several of the Mandans, though eight of them were killed and scalped by the way.

So ended that day and the hunt; but many a day and sad, will last the grief of those whose hearts were broken on that unlucky occasion.

This day, though, my readers, has been one of a more joyful kind, for the Great Spirit, who was indignant at so flagrant an injustice, has sent the Mandans an abundance of buffaloes; and all hearts have joined in a general thanksgiving to Him for his goodness and justice.

LETTER—NO. 19.

◄———————————————————►

Mandan Village, Upper Missouri.

... *T*he games and amusements of these people are in most respects like those of the other tribes, consisting of ball plays—game of the moccasin, of the platter—feats of archery—horse-racing, &c.; and they have yet another, which may be said to be their favourite amusement, and unknown to the other tribes about them. The game of Tchung-kee, a beautiful athletic exercise, which they seem to be almost unceasingly practising whilst the weather is fair, and they have nothing else of moment to demand their attention. This game is decidedly their favourite amusement, and is played near to the village on a pavement of clay, which has been used for that purpose until it has become as smooth and hard as a floor. For this game two champions form their respective parties, by choosing alternately the most famous players, until their requisite numbers are made up. Their bettings are then made, and their stakes are held by some of the chiefs or others present The play commences with two (one from each party), who start off upon a trot, abreast of each other, and one of them rolls in advance of them, on the pavement, a little ring of two or three inches in diameter, cut out of a stone; and each one follows it up with his "tchung-kee" (a stick of six feet in length, with little bits of leather projecting from its sides of an inch or more in length), which he throws before him as he runs, sliding it along upon the ground after the ring, endeavouring to place it in such a position when it stops, that the ring may fall upon it, and receive one of the little projections of leather through it, which counts for game, one, or two, or four, according to the position of the leather on which the ring is lodged. The last winner always has the rolling of the ring, and both start and throw the tchung-kee together; if either fails to receive the ring or to lie in a certain position, it is a forfeiture of the amount of the number he was nearest to, and he loses his throw; when another steps into his place. This game is a very difficult one to describe, so as to give an exact idea of it, unless one can see it played—it is a game of great beauty and fine bodily exercise, and these people become excessively fascinated with it; often gambling away every thing they possess, and even sometimes, when everything else was gone, have been known to stake their liberty upon the issue of these games, offering themselves as slaves to their opponents in case they get beaten.

Feasting and *fasting* are important customs observed by the Mandans, as well as by most other tribes, at stated times and for particular purposes. These observances are strictly religious and rigidly observed ... *Sacrificing* is also a religious custom with these people, and is performed in many different modes, and on numerous occasions. Of this custom I shall also speak more fully hereafter, merely noticing at present, some few of the hundred modes in which these offerings are made to the Good and Evil Spirits. Human sacrifices have never been made by the Mandans, not by any of the northwestern tribes (so far as I can learn), excepting the Pawnees of the Platte; who have, undoubtedly, observed such an inhuman practice in former times, though they have relinquished it of late. The Mandans sacrifice their fingers to the Great Spirit, and of their worldly goods, the best and the most costly; if a horse or a dog, it must be the favourite one; if it is an arrow from their quiver, they will select the most perfect one as the most effective gift; if it is meat, it is the choicest piece cut from the buffalo or other animal; if it is anything from the stores of the Traders, it is the most costly—it is blue or scarlet cloth, which costs them in this country an enormous price, and is chiefly used for the purpose of hanging over their wigwams to decay, or to cover the scaffolds where rest the bones of their departed relations.

Of these kinds of sacrifices there are three of an interesting nature, erected over the great medicine-lodge in the centre of the village— they consist of ten or fifteen yards of blue and black cloth each, purchased from the Fur Company at fifteen or twenty dollars per yard, which are folded up so as to resemble human figures, with quills in their heads and masks on their faces. These singular-looking figures, like *"scare crows"* are erected on poles about thirty feet high, over the door of the mystery-lodge, and there are left to decay. There hangs now by the side of them another, which was added to the number a few days since, of the skin of a white buffalo . . .

This beautiful and costly skin, when its history is known, will furnish a striking proof of the importance which they attach to these propitiatory offerings. But a few weeks since, a party of Mandans returned from the Mouth of the Yellow Stone, two hundred miles above, with information that a party of Blackfeet were visiting that place on business with the American Fur Company; and that they had with them a white buffalo robe for sale. This was looked upon as a subject of great importance by the chiefs, and one worthy of public consideration. A white buffalo robe is a great curiosity, even in the country of buffaloes, and will always command an almost incredible price, from its extreme scarcity; and then, from its being the most costly article of traffic in these regions, it is usually converted into a *sacrifice*, being offered to the Great Spirit, as the most acceptable gift that can be procured. Amongst the vast herds of buffaloes which graze on these boundless prairies, there is not one in an hundred thousand, perhaps, that is white; and when such an one is obtained, it is considered great *medicine* or mystery.

On the receipt of the intelligence above-mentioned, the chiefs convened in council, and deliberated on the expediency of procuring the white robe from the Blackfeet; and also of appropriating the requisite means, and devising the proper mode of procedure for effecting the purchase. At the close of their deliberations, eight men were fitted out on eight of their best horses, who took from the Fur Company's store, on the credit of the chiefs, goods exceeding even the value of their eight horses; and they started for the Mouth of the Yellow Stone, where they arrived in due time, and made the purchase, by leaving the eight horses and all the goods which they carried; returning on foot to their own village, bringing home with them the white robe, which was looked upon by all eyes of the villagers as a thing that was vastly curious, and containing (as they express it) something of the Great Spirit. This wonderful anomaly laid several days in the chief's lodge, until public curiosity was gratified; and then it was taken by the doctors or high-priests, and with a great deal of form and mystery consecrated, and raised on the top of a long pole over the *medicine-lodge*; where it now stands in a group with the others, and will stand as an offering to the Great Spirit, until it decays and falls to the ground . . .

. . . The Mandans, as I have said in a former Letter, raise a great deal of corn; and sometimes a most disastrous drought will be visited on the land, destructive to their promised harvest. Such was the case when I arrived at the Mandan village on the stream-boat, Yellow-Stone. Rain had not fallen for many a day, and the dear little girls and the ugly old squaws, altogether (all of whom had fields of corn), were groaning and crying to their lords, and imploring them to intercede for rain, that their little respective patches, which were now turning pale and yellow, might not be withered, and they be deprived of the pleasure of their customary annual festivity, and the joyful occasion of the "roasting ears," and the "green corn dance."

The chiefs and doctors sympathized with the plaints of the women, and recommended patience. Great deliberation, they said, was necessary in these cases; and though they resolved on making the attempt to produce rain for the benefit of the corn; yet they very wisely resolved that to begin too soon might ensure their entire defeat in the endeavour; and that the longer they put it off, the more certain they would feel of ultimate success. So, after a few days of further delay, when the importunities of the women had become clamorous, and even mournful, and almost insupportable, the *medicine-men* assembled in the council-house, with all their mystery apparatus about them—with an abundance of wild sage, and other aromatic herbs, with a fire prepared to burn them, that their savoury odours might be sent forth to the Great Spirit. The lodge was closed to all the villagers, except some ten or fifteen young men, who were willing to hazard the dreadful alternative of making it rain, or suffer the everlasting disgrace of having made a fruitless essay.

They, only, were allowed as witnesses to the *hocus pocus* and *conjuration* devised by the doctors inside of the medicine-lodge; and they were called up by lot, each one in his turn, to spend a day upon the top of the lodge, to test the potency of his medicine; or, in other words, to see how far his voice might be heard and obeyed amongst the clouds of the heavens; whilst the doctors were burning incense in the wigwam below, and with their songs and prayers to the Great Spirit for success, were sending forth grateful fumes and odours to Him "who lives in the sun and commands the thunders of Heaven." Wah-kee (the shield) was the first who ascended the wigwam at sunrise; and he stood all day, and looked foolish, as he was counting over and over his string of mystery-beads—the whole village were assembled around him, and praying for his success. Not a cloud appeared—the day was calm and hot; and at the setting of the sun, he descended from the lodge and went home—"his *medicine* was not good," nor can he ever be a *medicine-man*.

Om-pah (the elk) was the next; he ascended the lodge at sunrise the next morning. His body was entirely naked, being covered with yellow clay. On his left arm he carried a beautiful shield, and a long lance in his right; and on his head the skin of a raven, the bird that soars amidst the clouds, and above the lightning's glare—he flourished his shield and brandished his lance, and raised his voice, but in vain; for at sunset the ground was dry and the sky was clear; the squaws were crying, and their corn was withering at its roots.

War-rah-pa (the beaver) was next; he also spent his breath in vain upon the empty air, and came down at night—and Wak-a-dah-ha-hee (the white buffalo's hair) took the stand the next morning. He is a small, but beautifully proportioned young man. He was dressed in a tunic and leggings of the skins of the mountain-sheep, splendidly garnished with quills of the porcupine, and fringed with locks of hair taken by his own hand from the heads of his enemies. On his arm he carried his shield, made of the buffalo's hide—its boss was the head of the war-eagle—and its front was ornamented with "red chains of lightning." In his left hand he clenched his sinewy bow and one single arrow. The villagers were all gathered about him; when he threw up a feather to decide on the course of the wind, and he commenced thus:—"My friends! people of the pheasants! you see me here a sacrifice—I shall this day relieve you from great distress, and bring joy amongst you; or I shall descend from this lodge when the sun goes down, and live amongst the dogs and old women all my days. My friends! you saw which way the feather flew, and I hold my shield this day in the direction where the wind comes—the lightning on my shield will draw a great cloud, and this arrow, which is selected from my quiver, and which is feathered with the quill of the white swan, will make a hole in it. My friends! this hole in the lodge at my feet, shows me the medicine-men, who are seated in the lodge below me and crying to the Great Spirit; and through it comes and passes into my nose delightful odours, which you see rising in the smoke to the Great Spirit above, who rides in the clouds and commands the winds! Three days they have sat here, my friends, and nothing has been done to relieve your distress. On the first day was Wah-kee (the shield), he could do nothing; he counted his beads and came down—his medicine was not good—his name was bad, and it kept off the rain. The next was Om-pah (the elk); on his head the raven was seen, who flies *above* the storm, and he failed. War-rah-pa (the beaver) was the next, my friends; the beaver lives *under* the *water*, and he never wants it to rain. My friends! I see you are in great distress, and nothing has yet been done; this shield belonged to my father the White Buffalo; and the lightning you see on it is red; it was taken from a black cloud, and that cloud will come over us to-day. I am the white buffalo's hair—and I am the son of my father."

In this manner flourished and manœuvred Wak-a-dah-ha-hee (the white buffalo's hair), alternately addressing the audience and the heavens—and holding converse with the winds and the "*je-bi*" (spirits) that are floating about in them—stamping his foot over the heads of the *magi*, who were involved in mysteries beneath him, and invoking the spirits of darkness and light to send rain, to gladden the hearts of the Mandans.

It happened on this memorable day about noon, that the steamboat Yellow Stone, on her first trip up the Missouri River, approached and landed at the Mandan Village, as I have described in a former epistle. I was lucky enough to be a passenger on this boat, and helped to fire a salute of twenty guns of twelve pounds calibre, when we first came in sight of the village, some three or four miles below. These guns introduced a *new sound* into this strange country, which the Mandans at first supposed to be thunder; and the young man upon the lodge, who turned it to good account, was gathering fame in rounds of applause, which were repeated and echoed through the whole village; all eyes were centred upon him—chiefs envied him—mothers' hearts were beating high whilst they were decorating and leading up their fair daughters to offer him in marriage, on his signal success. The medicine-men had left the lodge, and came out to bestow upon him the envied title of "*medicine-man*," or "doctor," which he had so deservedly won—wreaths were prepared to decorate his brows, and eagle's plumes and calumets were in readiness for him; his friends were all rejoiced—his enemies wore on their faces a silent gloom and hatred; and his old sweethearts, who had formerly cast him off, gazed intensely upon him, as they glowed with the burning fever of repentance.

During all this excitement, Wak-a-dah-ha-hee kept his position, assuming the most commanding and threatening attitudes; brandishing his shield in the direction of the thunder (Illustration 21), although there was not a cloud to be seen, until he (poor fellow), being elevated above the rest of the village, espied, to his inexpressible amazement, the steam-boat ploughing its way up the windings of the river below; puffing her steam from her pipes, and sending forth the thunder from a twelve-pounder on her deck! * * * The White Buffalo's Hair stood motionless and turned pale, he looked awhile, and turned to the chief and to the multitude, and addressed them with a trembling lip—"My friends, we will get no rain!—there are, you see, no clouds; but my medicine is great—I have brought a *thunder boat!* look and see it! the thunder you hear is out of her mouth, and the lightning which you see is on the waters!"

At this intelligence, the whole village flew to the tops of their wigwams, or to the bank of the river, from whence the steamer was in full view, and ploughing along, to their utter dismay and confusion.

In this promiscuous throng of chiefs, doctors, women, children and dogs, was mingled Wak-a-dah-ha-hee (the white buffalo's hair), having descended from his high place to mingle with the frightened throng.

Dismayed at the approach of so strange and unaccountable an object, the Mandans stood their ground but a few moments; when, by an order of the chiefs, all hands were ensconced within the piquets of their village, and all the warriors armed for desperate

Illustration 21. Rainmaking among the Mandans.

defence. A few moments brought the boat in front of the village, and
all was still and quiet as death; not a Mandan was to be seen upon
the banks. The steamer was moored, and three or four of the chiefs
soon after, walked boldly down the bank and on to her deck, with a
spear in one hand and the calumet or pipe of peace in the other.
The moment they stepped on board they met (to their great surprise
and joy) their old friend, Major Sanford, their agent, which circumstance put an instant end to all their fears. The villagers were soon
apprized of the fact, and the whole race of the beautiful and friendly
Mandans was paraded on the bank of the river, in front of the steamer.

The "rain maker," whose apprehensions of a public calamity
brought upon the nation by his extraordinary *medicine*, had, for the
better security of his person from apprehended vengeance, secreted
himself in some secure place, and was the last to come forward, and
the last to be convinced that this visitation was a friendly one from
the white people; and that his *medicine* had not in the least been
instrumental in bringing it about. This information, though received
by him with much caution and suspicion, at length gave him great
relief, and quieted his mind as to his danger. Yet still in his breast
there was a rankling thorn, though he escaped the dreaded vengeance which he had a few moments before apprehended as at hand;
as he had the mortification and disgrace of having failed in his
mysterious operations. He set up, however (during the day, in his
conversation about the strange arrival), his *medicines*, as the cause of
its approach; asserting everywhere and to everybody, that he knew of
its coming, and that he had by his magic brought the occurrence
about. This plea, however, did not get him much audience; and in
fact, everything else was pretty much swallowed up in the guttural
talk, and bustle, and gossip about the mysteries of the "thunder-
boat;" and so passed the day, until just at the approach of evening,
when the "White Buffalo's Hair" (more watchful of such matters on
this occasion than most others) observed that a black cloud had been
jutting up in the horizon, and was almost directly over the village! In
an instant his shield was on his arm, and his bow in his hand, and
he again upon the lodge! stiffened and braced to the last sinew, he
stood, with his face and his shield presented to the cloud, and his
bow drawn. He drew the eyes of the whole village upon him as he

vaunted forth his super-human powers, and at the same time commanding the cloud to come nearer, that he might draw down its contents upon the heads and the corn-fields of the Mandans! In this wise he stood, waving his shield over his head, stamping his foot and frowning as he drew his bow and threatened the heavens, commanding it to rain—his bow was bent, and the arrow drawn to its head, was sent to the cloud, and he exclaimed, "My friends, it is done! Wak-a-dah-ha-hee's arrow has entered that black cloud, and the Mandans will be wet with the water of the skies!" His predictions were true;—in a few moments the cloud was over the village, and the rain fell in torrents. He stood for some time wielding his weapons and presenting his shield to the sky, while he boasted of his power and the efficacy of his *medicine,* to those who had been about him, but were now driven to the shelter of their wigwams. He, at length, finished his vaunts and his threats, and descended from his high place (in which he had been perfectly drenched), prepared to receive the honours and the homage that were due to one so potent in his mysteries; and to receive the style and title of *"medicine-man."* This is one of a hundred different modes in which a man in Indian countries acquires the honourable appellation.

This man had "made it rain," and of course was to receive more than usual honours, as he had done much more than ordinary men could do. All eyes were upon him, and all were ready to admit that he was skilled in the magic art; and must be so nearly allied to the Great or Evil Spirit, that he must needs be a man of great and powerful influence in the nation, and well entitled to the style of doctor or *medicine-man.*

Readers, there are two facts relative to these strange transactions, which are infallibly true, and should needs be made known. The first is, that when the Mandans undertake to make it rain, *they never fail to succeed,* for their ceremonies never stop until rain begins to fall. The second is equally true, and is this:—that he who has once *"made it rain,"* never attempts it again; his medicine is undoubted—and on future occasions of the kind, he stands aloof, who has once done it in presence of the whole village, giving an opportunity to other young men who are ambitious to signalize themselves in the same way.

During the memorable night of which I have just spoken, the steam-boat remained by the side of the Mandan village, and the rain that had commenced falling continued to pour down its torrents until midnight; black thunder roared, and livid lightning flashed until the heavens appeared to be lit up with one unceasing and appalling glare. In this frightful moment of consternation, a flash of lightning buried itself in one of the earth-covered lodges of the Mandans, and killed a beautiful girl. Here was food and fuel fresh for their superstitions; and a night of vast tumult and excitement ensued. The dreams of the new-made medicine-man were troubled, and he had dreadful apprehensions for the coming day—for he knew that he was subject to the irrevocable decree of the chiefs and doctors, who canvass every strange and unaccountable event, with close and superstitious scrutiny, and let their vengeance fall without mercy upon its immediate cause.

He looked upon his well-earned fame as likely to be withheld from him; and also considered that his life might perhaps be demanded as the forfeit for this girl's death, which would certainly be charged upon him. He looked upon himself as culpable, and supposed the accident to have been occasioned by his criminal desertion of his post, when the steam-boat was approaching the village. Morning came, and he soon learned from some of his friends, the opinions of the wise men; and also the nature of the tribunal that was preparing for him; he sent to the prairie for his three horses, which were brought in, and he mounted the *medicine-lodge,* around which, in a few moments, the villagers were all assembled. "My friends! (said he) I see you all around me, and I am before you; my medicine, you see, is great—it is *too great*—I am young, and I was too fast—I knew not when to stop. The wigwam of Mah-sish is laid low, and many are the eyes that weep for Ko-ka (the antelope:) Wak-a-dah-ha-hee gives three horses to gladden the hearts of those who weep for Ko-ka; his medicine was great—his arrow pierced the black cloud, and the lightning came, and the *thunder-boat* also! who says the medicine of Wak-a-dah-ha-hee is not strong?"

At the end of this sentence an unanimous shout of approbation ran through the crowd, and the "Hair of the White Buffalo" descended amongst them, where he was greeted by shakes of the hand; and amongst whom he now lives and thrives under the familiar and honourable appellation of the "BIG DOUBLE MEDICINE."

LETTER—NO. 20.

Mandan Village, Upper Missouri.

... *I* have seen a fair exhibition of [the Mandans'] archery this day, in a favourite amusement which they call the *"game of the arrow,"* where the young men who are the most distinguished in this exercise, assemble on the prairie at a little distance from the village, and having paid, each one, his "entrance-fee," such as a shield, a robe, a pipe, or other article, step forward in turn, shooting their arrows into the air, endeavouring to see who can get the greatest number flying in the air at one time, thrown from the same bow. For this, the number of eight or ten arrows are clenched in the left hand with the bow, and the first one which is thrown is elevated to such a degree as will enable it to remain the longest time possible in the air, and while it is flying, the others are discharged as rapidly as possible; and he who succeeds in getting the greatest number up at once, is "best," and takes the goods staked.

In looking on at this amusement, the spectator is surprised; not at the great distance to which the arrows are actually sent; but at the quickness of fixing them on the string, and discharging them in succession; which is no doubt, the result of great practice, and enables the most expert of them to get as many as eight arrows up before the first one reaches the ground.

For the successful use of the bow, as it is used through all this region of country on horseback, and that invariably at full speed, the great object of practice is to enable the bowman to draw the bow with suddenness and instant effect; and also to repeat the shots in the most rapid manner. As their game is killed from their horses' backs while at the swiftest rate—and their enemies fought in the same way; and as the horse is the swiftest animal of the prairie, and always able to bring his rider alongside, within a few paces of his victim; it will easily be seen that the Indian has little use in throwing his arrow more than a few paces; when he leans quite low on his horse's side, and drives it with astonishing force, capable of producing instant death to the buffalo, or any other animal in the country . . . Dashing forward at fullest speed on the wild horse, without the use of the rein, when the shot is required to be made with the most instantaneous effect, I scarcely think it possible that any people can be found more skilled, and capable of producing more deadly effects with the bow.

The horses which the Indians ride in this country are invariably the wild horses, which are found in great numbers on the prairies; and have, unquestionably, strayed from the Mexican borders, into which they were introduced by the Spanish invaders of that country; and now range and subsist themselves, in winter and summer, over the vast plains of prairie that stretch from the Mexican frontiers to Lake Winnipeg on the North, a distance of 3000 miles. These horses are all of small stature, of the pony order; but a very hardy and tough animal, being able to perform for the Indians a continual and essential service. They are taken with the *laso*, which is a long halter or thong, made of raw-hide, of some fifteen or twenty yards in length, and which the Indians throw with great dexterity; with a noose at one end of it, which drops over the head of the animal they wish to catch, whilst running at full speed—when the Indian dismounts from his own horse, and holding to the end of the laso, choaks the animal down, and afterwards tames and converts him to his own use.

Scarcely a man in these regions is to be found, who is not the owner of one or more of these horses; and in many instances of eight, ten, or even twenty, which he values as his own personal property.

The Indians are hard and cruel masters; and, added to their cruelties is the sin that is familiar in the Christian world, of sporting with the limbs and the lives of these noble animals. *Horse-racing* here, as in all more enlightened communities, is one of the most exciting amusements, and one of the most extravagant modes of gambling . . .

Besides these, many have been the amusements of this day, to which I have been an eye-witness; and since writing the above, I have learned have the cause of this unusual expression of hilarity and mirth; which was no more nor less than the safe return of a small war-party, who had been so long out without any tidings having been received of them—that they had long since been looked upon as sacrificed to the fates of war and lost. This party was made up of the most distinguished and desperate young men of the tribe, who had sallied out against the Riccarees, and taken the most solemn oath amongst themselves never to return without achieving a victory. They had wandered long and faithfully about the country, following the trails of their enemy; when they were attacked by a numerous party, and lost several of their men and all their horses. In this condition, to evade the scrutiny of their enemy, who were closely investing the natural route to their village; they took a circuitous range of the country, to enable them to return with their lives, to their village.

In this plight, it seems, I had dropped my little canoe alongside of them, while descending from the Mouth of Yellow Stone to this place, not many weeks since; where they had bivouacked or halted, to smoke and consult on the best and safest mode of procedure. At the time of meeting them, not knowing anything of their language, they were unable to communicate their condition to me, and more probably were afraid to do so even if they could have done it, from apprehension that we might have given some account of them to their enemies. I rested my canoe an hour or so with them, during which time they treated us with an indifferent reserve, yet respect-fully; and we passed on our way, without further information of them or their plans than the sketch that I there made (Illustration 22) and which I shall preserve and value as one of the most pleasing groups I ever have had the pleasure to see. Seated on their buffalo robes, which were spread upon the grass, with their respective weapons laying about them, and lighting their pipes at a little fire which was kindled in the centre—the chief or leader of the party, with his arms stacked behind him, and his long head-dress of war-eagles' quills and ermine falling down over his back, whilst he sat in a contemplative and almost desponding mood, was surely one

Illustration 22. Mandan war party in council.

of the most striking and beautiful illustrations of a natural hero that I ever looked upon.

These gallant fellows got safely home to their village, and the numerous expressions of joy for their return, which I have this day witnessed, have so much fatigued me that I write brief, and close my Letter here.

Mandan Village, Upper Missouri.

*T*he *annual religious ceremony*, of four days, of which I have
. . . so often spoken, and which I have so long been wishing
to see, has at last been enacted in this village; and I have, fortu-
nately, been able to see and to understand it in most of its bearings,
which was more than I had reason to expect; for no white man, in all
probability, has ever been before admitted to the *medicine-lodge*
during these most remarkable and appalling scenes . . .

The Mandans believe in the existence of a Great (or Good) Spirit,
and also of an Evil Spirit, who they say existed long before the Good
Spirit, and is far superior in power. They all believe also in a future
state of existence, and a future administration of rewards and punishments, and (so do all other tribes that I have yet visited) they
believe those punishments are not eternal, but commensurate with
their sins.

These people living in a climate where they suffer from cold in the
severity of their winters, have very naturally reversed our ideas of
Heaven and Hell. The latter they describe to be a country very far to
the north, of barren and hideous aspect, and covered with eternal
snows and ice. The torments of this freezing place they describe as
most excruciating; whilst Heaven they suppose to be in a warmer
and delightful latitude, where nothing is felt but the keenest enjoyment, and where the country abounds in buffaloes and other luxuries of life. The Great or Good Spirit they believe dwells in the
former place for the purpose of there meeting those who have
offended him; increasing the agony of their sufferings, by being
himself present, administering the penalties. The Bad or Evil Spirit

they are the same time suppose to reside in Paradise, still tempting the happy; and those who have gone to the regions of punishment they believe to be tortured for a time proportioned to the amount of their transgressions, and that they are then to be transferred to the land of the happy, where they are again liable to the temptations of the Evil Spirit, and answerable again at a future period for their new offences.

Such is the religious creed of the Mandans, and for the purpose of appeasing the Good and Evil Spirits, and to secure their entrance into those "fields Elysian," or beautiful hunting grounds, do the young men subject themselves to the horrid and sickening cruelties to be described in the following pages.

There are other three distinct objects (yet to be named) for which these religious ceremonies are held, which are as follow:—

First, they are held annually as a celebration of the event of the subsiding of the Flood, which they call *Mee-nee-ro-ka-ha-sha,* (sinking down or settling of the waters).

Secondly, for the purpose of dancing what they call *Bel-lohck-na-pic* (the bull-dance); to the strict observance of which they attribute the coming of buffaloes to supply them with food during the season; and

Thirdly and lastly, for the purpose of conducting all the young men of the tribe, as they annually arrive to the age of manhood, through an ordeal of privation and torture, which, while it is supposed to harden their muscles and prepare them for extreme endurance, enables the chiefs who are spectators to the scene, to decide upon their comparative bodily strength and ability to endure the extreme privations and sufferings that often fall to the lots of Indian warriors; and that they may decide who is the most hardy and best able to lead a war-party in case of extreme exigency.

This part of the ceremony, as I have just witnessed it, is truly shocking to behold, and will almost stagger the belief of the world when they read of it. The scene is too terrible and too revolting to be seen or to be told, were it not an essential part of a whole, which will be new to the civilized world, and therefore worth their knowing.

The bull-dance, and many other parts of these ceremonies are exceedingly grotesque and amusing, and that part of them which has a relation to the Deluge is harmless and full of interest.

In the centre of the Mandan village is an open, circular area of 150 feet diameter, kept always clear, as a public ground, for the display of all their public feasts, parades, &c. and around it are their wigwams placed as near to each other as they can well stand, their doors facing the centre of this public area.

In the middle of this ground, which is trodden like a hard pavement, is a curb (somewhat like a large hogshead standing on its end) made of planks (and bound with hoops), some eight or nine feet high, which they religiously preserve and protect from year to year, free from mark or scratch, and which they call the "big canoe"—it is undoubtedly a symbolic representation of a part of their traditional history of the Flood; which it is very evident, from this and numerous other features of this grand ceremony, they have in some way or other received, and are here endeavouring to perpetuate by vividly impressing it on the minds of the whole nation. This object of superstition, from its position, as the very centre of the village is the rallying point of the whole nation. To it their devotions are paid on various occasions of feasts and religious exercises during the year; and in this extraordinary scene it was often the nucleus of their mysteries and cruelties, as I shall shortly describe them, and becomes an object worth bearing in mind, and worthy of being understood.

This exciting and appalling scene . . . commences, not on a particular day . . . but at a particular season, which is designated by the full expansion of the willow leaves under the bank of the river; for according to their tradition, "the twig that the bird brought home was a willow bough, and had full-grown leaves on it," and the bird to which they allude, is the mourning or turtle-dove, which they took great pains to point out to me, as it is often to be seen feeding on the sides of their earth-covered lodges, and which, being, as they call it, a *medicine-bird,* is not to be destroyed or harmed by any one, and even their dogs are instructed not to do it injury.

On the morning on which this strange transaction commenced, I was sitting at breakfast in the house of the Trader, Mr. Kipp, when at sun-rise, we were suddenly startled by the shrieking and screaming of the women, and barking and howling of dogs, as if an enemy were actually storming their village.

"Now we have it! (exclaimed *mine host*, as he sprang from the table), the grand ceremony has commenced!—drop your knife and fork, Monsr. and get your sketch-book as soon as possible, that you may lose nothing, for the very moment of *commencing* is as curious as anything else of this strange affair." I seized my sketch-book, and all hands of us were in an instant in front of the medicine-lodge, ready to see and to hear all that was to take place. Groups of women and children were gathered on the tops of their earth-covered wigwams, and all were screaming, and dogs were howling, and all eyes directed to the prairies in the West, where was beheld at a mile distant, a solitary individual descending a prairie bluff, and making his way in a direct line towards the village!

The whole community joined in the general expression of great alarm, as if they were in danger of instant destruction; bows were strung and thrummed to test their elasticity—their horses were caught upon the prairie and run into the village—warriors were blackening their faces, and dogs were muzzled, and every preparation made, as if for instant combat.

During this deafening din and confusion within the piquets of the village of the Mandans, the figure discovered on the prairie continued to approach with a dignified step and in a right line towards the village; all eyes were upon him, and he at length made his appearance (without opposition) within the piquets, and proceeded towards the centre of the village, where all the chiefs and braves stood ready to receive him, which they did in a cordial manner, by shaking hands with him, recognizing him as an old acquaintance, and pronouncing his name *Nu-mohk-muck-a-nah* (the first or only man). The body of this strange personage, which was chiefly naked, was painted with white clay, so as to resemble at a little distance, a white man; he wore a robe of four white wolf skins falling back over his shoulders; on his head he had a splendid head-dress made of two ravens' skins, and in his left hand he cautiously carried a large pipe, which he seemed to watch and guard as something of great importance. After passing the chiefs and braves as described, he approached the *medicine* or mystery lodge, which he had the means of opening, and which had been religiously closed during the year except for the performance of these religious rites.

Having opened and entered it, he called in four men whom he appointed to clean it out, and put it in readiness for the ceremonies, by sweeping it and strewing a profusion of green willow-boughs over its floor; and over these were arranged a curious group of buffalo and human skulls, and other articles, which were to be used during this strange and unaccountable transaction.

During the whole of his day, and while these preparations were making in the *medicine-lodge,* Nu-mohk-muck-a-nah (the first or only man) travelled through the village, stopping in front of every man's lodge, and crying until the owner of the lodge came out, and asked who he was, and what was the matter? to which he replied by relating the sad catastrophe which had happened on the earth's surface by the overflowing of the waters, saying that "he was the only person saved from the universal calamity; that he landed his big canoe on a high mountain in the west, where he now resides; that he had come to open the *medicine-lodge,* which must needs receive a present of some edged-tool from the owner of every wigwam, that it may be sacrificed to the water;" for he says, "if this is not done, there will be another flood, and no one will be saved, as it was with such tools that the big canoe was made."

Having visited every lodge or wigwam in the village, during the day, and having received such a present at each, as a hatchet, a knife, &c. (which is undoubtedly always prepared and ready for the occasion), he returned at evening and deposited them in the *medicine-lodge,* where they remained until the afternoon of the last day of the ceremony, when, as the final or closing scene, they were thrown into the river in a deep place, from a bank thirty feet high, and in presence of the whole village; from whence they can never be recovered, and where they were, undoubtedly, *sacrificed* to the Spirit of the Water.

During the first night of this strange character in the village, no one could tell where he slept; and every person, both old and young, and dogs, and all living things were kept within doors, and dead silence reigned every where. On the next morning at sunrise, however, he made his appearance again, and entered the *medicine-lodge;* and at his heels (in *"Indian file,"* *i.e.* single file, one following in another's tracks) all the young men who were candidates for the self-tortures which were to be inflicted, and for the honours that were to be bestowed by the chiefs on those who could most manfully endure them. There were on this occasion about fifty young men who entered the lists, and as they went into the sacred lodge, each one's body was chiefly naked, and covered with clay of different colours; some were red, others were yellow, and some were covered with white clay, giving them the appearance of white men. Each one of them carried in his right hand his *medicine-bag*—on his left arm, his shield of the bull's hide—in his left hand, his bow and arrows, with his quiver slung on his back.

When all had entered the lodge, they placed themselves in reclining postures around its sides, and each one had suspended over his head his respective weapons and *medicine*, presenting altogether, one of the most wild and picturesque scenes imaginable.

Nu-mohk-muck-a-nah (the first or only man) was in the midst of them, and having lit and smoked his medicine-pipe for their success; and having addressed them in a short speech, stimulating and encouraging them to trust to the Great Spirit for His protection during the severe ordeal they were about to pass through; he called into the lodge an old medicine or mystery-man, whose body was painted yellow, and whom he appointed master of ceremonies during this occasion, whom they denominated in their language *O-kee-pah Ka-se-kah* (keeper or conductor of the ceremonies). He was appointed, and the authority passed by the presentation of the medicine-pipe, on which they consider hangs all the power of holding and conducting all these rites.

After this delegated authority had thus passed over to the medicine-man; Nu-mohk-muck-a-nah shook hands with him, and bade him good bye, saying "that he was going back to the mountains in the west, from whence he should assuredly return in just a year from that time, to open the lodge again." He then went out of the lodge, and passing through the village, took formal leave of the chiefs in the same manner, and soon disappeared over the bluffs from whence he came . . .

To return to the lodge,—the medicine or mystery-man just appointed, and who had received his injunctions from Nu-mohk-muck-a-nah, was left sole conductor and keeper; and according to those

injunctions, it was his duty to lie by a small fire in the centre of the
lodge, with his medicine-pipe in his hand, crying to the Great Spirit
incessantly, watching the young men, and preventing entirely their
escape from the lodge, and all communication whatever with people
outside, for the space of four days and nights, during which time they
were not allowed to *eat*, to *drink*, or to *sleep*, preparatory to the
excruciating self-tortures which they were to endure on the fourth day.

I mentioned that I had made four paintings of these strange
scenes, and the first one exhibits the interior of the medicine-lodge
at this moment; with the young men all reclining around its sides,
and the conductor or mystery-man lying by the fire, crying to the
Great Spirit. It was just at this juncture that I was ushered into this
sacred temple of their worship, with my companions, which was,
undoubtedly, the first time that their devotions had ever been trespassed upon by the presence of pale faces; and in this instance had
been brought about in the following strange and unexpected manner.

I had most luckily for myself, painted a full-length portrait of this
great magician or high-priest, but a day previous to the commencement of the ceremonies (in which I had represented him in the
performance of some of his mysteries), with which he had been so
exceedingly pleased as well as astonished (as "he could see its eyes
move"), that I must needs be, in his opinion, deeply skilled in magic
and mysteries, and well-entitled to a respectable rank in the craft, to
which I had been at once elevated by the unanimous voice of the
doctors, and regularly initiated, and styled *Te-ho-pee-nee-wash-ee-
waska-pooska*, the *white medicine* (or Spirit) *painter*.

With this very honourable degree which had just been conferred
upon me, I was standing in front of the medicine-lodge early in the
morning, with my companions by my side, endeavouring to get a
peep, if possible, into its sacred interior; when this *master of ceremonies*, guarding and conducting its secrets, as I before described,
came out of the door and taking me with a firm *professional* affection
by the arm, led me into this *sanctum sanctorum*, which was strictly
guarded from, even a peep or a gaze from the vulgar, by a vestibule
of eight or ten feet in length, guarded with a double screen or door,
and two or three dark and frowning centinels with spears or war-
clubs in their hands. I gave the wink to my companions as I was

passing in, and the potency of my *medicine* was such as to gain them a quiet admission, and all of us were comfortably placed on elevated seats, which our conductor soon prepared for us.

We were then in full view of everything that transpired in the lodge, having before us the scene exactly, which is represented in the first of the four pictures. To this seat we returned every morning at sunrise, and remained until sun-down for four days, the whole time which these strange scenes occupied.

In addition to the preparations and arrangements of the interior of this sanctuary, as above described, there was a curious, though a very strict arrangement of buffalo and human skulls placed on the floor of the lodge, and between them (which were divided into two parcels), and in front of the reclining group of young candidates, was a small and very delicate scaffold, elevated about five feet from the ground, made of four posts or crotches, not larger than a gun-rod, and placed some four or five feet apart, supporting four equally delicate rods, resting in the crotches; thus forming the frame of the scaffold, which was completed by a number of still smaller and more delicate sticks, transversely resting upon them. On the centre of this little frame rested some small object, which I could not exactly understand from the distance of twenty or thirty feet which intervened between it and my eye. I started several times from my seat to approach it, but all eyes were instantly upon me, and every mouth in the assembly sent forth a hush—sh—! which brought me back to my seat again; and I at length quieted my stifled curiosity as well as I could, upon learning the fact, that so sacred was that object, and so important its secrets or mysteries, that not *I* alone, but even the young men, who were passing the ordeal, and all the village, save the conductor of the mysteries, were stopped from approaching it, or knowing what it was.

This little mystery-thing, whatever it was, had the appearance from where I sat, of a small tortoise or frog lying on its back, with its head and legs quite extended, and wound and tasselled off with exceedingly delicate red and blue, and yellow ribbons or tassels, and other bright coloured ornaments; and seemed, from the devotions paid to it, to be the very nucleus of their mysteries—the *sanctissimus sanctorum*, from which seemed to emanate all the sanctity of their proceedings, and to which, all seemed to be paying the highest devotional respect.

This strange, yet important *essence* of their mysteries, I made every enquiry about; but got no further information of, than what I could learn by my eyes, at the distance at which I saw it, and from the silent respect which I saw paid to it. I tried with the doctors, and all of the *fraternity* answered me, that that was "*great medicine*," assuring me that it "could not be told." So I quieted my curiosity as well as I could, by the full conviction that I had a *degree* or two yet to take before I could fathom all the arcana of Indian superstitions; and that this little, seemingly wonderful relic of antiquity, symbol of some grand event, or "secret too valuable to be told," might have been at last nothing but a silly bunch of strings and toys, to which they pay some great peculiar regard; giving thereby to some favourite Spirit or essence an ideal existence, and which, when called upon the describe, they refuse to do so, calling it "*Great Medicine*," for the very reason that there is nothing in it to reveal or describe.

Immediately under the little frame or scaffold described, and on the floor of the lodge was placed a knife, and by the side of it a bundle of splints or skewers, which were kept in readiness for the infliction of the cruelties directly to be explained. There were seen also, in this stage of the affair, a number of cords of rawhide hanging down from the top of the lodge, and passing through its roof, with which the young men were to be suspended by the splints passed through their flesh, and drawn up by men placed on the top of the lodge for the purpose, as will be described in a few moments.

There were also four articles of great veneration and importance lying on the floor of the lodge, which were sacks, containing in each some three or four gallons of water. These also were objects of superstitious regard, and made with great labour and much ingenuity; each one of them being constructed of the skin of the buffalo's neck, and most elaborately sewed together in the form of a large tortoise lying on its back, with a bunch of eagle's quills appended to it as a tail; and each of them having a stick, shaped like a drum-stick, lying on them, with which, in a subsequent stage of these ceremonies, as will be seen, they are beaten upon by several of their mystery-men, as a part of the music for their strange dances and mysteries. By the side of these sacks which they call *Eeh-teeh-ka*, are two other articles of equal importance, which they call *Eeh-na-dee* (rattles), in the form of a gourd-shell made also of dried skins, and used at the same time as the others, in the music (or rather *noise* and *din*) for their dances, &c.

These four sacks of water have the appearance of very great antiquity; and by enquiring of my very ingenious friend and patron, the *medicine-man*, after the ceremonies were over, he very gravely told me, that "those four tortoises contained the waters from the four quarters of the world—that these waters had been contained therein ever since the settling down of the waters!" I did not think it best to advance any argument against so ridiculous a theory, and therefore could not even enquire or learn, at what period they had been instituted, or how often, or on what occasions, the water in them had been changed or replenished.

I made several propositions, through my friend Mr. Kipp, the trader and interpreter, to purchase one of these strange things by offering them a very liberal price; to which I received in answer that these, and all the very numerous articles used in these ceremonies, being a *society property* were *medicine*, and could not be sold for any consideration; so I abandoned all thoughts of obtaining anything, except what I have done by the *medicine* operation of my pencil, which was applied to everything, and even upon that they looked with decided distrust and apprehension, as a sort of theft or sacrilege.

Such then was the group, and such the appearance of the interior of the medicine-lodge during the three first, and part of the fourth day also, of the Mandan religious ceremonies. The medicine-man with a group about him, of young aspirants who were under his sole controul, as was every article and implement to be used, and the sanctity of this solitary and gloomy looking place, which could not be trespassed upon by any man's presence without his most sovereign permission.

During the three first days of this solemn conclave, there were many very curious forms and amusements enacted in the open area in the middle of the village, and in front of the medicine-lodge, by other members of the community, one of which formed a material part or link of these strange ceremonials. This very curious and exceedingly grotesque part of their performance, which they denominated *Bel-lohck nah-pick* (the bull-dance) of which I have before spoken, as one of the avowed objects for which they held this annual fête; and to the strictest observance of which they attribute the coming of buffaloes to supply them with food during the season—is repeated four times during the first day, eight times on the second day, twelve times on the third day, and sixteen times on the fourth day; and always around the curb, or *"big canoe,"* of which I have before spoken.

This subject I have selected for my second picture, and the principal actors in it were eight men, with the entire skins of buffaloes thrown over their backs, with the horns and hoofs and tails remaining on; their bodies in a horizontal position, enabling them to imitate the actions of the buffalo, whilst they were looking out of its eyes as through a mask. The bodies of these men were chiefly naked and all painted in the most extraordinary manner, with the nicest adherence to exact similarity; their limbs, bodies and faces, being in every part covered, either with black, red, or white paint. Each one of these strange characters had also a lock of buffalo's hair tied around his ancles—in his right hand a rattle, and a slender white rod or staff, six feet long, in the other; and carried on his back, a bunch of green willow boughs about the usual size of a bundle of straw. These eight men, being divided into four pairs, took their positions on the four different sides of the curb or big canoe, representing thereby the four cardinal points; and between each group of them, with the back turned to the big canoe, was another figure, engaged in the same dance, keeping step with them, with a similar staff or wand in one hand and a rattle in the other, and (being four in number) answering again to the four cardinal points. The bodies of these four young men were chiefly naked, with no other dress upon them than a beautiful kelt (or quartz-quaw), around the waist, made of eagles quills and ermine, and very splendid head-dresses made of the same materials. Two of these figures were painted entirely black with pounded charcoal and grease, whom they called the "firmament or night," and the numerous white spots which were dotted all over their bodies, they called "stars." The other two were painted from head to foot as red as vermilion could make them; these they said represented the day, and the white streaks which were painted up and down over their bodies, were "ghosts which the morning rays were chasing away."

These twelve are the only persons actually engaged in this strange dance, which is each time repeated in the same form, without the slightest variation. There are, however, a great number of characters engaged in giving the whole effect and wildness to this strange and laughable scene, each one acting well his part, and whose offices, strange and inexplicable as they are, I will endeavour to point out and explain as well as I can, from what I saw, elucidated by their own descriptions.

This most remarkable scene, then, which is witnessed more or less often on each day, takes place in presence of the whole nation, who are generally gathered around, on the tops of the wigwams or otherwise, as spectators, whilst the young men are reclining and fasting in the lodge as above described. On the first day, this *"bull-dance"* is given *once* to each of the cardinal points and the medicine-man smokes his pipe in those directions. On the second day, *twice* to each; *three times* to each on the third day, and *four times* to each on the fourth. As a signal for the dancers and other characters (as well as the public) to assemble, the old man, master of ceremonies, with the medicine-pipe in hand, dances out of the lodge, singing (or rather crying) forth a most pitiful lament, until he approaches the big canoe, against which he leans, with the pipe in his hand, and continues to cry. At this instant, four very aged and patriarchal looking men, whose bodies are painted red, and who have been guarding the four sides of the lodge, enter it and bring out the four sacks of water, which they place near the big canoe, where they seat themselves by the side of them and commence thumping on them with the mallets or drumsticks which have been lying on them; and another brandishes and shakes the *eeh-na-dees* or rattles, and all unite to them their voices, raised to the highest pitch possible, as the music for the *bull-dance*, which is then commenced and continued for fifteen minutes or more in perfect time, and without cessation or intermission. When the music and dancing stop, which are always perfectly simultaneous, the whole nation raise the huzza! and a deafening shout of approbation; the master of ceremonies dances back to the medicine-lodge, and the old men return to their former place; the sacks of water, and all rest as before, until by the same method, they are again called into a similar action.

The supernumeraries or other characters who play their parts in this grand spectacle, are numerous and well worth description. By the side of the big canoe are seen two men with the skins of grizzly bears thrown over them, using the skins as a mask, over their heads. These ravenous animals are continually growling and threatening to devour everything before them and interfering with the forms of their religious ceremony. To appease them, the women are continually bringing and placing before them dishes of meat, which are as often snatched up and carried to the prairie, by two men whose bodies are painted black and their heads white, whom they call bald eagles, who are darting by them and grasping their food from before them as they pass. These are again chased upon the plains by a hundred or more small boys, who are naked, with their bodies painted yellow and their heads white, whom they call *Cabris* or antelopes; who at length get the food away from them and devour it; thereby inculcating (perhaps) the beautiful moral, that by the dispensations of Providence, his bountiful gifts will fall at last to the hands of the innocent.

During the intervals between these dances, all these characters, except those from the medicine-lodge, retire to a wigwam close by, which they use on the occasion also as a sacred place, being occupied exclusively by them while they are at rest, and also for the purpose of painting and ornamenting their bodies for the occasion.

During each and every one of these dances, the old men who beat upon the sacks and sing, are earnestly chanting forth their supplications to the Great Spirit, for the continuation of his influence in sending them buffaloes to supply them with food during the year; they are administering courage and fortitude to the young men in the lodge, by telling them, that "the Great Spirit has opened his ears in their behalf—that the very atmosphere all about them is peace—that their women and children can hold the mouth of the grizzly bear—that they have invoked from day to day O-kee-hee-de (the Evil Spirit)—that they are still challenging him to come, and yet he has not dared to make his appearance!"

But alas! in the last of these dances, on the fourth day, in the midst of all their mirth and joy, and about noon, and in the height of all these exultations, an instant scream burst forth from the tops of the lodges!—men, women, dogs and all, seemed actually to howl and shudder with alarm, as they fixed their glaring eye-balls upon the prairie bluff, about a mile in the west, down the side of which a man was seen descending at full speed towards the village! This strange character darted about in a zig-zag course in all directions on the prairie, like a boy in pursuit of a butterfly, until he approached the piquets of the village, when it was discovered that his body was entirely naked, and painted as black as a negro, with pounded charcoal and bear's grease; his body was therefore everywhere of shining black, except occasionally white rings of an inch or more in diameter, which were marked here and there all over him; and frightful indentures of white around his mouth, resembling canine teeth. Added to his hideous appearance, he gave the most frightful shrieks and screams as he dashed through the village and entered the terrified group, which was composed (in that quarter) chiefly of females, who had assembled to witness the amusements which were transpiring around the "big canoe."

This unearthly looking creature carried in his two hands a wand or staff of eight or nine feet in length, with a red ball at the end of it, which he continually slid on the ground a-head of him as he ran. All eyes in the village, save those of the persons engaged in the dance, were centred upon him, and he made a desperate rush towards the women, who screamed for protection as they were endeavouring to retreat; and falling in groups upon each other as they were struggling to get out of his reach. In this moment of general terror and alarm there was an instant check! and all for a few moments were as silent as death.

The old master of ceremonies, who had run from his position at the big canoe, had met this monster of fiends, and having thrust the *medicine-pipe* before him, held him still and immoveable under its charm! This check gave the females an opportunity to get out of his reach, and when they were free from their danger, though all hearts beat yet with the instant excitement, their alarm soon cooled down into the most exorbitant laughter and shouts of applause at his sudden defeat, and the awkward and ridiculous posture in which he was stopped and held. The old man was braced stiff by his side, with his eye-balls glaring him in the face, whilst the medicine-pipe held in its mystic chains his *Satanic* Majesty, annulling all the powers of his magical wand, and also depriving him of the powers of locomotion! Surely no two human beings ever presented a more striking group than these two individuals did for a few moments, with their eye-balls set in direst mutual hatred upon each other; both struggling for the supremacy, relying on the potency of their medicine or mystery. The one held in check, with his body painted black, representing (or rather assuming to be) his sable majesty, O-kee-hee-de (the Evil Spirit), frowning everlasting vengeance on the other, who sternly gazed him back with a look of exultation and contempt, as he held him in check and disarmed under the charm of his sacred mystery-pipe.

When the superior powers of the medicine-pipe (on which hang all these annual mysteries) had been thus fully tested and acknowledged, and the women had had requisite time to withdraw from the reach of this fiendish monster, the pipe was very gradually withdrawn from before him, and he seemed delighted to recover the use of his limbs again, and power of changing his position from the exceedingly unpleasant and really ridiculous one he appeared in, and was compelled to maintain, a few moments before; rendered more superlatively ridiculous and laughable, from the further information, which I am constrained to give, of the plight in which this demon of terror and vulgarity made his *entrée* into the midst of the Mandan village, and to the centre and nucleus of their first and greatest religious ceremony.

Then, to proceed: I said that this strange personage's body was naked—was painted jet black with charcoal and bear's grease, with a wand in his hands of eight feet in length with a red ball at the end of it, which he was rubbing about on the ground in front of him as he ran . . .

In this plight . . . he pursued the groups of females, spreading dismay and alarm wherever he went, and consequently producing the awkward and exceedingly laughable predicament in which he was placed by the sudden check from the medicine-pipe, as I have above stated, when all eyes were intently fixed upon him, and all joined in rounds of applause for the success of the magic spell that was placed upon him; all voices were raised in shouts of satisfaction at his defeat, and all eyes gazed upon him; of chiefs and of warriors—matrons and even of their tender-aged and timid daughters, whose education had taught them to receive the *moral* of these scenes without the shock of impropriety, that would have startled a more fastidious and consequently sensual-thinking people.

After repeated attempts thus made, and thus defeated in several parts of the crowd, this blackened monster was retreating over the ground where the buffalo-dance was going on, and having (apparently, par accident) swaggered against one of the men placed under the skin of a buffalo and engaged in the "bull dance," he started back, and placing himself in the attitude of a buffalo . . .

After this he paid his visits to three others of the eight, in succession, receiving as before the deafening shouts of approbation which pealed from every mouth in the multitude, who were all praying to the Great Spirit to send them buffaloes to supply them with food during the season, and who attribute the coming of buffaloes for this purpose entirely to the strict and critical observance of this ridiculous and disgusting part of the ceremonies.

During the half hour or so that he had been jostled about amongst man and beasts, to the great amusement and satisfaction of the lookers-on, he seemed to have become exceedingly exhausted, and anxiously looking out for some feasible mode of escape.

In this awkward predicament he became the laughing-stock and butt for the women, who being no longer afraid of him, were gathering in groups around, to tease and tantalize him; and in the midst of this dilemma, which soon became a very sad one—one of the women, who stole up behind him with both hands full of yellow dirt—dashed it into his face and eyes, and all over him, and his body being covered with grease, took instantly a different hue. He seemed heart-broken at this signal disgrace, and commenced crying most vehemently, when, *à l'instant*, another caught his *wand* from his hand, and broke it across her knee. It was snatched for by others, who broke it still into bits, and then threw them at him. His power was now gone—his bodily strength was exhausted, and he made a bolt for the prairie—he dashed through the crowd, and made his way through the piquets on the back part of the village, where were placed for the purpose, an hundred or more women and girls, who escorted him as he ran on the prairie for half a mile or more, beating him with sticks, and stones, and dirt, and kicks, and cuffs, until he was at length seen escaping from their clutches, and making the best of his retreat over the prairie bluffs, from whence he first appeared.

At the moment of this signal victory, and when all eyes lost sight of him as he disappeared over the bluffs, the whole village united their voices in shouts of satisfaction. The bull-dance then stopped, and preparations were instantly made for the commencement of the cruelties which were to take place within the lodge, leaving us to draw, from what had just transpired, the following beautiful moral:—

That in the midst of their religious ceremonies, the Evil Spirit (O-kee-hee-de) made his entrée for the purpose of doing mischief, and of disturbing their worship—that he was held in check, and defeated by the superior influence and virtue of the *medicine-pipe*, and at last, driven in disgrace our of the village, by the very part of the community whom he came to abuse.

At the close of this exciting scene, preparations were made, as above stated, by the return of the master of ceremonies and musicians to the medicine-lodge, where also were admitted at the same time a number of men, who were to be instruments of the cruelties to be inflicted; and also the chief and doctors of the tribe, who were to look on, and bear witness to, and decide upon, the comparative degree of fortitude, with which the young men sustain themselves in this most extreme and excruciating ordeal. The chiefs having seated themselves on one side of the lodge, dressed out in their robes and splendid head-dresses—the band of music seated and arranged themselves in another part; and the old master of ceremonies having placed himself in front of a small fire in the centre of the lodge, with his "big pipe" in his hands, and having commenced smoking to the Great Spirit, with all possible vehemence for the success of these aspirants, presented the subject for the third picture, which they call "*pohk-hong*," the cutting scene. Around the sides of the lodge are seen, still reclining, as I have before mentioned, a part of the group, whilst others of them have passed the ordeal of self-tortures, and have been removed out of the lodge; and others still are seen in the very act of submitting to them, which were inflicted in the following manner: —After having removed the *sanctissimus sanctorum*, or little scaffold, of which I before spoke, and having removed also the buffalo and human skulls from the floor, and attached them to the posts of the lodge; and two men having taken their positions near the middle of the lodge, for the purpose of inflicting the tortures—the one with the scalping-knife, and the other with the bunch of splints (which I have before mentioned) in his hand; one at a time of the young fellows, already emaciated with fasting, and thirsting, and waking, for nearly four days and nights, advanced from the side of the lodge, and placed himself on his hands and feet, or otherwise, as best suited for the performance of the operation, where he submitted to the cruelties in the following manner:—An inch or more of the flesh on each shoulder, or each breast was taken up between the thumb and finger by the man who held the knife in his right hand; and the knife, which had been ground sharp on both edges, and then hacked and notched with the blade of another, to make it produce as much pain as possible, was forced through the flesh below the fingers, and being withdrawn, was followed with a splint or skewer, from the other, who held a bunch of such in his left hand, and was ready to force them through the wound. There were then two cords lowered down from the top of the lodge (by men who were placed on the lodge outside, for the purpose), which were fastened to these splints or skewers, and they instantly began to haul him up; he was thus raised until his body was suspended from the ground where he rested, until the knife and a splint were passed through the flesh or integuments in a similar manner on each arm below the shoulder (over the *brachialis externus*), below the elbow (over the *extensor carpi radialis*), on the thighs (over the *vastus externus*), and below the knees (over the *peroneus*).

In some instances they remained in a reclining position on the ground until this painful operation was finished, which was performed, in all instances, exactly on the same parts of the body and limbs; and which, in its progress, occupied some five or six minutes.

Each one was then instantly raised with the cords, until the weight of his body was suspended by them, while the blood was streaming down their limbs, the bystanders hung upon the splints each man's appropriate shield, bow and quiver, &c.; and in many instances, the skull of a buffalo with the horns on it, was attached to each lower arm and each lower leg, for the purpose, probably, of preventing by their great weight, the struggling, which might otherwise have taken place to their disadvantage whilst they were hung up.

When these things were all adjusted, each one was raised higher by the cords, until these weights all swung clear from the ground, leaving his feet, in most cases, some six or eight feet above the ground. In this plight they at once became appalling and frightful to look at—the flesh, to support the weight of their bodies, with the additional weights which were attached to them, was raised six or eight inches by the skewers; and their heads sunk forward on the breasts, or thrown backwards, in a much more frightful condition, according to the way in which they were hung up.

The unflinching fortitude, with which every one of them bore this part of the torture surpassed credulity; each one as the knife were passed through his flesh sustained an unchangeable countenance; and several of them, seeing me making sketches, beckoned me to look at their faces, which I watched through all this horrid operation, without being able to detect anything but the pleasantest smiles as they looked me in the eye, while I could hear the knife rip through the flesh, and feel enough of it myself, to start involuntary and uncontroullable tears over my cheeks.

When raised to the condition above described, and completely suspended by the cords, the sanguinary hands, through which he had just passed, turned back to perform a similar operation on another who was ready, and each one in his turn passed into the charge of others, who instantly introduced him to a new and improved stage of their refinements in cruelty.

Surrounded by imps and demons as they appear, a dozen or more, who seem to be concerting and devising means for his exquisite agony, gather around him, when one of the number advances towards him in a sneering manner, and commences turning him around with a pole which he brings in this hand for the purpose. This is done in a gentle manner at first; but gradually increased, when the brave fellow, whose proud spirit can controul its agony no longer, burst out in the most lamentable and heart-rending cries that the human voice is capable of producing, crying forth a prayer to the Great Spirit to support and protect him in this dreadful trial; and continually repeating his confidence in his protection. In this condition he is continued to be turned, faster and faster—and there is no hope of escape from it, nor chance for the slightest relief, until by fainting, his voice falters, and his struggling ceases, and he hangs, apparently, a still and lifeless corpse! When he is, by turning, gradually brought to this condition, which is generally done within ten or fifteen minutes, there is a close scrutiny passed upon him among his tormentors, who are checking and holding each other back as long as the least struggling or tremour can be discovered, lest he should be removed before he is (as they term it) "entirely dead."

When brought to this alarming and most frightful condition, and the turning has gradually ceased, as his voice and his strength have given out, leaving him to hang entirely still, and apparently lifeless; when his tongue is distended from his mouth, and his *medicine-bag*, which he has affectionately and superstitiously clung to with his left hand, has dropped to the ground; the signal is given to the men on top of the lodge, by gently striking the cord with the pole below, when they very gradually and carefully lower him to the ground.

In this helpless condition he lies, like a loathsome corpse to look at, though in the keeping (as they call it) of the Great Spirit, whom he trusts will protect him, and enable him to get up and walk away. As soon as he is lowered to the ground thus, one of the bystanders advances, and pulls out the two splints or pins from the breasts and shoulders, thereby disengaging him from the cords by which he has been hung up; but leaving all the others with their weights, &c. hanging to his flesh.

In this condition he lies for six or eight minutes, until he gets strength to rise and move himself, for no one is allowed to assist or offer him aid, as he is here enjoying the most valued privilege which a Mandan can boast of, that of "trusting his life to the keeping of the Great Spirit," in this time of extreme peril.

As soon as he is seen to get strength enough to rise on his hands and feet, and drag his body around the lodge, he crawls with the weights still hanging to his body, to another part of the lodge, where there is another Indian sitting with a hatchet in his hand, and a dried buffalo skull before him; and here, in the most earnest and humble manner, by holding up the little finger of his left hand to the Great Spirit, he expresses to Him, in a speech of a few words, his willingness to give it as a sacrifice; when he lays it on the dried buffalo skull, where the other chops it off near the hand, with a blow of the hatchet!

Nearly all of the young men whom I saw passing this horrid ordeal, gave in the above manner, the little finger of the left hand; and I saw also several, who immediately afterwards (and apparently with very little concern or emotion), with a similar speech, extended in the same way, the *fore*-finger of the same hand, and that too was struck off; leaving on the left hand only the two middle fingers and the thumb; all which they deem absolutely essential for holding the bow, the only weapon for the left hand.

One would think that this mutilation had thus been carried quite far enough; but I have since examined several of the head chiefs and dignitaries of the tribe, who have also given, in this manner, the little finger of the right hand, which is considered by them to be a much greater sacrifice than both of the others; and I have found also a number of their most famous men, who furnish me incontestible proof, by five or six corresponding scars on each arm, and each breast, and each leg, that they had so many times in their lives submitted to this almost incredible operation, which seems to be optional with them; and the oftener they volunteer to go through it, the more famous they become in the estimation of their tribe.

No bandages are applied to the fingers which have been amputated, nor any arteries taken up; nor is any attention whatever, paid to them or the other wounds; but they are left (as they say) "for the Great Spirit to cure, who will surely take good care of them." It is a remarkable fact (which I learned from a close inspection of their wounds from day to day) that the bleeding is but very slight and soon ceases, probably from the fact of their extreme exhaustion and debility, caused by want of sustenance and sleep, which checks the natural circulation, and admirably at the same time prepares them to meet the severity of these tortures without the same degree of sensibility and pain, which, under other circumstances, might result in inflammation and death.

During the whole of the time of this cruel part of these most extraordinary inflictions, the chiefs and dignitaries of the tribe are looking on, to decide who are the hardiest and "stoutest hearted"—who can hang the longest by his flesh before he faints, and who will be soonest up, after he has been down; that they may know whom to appoint to lead a war-party, or place at the most honourable and desperate post. The four old men are incessantly beating upon the sacks of water and singing the whole time, with their voices strained to the highest key, vaunting forth, for the encouragement of the young men, the power ad efficacy of the *medicine-pipe*, which has disarmed the monster O-kee-hee-de (or Evil Spirit), and driven him from the village, and will be sure to protect them and watch over them through their present severe trial.

As soon as six or eight had passed the ordeal as above described, they were led out of the lodge, with their weights hanging to their flesh, and dragging on the ground, to undergo another, and a still more appalling mode of suffering in the centre of the village, and in presence of the whole nation, in the manner as follows:—

The signal for the commencement of this part of the cruelties was given by the old master of ceremonies, who again ran out as in the buffalo-dance, and leaning against the big canoe, with his *medicine-pipe* in his hand, began to cry. This was done several times in the afternoon, as often as there were six or eight who had passed the ordeal just described within the lodge, who were then taken out in the open area, in the presence of the whole village, with the buffalo skulls and other weights attached to their flesh, and dragging on the ground! There were then in readiness, and prepared for the purpose, about twenty young men, selected of equal height and equal age; with their bodies chiefly naked, with beautiful (and similar) head-dresses of war-eagles' quills, on their heads, and a wreath made of willow boughs held in the hands between them, connecting them in a chain or circle in which they ran around the *big canoe*, with all possible speed, raising their voices in screams and yelps to the highest pitch that was possible, and keeping the curb or big canoe in the centre, as their nucleus.

Then were led forward the young men who were further to suffer, and being placed at equal distances apart, and outside of the ring just described, each one was taken in charge of two athletic young men, fresh and strong, who stepped up to him, one on each side, and by wrapping a broad leather strap around his wrists, without tying it, grasped it firm underneath the hand, and stood prepared for what they call *Eh-ke-nah-ka-nah-pick* (the last race. Illustration 23). This, the spectator looking on would suppose was most correctly named, for he would think it was the last race they could possibly run in this world.

In this condition they stand, pale and ghastly, from abstinence and loss of blood, until all are prepared, and the word is given, when all start and run around, outside of the other ring; and each poor fellow, with his weights dragging on the ground, and his furious conductors by his side, who hurry him forward by the wrists, struggles in the desperate emulation to run longer without "dying" (as they call it) than his comrades, who are fainting around him and sinking down, like himself, where their bodies are dragged with all possible speed, and often with their faces in the dirt. In the commencement of this dance or race they all start at a moderate pace, and their speed being gradually increased, the pain becomes so excruciating that their languid and exhausted frames give out, and they are dragged by their wrists until they are disengaged from the weights that were attached to their flesh, and this must be done by such violent force as to tear the flesh out with the splint, which (as they say) can never be pulled out endwise, without greatly offending the Great Spirit and defeating the object for which they have thus far suffered. The splints of skewers which are put through the breast and the shoulders, take up a part of the pectoral or trapezius muscle, which is necessary for the support of the great weight of their bodies, and which, as I have before mentioned, are withdrawn as soon as he is lowered down—but all the others, on the legs and arms, seem to be very ingeniously passed through the flesh and integuments without taking up the muscle, and even these, to be broken out, require so strong and so violent a force that most of the poor fellows fainted under the operation, and when they were freed from the last of the buffalo skulls and other weights, (which was often done by some of

Illustration 23. The Last Race.

the bystanders throwing the weight of their bodies on to them as they were dragging on the ground) they were in every instance dropped by the persons who dragged them, and their bodies were left, appearing like nothing but a mangled and a loathsome corpse! At this strange and frightful juncture, the two men who had dragged them, fled through the crowd and away upon the prairie, as if they were guilty of some enormous crime, and were fleeing from summary vengeance.

Each poor fellow, having thus patiently and manfully endured the privations and tortures devised for him, and (in this last struggle with the most appalling effort) torn himself loose from them and his tormentors, he lies the second time, in the "keeping (as he terms it) of the Great Spirit," to whom he issues his repeated prayers, and entrusts his life: and in whom he reposes the most implicit confidence for his preservation and recovery. As an evidence of this, and of the high value which these youths set upon this privilege, there is no person, not a relation or a chief of the tribe, who is allowed, or who would dare, to step forward to offer an aiding hand, even to save his life; for not only the rigid customs of the nation, and the pride of the individual who has entrusted his life to the keeping of the Great Spirit, would sternly reject such a tender; but their superstition, which is the strongest of all arguments in an Indian community, would alone, hold all the tribe in fear and dread of interfering, when they consider they have so good a reason to believe that the Great Spirit has undertaken the special care and protection of his devoted worshippers.

In this "last race," which was the struggle that finally closed their sufferings, each one was dragged until he fainted, and was thus left, looking more like the dead than the living: and thus each one laid, until, by the aid of the Great Spirit, he was in a few minutes seen gradually rising, and at last reeling and staggering, like a drunken man, through the crowd (which made way for him) to his wigwam, where his friends and relatives stood ready to take him into hand and restore him.

In this frightful scene, as in the buffalo-dance, the whole nation was assembled as spectators, and all raised the most piercing and violent yells and screams they could possibly produce, to drown the cries of the suffering ones, that no heart could even be touched with sympathy for them. I have mentioned before, that six or eight of the young men were brought from the medicine-lodge at a time, and when they were thus passed through this shocking ordeal, the medicine-men and the chiefs returned to the interior, where as many more were soon prepared, and underwent a similar treatment; and after that another batch, and another, and so on, until the whole number, some forty-five or fifty had run in this sickening circle, and, by leaving their weights, had opened the flesh for honourable scars. I said *all*, but there was one poor fellow though (and I shudder to tell it), who was dragged around and around the circle, with the skull of an elk hanging to the flesh on one of his legs,—several had jumped upon it, but to no effect, for the splint was under the sinew, which could not be broken. The dragging became every instant more and more furious, and the apprehensions for the poor fellow's life, apparent by the piteous howl which was set up for him by the multitude around; and at last the medicine-man ran, with his medicine-pipe in his hand, and held them in check, when the body was dropped, and left upon the ground, with the skull yet hanging to it. The boy, who was an extremely interesting and fine-looking youth, soon recovered his senses and his strength, looking deliberately at his torn and bleeding limbs; and also with the most pleasant smile of defiance, upon the misfortune which had now fallen to his peculiar lot, crawled through the crowd (instead of walking, which they are never again at liberty to do until the flesh is torn out, and the article left) to the prairie, and over which, for the distance of half a mile, to a sequestered spot, without any attendant, where he laid three days and three nights, yet longer, without food, and praying to the Great Spirit, until suppuration took place in the wound, and by the decaying of the flesh the weight was dropped, and the splint also, which he dare not extricate in another way. At the end of this, he crawled back to the village on his hands and knees, being too much emaciated to walk, and begged for something to eat, which was at once given him, and he was soon restored to health . . .

After these young men, who had for the last four days occupied the medicine-lodge, had been operated on, in the manner above described, and taken out of it, the old medicine-man, master of ceremonies, returned, (still crying to the Great Spirit) sole tenant of that sacred place, and brought out the "edged tools," which I before said had been collected at the door of every man's wigwam, to be given as a sacrifice to the water, and leaving the lodge securely fastened, he approached the bank of the river, when all the medicine-men attended him, and all the nation were spectators; and in their presence he threw them from a high bank into very deep water, from which they cannot be recovered, and where they are, correctly speaking, made a sacrifice to the water. This part of the affair took place just exactly at sun-down, and closed the scene, being the end or finale of the *Mandan religious ceremony* . . .

That these people should have a tradition of the Flood is by no means surprising; as I have learned from every tribe I have visited, that they all have some high mountain in their vicinity, where they insist upon it the big canoe landed; but that these people should hold an annual celebration of the event, and the season of that decided by such circumstances as the full leaf of the willow, and the medicine-lodge opened by such a man as Nu-mohk-muck-a-nah (who appears to be a white man), and making his appearance "from the high-mountains in the West;" and some other circumstances, is surely a very remarkable thing, and requires some extraordinary attention.

This Nu-mohk-muck-a-nah (first or only man) is undoubtedly some mystery or medicine-man of the tribe, who has gone out on the prairie on the evening previous, and having dressed and painted himself for the occasion, comes into the village in the morning, endeavouring to keep up the semblance of reality; for their tradition says, that at a very ancient period such a man did actually come from the West—that his body was of the white colour, as this man's body is represented—that he wore a robe of four white wolf skins—his head-dress was made of two raven's skins—and in his left hand was a huge pipe. He said, "he was at one time the only man—he told them of the destruction of every thing on the earth's surface by water—that he stopped in his *big canoe* on a high mountain in the West, where he landed and was saved."

"That the Mandans, and all other people were bound to make yearly sacrifices of some edged-tools to the water, for of such things the big canoe was made. That he instructed the Mandans how to build their medicine-lodge, and taught them also the forms of these annual ceremonies; and told them that as long as they made these sacrifices, and performed their rites to the full letter, they might be assured of the fact, that they would be the favourite people of the Almighty, and would always have enough to eat and drink; and that so soon as they should depart in one tittle from these forms, they might be assured, that their race would decrease, and finally run out; and that they might date their nation's calamity to that omission or neglect."

These people have, no doubt, been long living under the dread of such an injunction, and in the fear of departing from it; and while they are living in total ignorance of its origin, the world must remain equally ignorant of much of its meaning, as they needs must be of all Indian customs resting on ancient traditions, which soon run into fables, having lost all their system, by which they might have been construed.

This strange and unaccountable custom, is undoubtedly peculiar to the Mandans; although, amongst the Minatarees, and some others of the neighbouring tribes, they have seasons of abstinence and self-torture, somewhat similar, but bearing no other resemblance to this than a mere feeble effort or form of imitation.

It would seem from their tradition of the willow branch, and the dove, that these people must have had some proximity to some part of the civilized world; or that missionaries or others have been formerly among them, inculcating the Christian religion and the Mosaic account of the Flood; which is, in this and some other respects, decidedly different from the theory which most natural people have distinctly established of that event.

There are other strong, and almost decisive proofs in my opinion, in support of the assertion, which are to be drawn from the diversity of colour in their hair and complexions, as I have before described, as well as from their tradition just related, of the "*first or only man*," whose body was white, and who came from the West, telling them of the destruction of the earth by water, and instructing them in the forms of these mysteries; and, in addition to the above, I will add the two following very curious stories, which I had from several of their old and dignified chiefs, and which are, no doubt, standing and credited traditions of the tribe.

"The Mandans (people of the pheasants) were the first people created in the world, and they originally lived inside of the earth; they raised many vines, and one of them had grown up through a hole in the earth, over head, and one of their young men climbed up it until he came out on the top of the ground, on the bank of the river, where the Mandan village stands. He looked around, and admired the beautiful country and prairies about him—saw many buffaloes—killed one with his bow and arrows, and found that its meat was good to eat. He returned, and related what he had seen; when a number of others went up the vine with him, and witnessed the same things. Amongst those who went up, were two very pretty young women, who were favourites of the chiefs, because they were virgins; and amongst those who were trying to get up, was a very large and fat woman, who was ordered by the chiefs not to go up, but whose curiosity led her to try it as soon as she got a secret opportunity, when there was no one present. When she got part of the way up, the vine broke under the great weight of her body, and let her down. She was very much hurt by the fall, but did not die. The Mandans were very sorry about this; and she was disgraced for being the cause of a very great calamity, which she had brought upon them, and which could never be averted; for no more could ever ascend, nor could those descend who had got up; but they built the Mandan village, where it formerly stood, a great ways below on the river; and the remainder of the people live under ground to this day."

The above tradition is told with great gravity by their chiefs and doctors or mystery-men; and the latter profess to hear their friends talk through the earth at certain times and places, and even consult them for their opinions and advice on many important occasions.

The next tradition runs thus:—

"At a very ancient period, O-kee-hee-de (the Evil Spirit, the black fellow mentioned in the religious ceremonies) came to the Mandan village with Nu-mohk-muck-a-nah (the first or only man) from the West, and sat down by a woman who had but one eye, and was hoeing corn. Her daughter, who was very pretty came up to her, and the Evil Spirit desired her to go and bring some water; but wished that before she started, she would come to him and eat some buffalo meat. He told her to take a piece out of his side, which she did and ate it, which proved to be buffalo-fat. She then went for the water, which she brought, and met them in the village where they had walked, and they both drank of it—nothing more was done.

"The friends of the girl soon after endeavoured to disgrace her, by telling her that she was *enciente* [pregnant] which she did not deny. She declared her innocence at the same time, and boldly defied any man in the village to come forward and accuse her. This raised a great excitement in the village, and as no one could stand forth to accuse her, she was looked upon as *great medicine*. She soon after went off secretly to the upper Mandan village, where the child was born.

"Great search was made for her before she was found; as it was expected that the child would also be great *medicine* or mystery, and of great importance to the existence and welfare of the tribe. They were induced to this belief from the very strange manner of its conception and birth, and were soon confirmed in it from the wonderful things which it did at an early age. They say, that amongst other miracles which he performed, when the Mandans were like to starve, he gave them four buffalo bulls, which filled the whole village—leaving as much meat as there was before they had eaten; saying that these four bulls would supply them for ever. Nu-mohk-muck-a-nah (the first or only man) was bent on the destruction of the child, and after making many fruitless searches for it, found it hidden in a dark place, and put it to death by throwing it into the river.

"When O-kee-hee-de (the Evil Spirit) heard of the death of this child, he sought for Nu-mohk-muck-a-nah with intent to kill him. He traced him a long distance, and at length found him at *Heart River*, about seventy miles below the village, with the big medicine-pipe in his hand, the charm or mystery of which protects him from all of his enemies. They soon agreed, however, to become friends, smoked the big pipe together, and returned to the Mandan village. The Evil Spirit was satisfied; and Nu-mohk-muck-a-nah told the Mandans never to pass Heart River to live, for it was the centre of the world, and to live beyond it would be destruction to them; and he named it *Nat-com-pa-sa-hah* (heart or centre of the world)" . . .

I am not yet able to learn from these people whether they have any distinct theory of the creation; as they seem to date nothing further back than their own existence as a people; saying (as I have before mentioned), that they were the first people created; involving the glaring absurdities that they were the only people on earth before the Flood, and the only one saved was a white man; or that they were created inside of the earth, as their tradition says; and that they did not make their appearance on its outer surface until after the Deluge. When an Indian story is told, it is like all other gifts, "to be taken for what it is worth," and for any seeming inconsistency in their traditions there is no remedy; for as far as I have tried to reconcile them by reasoning with, or questioning them, I have been entirely defeated; and more than that, have generally incurred their distrust and ill-will. One of the Mandan doctors told me very gravely a few days since, that the earth was a large tortoise, that it carried the dirt on its back—that a tribe of people, who are now dead, and whose faces were white, used to dig down very deep in this ground to catch *badgers*; and that one day they stuck a knife through the tortoise-shell, and it sunk down so that the water ran over its back, and drowned all but one man. And on the next day while I was painting his portrait, he told me there were *four tortoises*,—one in the North—one in the East—one in the South, and one in the West; that each one of these rained ten days, and the water covered over the earth . . .

The Mandan chiefs and doctors, in all their feasts, where the pipe is lit and about to be passed around, deliberately propitiate the good-will and favour of the Great Spirit, by extending the stem of the pipe *upwards* before they smoke it themselves; and also as deliberately and as strictly offering the stem to the four *cardinal points* in succession, and then drawing a whiff through it, passing it around amongst the group.

The *annual religious ceremony* invariably lasts *four* days, and the other following circumstances attending these strange forms, and seeming to have some allusion to the *four* cardinal points, or the "four tortoises," seem to me to be worthy of further notice. *Four* men are selected by Nu-mohk-muck-a-nah (as I have before said), to cleanse out and prepare the medicine-lodge for the occasion—one he calls from the *north* part of the village—one from the *east*—one from the *south*, and one from the *west*. The *four* sacks of water, in form of large tortoises, resting on the floor of the lodge and before described, would seem to be typical of the same thing; and also the *four* buffalo, and the *four* human skulls resting on the floor of the same lodge—the *four* couples of dancers in the "bull-dance," as before described; and also the *four* intervening dancers in the same dance, and also described . . .

I have dwelt longer on the history and customs of these people than I have or shall on any other tribe, in all probability, and that from the fact that I have found them a very peculiar people, as will have been seen by my notes.

From these very numerous and striking peculiarities in their personal appearance—their customs—traditions and language, I have been led conclusively to believe that they are a people of decidedly a different origin from that of any other tribe in these regions.

From these reasons, as well as from the fact that they are a small and feeble tribe, against whom the powerful tribe of Sioux are waging a deadly war with the prospect of their extermination; and who with their limited numbers, are not likely to hold out long in their struggle for existence, I have taken more pains to pourtray their whole character, than my limited means will allow me to bestow upon other tribes.

From the ignorant and barbarous and disgusting customs just recited, the world would naturally infer, that these people must be the most cruel and inhuman beings in the world—yet, such is not the case, and it becomes my duty to say it; a better, more honest, hospitable and kind people, as a community, are not to be found in the world. No set of men that ever I associated with have better hearts than the Mandans, and none are quicker to embrace and welcome a white man than they are—none will press him closer to his bosom, that the pulsation of his heart may be felt, than a Mandan; and no man in any country will keep his word and guard his honour more closely . . .

. . . Severed as they are from the contaminating and counteracting vices which oppose and thwart most of the best efforts of the

Missionaries along the frontier, and free from the almost fatal prejudices which they have there to contend with; they present a better
field for the labours of such benevolent teachers than they have yet
worked in, and a far better chance than they have yet had of proving
to the world that the poor Indian is not a brute—that he is a human
and humane being, that he is capable of improvement—and that his
mind is a beautiful blank on which anything can be written if the
proper means be taken.

The Mandans being but a small tribe, of two thousand only, and
living all in two villages, in sight of each other, and occupying these
permanently, without roaming about like other neighbouring tribes,
offer undoubtedly, the best opportunity for such an experiment of
any tribe in the country. The land about their villages is of the best
quality for ploughing and grazing, and the water just such as would
be desired. Their villages are fortified with piquets or stockades,
which protect them from the assaults of their enemies at home; and
the introduction of agriculture (which would supply them with the
necessaries and luxuries of life, without the necessity of continually
exposing their lives to their more numerous enemies on the plains,
when they are seeking in the chase the means of their subsistence)
would save them from the continual wastes of life, to which, in their
wars and the chase they are continually exposed, and which are
calculated soon to result in their extinction.

I deem it not folly nor idle to say that these people *can be saved*,
nor officious to suggest to some of the very many excellent and pious
men, who are almost throwing away the best energies of their lives
along the debased frontier, that if they would introduce the ploughshare
and their prayers amongst these people, who are so far separated
from the taints and contaminating vices of the frontier, they would
soon see their most ardent desires accomplished and be able to solve
to the world the perplexing enigma, by presenting a nation of
savages, civilized and christianized (and consequently *saved*), in the
heart of the American wilderness.

In taking this final leave of [the Mandans], which will be done
with some decided feelings of regret, and in receding from their
country, I shall look back and reflect upon them and their curious and

peculiar modes with no small degree of pleasure, as well as surprise; inasmuch as their hospitality and friendly treatment have fully corroborated my fixed belief that the North American Indian in his primitive state is a high-minded, hospitable and honourable being— and their singular and peculiar customs have raised an irresistible belief in my mind that they have had a different origin, or are of a different compound of character from any other tribe that I have yet seen, or that can be probably seen in North America.

In coming to such a conclusion as this, the mind is at once filled with a flood of enquiries as to the source from which they have sprung, and eagerly seeking for the evidence which is to lead it to the most probable and correct conclusion. Amongst these evidences of which there are many, and forcible ones to be met with amongst these people, and many of which I have named in my former epistles, the most striking ones are those which go, I think, decidedly bearing incontestable proofs of an amalgam of civilized and savage; and that in the absence of all proof of any recent proximity of a civilized stock that could in any way have been engrafted upon them.

These facts then, with the host of their peculiarities which stare a traveller in the face, lead the mind back in search of some more remote and rational cause for such striking singularities; and in this dilemma, I have been almost disposed (not to advance it as a *theory*, but) to enquire whether here may not be found, yet existing, the remains of the *Welsh colony*—the followers of Madoc; who history tells us, if I recollect right, started with ten ships, to colonize a country which he had discovered in the Western Ocean; whose expedition I think has been pretty clearly traced to the mouth of the Mississippi, or the coast of Florida, and whose fate further than this seems sealed in unsearchable mystery.

I am travelling in this country as I have before said, not to advance or to prove *theories*, but to see all that I am able to see, and to tell it in the simplest and most intelligible manner I can to the world, for their own conclusions, or for theories I may feel disposed to advance, and be better able to defend after I get out of this singular country; where all the powers of ones faculties are required, and much better employed I consider, in helping him along and in gathering materials, than in stopping to draw too nice and delicate conclusions by the way.

If my indefinite recollections of the fate of that colony, however, as recorded in history be correct, I see no harm in suggesting the inquiry, whether they did not sail up the Mississippi river in their ten ships, or such number of them as might have arrived safe in its mouth; and having advanced up the Ohio from its junction, (as they naturally would, it being the widest and most gentle current) to a rich and fertile country, planted themselves as agriculturalists on its rich banks, where they lived and flourished, and increased in numbers, until they were attacked, and at last besieged by the numerous hordes of savages who were jealous of their growing condition; and as a protection against their assaults, built those numerous *civilized* fortifications, the ruins of which are now to be seen on the Ohio and the Muskingum, in which they were at last all destroyed, except some few families who had intermarried with the Indians, and whose offspring, being half-breeds, were in such a manner allied to them that their lives were spared; and forming themselves into a small and separate community, took up their residence on the banks of the Missouri; on which, for the want of a permanent location, being on the lands of their more powerful enemies, were obliged repeatedly to remove; and continuing their course up the river, have in time migrated to the place where they are now living, and consequently found with the numerous and almost unaccountable peculiarities of which I have before spoken, so inconsonant with the general character of the North American Indians; with complexions of every shade; with hair of all the colours in civilized society, and many with hazel, with grey, and with blue eyes.

The above is a suggestion of a *moment*; and I wish the reader to bear it in mind, that if I ever advance such as a *theory*, it will be after I have collected other proofs, which I shall take great pains to do; after I have taken a vocabulary of their language, and also in my transit down the river in my canoe, I may be able from my own examinations of the ground, to ascertain whether the shores of the Missouri bear evidences of their former locations; or whether amongst the tribes who inhabit the country below, there remain any satisfactory traditions of their residences in, and transit through their countries.*

*For Catlin's further comments on the Mandans, See Appendix, pp. 487–497.—ed.

LETTER—NO. 23.

◄————————►

Minataree Village, Upper Missouri.

*T*he village of the Minatarees . . . is also located on the
... west bank of the Missouri river, and only eight miles
above the Mandans. On my way down the river in my canoe, I
passed this village without attending to their earnest and clamorous
invitations for me to come ashore, and it will thus be seen that I am
retrograding a little, to see all that is to be seen in this singular
country . . .

The Minatarees (people of the willows) are a small tribe of about
1500 souls, residing in three villages of earth-covered lodges, on the
banks of Knife river; a small stream, so called, meandering through a
beautiful and extensive prairie, and uniting its waters with the
Missouri.

This small community is undoubtedly a part of the tribe of
Crows, of whom I have already spoken, living at the base of the
Rocky Mountains, who have at some remote period, either in their
war or hunting excursions, been run off by their enemy, and their
retreat having been prevented, have thrown themselves upon the
hospitality of the Mandans, to whom they have looked for protection,
and under whose wing they are now living in a sort of confederacy,
ready to intermarry and also to join, as they often have done, in the
common defence of their country.

In language and personal appearance, as well as in many of their
customs, they are types of the Crows; yet having adopted and so long
lived under its influence, the system of the Mandans, they are much
like them in many respects, and continually assimilating to the
modes of their patrons and protectors. Amongst their vague and

various traditions they have evidently some disjointed authority for the manner in which they came here; but no account of the time. They say, that they came poor—without wigwams or horses—were nearly all women, as their warriors had been killed off in their flight; that the Mandans would not take them into their village, nor let them come nearer than where they are now living, and there assisted them to build their villages. From these circumstances their wigwams have been constructed exactly in the same manner as those of the Mandans, which I have already described, and entirely distinct from any custom to be seen in the Crow tribe.

Notwithstanding the long familiarity in which they have lived with the Mandans, and the complete adoption of most of their customs, yet it is almost an unaccountable fact, that there is scarcely a man in the tribe who can speak half a dozen words of the Mandan language; although on the other hand, the Mandans are most of them able to converse in the Minataree tongue; leaving us to conclude, either that the Minatarees are a very inert and stupid people, or that the Mandan language (which is most probably the case) being different from any other language in the country, is an exceedingly difficult one to learn.

The principal village of the Minatarees which is built upon the bank of the Knife river, contains forty or fifty earth-covered wigwams, from forty to fifty feet in diameter, and being elevated, overlooks the other two, which are on lower ground and almost lost amidst their numerous corn fields and other profuse vegetation which cover the earth with their luxuriant growth.

The scenery along the banks of this little river, from village to village, is quite peculiar and curious; rendered extremely so by the continual wild and garrulous groups of men, women, and children, who are wending their way along its winding shores, or dashing and plunging through its blue waves, enjoying the luxury of swimming, of which both sexes seem to be passionately fond. Others are paddling about in their tub-like canoes, made of the skins of buffaloes; and every now and then, are to be seen their sudatories, or vapour-baths, where steam is raised by throwing water on to heated stones; and the patient jumps from his sweating-house and leaps into the river in the highest state of perspiration, as I have more fully described whilst speaking of the bathing of the Mandans.

The chief sachem of this tribe is a very ancient and patriarchal looking man, by the name of Eeh-tohk-pah-shee-pee-shah (the black moccasin), and counts, undoubtedly, more than an hundred *snows*. I have been for some days an inmate of his hospitable lodge, where he sits tottering with age, and silently reigns sole monarch of his little community around him, who are continually dropping in to cheer his sinking energies, and render him their homage. His voice and his sight are nearly gone; but the gestures of his hands are yet energetic and youthful, and freely speak the language of his kind heart.

I have been treated in the kindest manner by this old chief; and have painted his portrait (Illustration 24) as he was seated on the floor of his wigwam, smoking his pipe, whilst he was recounting over to me some of the extraordinary feats of his life, with a beautiful Crow robe wrapped around him, and his hair wound up in a conical form upon his head, and fastened with a small wooden pin, to keep it in its place.

This man has many distinct recollections of Lewis and Clarke, who were the first explorers of this country, and who crossed the Rocky Mountains thirty years ago. It will be seen by reference to their very interesting history of their tour, that they were treated with great kindness by this man; and that they in consequence constituted him chief of the tribe, with the consent of his people; and he has remained their chief ever since. He enquired very earnestly for "Red Hair" and "Long Knife" (as he had ever since termed Lewis and Clarke), from the fact, that one had red hair (an unexampled thing in his country), and the other wore a broad sword which gained for him the appellation of "Long Knife."

I have told him that "Long Knife" has been many years dead; and that "Red Hair" is yet living in St. Louis, and no doubt, would be glad to hear of him; at which he seemed much pleased, and has signified to me that he will make me bearer of some peculiar dispatches to him.*

*About a year after writing the above, and whilst I was in St. Louis, I had the pleasure of presenting the compliments of this old veteran to General Clarke; and also of shewing to him the portrait, which he instantly recognized amongst hundreds of others; saying, that "they had considered the Black Moccasin quite an old man when they appointed him chief thirty-two years ago."

Illustration 24. Eeh-tohk-pah-shee-pee-shah, Black Moccasin.

The name by which these people are generally called (Grosventres) is one given them by the French Traders, and has probably been applied to them with some degree of propriety or fitness, as contradistinguished from the Mandans, amongst whom these Traders were living; and who are a small race of Indians, being generally at or below the average stature of man; whilst the Minatarees are generally tall and heavily built. There is no tribe in the western wilds, perhaps, who are better entitled to the style of warlike, than the Minatarees; for they, unlike the Mandans, are continually carrying war into their enemies' country; oftentimes drawing the poor Mandans into unnecessary broils, and suffering so much themselves in their desperate war-excursions, that I find the proportion of women to the number of men as two or three to one, through the tribe.

The son of Black Moccasin, whose name is Ee-a-chin-che-a (the red thunder), and who is reputed one of the most desperate warriors of his tribe, I have also painted at full length, in his war-dress, with his bow in his hand, his quiver slung, and his shield upon his arm. In this plight, *sans* head-dress, *sans* robe, and *sans* everything that might be an useless incumbrance—with the body chiefly naked, and profusely bedaubed with red and black paint, so as to form an almost perfect disguise, the Indian warriors invariably sally forth to war; save the chief, who always plumes himself, and leads on his little band, tendering himself to his enemies a conspicuous mark, with all his ornaments and trophies upon him; that his enemies, if they get him, may get a prize worth the fighting for.

Besides chiefs and warriors to be admired in this little tribe, there are many beautiful and voluptuous looking women, who are continually crowding in throngs, and gazing upon a stranger; and possibly shedding more bewitching smiles from a sort of necessity, growing out of the great disparity in numbers between them and the rougher sex, to which I have before alluded.

From the very numerous groups of these that have from day to day constantly pressed upon me, overlooking the operations of my brush; I have been unable to get more than one who would consent to have her portrait painted, owing to some fear or dread of harm that might eventually ensue in consequence; or from a natural coyness or timidity, which is surpassing all description amongst these wild tribes, when in presence of strangers.

The one whom I have painted is a descendant from the old chief; and though not the most beautiful, is yet a fair sample of them, and dressed in a beautiful costume of the mountain-sheep skin, handsomely garnished with porcupine quills and beads. This girl was almost *compelled* to stand for her picture by her relatives who urged her on, whilst she modestly declined, offering as her excuse that "she was not pretty enough, and that her picture would be laughed at." This was either ignorance or excessive art on her part; for she was certainly more than comely, and the beauty of her name, Seet-se-be-a (the midday sun) is quite enough to make up for a deficiency, if there were any, in the beauty of her face.

I mentioned that I found these people raising abundance of corn or maize: and I have happened to visit them in the season of their festivities, which annually take place when the ears of corn are of the proper size for eating. The green corn is considered a great luxury by all those tribes who cultivate it; and is ready for eating as soon as the ear is of full size, and the kernels are expanded to their full growth, but are yet soft and pulpy. In this green state of the corn, it is boiled and dealt out in great profusion to the whole tribe, who feast and surfeit upon it whilst it lasts; rendering thanks to the *Great Spirit* for the return of this joyful season, which they do by making sacrifices, by dancing, and singing songs of thanksgiving. This joyful occasion is one valued alike, and conducted in a similar manner, by most of the tribes who raise the corn, however remote they may be from each other. It lasts but for a week or ten days; being limited to the longest term that the corn remains in this tender and palatable state; during which time all hunting, and all war-excursions, and all other avocations, are positively dispensed with; and all join in the most excessive indulgence of gluttony and conviviality that can possibly be conceived. The fields of corn are generally pretty well stripped during this excess; and the poor improvident Indian thanks the Great Spirit for the indulgence he has had, and is satisfied to ripen merely the few ears that are necessary for his next year's planting, without reproaching himself for his wanton lavishness, which has laid waste his fine fields, and robbed him of the golden harvest, which might have gladdened his heart, with those of his wife and little children, through the cold and dreariness of winter.

The most remarkable feature of these joyous occasion is the *green corn-dance*, which is always given as preparatory to the feast, and by most of the tribes in the following manner:—

At the usual season, and the time when from outward appearance of the stalks and ears of the corn, it is supposed to be nearly ready for use, several of the old women who are the owners of fields or patches of corn (for such are the proprietors and cultivators of all crops in Indian countries, the men never turning their hands to such degrading occupations) are delegated by the medicine-men to look at the corn fields every morning at sun-rise, and bring into the council-house, where the kettle is ready, several ears of corn, the husks of which the women are not allowed to break open or even to peep through. The women then are from day to day discharged and the doctors left to decide, until from repeated examinations they come to the decision that it will do; when they dispatch *runners* or *criers*, announcing to every part of the village or tribe that the Great Spirit has been kind to them, and they must all meet on the next day to return thanks for his goodness. That all must empty their stomachs, and prepare for the feast that is approaching.

On the day appointed by the doctors, the villagers are all assembled, and in the midst of the group a kettle is hung over a fire and filled with the green corn, which is well boiled, to be given to the Great Spirit, as a sacrifice necessary to be made before any one can indulge the cravings of his appetite. Whilst this first kettleful is boiling, four medicine-men with a stalk of the corn on one hand and a rattle (she-she-quoi) in the other, with their bodies painted with white clay, dance around the kettle, chanting a song of thanksgiving to the Great Spirit to whom the offering is to be made. At the same time a number of warriors are dancing around in a more extended circle, with stalks of the corn in their hands, and joining also in the song of thanksgiving, whilst the villagers are all assembled and looking on. During this scene there is an arrangement of wooden bowls laid upon the ground, in which the feast is to be dealt out, each one having in it a spoon made of the buffalo or mountain-sheep's horn.

In this wise the dance continues until the doctors decide that the corn is sufficiently boiled; it then stops for a few moments, and again assumes a different form and a different song, whilst the doctors are placing the ears on a little scaffold of sticks, which they erect immediately over the fire where it is entirely consumed, as they join again in the dance around it.

The fire is then removed, and with it the ashes, which together are buried in the ground, and *new fire* is originated on the same spot where the old one was, by friction, which is done by a desperate and painful exertion by three men seated on the ground, facing each other and violently drilling the end of a stick into a hard block of wood by rolling it between the hands, each one catching it in turn from the others without allowing the motion to stop until smoke, and at last a spark of fire is seen and caught in a piece of spunk, when there is great rejoicing in the crowd. With this a fire is kindled, and the kettleful of corn again boiled for the feast, at which the chiefs, doctors, and warriors are seated; and after this an unlimited licence is given to the whole tribe, who surfeit upon it and indulge in all their favourite amusements and excesses, until the fields of corn are exhausted.

LETTER—NO. 24.

◀——————————————▶

Minataree Village, Upper Missouri.

*E*pistles from such a strange place as this, where I have no
... *E* desk to write from, or mail to send them by, are hastily
scribbled off in my notebook ... the only place where I can
satisfactorily make these entries is in the shade of some sequestered
tree, to which I occasionally resort, or more often from my bed
(from which I am now writing), enclosed by a sort of curtains made
of the skins of elks or buffaloes, completely encompassing me, where
I am reclining on a sacking-bottom, made of the buffalo's hide;
making my entries and notes of the incidents of the past day, amidst
the roar and unintelligible din of savage conviviality that is going on
under the same roof, and under my own eye, whenever I feel
disposed to apply it to a small aperture which brings at once the
whole interiour and all its inmates within my view.

There are at this time some distinguished guests, besides *myself*,
in the lodge of the Black Moccasin; two chiefs or leaders of a party of
Crows, who arrived here a few days since, on a visit to their ancient
friends and relatives. The consequence has been, that feasting and
carousing have been the "order of the day" here for some time; and I
have luckily been a welcome participator in their entertainments. A
distinguished chief of the Minatarees, with several others in company, has been for some months past on a visit to the Crows and
returned, attended by some remarkably fine-looking fellows, all
mounted on fine horses ... They may be justly said to be the most
beautifully clad of all the Indians in these regions, and bringing from
the base of the Rocky Mountains a fine and spirited breed of the

wild horses, have been able to create a great sensation amongst the Minatarees, who have been paying them all attention and all honours for some days past . . .

The upper town of the Minatarees . . . is half a mile or more distant, and on the other bank of the Knife River, which we crossed in the following manner:—The old chief, having learned that we were to cross the river, gave direction to one of the women of his numerous household, who took upon her head a skin-canoe (more familiarly called in this country, a bull-boat), made in the form of a large tub, of a buffalo's skin, stretched on a frame of willow boughs, which she carried to the water's edge; and placing it in the water, made signs for us three to get into it. When we were in, and seated flat on its bottom, with scarce room in any way to adjust our legs and our feet (as we sat necessarily facing each other), she stepped before the boat, and pulling it along, waded towards the deeper water, with her back towards us, carefully with the other hand attending to her dress, which seemed to be but a light slip, and floating upon the surface until the water was above her waist, when it was instantly turned off, over her head, and thrown ashore; and she boldly plunged forward, swimming and drawing the boat with one hand, which she did with apparent ease. In this manner we were conveyed to the middle of the stream, where we were soon surrounded by a dozen or more beautiful girls, from twelve to fifteen and eighteen years of age, who were at that time bathing on the opposite shore.

They all swam in a bold and graceful manner, and as confidently as so many otters or beavers; and gathering around us, with their long black hair floating about on the water, whilst their faces were glowing with jokes and fun, which they were cracking about us, and which we could not understand.

In the midst of this delightful little aquatic group, we three sat in our little skin-bound tub (like the "three wise men of Gotham, who went to sea in a bowl," &c.), floating along down the current, losing sight, and all thoughts, of the shore, which was equi-distant from us on either side; whilst we were amusing ourselves with the playfulness of these dear little creatures who were floating about under the clear blue water, catching their hands on to the sides of our boat; occasionally raising one-half of their bodies out of the water, and sinking again, like so many mermaids . . . I had some awls in my pockets, which I presented to them, and also a few strings of beautiful beads, which I placed over their delicate necks as they raised them out of the water by the side of our boat; after which they all joined in conducting our craft to the shore, by swimming by the sides of, and behind it, pushing it along in the direction where they designed to land it, until the water became so shallow, that their feet were upon the bottom, when they waded along with great coyness, dragging us towards the shore, as long as their bodies, in a crouching position, could possibly be half concealed under the water, when they gave our boat the last push for the shore, and raising a loud and exulting laugh, plunged back again into the river; leaving us the only alternative of sitting still where we were, or of stepping out into the water at half leg deep, and of wading to the shore, which we at once did . . . on our way to the upper village, which I have before mentioned . . .

The Minatarees, as I have before said, are a bold, daring, and warlike tribe; quite different in these respects from their neighbours the Mandans, carrying war continually in their enemies' country, thereby exposing their lives and diminishing the number of their warriors to that degree that I find two or three women to a man, through the tribe. They are bold and fearless in the chase also, and in their eager pursuits of the bison, or buffaloes, their feats are such as to excite the astonishment and admiration of all who behold them. Of these scenes I have witnessed many since I came into this country, and amongst them all, nothing have I seen to compare with one to which I was an eye-witness a few mornings since, and well worthy of being described.

The Minatarees, as well as the Mandans, had suffered for some months past for want of meat, and had indulged in the most alarming fears, that the herds of buffaloes were emigrating so far off from them, that there was great danger of their actual starvation, when it was suddenly announced through the village one morning at an early hour, that a herd of buffaloes was in sight, when an hundred or more young men mounted their horses with weapons in hand and steered their course to the prairies. The chief informed me that one of his horses was in readiness for me at the door of his wigwam, and that I had better go and see the curious affair. I accepted his polite offer, and mounting the steed, galloped off with the hunters to the prairies, where we soon descried at a distance, a fine herd of buffaloes grazing, when a halt and a council were ordered, and the mode of attack was agreed upon. I had armed myself with my pencil and my sketch-book only, and consequently took my position generally in the rear, where I could see and appreciate every manœuvre.

The plan of attack, which in this country is familiarly called a "*surround,*" was explicitly agreed upon, and the hunters who were all mounted on their "buffalo horses" and armed with bows and arrows or long lances, divided into two columns, taking opposite directions, and drew themselves gradually around the herd at a mile or more distance from them; thus forming a circle of horsemen at equal distances apart, who gradually closed in upon them with a moderate pace, at a signal given. The unsuspecting herd at length "got the wind" of the approaching enemy and fled in a mass in the greatest confusion. To the point where they were aiming to cross the line, the horsemen were seen at full speed, gathering and forming in a column, brandishing their weapons and yelling in the most frightful manner, by which means they turned the black and rushing mass which moved off in an opposite direction where they were again met and foiled in a similar manner, and wheeled back in utter confusion; by which time the horsemen had closed in from all directions, forming a continuous line around them, whilst the poor affrighted animals were eddying about in a crowded and confused mass, hooking and climbing upon each other; when the work of death commenced. I had rode up in the rear and occupied an elevated position at a few rods distance, from which I could (like the general of a battle field) survey from my horse's back, the nature and the progress of the grand mêleé; but (unlike him) without the power of issuing a command or in any way directing its issue.

In this grand turmoil (Illustration 25), a cloud of dust was soon raised, which in parts obscured the throng where the hunters were galloping their horses around and driving the whizzing arrows or their long lances to the hearts of these noble animals; which in many instances, becoming infuriated with deadly wounds in their sides, erected their shaggy manes over their blood-shot eyes and furiously plunged forwards at the sides of their assailants' horses, sometimes goring them to death at a lunge, and putting their dismounted riders to flight for their lives; sometimes their dense crowd was opened, and the blinded horsemen, too intent on their prey amidst the cloud of dust, were hemmed and wedged in amidst the crowding beasts, over whose backs they were obliged to leap for security, leaving their horses to the fate that might await them in the results of this wild and desperate war. Many were the bulls that turned upon their assailants and met them with desperate resistance; and many were the warriors who were dismounted, and saved themselves by the superior muscles of their legs; some who were closely pursued by the bulls, wheeled suddenly around and snatching the part of a buffalo robe from around their waists, threw it over the horns and the eyes of the infuriated beast, and darting by its side drove the arrow or the lance to its heart. Others suddenly dashed off upon the prairies by the side of the affrighted animals which had escaped from the throng, and closely escorting them for a few rods, brought down their hearts blood in streams, and their huge carcasses upon the green and enamelled turf.

In this way this grand hunt soon resolved itself into a desperate battle: and in the space of fifteen minutes, resulted in the total destruction of the whole herd, which in all their strength and fury were doomed, like every beast and living thing else, to fall before the destroying hands of mighty man.

I had sat in trembling silence upon my horse, and witnessed this extraordinary scene, which allowed not one of these animals to escape out of my sight. Many plunged off upon the prairie for a distance, but were overtaken and killed; and although I could not distinctly estimate the number that were slain, yet I am sure that some hundreds of these noble animals fell in this grand mêlée.

The scene after the battle was over was novel and curious in the extreme; the hunters were moving about amongst the dead and dying animals, leading their horses by their halters, and claiming their victims by their private marks upon their arrows, which they were drawing from the wounds in the animals' sides.

Amongst the poor affrighted creatures that had occasionally dashed through the ranks of their enemy, and sought safety in flight upon

Illustration 25. A buffalo chase.

the prairie (and in some instances, had undoubtedly gained it), I saw them stand awhile, looking back, when they turned, and, as if bent on their own destruction, retraced their steps, and mingled themselves and their deaths with those of the dying throng. Others had fled to a distance on the prairies, and for want of company, of friends or of foes, had stood and gazed on till the battle-scene was over; seemingly taking pains to stay, and hold their lives in readiness for their destroyers, until the general destruction was over, when they fell easy victims to their weapons—making the slaughter complete.

After this scene, and after arrows had been claimed and recovered, a general council was held, when all hands were seated on the ground, and a few pipes smoked; after which, all mounted their horses and rode back to the village.

A deputation of several of the warriors was sent to the chief, who explained to him what had been their success; and the same intelligence was soon communicated by little squads to every family in the village; and preparations were at once made for securing the meat. For this purpose, some hundreds of women and children, to whose lots fall all the drudgeries of Indian life, started out upon the trail, which led them to the battle-field, where they spent the day in skinning the animals, and cutting up the meat, which was mostly brought into the villages on their backs, as they tugged and sweated under their enormous and cruel loads.

I rode out to see this curious scene; and I regret exceedingly that I kept no memorandum of it in my sketch-book. Amidst the throng of women and children, that had been assembled, and all of whom seemed busily at work, were many superannuated and disabled nags, which they had brought out to assist in carrying in the meat; and at least, one thousand semi-loup dogs, and whelps, whose keen appetites and sagacity had brought them out, to claim their shares of this abundant and sumptuous supply.

I stayed and inspected this curious group for an hour or more, during which time, I was almost continually amused by the clamorous contentions that arose, and generally ended, in desperate combats; both amongst the dogs and women, who seemed alike tenacious of their local and recently acquired rights; and disposed to settle their claims by "tooth and nail"—by manual and brute force.

When I had seen enough of this I rode to the top of a beautiful prairie bluff, a mile or two from the scene, where I was exceedingly amused by overlooking the route that laid between this and the village, which was over the undulating green fields for several miles, that laid beneath me; over which there seemed a continual string of women, dogs and horses, for the rest of the day, passing and repassing as they were busily bearing home their heavy burthens to their village, and in their miniature appearance, which the distance gave them, not unlike to a busy community of ants as they are sometimes seen, sacking and transporting the treasures of a cupboard, or the sweets of a sugar bowl . . .

The Riccaree [Arikara] village . . . is beautifully situated on the west bank of the river, 200 miles below the Mandans; and built very much in the same manner; being constituted of 150 earth-covered lodges, which are in part surrounded by an imperfect and open barrier of piquets set firmly in the ground, and of ten or twelve feet in height.

This village is built upon an open prairie, and the gracefully undulating hills that rise in distance behind it are everywhere covered with a verdant green turf, without a tree or a bush anywhere to be seen. This view was taken from the deck of the steamer when I was on my way up the river; and probably it was well that I took it then, for so hostile and deadly are the feelings of these people towards the *pale faces*, at this time, that it may be deemed most prudent for me to pass them on my way down the river, without stopping to make them a visit. They certainly are harbouring the most resentful feelings at this time towards the Traders, and others passing on the river; and no doubt, that there is great danger of the lives of any white men, who unluckily fall into their hands. They have recently sworn death and destruction to every white man, who comes in their way; and there is no doubt, that they are ready to execute their threats.

When Lewis and Clarke first visited these people thirty years since, it will be found by a reference to their history, that the Riccarees received and treated them with great kindness and hospitality; but owing to the system of trade, and the manner in which it has been conducted in this country, they have been inflicted with real or imaginary abuses, of which they are themselves, and the Fur Traders, the best judges; and for which they are now harbouring the most inveterate feelings towards the whole civilized race.

The Riccarees are unquestionably a part of the tribe of Pawnees, living on the Platte River, some hundreds of miles below this, inasmuch as their language is nearly or quite the same; and their personal appearance and customs as similar as could be reasonably expected amongst a people so long since separated from their parent tribe, and continually subjected to innovations from the neighbouring tribes around them; amongst whom, in their erratic wanderings in search of a location, they have been jostled about in the character, alternately, of friends and of foes.

I shall resume my voyage down the river in a few days in my canoe; and I may, perhaps, stop and pay these people a visit, and consequently, be able to say more of them; or, I may be *hauled in*, to the shore, and my boat plundered, and my "*scalp danced*," as they have dealt quite recently with the *last trader*, who has dared for several years past, to continue his residence with them, after they had laid fatal hands on each one of his comrades before him, and divided and shared their goods.

LETTER—NO. 26.

◄———————————————►

Mouth of Teton River, Upper Missouri.

*S*ince writing the above Letter I have descended the Missouri, a distance of six or seven hundred miles, in my little bark, with Bátiste and Bogard, my old *"compagnons du voyage"* . . . I am now in the heart of the country belonging to the numerous tribe of Sioux or Dahcotas, and have Indian faces and Indian customs in abundance around me. This tribe is one of the most numerous in North America, and also one of the most vigorous and warlike tribes to be found, numbering some forty or fifty thousand, and able undoubtedly to muster, if the tribe could be moved simultaneously, at least eight or ten thousand warriors, well mounted and well armed. This tribe take vast numbers of the wild horses on the plains towards the Rocky Mountains, and many of them have been supplied with guns; but the greater part of them hunt with their bows and arrows and long lances, killing their game from their horses' backs while at full speed.

The name Sioux (pronounced *see-oo*) by which they are familiarly called, is one that has been given to them by the French traders, the meaning of which I never have learned; their own name being, in their language, Dah-co-ta. The personal appearance of these people is very fine and prepossessing, their persons tall and straight, and their movements elastic and graceful. Their stature is considerably above that of the Mandans and Riccarees, or Blackfeet; but about equal to that of the Crows, Assinneboins and Minatarees, furnishing at least one half of their warriors of six feet or more in height.

I am here living with, and enjoying the hospitality of a gentleman by the name of *Laidlaw*, a Scotchman, who is attached to the

American Fur Company ... This gentleman has a finely-built Fort here, of two or three hundred feet square, enclosing eight or ten of their factories, houses and stores, in the midst of which he occupies spacious and comfortable apartments, which are well supplied with the comforts and luxuries of life and neatly and respectably conducted by a fine looking, modest, and dignified Sioux woman, the kind and affectionate mother of his little flock of pretty and interesting children.

This Fort is undoubtedly one of the most important and productive of the American Fur Company's posts, being in the centre of the great Sioux country, drawing from all quarters an immense and almost incredible number of buffalo robes, which are carried to the New York and other Eastern markets, and sold at a great profit. This post is thirteen hundred miles above St. Louis, on the west bank of the Missouri, on a beautiful plain near the mouth of the Teton river [now called Bad River] which empties into the Missouri from the West, and the Fort has received the name of Fort Pierre in compliment to Monsr. Pierre Chouteau, who is one of the partners in the Fur Company, residing in St. Louis ...

... The Fort is in the centre of one of the Missouri's most beautiful plains, and hemmed in by a series of gracefully undulating, grass-covered hills, on all sides; rising like a series of terraces, to the summit level of the prairies, some three or four hundred feet in elevation, which then stretches off in an apparently boundless ocean of gracefully swelling waves and fields of green. On my way up the river I made a painting of this lovely spot, taken from the summit of the bluffs, a mile or two distant (Illustration 26), shewing an encampment of Sioux, of six hundred tents or skin lodges, around the Fort, where they had concentrated to make their spring trade ...

The great family of Sioux who occupy so vast a tract of country, extending from the banks of the Mississippi river to the base of the Rocky Mountains, are everywhere a migratory or roaming tribe, divided into forty-two bands or families, each having a chief who all acknowledge a superior or head chief, to whom they all are held subordinate ...

There is no tribe on the Continent, perhaps, of finer looking men than the Sioux; and few tribes who are better and more comfortably

Illustration 26. Fort Pierre, mouth of the Teton River.

clad, and supplied with the necessaries of life. There are no parts of the great plains of America which are more abundantly stocked with buffaloes and wild horses, nor any people more bold in destroying the one for food, and appropriating the other to their use. There has gone abroad, from the many histories which have been written of these people, an opinion which is too current in the world, that the Indian is necessarily a poor, drunken, murderous wretch; which account is certainly unjust as regards the savage, and doing less than justice to the world for whom such histories have been prepared. I have travelled several years already amongst these people and I have not had my scalp taken, nor a blow struck me; nor had occasion to raise my hand against an Indian; nor has my property been stolen, as yet to my knowledge, to the value of a shilling; and that in a country where no man is punishable by law for the crime of stealing; still some of them steal, and murder too; and if white men did not do the same, and that in defiance of the laws of God and man, I might take satisfaction in stigmatizing the Indian character as thievish and murderous. That the Indians in their *native state* are "*drunken*," is false; for they are the only temperance people, literally speaking, that ever I saw in my travels, or ever expect to see. If the civilized world are startled at this, it is the *fact* that they must battle with, not with me; for these people manufacture no spirituous liquor themselves, and know nothing of it until it is brought into their country and tendered to them by Christians. That these people are "*naked*" is equally untrue, and as easily disproved; for I am sure that with the paintings I have made amongst the Mandans and Crows, and other tribes; and with their beautiful costumes which I have procured and shall bring home, I shall be able to establish the fact that many of these people dress, not only with clothes comfortable for any latitude, but that they also dress with some considerable taste and elegance. Nor am I quite sure that they are entitled to the name of "*poor*," who live in a boundless country of green fields, with good horses to ride; where they are all joint tenants of the soil, together; where the Great Spirit has supplied them with an abundance of food to eat—where they are all indulging in the pleasures and amusements of a lifetime of idleness and ease, with no business hours to attend to, or professions to learn—where they have no notes in bank or other debts to pay—no taxes, no tithes, no rents, nor beggars to touch and tax the sympathy of their souls at every step they go. Such might be poverty in the Christian world, but is sure to be a blessing where the pride and insolence of comparative wealth are unknown.

I mentioned that this is the nucleus or place of concentration of the numerous tribe of the Sioux, who often congregate here in great masses to make their trades with the American Fur Company; and that on my way up the river, some months since, I found here encamped, six hundred families of Sioux, living in tents covered with buffalo hides. Amongst these there were twenty or more of the different bands, each one with their chief at their head, over whom was a *superior chief* and leader, a middle-aged man, of middling stature, with a noble countenance, and a figure almost equalling the Apollo, and I painted his portrait (Illustration 27). The name of the chief is Ha-wan-je-tah (the one horn) of the Mee-ne-cow-e-gee band, who has risen rapidly to the highest honours in the tribe, from his own extraordinary merits, even at so early an age . . . This extraordinary man, before he was raised to the dignity of chief, was the renowned of his tribe for his athletic achievements. In the chase he was foremost; he could run down a buffalo, which he often had done, on his own legs, and drive his arrow to the heart. He was the fleetest in the tribe; and in the races he had run, he had always taken the prize. It was proverbial in his tribe, that Ha-wan-je-tah's bow never was drawn in vain, and his wigwam was abundantly furnished with scalps that he had taken from his enemies' heads in battle.

Having descended the river thus far, then, and . . . taken up my quarters for awhile . . . and having introduced my readers to the country and the people, and more particularly to the chief dignitary of the Sioux; and having promised in the beginning of this Letter also, that I should give them some amusing and curious information that we picked up, and incidents that we met with, on our voyage from the Mandans to this place; I have again to beg that they will pardon me for withholding from them yet awhile longer, the incidents of that curious and most important part of my Tour, the absence of which, at this time, seems to make a "hole in the ballad,"

Illustration 27. Ha-wan-je-tah, One Horn.

though I promise my readers they are written, and will appear in the book in a proper and appropriate place.

Taking it for granted then, that I will be indulged in this freak, I am taking the liberty of presuming on my readers' patience in proposing another, which is to offer them here an extract from my Notes, which were made on my journey of 1300 miles from St. Louis to this place,* where I stopped, as I have said, amongst several thousands of Sioux; where I remained for some time . . .

On the long and tedious route that lies between St. Louis and this place, I passed the Sacs and Ioways—the Konzas [Kansas]—the Omahaws, and the Ottoes (making notes on them all, which are reserved for another place), and landed at the Puncahs, a small tribe residing in one village, on the west bank of the river, 300 miles below this, and 1000 from St. Louis.

The Puncahs are all contained in seventy-five or eighty lodges, made of buffalo skins, in the form of tents; the frames for which are poles of fifteen or twenty feet in length, with the butt ends standing on the ground, and the small ends meeting at the top, forming a cone, which sheds off the rain and wind with perfect success. This small remnant of a tribe are not more than four or five hundred in numbers; and I should think, at least, two-thirds of those are women. This disparity in numbers having been produced by the continual losses which their men suffer, who are penetrating the buffalo country for meat, for which they are now obliged to travel a great way (as the buffaloes have recently left their country), exposing their lives to their more numerous enemies about them.

The chief of this tribe, whose name is Shoo-de-ga-cha (smoke) . . . is a noble specimen of native dignity and philosophy. I conversed much with him; and from his dignified manners, as well as from the soundness of his reasoning, I became fully convinced that he deserved to be the sachem of a more numerous and prosperous tribe. He related to me with great coolness and frankness, the poverty and distress of his nation; and with the method of a philosopher, predicted the certain and rapid extinction of his tribe, which he had not the power to avert. Poor, noble chief; who was equal to,

*See footnote on p. 9.

and worthy of a greater empire! He sat upon the deck of the steamer, overlooking the little cluster of his wigwams mingled amongst the trees; and . . . shed tears as he was descanting on the poverty of his ill-fated little community, which he told me "had once been powerful and happy; that the buffaloes which the Great Spirit had given them for food, and which formerly spread all over their green prairies, had all been killed or driven out by the approach of white men, who wanted their skins; that their country was now entirely destitute of game, and even of roots for their food, as it was one continued prairie; and that his young men penetrating the countries of their enemies for buffaloes, which they were obliged to do, were cut to pieces and destroyed in great numbers. That his people had foolishly become fond of *fire-water* (whiskey), and had given away everything in their country for it—that it had destroyed many of his warriors, and soon would destroy the rest—that his tribe was too small, and his warriors too few to go to war with the tribes around them; that they were met and killed by the Sioux on the North, by the Pawnees on the West; and by the Osages and Konzas on the South; and still more alarmed from the constant advance of the pale faces—their enemies from the East, with whiskey and small-pox, which already had destroyed four-fifths of his tribe, and soon would impoverish, and at last destroy the remainder of them."

In this way did this shrewd philosopher lament over the unlucky destiny of his tribe; and I pitied him with all my heart. I have no doubt of the correctness of his representations; and I believe there is no tribe on the frontier more in want, nor any more deserving of the sympathy and charity of the government and Christian societies of the civilized world.

The son of this chief, a youth of eighteen years, and whose portrait I painted, distinguished himself in a singular manner the day before our steamer reached their village, by taking to him *four wives in one day!* This extraordinary and unprecedented freak of his, was just the thing to make him the greatest sort of *medicine* in the eyes of his people; and probably he may date much of his success and greatness through life, to this bold and original step, which suddenly raised him into notice and importance.

The old chief Shoo-de-ga-cha, of whom I have spoken above, considering his son to have arrived to the age of maturity, fitted him out for house-keeping, by giving him a handsome wigwam to live in, and nine horses, with many other valuable presents; when the boy, whose name is Hongs-kay-de (the great chief), soon laid his plans for the proud and pleasant epoch in his life, and consummated them in the following ingenious and amusing manner.

Wishing to connect himself with, and consequently to secure the countenance of some of the most influential men in the tribe, he had held an interview with one of the most distinguished; and easily (being the son of a chief), made an arrangement for the hand of his daughter, which he was to receive on a certain day, and at a certain hour, for which he was to give two horses, a gun, and several pounds of tobacco. This was enjoined on the father as a profound secret, and as a condition of the espousal. In like manner he soon made similar arrangements with three other leading men of the tribe, each of whom had a young and beautiful daughter, of marriageable age. To each of the fathers he had promised two horses, and other presents similar to those stipulated for in the first instance, and all under the same injunctions of secresy, until the hour approached, when he had announced to the whole tribe that he was to be married. At the time appointed, they all assembled, and all were in ignorance of the fair hand that was to be placed in his on this occasion. He had got some of his young friends who were prepared to assist him, to lead up the eight horses. He took two of them by the halters, and the other presents agreed upon in his other hand, and advancing to the first of the parents, whose daughter was standing by the side of him, saying to him, "you promised me the hand of your daughter on this day, for which I was to give you two horses." The father assented with a "ugh!" receiving the presents, and giving his child; when some confusion ensued from the simultaneous remonstrances, which were suddenly made by the other three parents, who had brought their daughters forward, and were shocked at this sudden disappointment, as well as by the mutual declarations they were making, of similar contracts that each one had entered into with him! As soon as they could be pacified, and silence was restored, he exultingly replied, "You have all acknowledged in public your promises with me, which I shall expect you to fulfil. I am here to perform all the engagements which I have made, and I expect you all to do the same"—No more was said. He led up the two horses for each, and delivered the other presents; leading off to his wigwam his four brides—taking two in each hand, and commenced at once upon his new mode of life; reserving only one of his horses for his own daily use.

I visited the wigwam of this young installed *medicine-man* several times, and saw his four modest little wives seated around the fire, where all seemed to harmonize very well; and for aught I could discover, were entering very happily on the duties and pleasures of married life . . . The ages of these young brides were probably all between twelve and fifteen years, the season of life in which most of the girls in this wild country contract marriage.

It is a surprising fact, that women mature in these regions at that early age, and there have been some instances where marriage has taken place, even at eleven; and the juvenile mother has been blest with her first offspring at the age of twelve!

These facts are calculated to create surprise and almost incredulity in the mind of the reader, but there are circumstances for his consideration yet to be known, which will in a manner account for these extraordinary facts.

There is not a doubt but there is a more early approach to maturity amongst the females of this country than in civilized communities, owing either to a natural and constitutional difference, or to the exposed and active life they lead. Yet there is another and more general cause of early marriages (and consequently apparent maturity), which arises out of the modes and forms of the country, where most of the marriages are contracted with the parents, hurried on by the impatience of the applicant, and prematurely accepted and consummated on the part of the parents, who are often impatient to be in receipt of the presents they are to receive as the price of their daughters. There is also the facility of dissolving the marriage contract in this country, which does away with one of the most serious difficulties which lies in the way in the civilized world, and calculated greatly to retard its consummation, which is not an equal objection in Indian communities. Education and accomplishments, again, in the fashionable world, and also a time and a season to flourish and show them off, necessarily engross that part of a young lady's life, when the poor Indian girl, who finds herself weaned from the familiar embrace of her parents, with her mind and her body maturing, and her thoughts and her passions straying away in the world for some theme or some pleasure to cling to, easily follows their juvenile and ardent dictates, prematurely entering on that system of life, consisting in reciprocal dependence and protection.

In the instance above described, the young man was in no way censured by his people, but most loudly applauded; for in this country polygamy is allowed; and in this tribe, where there are two or three times the number of women that there are of men, such an arrangement answers a good purpose, whereby so many of the females are provided for and taken care of; and particularly so, and to the great satisfaction of the tribe, as well as of the parties and families concerned, when so many fall to the lot of a chief, or the son of a chief, into whose wigwam it is considered an honour to be adopted, and where they are the most sure of protection.

LETTER—NO. 27.

◄───────►

Mouth of Teton River, Upper Missouri.

When we were about to start on our way up the river from the village of the Puncahs, we found that they were packing up all their goods and preparing to start for the prairies, farther to the West, in pursuit of buffaloes, to dry meat for their winter's supplies. They took down their wigwams of skins to carry with them, and all were flat to the ground and everything packing up ready for the start. My attention was directed by Major Sanford, the Indian Agent, to one of the most miserable and helpless looking objects that I ever had seen in my life, a very aged and emaciated man of the tribe, who he told me was to be *exposed*.

The tribe were going where hunger and dire necessity compelled them to go, and this pitiable object, who had once been a chief, and a man of distinction in his tribe, who was now too old to travel, being reduced to mere skin and bones, was to be left to starve, or meet with such death as might fall to his lot, and his bones to be picked by the wolves! I lingered around this poor old forsaken patriarch for hours before we started, to indulge the tears of sympathy which were flowing for the sake of this poor benighted and decrepit old man, whose worn-out limbs were no longer able to support him; their kind and faithful offices having long since been performed, and his body and his mind doomed to linger into the withering agony of decay, and gradual solitary death. I wept, and it was a pleasure to weep, for the painful looks, and the dreary prospects of this old veteran, whose eyes were dimmed, whose venerable locks were whitened by an hundred years, whose limbs were almost naked, and trembling as he sat by a small fire which his

friends had left him, with a few sticks of wood within his reach and
a buffalo's skin stretched upon some crotches over his head. Such
was to be his only dwelling, and such the chances for his life, with
only a few half-picked bones that were laid within his reach, and a
dish of water, without weapons or means of any kind to replenish
them, or strength to move his body from its fatal locality. In this sad
plight I mournfully contemplated this miserable remnant of existence, who had unluckily outlived the fates and accidents of wars to
die alone, at death's leisure. His friends and his children had all left
him, and were preparing in a little time to be on the march. He had
told them to leave him, "he was old," he said, "and too feeble to
march." "My children," said he, "our nation is poor, and it is
necessary that you should all go to the country where you can get
meat,—my eyes are dimmed and my strength is no more; my days
are nearly all numbered, and I am a burthen to my children—I
cannot go, and I wish to die. Keep your hearts stout, and think not
of me; I am no longer good for anything." In this way they had
finished the ceremony of *exposing* him, and taken their final leave of
him. I advanced to the old man, and was undoubtedly the last
human being who held converse with him. I sat by the side of him,
and though he could not distinctly see me, he shook me heartily by
the hand and smiled, evidently aware that I was a white man, and
that I sympathized with his inevitable misfortune. I shook hands
again with him, and left him, steering my course towards the steamer
which was a mile or more from me, and ready to resume her voyage
up the Missouri.*

This cruel custom of exposing their aged people, belongs, I think,
to all the tribes who roam about the prairies, making severe marches,
when such decrepit persons are totally unable to go, unable to ride
or to walk,—when they have no means of carrying them. It often
becomes absolutely necessary in such cases that they should be left;

*When passing by the site of the Puncah village a few months after this, in my
canoe, I went ashore with my men, and found the poles and the buffalo skin,
standing as they were left, over the old man's head. The firebrands were lying nearly
as I had left them, and I found at a few yards distant the skull, and others of his
bones, which had been picked and cleaned by the wolves; which is probably all that
any human being can ever know of his final and melancholy fate.

and they uniformly insist upon it, saying as this old man did, that they are old and of no further use—that they left their fathers in the same manner—that they wish to die, and their children must not mourn for them.

From the Puncah village, our steamer made regular progress from day to day towards the mouth of the Teton, from where I am now writing; passing the whole way a country of green fields, that come sloping down to the river on either side, forming the loveliest scenes in the world.

From day to day we advanced, opening our eyes to something new and more beautiful every hour that we progressed, until at last our boat was aground; and a day's work of sounding told us at last, that there was no possibility of advancing further, until there should be a rise in the river, to enable the boat to get over the bar. After laying in the middle of the river about a week, in this unpromising dilemma, Mr. Chouteau started off twenty men on foot, to cross the plains for a distance of 200 miles to Laidlaw's Fort, at the mouth of Teton river. To this expedition, I immediately attached myself; and having heard that a numerous party of Sioux were there encamped, and waiting to see the steamer, I packed on the backs, and in the hands of several of the men, such articles for painting, as I might want; canvass, paints, and brushes, with my sketch-book slung on my back, and my rifle in my hand, and I started off with them.

We took leave of our friends on the boat, and mounting the green bluffs, steered our course from day to day over a level prairie, without a tree or a bush in sight, to relieve the painful monotony, filling our canteens at the occasional little streams that we passed, kindling our fires with dried buffalo dung, which we collected on the prairie, and stretching our tired limbs on the level turf whenever we were overtaken by night.

We were six or seven days in performing this march; and it gave me a good opportunity of testing the muscles of my legs, with a number of half-breeds and Frenchmen, whose lives are mostly spent in this way, leading a novice, a cruel, and almost killing journey. Every rod of our way was over a continuous prairie, with a verdant green turf of wild grass of six or eight inches in height; and most of the way enamelled with wild flowers, and filled with a profusion of strawberries.

For two or three of the first days, the scenery was monotonous, and became exceedingly painful from the fact, that we were (to use a phrase of the country) "out of sight of land," *i.e.* out of sight of anything rising above the horizon, which was a perfect straight line around us, like that of the blue and boundless ocean. The pedestrian over such a discouraging sea of green, without a landmark before or behind him; without a beacon to lead him on, or define his progress, feels weak and overcome when night falls; and he stretches his exhausted limbs, apparently on the same spot where he has slept the night before, with the same prospect before and behind him; the same grass, and the same wild flowers beneath and about him; the same canopy over his head, and the same cheerless sea of green to start upon in the morning. It is difficult to describe the simple beauty and serenity of these scenes of solitude, or the feelings of feeble man, whose limbs are toiling to carry him through them—without a hill or tree to mark his progress, and convince him that he is not, like a squirrel in his cage, after all his toil, standing still. One commences on peregrinations like these, with a light heart, and a nimble foot, and spirits as buoyant as the very air that floats along by the side of him; but his spirit soon tires, and he lags on the way that is rendered more tedious and intolarable by the tantalizing *mirage* that opens before him beautiful lakes, and lawns, and copses; of by the *looming* of the prairie ahead of him, that seems to rise in a parapet, and decked with its varied flowers, phantom-like, flies and moves along before him.

I got on for a couple of days in tolerable condition, and with some considerable applause; but my half-bred companions took the lead at length, and left me with several other novices far behind, which gave me additional pangs; and I at length felt like giving up the journey, and throwing myself upon the ground in hopeless despair. I was not alone in my misery, however, but was cheered and encouraged by looking back and beholding several of our party half a mile or more in the rear of me, jogging along, and suffering more agony in their new experiment than I was suffering myself. Their loitering and my murmurs, at length, brought our leaders to a halt, and we held a sort of council, in which I explained that the pain in my feet was so intolerable, that I felt as if I could go no further; when one of our half-breed leaders stepped up to me, and addressing me in French, told me that I must "*turn my toes in*" as the Indians do, and that I could then go on very well. We halted a half-hour, and took a little refreshment, whilst the little Frenchman was teaching his lesson to the rest of my fellow-novices, when we took up our march again; and I soon found upon trial, that by turning my toes in, my feet went more easily through the grass; and by turning the weight of my body more equally on the toes (enabling each one to support its propor-tionable part of the load, instead of throwing it all on to the joints of the big toes, which is done when the toes are turned out); I soon got relief, and made my onward progress very well. I rigidly adhered to this mode, and found no difficulty on the third and fourth days, of taking the lead of the whole party, which I constantly led until our journey was completed.*

On this journey we saw immense herds of buffaloes; and although we had no horses to *run* them, we successfully *approached* them on foot, and supplied ourselves abundantly with fresh meat. After trav-elling for several days, we came in sight of a high range of blue hills in distance on our left, which rose to the height of several hundred feet above the level of the prairies. These hills were a conspicuous landmark at last, and some relief to us. I was told by our guide, that they were called the Bijou Hills, from a Fur Trader of that name, who had had his trading-house at the foot of them on the banks of the Missouri river, where he was at last destroyed by the Sioux Indians.

Not many miles back of this range of hills, we came in contact with an immense saline, or "salt meadow," as they are termed in this country, which turned us out of our path, and compelled us to travel

*On this march we were all travelling in moccasins, which being made without any soles, according to the Indian custom, had but little support for the foot underneath; and consequently, soon subjected us to excruciating pain, whilst walking according to the civilized mode, with the toes turned out. From this very painful experience I learned to my complete satisfaction, that man in a state of nature who walks on his naked feet, *must* walk with his toes turned in, that each may perform the duties assigned to it in proportion to its size and strength; and that civilized man *can* walk with his toes turned out if he chooses, if he will use a stiff sole under his feet, and will be content at last to put up with an acquired deformity of the big toe joint, which too many know to be a frequent and painful occurrence.

several miles out of our way, to get by it; we came suddenly upon a great depression of the prairie, which extended for several miles, and as we stood upon its green banks, which were gracefully sloping down, we could overlook some hundreds of acres of the prairie which were covered with an incrustation of salt, that appeared the same as if the ground was everywhere covered with snow.

These scenes, I am told are frequently to be met with in these regions, and certainly present the most singular and startling effect, by the sudden and unexpected contrast between their snow-white appearance, and the green fields that hem them in on all sides. Through each of these meadows there is a meandering small stream which arises from salt springs, throwing out in the spring of the year great quantities of water, which flood over these meadows to the depth of three or four feet; and during the heat of summer, being exposed to the rays of the sun, entirely evaporates, leaving the incrustation of *muriate* on the surface, to the depth of one or two inches. These places are the constant resort of buffaloes, which congregate in thousands about them, to lick up the salt; and on approaching the banks of this place we stood amazed at the almost incredible numbers of these animals, which were in sight on the opposite banks, at the distance of a mile or two from us, where they were lying in countless numbers, on the level prairie above, and stretching down by hundreds, to lick at the salt, forming in distance, large masses of black, most pleasingly to contrast with the snow white, and the vivid green, which I have before mentioned . . .

LETTER—NO. 28.

◀——————▶

Mouth of Teton River, Upper Missouri.

Whilst painting the portraits of the chiefs and braves of the Sioux, my painting-room was the continual rendezvous of the worthies of the tribe . . . About one in five or eight was willing to be painted, and the rest thought they would be much more sure of "sleeping quiet in their graves" after they were dead, if their pictures were not made. By this lucky difficulty I got great relief, and easily got through with those who were willing, and at the same time decided by the chiefs to be worthy, of so signal an honour.

After I had done with the chiefs and braves, and proposed to paint a few of the women, I at once got myself into a serious perplexity, being heartily laughed at by the whole tribe, both by men and by women . . . If I was to paint women and children, the sooner I destroyed *their* pictures, the better; for I had represented to them that I wanted their pictures to exhibit to white chiefs, to shew who were the most distinguished and worthy of the Sioux; and their women had never taken scalps, nor did anything better than make fires and dress skins. I was quite awkward in this dilemma, in explaining to them that I wanted the portraits of the women to hang *under* those of their husbands, merely to shew how their women *looked*, and how they *dressed*, without saying any more of them. After some considerable delay of my operations, and much deliberation on the subject, through the village, I succeeded in getting a number of women's portraits, of which the two above introduced are a couple.

The vanity of these men, after they had agreed to be painted was beyond all description, and far surpassing that which is oftentimes immodest enough in civilized society, where the sitter generally leaves the picture, when it is done to speak for, and to take care of, itself; while an Indian often lays down, from morning till night, in front of his portrait, admiring his own beautiful face, and faithfully guarding it from day to day, to save it from accident or harm . . .

I was for a long time at a loss for the true cause of so singular a peculiarity, but at last learned that it was owing to their superstitious notion, that there may be life to a certain extent in the picture; and that if harm or violence be done to it, it may in some mysterious way, affect their health or do them other injury.

After I had been several weeks busily at work with my brush in this village, and pretty well used to the modes of life in these regions . . . it was announced one day, that the steamer which we had left, was coming in the river below . . . All ears were listening; when, at length, we discovered the puffing of her steam; and, at last, heard the thundering of her cannon, which were firing from her deck.

The excitement and dismay caused amongst 6000 of these wild people, when the steamer came up in front of their village, was amusing in the extreme. The steamer was moored at the shore, however . . . and the whole village gathered in front of the boat, without showing much further amazement, or even curiosity about it.

The steamer rested a week or two at this place before she started on her voyage for the head-waters of the Missouri; during which time, there was much hilarity and mirth indulged in amongst the Indians, as well as with the hands employed in the service of the Fur Company. The appearance of a steamer in this wild country was deemed a wonderful occurrence, and the time of her presence here, looked upon, and used as a holiday. Some sharp encounters amongst the trappers, who come in here from the mountains, loaded with packs of furs, with sinews hardened by long exposure, and seemingly impatient for a *fight*, which is soon given them by some bullying fisticuff-fellow, who steps forward and settles the matter in a ring, which is made and strictly preserved for *fair play*, until hard raps, and bloody noses, and blind eyes "*settle the hash*," and satisfy his trappership to lay in bed a week or two, and then graduate, a sober and a civil man.

Amongst the Indians we have had numerous sights and amusements to entertain and some to shock us. Shows of dances—ball-plays—horse-racing—foot-racing, and wrestling in abundance. Feasting—fasting, and prayers we have also had; and penance and tortures, and almost every thing short of self-immolation.

Some few days after the steamer had arrived, it was announced that a grand feast was to be given to the *great white chiefs*, who were visitors amongst them; and preparations were made accordingly for it. The two chiefs, Ha-wan-je-tah and Tchan-dee, of whom I have before spoken, brought their two tents together, forming the two into a semi-circle, enclosing a space sufficiently large to accommodate 150 men; and sat down with that number of the principal chiefs and warriors of the Sioux nation; with Mr. Chouteau, Major Sanford, the Indian agent, Mr. M'Kenzie, and myself, whom they had invited in due time, and placed on elevated seats in the centre of the crescent; while the rest of the company all sat upon the ground, and mostly cross-legged, preparatory to the feast being dealt out.

In the centre of the semi-circle was erected a flag-staff, on which was waving a white flag, and to which also was tied the calumet, both expressive of their friendly feelings towards us. Near the foot of the flag-staff were placed in a row on the ground, six or eight kettles, with iron covers on them, shutting them tight, in which were prepared the viands for our *voluptuous* feast. Near the kettles, and on the ground also, bottomside upwards, were a number of wooden bowls, in which the meat was to be served out. And in front, two or three men, who were there placed as waiters, to light the pipes for smoking, and also to deal out the food.

In these positions things stood, and all sat, with thousands climbing and crowding around, for a peep at the grand pageant; when at length, Ha-wan-je-tah (the one horn), head chief of the nation, rose in front of the Indian agent, in a very handsome costume, and addressed him thus:—"My father, I am glad to see you here to-day—my heart is always glad to see my father when he comes—our Great Father, who sends him here is very rich, and we are poor. Our friend Mr. M'Kenzie, who is here, we are also glad to see; we know him well, and we shall be sorry when he is gone. Our friend who is on your right-hand we all know is very rich; and we have heard that he owns the great *medicine-canoe*; he is a good man, and a friend to the red men. Our friend the *White Medicine*, who sits with you, we did not know—he came amongst us a stranger, and he has made me very well—all the women know it, and think it very good; he has done many curious things, and we have all been pleased with him—he has made us much amusement—and we know he is great medicine.

"My father, I hope you will have pity on us, we are very poor—we offer you to-day, not the best that we have got; for we have a plenty of good buffalo hump and marrow—but we give you our hearts in this feast—we have killed our faithful dogs to feed you—and the Great Spirit will seal our friendship. I have no more to say."

After these words he took off his beautiful war-eagle head-dress—his shirt and leggings—his necklace of grizzly bears' claws and his moccasins; and tying them together, laid them gracefully down at the feet of the agent as a present; and laying a handsome pipe on top of them, he walked around into an adjoining lodge, where he got a buffalo robe to cover his shoulders, and returned to the feast, taking his seat which he had before occupied.

Major Sanford then rose and made a short speech in reply, thanking him for the valuable present which he had made him, and for the very polite and impressive manner in which it had been done; and sent to the steamer for a quantity of tobacco and other presents, which were given to him in return. After this, and after several others of the chiefs had addressed him in a similar manner; and, like the first, disrobed themselves, and thrown their beautiful costumes at his feet, one of the three men in front deliberately lit a handsome pipe, and brought it to Ha-wan-je-tah to smoke. He took it, and after presenting the stem to the North—to the South—to the East, and the West—and then to the Sun that was over his head, and pronounced the words "How—how—how!" drew a whiff or two of smoke through it, and holding the bowl of it in one hand, and its stem in the other, he then held it to each of our mouths, as we successively smoked it; after which it was passed around through the whole group, who all smoked through it, or as far as its contents lasted, when another of the three waiters was ready with a second, and at length a third one, in the same way, which lasted through the hands of the whole number of guests. This smoking was conducted with the strictest adherence to exact and established form, and the feast the whole way, to the most positive silence. After the pipe is charged, and is being lit, until the time that the chief has drawn the smoke through it, it is considered an evil omen for any one to speak; and if any one break silence in that time, even in a whisper, the pipe is instantly dropped by the chief, and their superstition is such, that they would not dare to use it on this occasion; but another one is called for and used in its stead. If there is no accident of the kind during the smoking, the waiters then proceed to distribute the meat, which is soon devoured in the feast.

In this case the lids were raised from the kettles, which were all filled with dogs' meat alone. It being well-cooked, and made into a sort of a stew, sent forth a very savoury and pleasing smell, promising to be an acceptable and palatable food. Each of us civilized guests had a large wooden bowl placed before us, with a huge quantity of dogs' flesh floating in a profusion of soup, or rich gravy, with a large spoon resting in the dish, made of the buffalo's horn. In this most difficult and painful dilemma we sat; all of us knowing the solemnity and good feeling in which it was given, and the absolute necessity of falling to, and devouring a little of it. We all tasted it a few times, and resigned our dishes, which were quite willingly taken, and passed around with others, to every part of the group, who all ate heartily of the *delicious viands*, which were soon dipped out of the kettles, and entirely devoured; after which each one arose as he felt disposed, and walked off without uttering a word. In this way the feast ended, and all retired silently, and gradually, until the ground was left vacant to the charge of the waiters or officers, who seemed to have charge of it during the whole occasion.

This feast was unquestionably given to us, as the most undoubted evidence they could give us of their friendship; and we, who knew the spirit and feeling in which it was given, could not but treat it respectfully, and receive it as a very high and marked compliment.

Since I witnessed it on this occasion, I have been honoured with numerous entertainments of the kind amongst the other tribes, which I have visited towards the sources of the Missouri, and all conducted in the same solemn and impressive manner; from which I feel authorized to pronounce the *dog-feast* a truly religious ceremony, wherein the poor Indian sees fit to sacrifice his faithful companion to bear testimony to the sacredness of his vows of friendship, and invite his friend to partake of its flesh, to remind him forcibly of the reality of the sacrifice, and the solemnity of his professions.

The dog, amongst all Indian tribes, is more esteemed and more valued than amongst any part of the civilized world; the Indian who has more time to devote to his company, and whose untutored mind more nearly assimilates to that of his faithful servant, keeps him closer company, and draws him nearer to his heart; they hunt together, and are equal sharers in the chase—their bed is one; and on the rocks, and on their coats of arms they carve his image as the symbol of fidelity. Yet, with all of these he will end his affection with this faithful follower, and with tears in his eyes, offer him as a sacrifice to seal the pledge he has made to man; because a feast of venison, or of buffalo meat, is what is due to every one who enters an Indian's wigwam; and of course, conveys but a passive or neutral evidence, that generally goes for nothing.

I have sat at many of these feasts, and never could but appreciate the moral and solemnity of them. I have seen the master take from the bowl the head of his victim, and descant on its former affection and fidelity with tears in his eyes. And I have seen guests at the same time by the side of me, jesting and sneering at the poor Indian's folly and stupidity; and I have said in my heart, that they never deserved a name so good or so honourable as that of the poor animal whose bones they were picking.

At the feast which I have been above describing, each of us tasted a little of the meat, and passed the dishes on to the Indians, who soon demolished everything they contained. We all agreed that the meat was well cooked, and seemed to be a well-flavoured and palatable food; and no doubt, could have been eaten with a good relish, if we had been hungry, and ignorant of the nature of the food we were eating.

The flesh of these dogs, though apparently relished by the Indians, is, undoubtedly, inferior to the venison and buffalo's meat, of which feasts are constantly made where friends are invited, as they are in civilized society, to a pleasant and convivial party; from which fact alone, it would seem clear, that they have some extraordinary motive, at all events, for feasting on the flesh of that useful and faithful animal; even when, as in the instance I have been describing, their village is well supplied with fresh and dried meat of the buffalo. The dog-feast is given, I believe, by all tribes in North America; and by them all, I think, this faithful animal, as well as the horse, is sacrificed in several different ways, to appease offended Spirits or Deities, whom it is considered necessary that they should conciliate in this way; and when done, is invariably done by giving the best in the herd or the kennel.

Mouth of Teton River, Upper Missouri.

*A*nother curious and disgusting scene I witnessed in the after part of the day on which we were honoured with the dog-feast. In this I took no part, but was sufficiently near to it, when standing some rods off, and witnessing the cruel operation. I was called upon by one of the clerks in the Establishment to ride up a mile or so, near the banks of the Teton River, in a little plain at the base of the bluffs, where were grouped some fifteen or twenty lodges of the Ting-ta-to-ah band, to see a man (as they said) *"looking at the sun!"* We found him naked, except his breech-cloth, with splints or skewers run through the flesh on both breasts, leaning back and hanging with the weight of his body to the top of a pole which was fastened in the ground, and to the upper end of which he was fastened by a cord which was tied to the splints. In this position he was leaning back, with nearly the whole weight of his body hanging to the pole, the top of which was bent forward, allowing his body to sink about half-way to the ground. His feet were still upon the ground, supporting a small part of his weight; and he held in his left hand his favourite bow, and in his right, with a desperate grip, his medicine-bag. In this condition, with the blood trickling down over his body, which was covered with white and yellow clay, and amidst a great crowd who were looking on, sympathizing with and encouraging him, he was hanging and "looking at the sun," without paying the least attention to any one about him. In the group that was reclining around him, were several mystery-men beating their drums and shaking their rattles, and singing as loud as they could yell, to encourage him and strengthen his heart to stand and look at the sun, from its rising in the morning 'till its setting at night; at which time, if his heart and his strength have not failed him, he is "cut down," receives the liberal donation of presents (which have been thrown into a pile before him during the day), and also the name and the style of a doctor, or *medicine-man* which lasts him, and ensures him respect, through life.

This most extraordinary and cruel custom I never heard of amongst any other tribe, and never saw an instance of it before or after the one I have just named. It is a sort of worship, or penance, of great cruelty; disgusting and painful to behold, with only one palliating circumstance about it, which is, that it is a voluntary torture and of very rare occurrence. The poor and ignorant, misguided and superstitious man who undertakes it, puts his everlasting reputation at stake upon the issue; for when he takes his stand, he expects to face the sun and gradually turn his body in listless silence, till he sees it go down at night; and if he faints and falls, of which there is imminent danger, he loses his reputation as a brave or mystery-man, and suffers a signal disgrace in the estimation of the tribe, like all men who have the presumption to set themselves up for braves or mystery-men, and fail justly to sustain the character.

The Sioux seem to have many modes of worshipping the Great or Good Spirit, and also of conciliating the Evil Spirit: they have numerous fasts and feasts, and many modes of sacrificing, but yet they seem to pay less strict attention to them than the Mandans do, which may perhaps be owing in a great measure to the wandering and predatory modes of life which they pursue, rendering it difficult to adhere so rigidly to the strict form and letter of their customs.

There had been, a few days before I arrived at this place, a great medicine operation held on the prairie, a mile or so back of the Fort, and which, of course, I was not lucky enough to see. The poles were still standing, and the whole transaction was described to me by my friend Mr. Halsey, one of the clerks in the Establishment. From the account given of it, it seems to bear some slight resemblance to that of the *Mandan religious ceremony*, but no nearer to it than a feeble effort by so ignorant and superstitious a people, to copy a custom which they most probably have had no opportunity to see themselves, but have endeavoured to imitate from hearsay. They had an awning of immense size erected on the prairie which is yet standing, made of willow bushes supported by posts, with poles and willow boughs laid over; under the centre of which there was a pile set firmly in the ground, from which many of the young men had suspended their bodies by splints run through the flesh in different parts, the numerous scars of which were yet seen bleeding afresh from day to day, amongst the crowds that were about me . . .

The luxury of smoking is known to all the North American Indians, in their primitive state, and that before they have any knowledge of tobacco; which is only introduced amongst them by civilized adventurers, who teach them the use and luxury of whiskey at the same time.

In their native state they are excessive smokers, and many of them (I would almost venture the assertion), would seem to be smoking one-half of their lives. There may be two good reasons for this, the first of which is, that the idle and leisure life that the Indian leads, (who has no trade or business to follow—no office hours to attend to, or profession to learn), induces him to look for occupation and amusement in so innocent a luxury, which again further tempts him to its excessive use, from its feeble and harmless effects on the system. There are many weeds and leaves, and barks of trees, which are narcotics, and of spontaneous growth in their countries, which the Indians dry and pulverize, and carry in pouches and smoke to great excess—and which in several of the languages, when thus prepared, is called *k'nick k'neck* . . .

The weapons of these people, like their pipes, are numerous, and mostly manufactured by themselves . . . The scalping-knives *a* and *b*, and tomahawks *e e e e* (Illustration 28) are of civilized manufacture, made expressly for Indian use, and carried into the Indian country by thousands and tens of thousands, and sold at an enormous price. The scabbards of the knives and handles for the tomahawks, the Indians construct themselves, according to their own taste, and oftentimes ornament them very handsomely. In his rude and unapproached condition, the Indian is a stranger to such weapons as these—he works not in the metals; and his untutored mind

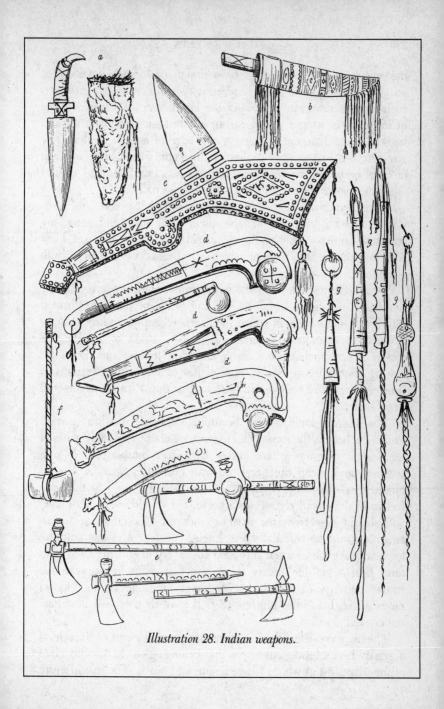

Illustration 28. Indian weapons.

has not been ingenious enough to design or execute anything so *savage* or destructive as these civilized *refinements on Indian barbarity*. In his native simplicity he shapes out his rude hatchet from a piece of stone, as in letter *f*, heads his arrows and spears with flints; and his knife is a sharpened bone, or the edge of a broken silex. The war-club *c* is also another civilized refinement, with a blade of steel, of eight or ten inches in length, and set in a club, studded around and ornamented with some hundreds of brass nails.

Their primitive clubs *d* are curiously carved in wood, and fashioned out with some considerable picturesque form and grace; are admirably fitted to the hand, and calculated to deal a deadly blow with the spike of iron or bone which is imbedded in the ball or bulb at the end.

Two of the tomahawks that I have named, marked *e*, are what are denominated "pipe-tomahawks," as the heads of them are formed into bowls like a pipe, in which their tobacco is put, and they smoke through the handle. These are the most valued of an Indian's weapons, inasmuch as they are a matter of luxury, and useful for cutting his fire-wood, &c. in time of peace; and deadly weapons in time of war, which they use in the hand, or throw with unerring and deadly aim.

The scalping-knife *b* in a beautiful scabbard, which is carried under the belt, is the form of knife most generally used in all parts of the Indian country, where knives have been introduced. It is a common and cheap butcher knife with one edge, manufactured at Sheffield, in England, perhaps, for sixpence; and sold to the poor Indian in these wild regions for a horse. If I should live to get home, and should ever cross the Atlantic with my Collection, a curious enigma would be solved for the English people, who may enquire for a scalping-knife, when they find that every one in my Collection (and hear also, that nearly every one that is to be seen in the Indian country, to the Rocky Mountains and the Pacific Ocean) bears on its blade the impress of G.R., which they will doubtless understand.

The huge two-edged knife, with its scabbard of a part of the skin of a grizzly bear's head, letter *a*, is one belonging to the famous chief of the Mandans, of whom I have before said much. The manufacture of this knife is undoubtedly American; and its shape differs altogether from those which are in general use.*

The above weapons, as well as the bow and lance, of which I have before spoken, are all carried and used on horseback with great effect. The Indians in this country of green fields, all *ride* for their enemies, and also for their game, which is almost invariably killed whilst their horses are at full-speed. They are all cruel masters for their horses; and in war or the chase goad them on with a heavy and cruel whip *g*, the handle of which is generally made of a large prong of the elk's horn or of wood, and the lashes of rawhide are very heavy; being braided, or twisted, or cut into wide straps. These are invariably attached to the wrist of the right arm by a tough thong, so that they can be taken up and used at any moment, and dropped the next, without being lost . . .

As I have introduced the *scalping-knife* above, it may be well for me to give some further account in this place of the custom and the mode of taking the scalp; a custom practiced by all the North American Indians, which is done when an enemy is killed in battle, by grasping the left hand into the hair on the crown of the head, and passing the knife around it through the skin, tearing off a piece of the skin with the hair, as large as the palm of the hand, or larger, which is dried, and often curiously ornamented and preserved, and highly valued as a trophy. The scalping is an operation not calculated of itself to take life, as it only removes the skin, without injuring the bone of the head; and necessarily, to be a genuine scalp, must contain and show the crown or centre of the head; that part of the

*This celebrated knife is now in My INDIAN MUSEUM, and there is no doubt, from its authentic history, that it has been several times plunged to the hearts of his enemies by the hand of Mah-to-toh-pa, who wielded it. Several years after I left that country, and one year after the destruction of the Mandans, I received the following letter from Mr. M'Kenzie, accompanying the knife and other things sent to me by him from that country: EXTRACT—"The poor Mandans are gone, and amongst them your old friend, Mah-to-toh-pa. I have been able to send you but a very few things, as the Riccarees immediately took possession of everything they had. Amongst the articles I have been able to procure, I send you the war-knife of Mah-to-toh-pa, which is now looked upon as the greatest *medicine in this country; and as you will recollect it, it will be highly appreciated by you.*"

skin which lies directly over what the phrenologists call "self-esteem," where the hair divides and radiates from the centre; of which they all profess to be strict judges, and be able to decide whether an effort has been made to produce two or more scalps from one head. Besides taking the scalp, the victor generally, if he has time to do it without endangering his own scalp, cuts off and brings home the rest of the hair, which his wife will divide into a great many small locks, and with them fringe off the seams of his shirt and his leggings, as will have been seen in many of the illustrations; which also are worn as trophies and ornaments to the dress, and then are familiarly called "*scalp-locks.*" Of these there are many dresses in my Collection, which exhibit a continuous row from the top of each shoulder, down the arms to the wrists, and down the seams of the leggings, from the hips to the feet, rendering them a very costly article to buy from the Indian, who is not sure that his success in his military exploits will ever enable him to replace them.

The scalp, then, is a patch of the skin taken from the head of an enemy killed in battle, and preserved and highly appreciated as the record of a death produced by the hand of the individual who possesses it; and may oftentimes during his life, be of great service to a man living in a community where there is no historian to enrol the names of the famous—to record the heroic deeds of the brave, who have gained their laurels in mortal combat with their enemies; where it is as lawful and as glorious to slay an enemy in battle, as it is in Christian communities; and where the poor Indian is bound to keep the record himself, or be liable to lose it and the honour, for no one in the tribe will keep it for him. As the scalp is taken then as the evidence of a death, it will easily be seen, that the Indian has no business or inclination to take it from the head of the living; which I venture to say is never done in North America, unless it be, as it sometimes has happened, where a man falls in the heat of battle, stunned with the blow of a weapon or a gunshot, and the Indian, rushing over his body, snatches off his scalp, supposing him dead, who afterwards rises from the field of battle, and easily recovers from this superficial wound of the knife, wearing a bald spot on his head during the remainder of his life, of which we have frequent occurrences on our Western frontiers. The scalp must be from the head of *an enemy* also, or it subjects its possessor to disgrace and infamy who carries it. There may be many instances where an Indian is justified in the estimation of his tribe in taking the life of one of his own people; and their laws are such, as oftentimes make it his imperative duty; and yet no circumstances, however aggravating, will justify him or release him from the disgrace of taking the scalp.

There is no custom practised by the Indians, for which they are more universally condemned, than that of taking the scalp; and, at the same time, I think there is some excuse for them, inasmuch as it is a general custom of the country, and founded, like many other apparently absurd and ridiculous customs of these people, in one of the necessities of Indian life, which necessities we are free from in the civilized world, and which customs, of course, we need not and do not practice. From an ancient custom, "time out of mind," the warriors of these tribes have been in the habit of going to war, expecting to take the scalps of their enemies whom they may slay in battle, and all eyes of the tribe are upon them, making it their duty to do it; so from custom it is every man's right, and his duty also, to continue and keep up a regulation of his society, which it is not in his power as an individual, to abolish or correct, if he saw fit to do it.

One of the principal denunciations against the custom of taking the scalp, is on account of its alleged *cruelty*, which it certainly has not; as the cruelty would be in the *killing*, and not in the act of cutting the skin from a man's head after he is dead. To say the most of it, it is a disgusting custom, and I wish I could be quite sure that the civilized and Christian world (who kill hundreds, to where the poor Indians kill one), do not often treat their *enemies dead*, in equally as indecent and disgusting a manner, as the Indian does by taking the scalp.

If the reader thinks that I am taking too much pains to defend the Indians for this, and others of their seemingly abominable customs, he will bear it in mind, that I have lived with these people, until I have learned the necessities of Indian life in which these customs are founded; and also, that I have met with so many acts of kindness and hospitality at the hands of the poor Indian, that I feel bound, when I can do it, to render what excuse I can for a people, who are dying with broken hearts, and never can speak in the civilized world in their own defence.

And even yet, reader, if your education, and your reading of Indian cruelties and Indian barbarities—of scalps, and scalping-knives, and scalping, should have ossified a corner of your heart against these unfortunate people, and would shut out their advocate, I will annoy you no longer on this subject, but withdraw, and leave you to cherish the very beautiful, humane and parental moral that was carried out by the United States and British Governments during the last, and the revolutionary wars, when they mutually employed thousands of their *"Red children,"* to aid and to bleed, in fighting their battles, and paid them, according to contract, so many pounds, shillings and pence or so many dollars and cents for every *"scalp"* of a "red" or a "blue coat" they could bring in!

. . . The most usual way of preparing and dressing the scalp is that of stretching it on a little hoop at the end of a stick two or three feet long (letter *a*), for the purpose of "dancing it," as they term it; which will be described in the *scalp-dance*, in a few moments. There are many again, which are small, and not "dressed;" sometimes not larger than a crown piece (letter *c*), and hung to different parts of the dress. In public shows and parades, they are often suspended from the bridle bits or halter when they are paraded and carried as trophies (letter *b*). Sometimes they are cut out, as it were into a string, the hair forming a beautiful fringe to line the handle of a war-club (letter *e*). Sometimes they are hung at the *end* of a club (letter *d*), and at other times, by the order of the chief, are hung out, over the wigwams, suspended from a pole, which is called the *"scalp-pole."* This is often done by the chief of a village, on a pleasant day, by his erecting over his wigwam a pole with all the scalps that he had taken, arranged upon it (letter *f*); at the sight of which all the chiefs and warriors of the tribe, who had taken scalps, "follow suit;" enabling every member of the community to stroll about the village on that day and "count scalps," learning thereby the standing of every warrior, which is decided in a great degree by the number of scalps they have taken in battles with their enemies . . .

So much for scalps and scalping, of which I shall yet say more, unless I should unluckily *lose one* before I get out of the country.

◄━━━━━━━━━━━━━━━━━━━━━━━━►

Mouth of Teton River, Upper Missouri.

*T*he Sioux *shield* is made of the skin of the buffalo's neck,
. . . hardened with the glue extracted from the hoofs and
joints of the same animal. The process of *"smoking the shield"* is a
very curious, as well as an important one, in their estimation. For
this purpose a young man about to construct him a shield, digs a
hole of two feet in depth, in the ground, and as large in diameter as
he designs to make his shield. In this he builds a fire, and over it, a
few inches higher than the ground, he stretches the raw hide hori-
zontally over the fire, with little pegs driven through holes made near
the edges of the skin. This skin is at first, twice as large as the size of
the required shield; but having got his particular and best friends
(who are invited on the occasion,) into a ring, to dance and sing
around it, and solicit the Great Spirit to instil into it the power to
protect him harmless against his enemies, he spreads over it the
glue, which is rubbed and dried in, as the skin is heated; and a
second busily drives other and other pegs, inside of those in the
ground, as they are gradually giving way and being pulled up by the
contraction of the skin. By this curious process, which is most
dexterously done, the skin is kept tight whilst it contracts to one-half
of its size, taking up the glue and increasing in thickness until it is
rendered as thick and hard as required (and his friends have pleaded
long enough to make it arrow, and almost ball proof), when the
dance ceases, and the fire is put out. When it is cooled and cut into
the shape that he desires, it is often painted with his *medicine* or
totem upon it, the figure of an eagle, an owl, a buffalo or other
animal, as the case may be, which he trusts will guard and protect

him from harm; it is then fringed with eagles' quills, or other ornaments he may have chosen, and *slung* with a broad leather strap that crosses his breast. These shields are carried by all the warriors in these regions, for their protection in battles, which are almost invariably fought from their horses' backs . . .

The *musical instruments* used amongst these people are few, and exceedingly rude and imperfect, consisting chiefly of rattles, drums, whistles, and lutes, all of which are used in the different tribes . . .

Dancing is one of the principal and most frequent amusements of all the tribes of Indians in America; and, in all of these, both vocal and instrumental music are introduced. These dances consist in about four different steps, which constitute all the different varieties: but the figures and forms of these scenes are very numerous, and produced by the most violent jumps and contortions, accompanied with the song and beats of the drum, which are given in exact time with their motions. It has been said by some travellers, that the Indian has neither harmony or melody in his music, but I am unwilling to subscribe to such an assertion; although I grant, that for the most part of their vocal exercises, there is a total absence of what the musical world would call melody; their songs being made up chiefly of a sort of violent chaunt of harsh and jarring gutturals, of yelps and barks, and screams, which are given out in perfect time, not only with "method (but with harmony) in their madness." There are times too, as every traveller of the Indian country will attest, if he will recall them to his recollection, when the Indian lays down by his fire-side with his drum in his hand, which he lightly and almost imperceptibly touches over, as he accompanies it with his stifled voice of dulcet sounds that might come from the most tender and delicate female.

These quiet and tender songs are very different from those which are sung at their dances, in full chorus and violent gesticulation; and many of them seem to be quite rich in plaintive expression and melody, though barren of change and variety.

Dancing, I have before said, is one of the principal and most valued amusements of the Indians, and much more frequently prac- tised by them than by any civilized society; inasmuch as it enters into their forms of worship, and is often their mode of appealing to the

Great Spirit—of paying their usual devotions to their *medicine*—and of honouring and entertaining strangers of distinction in their country.

Instead of the "giddy maze" of the quadrille or the country dance, enlivened by the cheering smiles and graces of silkened beauty, the Indian performs his rounds with jumps, and starts, and yells, much to the satisfaction of his own exclusive self, and infinite amusement of the gentler sex, who are always lookers on, but seldom allowed so great a pleasure, or so signal an honour, as that of joining with their lords in this or any other entertainment. Whilst staying with these people on my way up the river, I was repeatedly honoured with the dance, and I as often hired them to give them, or went to overlook where they were performing them at their own pleasure, in pursuance of their peculiar customs, or for their own amusement, that I might study and correctly herald them to future ages. I saw so many of their different varieties of dances amongst the Sioux, that I should almost be disposed to denominate them the *"dancing Indians."* It would actually seem as if they had dances for every thing. And in so large a village, there was scarcely an hour in any day or night, but what the beat of the drum could somewhere be heard. These dances are almost as various and different in their character as they are numerous—some of them so exceedingly grotesque and laughable, as to keep the bystanders in an irresistible roar of laughter—others are calculated to excite his pity, and forcibly appeal to his sympathies, whilst others disgust, and yet others terrify and alarm him with their frightful threats and contortions.

All the world have heard of the *"bear-dance,"* though I doubt whether more than a very small proportion have ever seen it. The Sioux, like all the others of these western tribes, are fond of bear's meat, and must have good stores of the "bear's-grease" laid in, to oil their long and glossy locks, as well as the surface of their bodies. And they all like the fine pleasure of a bear hunt, and also a participation in the bear dance, which is given several days in succession, previous to their starting out, and in which they all join in a song to the *Bear Spirit;* which they think holds somewhere an invisible existence, and must be consulted and conciliated before they can enter upon their excursion with any prospect of success. For this grotesque and amusing scene, one of the chief medicine-men, placed over his body the entire skin of a bear, with a war-eagle's quill on his head, taking the lead in the dance, and looking through the skin which formed a masque that hung over his face. Many others in the dance wore masques on their faces, made of the skin from the bear's head; and all, with the motions of their hands, closely imitated the movements of that animal; some representing its motion in running, and others the peculiar attitude and hanging of the paws, when it is sitting up on its hind feet, and looking out for the approach of an enemy. This grotesque and amusing masquerade oftentimes is continued at intervals, for several days previous to the starting of a party on the bear hunt, who would scarcely count upon a tolerable prospect of success, without a strict adherence to this most important and indispensible form!

Dancing is done here too, as it is oftentimes done in the enlightened world, to get favours—to buy the world's goods; and in both countries danced with about equal merit, except that the Indian has surpassed us in honesty by christening it in his own country, the *"beggar's dance."* This spirited dance was given, not by a set of *beggars* though, literally speaking, but by the first and most independent young men in the tribe, beautifully dressed, (*i.e.* not dressed at all, except with their breech clouts or *kelts*, made of eagles' and ravens' quills,) with their lances, and pipes, and rattles in their hands, and a medicine-man beating the drum, and joining in the song at the highest key of his voice. In this dance every one sings as loud as he can halloo; uniting his voice with the others, in an appeal to the Great Spirit, to open the hearts of the bystanders to give to the poor, and not to themselves; assuring them that the Great Spirit will be kind to those who are kind to the helpless and poor . . .

The *Scalp-dance* is given as a celebration of a victory; and amongst this tribe . . . danced in the night, by the light of their torches, and just before retiring to bed. When a war party returns from a war excursion, bringing home with them the scalps of their enemies, they generally "dance them" for fifteen nights in succession vaunting forth the most extravagant boasts of their wonderful prowess in war, whilst they brandish their war weapons in their hands. A number of young women are selected to aid (though they do not actually join in the dance), by stepping into the centre of the ring, and holding up the scalps that have been recently taken, whilst the warriors dance (or rather *jump*), around in a circle, brandishing their weapons, and barking and yelping in the most frightful manner, all jumping on both feet at a time, with a simultaneous stamp, and blow, and thrust of their weapons; with which it would seem as if they were actually cutting and carving each other to pieces. During these frantic leaps, and yelps, and thrusts, every man distorts his face to the utmost of his muscles, darting about his glaring eye-balls and snapping his teeth, as if he were in the heat (and actually breathing through his inflated nostrils the very hissing death) of battle! No description that can be written, could ever convey more than a feeble outline of the frightful effects of these scenes enacted in the dead and darkness of night, under the glaring light of their blazing flambeaux; nor could all the years allotted to mortal man, in the least obliterate or deface the vivid impress that one scene of this kind would leave upon his memory.

The precise object for which the scalp is taken, is one which is definitely understood, and has already been explained; but the motive (or motives), for which this strict ceremony is so scrupulously held by all the American tribes, over the scalp of an enemy, is a subject, as yet not satisfactorily settled in my mind. There is no doubt, but one great object in these exhibitions is public exultation; yet there are several conclusive evidences, that there are other and essential motives for thus formally and strictly displaying the scalp. Amongst some of the tribes, it is the custom to bury the scalps after they have gone through this series of public exhibitions; which may in a measure have been held for the purpose of giving them notoriety, and of awarding public credit to the persons who obtained them, and now, from a custom of the tribe, are obliged to part with them. The great respect which seems to be paid to them whilst they use them, as well as the pitying and mournful song which they howl to the *manes* of their unfortunate victims; as well as the precise care and solemnity with which they afterwards bury the scalps, sufficiently convince me that they have a superstitious dread of the spirits of their slain enemies, and many conciliatory offices to perform, to ensure their own peace; one of which is the ceremony above described.

. . . Whilst painting my portraits amongst the Sioux . . . I got the portrait of a noble Shienne chief, by the name of Nee-hee-o-eé-woo-tis, the wolf on the hill … The Shiennes are a small tribe of about 3000 in numbers, living neighbours to the Sioux, on the west of them, and between the Black Hills and the Rocky Mountains. There is no finer race of men than these in North America, and none superior in stature, excepting the Osages; scarcely a man in the tribe, full grown, who is less than six feet in height. The Shiennes are undoubtedly the richest in horses of any tribe on the Continent, living in a country as they do, where the greatest herds of wild horses are grazing on the prairies, which they catch in great numbers and vend to the Sioux, Mandans and other tribes, as well as to the Fur Traders.

These people are the most desperate set of horsemen, and warriors also, having carried on almost unceasing wars with the Pawnees and Blackfeet, "time out of mind" …

I painted the portrait of a celebrated warrior of the Sioux, by the name of Mah-to-chee-ga (the little bear), who was unfortunately slain in a few moments after the picture was done, by one of his own tribe; and which was very near costing me my life for having painted a side view of his face, leaving one-half of it out of the picture, which had been the cause of the affray; and supposed by the whole tribe to have been intentionally left out by me, as "good for nothing." This was the last picture that I painted amongst the Sioux, and the last, undoubtedly, that I ever shall paint in that place. So tremendous and so alarming was the excitement about it, that my brushes were instantly put away, and I embarked the next day on the steamer for the sources of the Missouri, and was glad to get underway.

The man who slew this noble warrior was a troublesome fellow of the same tribe, by the name of Shon-ka (the Dog). A "hue and cry" has been on his track for several months; and my life having been repeatedly threatened during my absence up the river, I shall defer telling the whole of this most extraordinary affair, until I see that my own scalp is safe, and I am successfully out of the country. A few weeks or months will decide how many are to fall victims to the vengeance of the relatives of this murdered brave; and if I outlive the affair, I shall certainly give some further account of it.

*   *   *

About four months previous . . . I had passed up the Missouri river by this place, on the steam-boat Yellow Stone, on which I ascended the Missouri to the mouth of Yellow Stone river. While going up, this boat, having on board the United States Indian agent, Major Sanford—Messrs. Pierre Chouteau, McKenzie of the American Fur Company, and myself, as passengers, stopped at this trading-post, and remained several weeks; where were assembled six hundred families of Sioux Indians, their tents being pitched in close order on an extensive prairie on the bank of the river.

This trading-post, in charge of Mr. Laidlaw, is the concentrating place, and principal trading depot, for this powerful tribe, who number, when all taken together, something like forty or fifty thousand. On this occasion, five or six thousand had assembled to see the steam-boat and meet the Indian agent, which, and whom they knew were to arrive about this time. During the few weeks that we remained there, I was busily engaged painting my portraits, for here were assembled the principal chiefs and *medicine-men* of the nation. To these people, the operations of my brush were entirely new and unaccountable, and excited amongst them the greatest curiosity imaginable. Every thing else (even the steam-boat) was abandoned for the pleasure of crowding into my painting-room, and witnessing the result of each fellow's success, as he came out from under the operation of my brush.

They had been at first much afraid of the consequences that might flow from so strange and unaccountable an operation; but having been made to understand my views, they began to look upon it as a great *honour*, and afforded me the opportunities that I desired; exhibiting the utmost degree of vanity for their appearance, both as to features and dress. The consequence was, that my room was filled with the chiefs who sat around, arranged according to the rank or grade which they held in the estimation of their tribe; and in this order it became necessary for me to paint them, to the exclusion of those who never signalized themselves, and were without any distinguishing character in society.

The first man on the list was *Ha-wan-ghee-ta* (one horn), head chief of the nation, of whom I have heretofore spoken; and after him the subordinate chiefs, or chiefs of bands, according to the estimation in which they were held by the chief and the tribe. My models were thus *placed* before me, whether ugly or beautiful, all the same, and I saw at once there was to be trouble somewhere, as I could not paint them all. The medicine-men or high priests, who are esteemed by many the oracles of the nation, and the most important men in it—becoming jealous, commenced their harangues, outside of the lodge, telling them that they were all fools—that those who were painted would soon die in consequence; and that these pictures, which had life to a considerable degree in them, would live in the hands of white men after they were dead, and make them sleepless and endless trouble.

Those whom I had painted, though evidently somewhat alarmed, were unwilling to acknowledge it, and those whom I had not painted, unwilling to be outdone in courage, allowed me the privilege; braving and defying the danger that they were evidently more or less in dread of. Feuds began to arise too, among some of the chiefs of the different bands, who (not unlike some instances amongst the chiefs and warriors of our own country), had looked upon their rival chiefs with unsleeping jealousy, until it had grown into disrespect and enmity. An instance of this kind presented itself at this critical juncture, in this assembly of inflammable spirits, which changed in a moment, its features, from the free and jocular garrulity of an Indian levee, to the frightful yells and agitated treads and starts of an Indian battle! I had in progress at this time a portrait of *Mah-to-tchee-ga* (little bear); of the *Onc-pa-pa band*, a noble fine fellow, who was sitting before me as I was painting. I was painting almost a profile view of his face, throwing a part of it into shadow, and had it nearly finished, when an Indian by the name of *Shon-ka* (the dog), chief of the *Caz-a-zshee-ta* band; an ill-natured and surly man—despised by the chiefs of every other band, entered the wigwam in a sullen mood, and seated himself on the floor in front of my sitter, where he could have a full view of the picture in its operation. After sitting a while with his arms folded, and his lips stiffly arched with contempt; he sneeringly spoke thus:—

"*Mah-to-tchee-ga* is but *half a man*." 　　* 　　* 　　* 　　*

* 　　* 　　Dead silence ensued for a moment, and nought was in motion save the eyes of the chiefs, who were seated around the room, and darting their glances about upon each other in listless anxiety to hear the sequel that was to follow! During this interval, the eyes of

Mah-to-tchee-ga had not moved—his lips became slightly curved, and he pleasantly asked, in low and steady accent, "Who says that?" "*Shon-ka* says it," was the reply; "and *Shon-ka* can prove it." At this the eyes of Mah-to-tchee-ga, which had not yet moved, began steadily to turn, and slow, as if upon pivots, and when they were rolled out of their sockets till they had fixed upon the object of their contempt; his dark and jutting brows were shoving down in trembling contention, with the blazing rays that were actually *burning* with contempt, the object that was before them. "*Why* does Shon-ka say it?"

"Ask *We-chash-a-wa-kon* (the painter), he can tell you; he knows you are but *half a man*—he has painted but one half of your face, and knows the other half is good for nothing!"

"Let the *painter* say it, and I will believe it; but when the Dog says it let him *prove* it."

"*Shon-ka* said it, and *Shon-ka* can prove it; if *Mah-to-tchee-ga* be a man, and wants to be honoured by the white men, let him not be ashamed; but let him do as *Shon-ka* has done, give the white man a horse, and then let him see the *whole of your face* without being ashamed."

"When *Mah-to-tchee-ga* kills a white man and *steals* his horses, he may be ashamed to look at a white man until he brings him a horse! When *Mah-to-tchee-ga* waylays and murders an honourable and a brave Sioux, because he is a coward and not brave enough to meet him in fair combat, *then* he may be ashamed to look at a white man till he has given him a horse! *Mah-to-tchee-ga* can look at any one; and he is now looking at an *old woman* and a *coward*!"

This repartee, which had lasted for a few minutes, to the amusement and excitement of the chiefs, being ended thus:—The Dog rose suddenly from the ground, and wrapping himself in his robe, left the wigwam, considerably agitated, having the laugh of all the chiefs upon him.

The Little Bear had followed him with his piercing eyes until he left the door, and then pleasantly and unmoved, resumed his position, where he sat a few minutes longer, until the portrait was completed. He then rose, and in the most graceful and gentlemanly manner, presented to me a very beautiful shirt of buckskin, richly garnished with quills of the porcupine, fringed with scalp-locks (honourable memorials) from his enemies' heads, and painted, with all his battles emblazoned on it. He then left my wigwam, and a few steps brought him to the door of his own, where the Dog intercepted him, and asked, "What meant *Mah-to-tchee-ga* by the last words that he spoke to *Shon-ka?*" "*Mah-to-tchee-ga* said it, and *Shon-ka* is not a fool—that is enough." At this the Dog walked violently to his own lodge; and the Little Bear retreated into his, both knowing from looks and gestures what was about to be the consequence of their altercation.

The Little Bear instantly charged his gun, and then (as their custom is) threw himself upon his face, in humble supplication to the Great Spirit for his aid and protection. His wife, in the meantime, seeing him agitated, and fearing some evil consequences, without knowing anything of the preliminaries, secretly withdrew the bullet from his gun, and told him not of it.

The Dog's voice, at this moment, was heard, and recognized at the door of Mah-to-tchee-ga's lodge,—"If Mah-to-tchee-ga be a *whole* man, let him come out and prove it; it is *Shon-ka* that calls him!"

His wife screamed; but it was too late. The gun was in his hand, and he sprang out of the door—both drew and simultaneously fired! The Dog fled uninjured; but the Little Bear lay weltering in his blood (strange to say!) with all that side of his face entirely shot away, which had been left out of the picture; and, according to the prediction of the Dog, "*good for nothing;*" carrying away one half of the jaws, and the flesh from the nostrils and corner of the mouth, to the ear, including one eye, and leaving the jugular vein entirely exposed. Here was a "coup;" and any one accustomed to the thrilling excitement that such scenes produce in an Indian village, can form *some* idea of the frightful agitation amidst several thousand Indians, who were divided into jealous bands or clans, under ambitious and rival chiefs! In one minute, a thousand guns and bows were seized! A thousand thrilling yells were raised; and many were the fierce and darting warriors who sallied round the Dog for his protection—he fled amidst a shower of bullets and arrows; but his braves were about him! The blood of the *Onc-pa-pas* was roused, and the indignant braves of that gallant band rushed forth from all quarters, and, swift upon their heels, were hot for vengeance! On the plain, and in full view of us, for some time, the whizzing arrows flew, and so did bullets, until the Dog and his brave followers were lost in distance on the prairie! In this rencontre, the Dog had his left arm broken; but succeeded, at length, in making his escape.

On the next day after this affair took place, the Little Bear died of his wound, and was buried amidst the most pitiful and heart-rending cries of his distracted wife, whose grief was inconsolable at the thought of having been herself the immediate and innocent cause of his death, by depriving him of his supposed protection.

This marvellous and fatal transaction was soon talked through the village, and the eyes of all this superstitious multitude were fixed upon me as the cause of the calamity—my paintings and brushes were instantly packed, and all hands, both Traders and Travellers, assumed at once a posture of defence.

I evaded, no doubt, in a great measure, the concentration of their immediate censure upon me, by expressions of great condolence, and by distributing liberal presents to the wife and relations of the deceased; and by uniting also with Mr. Laidlaw and the other gentlemen, in giving him honourable burial, where we placed over his grave a handsome Sioux lodge, and hung a white flag to wave over it.

On this occasion, many were the tears that were shed for the brave and honourable Mah-to-tchee-ga, and all the warriors of his band swore sleepless vengeance on the Dog, until his life should answer for the loss of their chief and leader.

On the day that he was buried, I started for the mouth of Yellow Stone, and while I was gone, the spirit of vengeance had pervaded nearly all the Sioux country in search of the Dog, who had evaded pursuit. His brother, however, a noble and honourable fellow, esteemed by all who knew him, fell in their way in an unlucky hour, when their thirst for vengeance was irresistible, and they slew him. Repentance deep, and grief were the result of so rash an act, when they beheld a brave and worthy man fall for so worthless a character; and as they became exasperated, the spirit of revenge grew more desperate than ever, and they swore they never would lay down their arms or embrace their wives and children until vengeance, full and complete, should light upon the head that deserved it. This brings us again to the first part of my story, and in this state were things in that part of the country, when I was descending the river, four months afterwards, and landed my canoe as I before stated, at Laidlaw's trading-house.

The excitement had been kept up all summer amongst these people, and their superstitions bloated to the full brim, from circumstances so well calculated to feed and increase them. Many of them looked to me at once as the author of all these disasters, considering I knew that one half of the man's face was *good for nothing,* or that I would not have left it out of the picture, and that I must therefore have foreknown the evils that were to flow from the omission; they consequently resolved that I was a dangerous man, and should suffer for my temerity in case the Dog could not be found. Councils had been held, and in all the solemnity of Indian *medicine* and *mystery,* I had been doomed to die! At one of these, a young warrior of the *Onc-pa-pa* band, arose and said, "The blood of two chiefs has just sunk into the ground, and an hundred bows are bent which are ready to shed more! on whom shall we bend them? I am a friend to the white men, but here is one whose *medicine* is too great—he is a great *medicine-man*! his *medicine* is too great! he was the death of Mah-to-tchee-ga! he made only one side of his face! he would not make the other—the side that he made was alive; the other was dead, and Shonka shot it off! How is this? Who is to die?"

After him, *Tah-zee-kee-da-cha* (torn belly), of the *Yankton* band, arose and said— "Father, this medicine-man has done much harm! You told our chiefs and warriors, that they must be painted—you said he was a good man, and we believed you!—you thought so, my father, but you see what he has done!—he looks at our chiefs and our women and then makes them alive!! In this way he has taken our chiefs away, and he can trouble their spirits when they are dead! —they will be unhappy. If he can make them alive by looking at them, he can do us much harm!—you tell us that they are not alive—we see their eyes move!—their eyes follow us wherever we go, that is enough! I have no more to say!" After him, rose a young man of the Onc-pa-pa band. "Father! you know that I am the brother of *Mah-to-tchee-ga*!—you know that I loved him—both sides of his face were good, and the medicine-man knew it also! Why was half of his face left out? He never was ashamed, but always looked white man in the face! Why was that side of his face shot off? Your friend is not our friend, and has forfeited his life—we want you to tell us where he is—we want to see him!"

Then rose Toh-ki-e-to (a *medicine-man*) of the Yankton band, and principal orator of the nation. "My friend, these are young men that speak—I am not afraid! your white medicine-man painted my picture, and it was good—I am glad of it—I am very glad to see that I shall live after I am dead!—I am old and not afraid!—some of our young men are foolish. I know that this man *put many of our buffaloes in his book*! for I was with him, and we have had no buffaloes since to eat, it is true—but I am not afraid!! *his medicine* is great and I wish him well—we are friends!"

In this wise was the subject discussed by these superstitious people during my absence, and such were the reasons given by my friend Mr. Laidlaw, for his friendly advice; wherein he cautioned me against exposing my life in their hands, advising me to take some other route than that which I was pursuing down the river, where I would find encamped at the mouth of Cabri river, eighty miles below, several hundred Indians belonging to the Little Bear's band, and I might possibly fall a victim to their unsatiated revenge. I resumed my downward voyage in a few days, however, with my little canoe, which "Ba'tiste and Bogard paddled and I steered," and passed their encampment in peace, by taking the opposite shore. The usual friendly invitation however, was given (which is customary on that river), by skipping several rifle bullets across the river, a rod or two ahead of us. To those invitations we paid no attention, and (not suspecting who we were), they allowed us to pursue our course in peace and security. Thus rested the affair of the Dog and its consequences, until I conversed with Major Bean, the agent for these people, who arrived in St. Louis some weeks after I did, bringing later intelligence from them, assuring me that "*the Dog had at length been overtaken and killed*, near the Black-hills, and that the affair might now for ever be considered as settled" . . .

LETTER—NO. 31.

←———————→

Mouth of Teton River, Upper Missouri.

The *Bisons*, or (as they are more familiarly denominated in . . . this country) *Buffaloes* . . . inhabit these regions in numerous herds . . . These noble animals of the ox species . . . are a subject of curious interest and great importance in this vast wilderness; rendered peculiarly so at this time, like the history of the poor savage; and from the same consideration, that they are rapidly wasting away at the approach of civilized man—and like him and his character, in a very few years, to live only in books or on canvass.

. . . The American bison, or (as I shall hereafter call it) buffalo, is the largest of the ruminating animals that is now living in America; and seems to have been spread over the plains of this vast country, by the Great Spirit, for the use and subsistence of the red men, who live almost exclusively on their flesh, and clothe themselves with their skins . . . Their colour is a dark brown, but changing very much as the season varies from warm to cold; their hair or fur, from its great length in the winter and spring, and exposure to the weather, turning quite light, and almost to a jet black, when the winter coat is shed off, and a new growth is shooting out.

The buffalo bull often grows to the enormous weight of 2000 pounds, and shakes a long and shaggy black mane, that falls in great profusion and *confusion*, over his head and shoulders; and oftentimes falling down quite to the ground. The horns are short, but very large, and have but one turn, *i.e.* they are a simple arch, without the least approach to a spiral form, like those of the common ox, or of the goat species.

The female is much smaller than the male, and always distinguishable by the peculiar shape of the horns, which are much smaller and more crooked, turning their points more in towards the centre of the forehead.

One of the most remarkable characteristics of the buffalo, is the peculiar formation and expression of the eye, the ball of which is very large and white, and the iris jet black. The lids of the eye seem always to be strained quite open, and the ball rolling forward and down; so that a considerable part of the iris is hidden behind the lower lid, while the pure white of the eyeball glares out over it in an arch, in the shape of a moon at the end of its first quarter.

These animals are, truly speaking, gregarious, but not migratory—they graze in immense and almost incredible numbers at times, and roam about and over vast tracts of country, from East to West, and from West to East, as often as from North to South; which has often been supposed they naturally and habitually did to accommodate themselves to the temperature of the climate in the different latitudes. The limits within which they are found in America, are from the 30th to the 55th degrees of North latitude; and their extent from East to West, which is from the border of our extreme Western frontier limits, to the Western verge of the Rocky Mountains, is defined by quite different causes, than those which the degrees of temperature have prescribed to them on the North and the South. Within these 25 degrees of latitude, the buffaloes seem to flourish, and get their living without the necessity of evading the rigour of the climate, for which Nature seems most wisely to have prepared them by the greater or less profusion of fur, with which she has clothed them.

It is very evident that, as high North as Lake Winnepeg, seven or eight hundred miles North of this, the buffalo subsists itself through the severest winters; getting its food chiefly by browsing amongst the timber, and by pawing through the snow, for a bite at the grass, which in those regions is frozen up very suddenly in the beginning of the winter, with all its juices in it, and consequently furnishes very nutritious and efficient food; and often, if not generally, supporting the animal in better flesh during these difficult seasons of their lives, than they are found to be in, in the 30th degree of latitude, upon the borders of Mexico, where the severity of winter is not known, but during a long and tedious autumn, the herbage, under the influence of a burning sun, is gradually dried away to a mere husk, and its nutriment gone, leaving these poor creatures, even in the dead of winter, to bask in the warmth of a genial sun, without the benefit of a green or juicy thing to bite at.

The place from which I am now writing, may be said to be the very heart or nucleus of the buffalo country . . . The finest animals that graze on the prairies are to be found in this latitude; and I am sure I never could send from a better source, some further account of the death and destruction that is dealt among these noble animals, and hurrying on their final extinction.

The Sioux are a bold and desperate set of horsemen, and great hunters; and in the heart of their country is one of the most extensive assortments of goods, of whiskey, and other saleable commodities, as well as a party of the most indefatigable men, who are constantly calling for every robe that can be stripped from these animals' backs.

These are the causes which lead so directly to their rapid destruction; and which open to the view of the traveller so freshly, so vividly, and so familiarly, the scenes of archery—of lancing, and of death-dealing, that belong peculiarly to this wild and shorn country.

The almost countless herds of these animals that are sometimes met with on these prairies, have been often spoken of by other writers, and may yet be seen by any traveller who will take the pains to visit these regions. The *"running season,"* which is in August and September, is the time when they congregate into such masses in some places, as literally to blacken the prairies for miles together. It is no uncommon thing at this season, at these gatherings, to see several thousands in a mass, eddying and wheeling about under a cloud of dust, which is raised by the bulls as they are pawing in the dirt, or engaged in desperate combats, as they constantly are, plunging and butting at each other in the most furious manner. In these scenes, the males are continually following the females, and the whole mass are in constant motion; and all bellowing (or "roaring") in deep and hollow sounds; which, mingled altogether, appear, at the distance of a mile or two, like the sound of distant thunder.

During the season whilst they are congregated together in these dense and confused masses, the remainder of the country around for many miles, becomes entirely vacated; and the traveller may spend many a toilsome day, and many a hungry night, without being cheered by the sight of one; where, if he retraces his steps a few weeks after, he will find them dispersed, and grazing quietly in little families and flocks, and equally stocking the whole country. . . .

In the heat of summer, these huge animals, which, no doubt, suffer very much with the great profusion of their long and shaggy hair or fur, often graze on the low grounds in the prairies, where there is a little stagnant water lying amongst the grass, and the ground underneath being saturated with it, is soft, into which the enormous bull, lowered down upon one knee, will plunge his horns, and at last his head, driving up the earth, and soon making an excavation in the ground, into which the water filters from amongst the grass, forming for him in a few moments, a cool and comfortable bath, into which he plunges like a hog in his mire.

In this *delectable* laver, he throws himself flat upon his side, and forcing himself violently around, with his horns and his huge hump on his shoulders presented to the sides, he ploughs up the ground by his rotary motion, sinking himself deeper and deeper in the ground, continually enlarging his pool, in which he at length becomes nearly immersed; and the water and mud about him mixed into a complete mortar, which changes his colour, and drips in streams from every part of him as he rises up upon his feet, a hideous monster of mud and ugliness, too frightful and too eccentric to be described!

It is generally the leader of the herd that takes upon him to make this excavation; and if not (but another one opens the ground), the leader (who is conqueror) marches forward, and driving the other from it plunges himself into it; and having cooled his sides, and changed his colour to a walking mass of mud and mortar; he stands in the pool until inclination induces him to step out, and give place to the next in command, who stands ready; and another, and another, who advance forward in their turns, to enjoy the luxury of the wallow; until the whole band (sometimes an hundred or more) will pass through it in turn; each one throwing his body around in a similar manner; and each one adding a little to the dimensions of the pool, while he carries away in his hair an equal share of the clay, which dries to a grey or whitish colour, and gradually falls off. By this operation, which is done, perhaps, in the space of half an hour, a circular excavation of fifteen or twenty feet in diameter, and two feet in depth, is completed, and left for the water to run into, which soon fills it to the level of the ground.

To these sinks, the waters lying on the surface of the prairies, are continually draining, and in them lodging their vegetable deposits; which, after a lapse of years, fill them up to the surface with a rich soil, which throws up an unusual growth of grass and herbage; forming conspicuous circles which arrest the eye of the traveller, and are calculated to excite his surprise for ages to come.

Many travellers who have penetrated not quite far enough into the Western country to see the habits of these animals, and the manner in which these *mysterious* circles are made; but who have seen the prairies strewed with their bleached bones, and have beheld these strange circles, which often occur in groups, and of different sizes— have come home with beautiful and ingenious theories (which *must needs be made*), for the origin of these singular and unaccountable appearances . . .

The Indians in these parts are all mounted on small, but serviceable horses, which are caught by them on the prairies, where they are often running wild in numerous bands. The Indian, then, mounted on his little wild horse, which has been through some years of training, dashes off at full speed amongst the herds of buffaloes, elks, or even antelopes, and deals his deadly arrows to their hearts from his horse's back. The horse is the fleetest animal of the prairie, and easily brings his rider alongside of his game, which falls a certain prey to his deadly shafts, at the distance of a few paces.

In the chase of the buffalo, or other animal, the Indian generally "strips" himself and his horse, by throwing off his shield and quiver, and every part of his dress, which might be an encumbrance to him in running; grasping his bow in his left hand, with five or six arrows drawn from his quiver, and ready for instant use. In his right hand (or attached to the wrist) is a heavy whip, which he uses without mercy, and forces his horse alongside of his game at the swiftest speed.

These horses are so trained, that the Indian has little use for the rein, which hangs on the neck, whilst the horse approaches the animal on the right side, giving his rider the chance to throw his arrow to the left; which he does at the instant when the horse is passing—bringing him opposite to the heart, which receives the deadly weapon "to the feather." When pursuing a large herd, the Indian generally rides close in the rear, until he selects the animal he wishes to kill, which he separates from the throng as soon as he can, by dashing his horse between it and the herd, and forcing it off by itself; where he can approach it without the danger of being trampled to death, to which he is often liable by too closely escorting the multitude . . .

. . . [Notice] the striking disparity between the size of a huge bull of 2000 pounds weight, and the Indian horse, which, it will be borne in mind, is but a pony.

No bridle whatever is used in this country by the Indians, as they have no knowledge of a bit. A short halter, however, which answers in place of a bridle, is in general use; of which they usually form a nose around the under jaw of the horse, by which they get great power over the animal; and which they use generally to *stop* rather than *guide* the horse. This halter is called by the French Traders in the country, *l'arrrêt*, the stop, and has great power in arresting the speed of a horse; though it is extremely dangerous to use too freely as a guide, interfering too much with the freedom of his limbs, for the certainty of his feet and security of his rider.

When the Indian then has directed the course of his steed to the animal which he has selected, the training of the horse is such, that it knows the object of its rider's selection, and exerts every muscle to give it close company; while the halter lies loose and untouched upon its neck, and the rider leans quite forward, and off from the side of his horse, with his bow drawn, and ready for the deadly shot, which is given at the instant he is opposite to the animal's body. The horse being instinctively afraid of the animal (though he generally brings his rider within the reach of the end of his bow), keeps his eye strained upon the furious enemy he is so closely encountering; and the moment he has approached to the nearest distance required, and has passed the animal, whether the shot is given or not, he gradually sheers off, to prevent coming on to the horns of the infuriated beast, which often are instantly turned, and presented for the fatal reception of its too familiar attendant. These frightful collisions often take place, not withstanding the sagacity of the horse, and the caution of its rider; for in these extraordinary (and inexpressible) exhilarations of chase, which seem to drown the prudence alike, of instinct and reason, both horse and rider often seem rushing on to destruction, as if it were mere pastime and amusement.

I have always counted myself a prudent man, yet I have often *waked* (as it were) out of the delirium of the chase (into which I had fallen, as into an agitated sleep, and through which I had passed as through a delightful dream), where to have died would have been but to have remained, riding on, without a struggle or a pang.

In some of these, too, I have arisen from the prairie, covered with dirt and blood, having severed company with gun and horse, the one lying some twenty or thirty feet from me with a broken stalk, and the other coolly brousing on the grass at half a mile distance, without man, and without other beast remaining in sight.

For the novice in these scenes there is much danger of his limbs and his life, and he finds it a hard and a desperate struggle that brings him in at *the death* of these huge monsters, except where it has been produced by hands that have acquired more sleight and tact than his own.

With the Indian, who has made this the every day sport and amusement of his life, there is less difficulty and less danger; he rides without "losing his breath," and his unagitated hand deals *certainty* in its deadly blows.

In Illustration 29, I have represented a party of Indians in chase of a herd, some of whom are pursuing with lance and others with bows and arrows. The group in the foreground shews the attitude at the instant after the arrow has been thrown and driven to the heart; the Indian at full speed, and the *laso* dragging behind his horse's heels. The laso is a long thong of rawhide, of ten or fifteen yards in length, made of several braids or twists, and used chiefly to catch the wild horse, which is done by throwing over their necks a noose which is made at the end of the laso, with which they are "choked down." In running the buffaloes, or in time of war, the laso drags on the

Illustration 29. Buffalo chase with bows and lances.

ground at the horse's feet, and sometimes several rods behind, so that if a man is dismounted, which is often the case, by the tripping or stumbling of the horse, he has the power of grasping to the laso, and by stubbornly holding on to it, of stopping and securing his horse, on whose back he is instantly replaced, and continuing on in the chase.

In the dead of the winters, which are very long and severely cold in this country, where horses cannot be brought into the chase with any avail, the Indian runs upon the surface of the snow by the aid of his snow shoes, which buoy him up, while the great weight of the buffaloes, sinks them down to the middle of their sides, and completely stopping their progress, ensures them certain and easy victims to the bow or lance of their pursuers. The snow in these regions often lies during the winter, to the depth of three and four feet, being blown away from the tops and sides of the hills in many places, which are left bare for the buffaloes to graze upon, whilst it is drifted in the hollows and ravines to a very great depth, and rendered almost entirely impassable to these huge animals, which, when closely pursued by their enemies, endeavour to plunge through it, but are soon wedged in and almost unable to move, where they fall an easy prey to the Indian, who runs up lightly upon his snow shoes and drives his lance to their hearts. The skins are then stripped off, to be sold to the Fur Traders, and the carcasses left to be devoured by the wolves. This is the season in which the greatest number of these animals are destroyed for their robes—they are most easily killed at this time, and their hair or fur being longer and more abundant, gives greater value to the robe.

The Indians generally kill and dry meat enough in the fall, when it is fat and juicy, to last them through the winter; so that they have little other object for this unlimited slaughter, amid the drifts of snow, than that of procuring their robes for traffic with their Traders. The snow shoes are made in a great many forms, of two and three feet in length, and one foot or more in width, of a hoop or hoops bent around for the frame, with a netting or web woven across with strings of rawhide, on which the feet rest, and to which they are fastened with straps somewhat like a skate. With these the Indian will glide over the snow with astonishing quickness, without sinking down, or scarcely leaving his track where he has gone.

The poor buffaloes have their enemy *man*, besetting and beseiging them at all times of the year, and in all the modes that man in his superior wisdom has been able to devise for their destruction. They struggle in vain to evade his deadly shafts, when he dashes amongst them over the plains on his wild horse—they plunge into the snow-drifts where they yield themselves an easy prey to their destroyers, and they also stand unwittingly and behold him, unsuspected under the skin of a white wolf, insinuating himself and his fatal weapons into close company, when they are peaceably grazing on the level prairies, and shot down before they are aware of their danger.

There are several varieties of the wolf species in this country, the most formidable and most numerous of which are white, often sneaking about in gangs or families of fifty or sixty in numbers, appearing in distance, on the green prairies like nothing but a flock of sheep. Many of these animals grow to a very great size, being I should think, quite a match for the largest Newfoundland dog. At present, whilst the buffaloes are so abundant, and these ferocious animals are glutted with the buffalo's flesh, they are harmless, and everywhere sneak away from man's presence; which I scarcely think will be the case after the buffaloes are all gone, and they are left, as they must be, with scarcely anything to eat. They always are seen following about in the vicinity of herds of buffaloes and stand ready to pick the bones of those that the hunters leave on the ground, or to overtake and devour those that are wounded, which fall an easy prey to them. While the herd of buffaloes are together, they seem to have little dread of the wolf, and allow them to come in close company with them. The Indian then has taken advantage of this fact, and often places himself under the skin of this animal, and crawls for half a mile or more on his hands and knees, until he approaches within a few rods of the unsuspecting group, and easily shoots down the fattest of the throng.

The buffalo is a very timid animal, and shuns the vicinity of man with the keenest sagacity; yet, when overtaken, and harassed or wounded, turns upon its assailants with the utmost fury, who have only to seek safety in flight. In their desperate resistance the finest horses are often destroyed; but the Indian, with his superior sagacity and dexterity, generally finds some effective mode of escape.

During the season of the year whilst the calves are young, the male seems to stroll about by the side of the dam, as if for the purpose of protecting the young, at which time it is exceedingly hazardous to attack them, as they are sure to turn upon their pursuers, who have often to fly to each other's assistance. The buffalo calf, during the first six months is red, and has so much the appearance of a red calf in cultivated fields, that it could easily be mingled and mistaken amongst them. In the fall, when it changes its hair it takes a brown coat for the winter, which it always retains. In pursuing a large herd of buffaloes at the season when their calves are but a few weeks old, I have often been exceedingly amused with the curious manœuvres of these shy little things. Amidst the thundering confusion of a throng of several hundreds or several thousands of these animals, there will be many of the calves that lose sight of their dams; and being left behind by the throng, and the swift passing hunters, they endeavour to secrete themselves, when they are exceedingly put to it on a level prairie, where nought can be seen but the short grass of six or eight inches in height, save an occasional bunch of wild sage, a few inches higher, to which the poor affrighted things will run, and dropping on their knees, will push their noses under it, and into the grass, where they will stand for hours, with their eyes shut, imagining themselves securely hid, whilst they are standing up quite straight upon their hind feet and can easily be seen at several miles distance. It is a familiar amusement for us accustomed to these scenes, to retreat back over the ground where we have just escorted the herd, and approach these little trembling things, which stubbornly maintain their positions, with their noses pushed under the grass, and their eyes strained upon us, as we dismount from our horses and are passing around them. From this fixed position they are sure not to move, until hands are laid upon them, and then for the shins of a novice, we can extend our sympathy; or if he can preserve the skin on his bones for the furious buttings of its head, we know how to congratulate him on his signal success and good luck. In these desperate struggles, for a moment, the little thing is conquered, and makes no further resistance. And I have often, in concurrence with a known custom of the country, held my hands over the eyes of the calf, and breathed a few strong breaths into its nostrils; after which I have, with my hunting companions, rode several miles into our encampment, with the little prisoner busily following the heels of my horse the whole way, as closely and as affectionately as its instinct would attach it to the company of its dam!

This is one of the most extraordinary things that I have met with in the habits of this wild country, and although I had often heard of it, and felt unable exactly to believe it, I am now willing to bear testimony to the fact, from the numerous instances which I have witnessed since I came into the country . . .

It is truly a melancholy contemplation for the traveller in this country, to anticipate the period which is not far distant, when the last of these noble animals, at the hands of white and red men, will fall victims to their cruel and improvident rapacity; leaving these beautiful green fields, a vast and idle waste, unstocked and unpeopled for ages to come, until the bones of the one and the traditions of the other will have vanished, and left scarce an intelligible trace behind.

That the reader should not think me visionary in these contemplations, or romancing in making such assertions, I will hand him the following item of the extravagancies which are practiced in these regions, and rapidly leading to the results which I have just named.

When I first arrived at this place, on my way up the river, which was in the month of May, in 1832, and had taken up my lodgings in the Fur Company's fort, Mr. Laidlaw, of whom I have before spoken, and also his chief clerk, Mr. Halsey, and many of their men, as well as the chiefs of the Sioux, told me, that only a few days before I arrived, (when an immense herd of buffaloes had showed themselves on the opposite side of the river, almost blackening the plains for a great distance,) a party of five or six hundred Sioux Indians on horseback, forded the river about mid-day, and spending a few hours amongst them, recrossed the river at sun-down and came into the Fort with *fourteen hundred fresh buffalo tongues,* which were thrown down in a mass, and for which they required but a few gallons of whiskey, which was soon demolished, indulging them in a little, and harmless carouse.

This profligate waste of the lives of these noble and useful animals, when, from all that I could learn, not a skin or a pound of the meat (except the tongues), was brought in, fully supports me in the seemingly extravagant predictions that I have made as to their extinction, which I am certain is near at hand. In the above extravagant instance, at a season when their skins were without fur and not worth taking off, and their camp was so well stocked with fresh and dried meat, that they had no occasion for using the flesh, there is a fair exhibition of the improvident character of the savage, and also of his recklessness in catering for his appetite, so long as the present inducements are held out to him in his country, for its gratification.

In this singular country, where the poor Indians have no laws or regulations of society, making it a vice or an impropriety to drink to excess, they think it no harm to indulge in the delicious beverage, as long as they are able to buy whiskey to drink. They look to white men as wiser than themselves, and able to set them examples—they see none of these in their country but sellers of whiskey, who are constantly tendering it to them, and most of them setting the example by using it themselves; and they easily acquire a taste, that to be catered for, where whiskey is sold at sixteen dollars per gallon, soon impoverishes them, and must soon strip the skin from the last buffalo's back that lives in their country, to "be dressed by their squaws" and vended to the Traders for a pint of diluted alcohol.

From the above remarks it will be seen, that not only the red men, but red men and white, have aimed destruction at the race of these animals; and with them, *beasts* have turned hunters of buffaloes in this country, slaying them, however, in less numbers, and for far more laudable purpose than that of selling their skins. The white wolves, of which I have spoken in a former epistle, follow the herds of buffaloes as I have said, from one season to another, glutting themselves on the carcasses of those that fall by the deadly shafts of their enemies, or linger with disease or old age to be dispatched by these sneaking cormorants, who are ready at all times kindly to relieve them from the pangs of a lingering death.

Whilst the herd is together, the wolves never attack them, as they instantly gather for combined resistance, which they effectually make. But when the herds are travelling, it often happens that an aged or wounded one, lingers at a distance behind, and when fairly out of sight of the herd, is set upon by these voracious hunters, which often gather to the number of fifty or more, and are sure at last to torture him to death, and use him up at a meal. The buffalo, however, is a huge and furious animal, and when his retreat is cut off, makes desperate and deadly resistance, contending to the last moment for the right of life—and oftentimes deals death by wholesale, to his canine assailants, which he is tossing into the air or stamping to death under his feet.

During my travels in these regions, I have several times come across such a gang of these animals surrounding an old or a wounded bull, where it would seem, from appearances, that they had been for several days in attendance, and at intervals desperately engaged in the effort to take his life. But a short time since, as one of my hunting companions and myself were returning to our encampment with our horses loaded with meat, we discovered at a distance, a huge bull, encircled with a gang of white wolves; we rode up as near as we could without driving them away, and being within pistol shot, we had a remarkably good view, where I sat for a few moments and made a sketch in my note-book; after which, we rode up and gave the signal for them to disperse, which they instantly did, withdrawing themselves to the distance of fifty or sixty rods, when we found, to our great surprise, that the animal had made desperate resistance, until his eyes were entirely eaten out of his head—the grizzle of his nose was mostly gone—his tongue was half eaten off, and the skin and flesh of his legs torn almost literally into strings. In this tattered and torn condition, the poor old veteran stood bracing up in the midst of his devourers, who had ceased hostilities for a few minutes, to enjoy a sort of parley, recovering strength and preparing to resume the attack in a few moments again. In this group, some were reclining, to gain breath, whilst others were sneaking about and licking their chaps in anxiety for a renewal of the attack; and others, less lucky, had been crushed to death by the feet or the horns of the bull. I rode nearer to the pitiable object as he stood bleeding and trembling before me, and said to him, "Now is your time, old fellow, and you had better be off." Though blind and nearly destroyed, there seemed evidently to be a recognition of a friend in me, as he straightened up, and, trembling with excitement, dashed off at full speed upon the prairie, in a straight line. We turned our horses and resumed our march, and when we had advanced a mile or more, we looked back, and on our left, where we saw again the ill-fated animal surrounded by his tormentors, to whose insatiable voracity he unquestionably soon fell a victim . . .

It is not enough in this polished and extravagant age, that we get from the Indian his lands, and the very clothes from his back, but the food from their mouths must be stopped, to add a new and useless article to the fashionable world's luxuries. The ranks must be thinned, and the race exterminated, of this noble animal, and the Indians of the great plains left without the means of supporting life, that white men may figure a few years longer, enveloped in buffalo robes—that they may spread them, for their pleasure and elegance, over the backs of their sleighs, and trail them ostentatiously amidst the busy throng, as things of beauty and elegance that had been made for them!

Reader! listen to the following calculations, and forget them not. The buffaloes (the quadrupeds from whose backs your beautiful robes were taken, and whose myriads were once spread over the whole country, from the Rocky Mountains to the Atlantic Ocean) have recently fled before the appalling appearance of civilized man, and taken up their abode and pasturage amid the almost boundless prairies of the West. An instinctive dread of their deadly foes, who made an easy prey of them whilst grazing in the forest, has led them to seek the midst of the vast and treeless plains of grass, as the spot where they would be least exposed to the assaults of their enemies; and it is exclusively in those desolate fields of silence (yet of beauty) that they are to be found—and over these vast steppes, or prairies, have they fled, like the Indian, towards the "setting sun;" until their bands have been crowded together, and their limits confined to a narrow strip of country on this side of the Rocky Mountains.

This strip of country, which extends from the province of Mexico to Lake Winnepeg on the North, is almost one entire plain of grass, which is, and ever must be, useless to cultivating man. It is here, and here chiefly, that the buffaloes dwell; and with, and hovering about them, live and flourish the tribes of Indians, whom God made for the enjoyment of that fair land and its luxuries.

It is a melancholy contemplation for one who has travelled as I have, through these realms, and seen this noble animal in all its pride and glory, to contemplate it so rapidly wasting from the world, drawing the irresistible conclusion too, which one must do, that its species is soon to be extinguished, and with it the peace and happiness (if not the actual existence) of the tribes of Indians who are joint tenants with them, in the occupancy of these vast and idle plains.

And what a splendid contemplation too, when one (who has travelled these realms, and can duly appreciate them) imagines them as they *might* in future be seen, (by some great protecting policy of government) preserved in their pristine beauty and wildness, in a *magnificent park*, where the world could see for ages to come, the native Indian in his classic attire, galloping his wild horse, with sinewy bow, and shield and lance, amid the fleeting herds of elks and buffaloes. What a beautiful and thrilling specimen for America to preserve and hold up to the view of her refined citizens and the world, in future ages! A *nation's Park*, containing man and beast, in all the wild and freshness of their nature's beauty!

I would ask no other monument to my memory, nor any other enrolment of my name amongst the famous dead, than the reputation of having been the founder of such an institution.

Such scenes might easily have been preserved, and still could be cherished on the great plains of the West, without detriment to the country or its borders; for the tracts of country on which the buffaloes have assembled, are uniformly sterile, and of no available use to cultivating man.

It is on these plains, which are stocked with buffaloes, that the finest specimens of the Indian race are to be seen. It is here, that the savage is decorated in the richest costume. It is here, and here only, that his wants are all satisfied, and even the *luxuries* of life are afforded him in abundance. And here also is he the proud and honourable man (before he has had teachers or laws), above the imported wants, which beget meanness and vice; stimulated by ideas of honour and virtue, in which the God of Nature has certainly not curtailed him.

There are, by a fair calculation, more than 300,000 Indians, who are now subsisted on the flesh of the buffaloes, and by those animals supplied with all the luxuries of life which they desire, as they know of none others. The great variety of uses to which they convert the body and other parts of that animal, are almost incredible to the person who has not actually dwelt amongst these people, and closely studied their modes and customs. Every part of their flesh is converted into food, in one shape or another, and on it they entirely subsist. The robes of the animals are worn by the Indians instead of blankets—their skins when tanned, are used as coverings for their lodges, and for their beds; undressed, they are used for constructing canoes—for saddles, for bridles—l'arrêts, lasos, and thongs. The horns are shaped into ladles and spoons—the brains are used for dressing the skins—their bones are used for saddle trees—for war clubs, and scrapers for graining the robes—and others are broken up for the marrow-fat which is contained in them. Their sinews are used for strings and backs to their bows—for thread to string their beads and sew their dresses. The feet of the animals are boiled, with their hoofs, for the glue they contain, for fastening their arrow points, and many other uses. The hair from the head and shoulders, which is long, is twisted and braided into halters, and the tail is used for a fly brush. In this wise do these people convert and use the various parts of this useful animal, and with all these luxuries of life about them, and their numerous games, they are happy (God bless them) in the ignorance of the disastrous fate that awaits them.

Yet this interesting community, with its sports, its wildnesses, its languages, and all its manners and customs, could be perpetuated, and also the buffaloes, whose numbers would increase and supply them with food for ages and centuries to come, if a system of non-intercourse could be established and preserved. But such is not to be the case—the buffalo's doom is sealed, and with their extinction must assuredly sink into real despair and starvation, the inhabitants of these vast plains, which afford for the Indians, no other possible means of subsistence; and they must at last fall a prey to wolves and buzzards, who will have no other bones to pick.

It seems hard and cruel, (does it not?) that we civilized people with all the luxuries and comforts of the world about us, should be drawing from the backs of these useful animals the skins for our luxury, leaving their carcasses to be devoured by the wolves—that we should draw from that country, some 150 or 200,000 or their robes annually, the greater part of which are taken from animals that are killed expressly for the robe, at a season when the meat is not cured and preserved, and for each of which skins the Indian has received but a pint of whiskey!

Such is the fact, and that number or near it, are annually destroyed, in addition to the number that is necessarily killed for the subsistence of 300,000 Indians, who live entirely upon them. It may be said, perhaps, that the Fur Trade of these great western realms, which is now limited chiefly to the purchase of buffalo robes, is of great and national importance, and should and must be encouraged. To such a suggestion I would reply, by merely enquiring, (independently of the poor Indians' disasters,) how much more advantageously would such a capital be employed, both for the weal of the country and for the owners, if it were invested in machines for the manufacture of *woollen robes*, of equal and superior value and beauty; thereby encouraging the growers of wool, and the industrious manufacturer, rather than cultivating a taste for the use of buffalo skins; which is just to be acquired, and then, from necessity, to be dispensed with, when a few years shall have destroyed the last of the animals producing them.

It may be answered, perhaps, that the necessaries of life are given in exchange for these robes; but what, I would ask, are the necessities in Indian life, where they have buffaloes in abundance to live on? The Indian's necessities are entirely artificial—are all created; and when the buffaloes shall have disappeared in his country, which will be within *eight* or *ten* years, I would ask, who is to supply him with the necessaries of life then? and I would ask, further, (and leave the question to be answered ten years hence), when the skin shall have been stripped from the back of the last animal, who is to resist the ravages of 300,000 starving savages; and in their trains, 1,500,000 wolves, whom direst necessity will have driven from their desolate and gameless plains, to seek for the means of subsistence along our exposed frontier? God has everywhere supplied man in a state of Nature, with the necessaries of life, and before we destroy the game of his country, or teach him new desires, he has no wants that are not satisfied.

Amongst the tribes who have been impoverished and repeatedly removed, the necessaries of life are extended with a better grace from the hands of civilized man; 90,000 of such have already been removed, and they draw from Government some 5 or 600,000 dollars annually in cash; *which money passes immediately into the hands of white men,* and for it the necessaries of life *may be* abundantly furnished. But who, I would ask, are to furnish the Indians who have been instructed in this unnatural mode—living upon *such* necessaries, and even luxuries of life, extended to them by the hands of white men, when those annuities are at an end, and the skin is stripped from the last of the animals which God gave them for their subsistence?

Reader, I will stop here, lest you might forget to answer these important queries—these are questions which I know will puzzle the world—and perhaps it is not right that I should ask them.   *   *
*   *   *   *   *   *   *   *   *   *

*   *   Thus much I wrote and painted at this place, whilst on my way up the river: after which I embarked on the steamer for the Yellow Stone, and the sources of the Missouri, through which interesting regions I have made a successful Tour; and have returned, as will have been seen by the foregoing narrations, in my canoe, to this place, from whence I am to descend the river still further in a few days. If I ever get time, I may give further Notes on this place, and of people and their doings, which I met with here; but at present, I throw my note-book, and canvass, and brushes into my canoe, which will be launched to-morrow morning, and on its way towards St. Louis, with myself at the steering-oar, as usual: and with Ba'tiste and Bogard to paddle, of whom, I beg the readers' pardon for having said nothing of late, though they have been my constant companions. Our way is now over the foaming and muddy waters of the Missouri, and amid snags and drift logs (for there is a sweeping freshet on her waters), and many a day will pass before other Letters will come from me; and possibly, the reader may have to look to my biographer for the rest. Adieu.

LETTER—NO. 32

◄––––––––––►

Fort Leavenworth, Lower Missouri.

*M*y voyage from the mouth of the Teton River . . . has been
. . . the most rugged, yet the most delightful, of my whole Tour.
Our canoe was generally landed at night on the point of some
projecting barren sand-bar, where we straightened our limbs on our
buffalo robes, secure from the annoyance of mosquitos, and out of
the walks of Indians and grizzly bears. In addition to the opportunity
which this descending Tour has afforded me, of visiting all the tribes
of Indians on the river, and leisurely filling my portfolio with the
beautiful scenery which its shores present—the sportsman's fever
was roused and satisfied; the swan, ducks, geese, and pelicans—the
deer, antelope, elk, and buffaloes, were *"stretched"* by our rifles; and
some times—"pull boys! pull!! a war party! for your lives pull! or we
are gone!"

I often landed my skiff, and mounted the green carpeted bluffs,
whose soft grassy tops, invited me to recline, where I was at once lost
in contemplation. Soul melting scenery that was about me! A place
where the mind could think volumes; but the tongue must be silent
that would *speak,* and the hand palsied that would *write.* A place
where a Divine would confess that he never had fancied Paradise—
where the painter's palette would lose its beautiful tints—the blood-
stirring notes of eloquence would die in their utterance—and even
the soft tones of sweet music would scarcely preserve a spark to
light the soul again that had passed this sweet delirium. I mean the
prairie, whose enamelled plains that lie beneath me, in distance
soften into sweetness, like an essence; whose thousand thousand
velvet-covered hills, (surely never formed by chance, but grouped in

one of Nature's sportive moods)—tossing and leaping down with
steep or graceful declivities to the river's edge, as if to grace its
pictured shores, and make it "a thing to look upon." I mean the
prairie at *sun-set;* when the green hill-tops are turned into gold—and
their long shadows of melancholy are thrown over the valleys—when
all the breathings of day are hushed, and nought but the soft notes of
the retiring dove can be heard; or the still softer and more plaintive
notes of the wolf, who sneaks through these scenes of enchantment,
and mournfully how—l—s, as if lonesome, and lost in the too
beautiful quiet and stillness about him. I mean *this* prairie; where
Heaven sheds its purest light, and lends its richest tints—*this round-
topp'd bluff,* where the foot treads soft and light—whose steep sides,
and lofty head, rear me to the skies, overlooking yonder pictured vale
of beauty—this solitary *cedar-post,* which tells a tale of grief—grief
that was keenly felt, and tenderly, but long since softened in the
march of time and lost. Oh, sad and tear-starting contemplation! sole
tenant of this stately mound, how solitary thy habitation! here Heaven
wrested from thee thy ambition, and made thee sleeping monarch of
this land of silence.

Stranger! oh, how the mystic web of sympathy links my soul to
thee and thy afflictions! I knew thee not, but it was enough; thy
tale was told, and I a solitary wanderer through thy land, have
stopped to drop familiar tears upon thy grave. Pardon this gush
from a stranger's eyes, for they are all that thou canst have in
this strange land, where friends and dear relations are not allowed
to pluck a flower, and drop a tear to freshen recollections of
endearments past.

Stranger! adieu. With streaming eyes I leave thee again, and thy
fairy land, to peaceful solitude. My pencil has faithfully traced thy
beautiful habitation; and long shall live in the world, and familiar,
the name of *"Floyd's Grave."*

Readers, pardon this digression. I have seated myself down, not
on a prairie, but at my table, by a warm and cheering fire, with my
journal before me to cull from it a few pages, for your entertainment;
and if there are spots of loveliness and beauty, over which I have
passed, and whose images are occasionally beckoning me into digres-
sions, you must forgive me.

Such is the spot I have just named, and some others, on to which I am instantly transferred when I cast my eyes back upon the enamelled and beautiful shores of the Upper Missouri; and I am constrained to step aside and give ear to their breathings, when their soft images, and cherished associations, so earnestly prompt me. "Floyd's Grave" is a name given to one of the most lovely and imposing mounds or bluffs on the Missouri River, about twelve hundred miles above St. Louis, from the melancholy fate of Serjeant Floyd, who was of Lewis and Clark's expedition, in 1806; who died on the way, and whose body was taken to this beautiful hill, and buried in its top, where now stands a cedar post, bearing the initials of his name (Illustration 30).

I landed my canoe in front of this grass-covered mound, and all hands being fatigued, we encamped a couple of days at its base. I several times ascended it and sat upon his grave, overgrown with grass and the most delicate wild flowers, where I sat and contemplated the solitude and stillness of this tenanted mound; and beheld from its top, the windings infinite of the Missouri, and its thousand hills and domes of green, vanishing into blue in distance, when nought but the soft-breathing winds were heard, to break the stillness and quietude of the scene. Where not the chirping of bird or sound of cricket, nor soaring eagle's scream, were interposed 'tween God and man; nor aught to check man's whole surrender of his soul to his Creator. I could not *hunt* upon this ground, but I roamed from hill-top to hill-top, and culled wild flowers, and looked into the valley below me, both up the river and down, and contemplated the thousand hills and dales that are now carpeted with green, streaked as they *will* be, with the plough, and yellow with the harvest sheaf; spotted with lowing kine—with houses and fences, and groups of hamlets and villas . . .

But a few miles from "Floyd's Bluff" we landed our canoe, and spent a day in the vicinity of the *"Black Bird's Grave."* This is a celebrated point on the Missouri, and a sort of telegraphic place, which all the travellers in these realms, both white and red, are in the habit of visiting: the one to pay respect to the bones of one of their distinguished leaders; and the others, to indulge their eyes on the lovely landscape that spreads out to an almost illimitable extent

Illustration 30. Grassy river bluffs, about 1300 miles above St. Louis.

in every direction about it. This elevated bluff, which may be distinguished for several leagues in distance, has received the name of the "Black Bird's Grave," from the fact, that a famous chief of the O-ma-haws, by the name of the Black Bird, was buried on its top, at his own peculiar request; over whose grave a cedar post was erected by his tribe some thirty years ago, which is still standing. The O-ma-haw village was about sixty miles above this place; and this very noted chief, who had been on a visit to Washington City, in company with the Indian agent, died of the small-pox, near this spot, on his return home. And, whilst dying, enjoined on his warriors who were about him, this singular request, which was literally complied with. He requested them to take his body down the river to this his favorite haunt, and on the pinnacle of this towering bluff, to bury him on the back of his favourite war-horse, which was to be buried alive, under him, from whence he could see, as he said, "the Frenchmen passing up and down the river in their boats." He owned, amongst many horses, a noble white steed that was led to the top of the grass-covered hill; and, with great pomp and ceremony, in presence of the whole nation, and several of the Fur Traders and the Indian agent, he was placed astride of his horse's back, with his bow in his hand, and his shield and quiver slung—with his pipe and his *medicine-bag*—with his supply of dried meat, and his tobacco-pouch replenished to last him through his journey to the "beautiful hunting grounds of the shades of his fathers"—with his flint and steel, and his tinder, to light his pipes by the way. The scalps that he had taken from his enemies' heads, could be trophies for nobody else, and were hung to the bridle of his horse—he was in full dress and fully equipped; and on his head waved, to the last moment, his beautiful head-dress of the war-eagle's plumes. In this plight, and the last funeral honours having been performed by the *medicine-men*, every warrior of his band painted the palm and fingers of his right hand with vermilion; which was stamped, and perfectly impressed on the milk-white sides of his devoted horse.

This all done, turfs were brought and placed around the feet and legs of the horse, and gradually laid up to its sides; and at last, over the back and head of the unsuspecting animal, and last of all, over the head and even the eagle plumes of its valiant rider, where altogether have smouldered and remained undisturbed to the present day.

This mound which is covered with a green turf, and spotted with wild flowers, with its cedar post in its centre, can easily be seen at the distance of fifteen miles, by the *voyageur,* and forms for him a familiar and useful land-mark.

Whilst visiting this mound in company with Major Sanford, on our way up the river, I discovered in a hole made in the mound, by a "ground hog" or other animal, the skull of the horse; and by a little pains, also came at the skull of the chief, which I carried to the river side, and secreted till my return in my canoe, when I took it in, and brought with me to this place, where I now have it, with others which I have collected on my route.

There have been some very surprising tales told of this man, which will render him famous in history, whether they be truth or matters of fiction. Of the many, one of the most current is, that he gained his celebrity and authority by the most diabolical series of murders in his own tribe; by administering arsenic (with which he had been supplied by the Fur Traders) to such of his enemies as he wished to get rid of—and even to others in his tribe whom he was willing to sacrifice, merely to establish his superhuman powers, and the most servile dread of the tribe, from the certainty with which his victims fell around him, precisely at the times he saw fit to predict their death! It has been said that he administered this potent drug, and to them unknown *medicine,* to many of his friends as well as to foes; and by such an inhuman and unparalleled depravity, succeeded in exercising the most despotic and absolute authority in his tribe, until the time of his death!

This story may be true, and it may not. I cannot contradict it; and I am sure the world will forgive me, if I say, I cannot believe it. If it be true, two things are also true; the one, not much to the credit of the Indian character; and the other, to the everlasting infamy of the Fur Traders. If it be true, it furnishes an instance of Indian depravity that I never have elsewhere heard of in my travels; and carries the most conclusive proof of the incredible enormity of white men's dealings in this country . . .

I have learned much of this noble chieftain, and at a proper time shall recount the modes of his civil and military life—how he exposed his life, and shed his blood in rescuing the victims to horrid torture, and abolished that savage custom in his tribe—how he led on and headed his brave warriors, against the Sacs and Foxes; and saved the butchery of his women and children—how he received the Indian agent, and entertained him in his hospitable wigwam, in his village—and how he conducted and acquitted himself on his embassy to the civilized world . . .

Book-making now-a-days, is done for money-making; and he who takes the Indian for his theme, and cannot go and see him, finds a poverty in his matter that naturally begets error, by grasping at every little tale that is brought or fabricated by their enemies. Such books are standards, because they are made for white man's reading only; and herald the character of a people who never can disprove them . . . The poor Indian who has no redress, stands stigmatized and branded, as a murderous wretch and beast.

If the system of book-making and newspaper printing were in operation in the Indian country awhile, to herald the iniquities and horrible barbarities of white men in these Western regions . . . chapters would soon be printed, which would sicken the reader to his heart, and set up the Indian, a fair and tolerable man.

There is no more beautiful prairie country than that which is to be seen in this vicinity. In looking back from this bluff, towards the West, there is, to an almost boundless extent, one of the most beautiful scenes imaginable. The surface of the country is gracefully and slightly undulating, like the swells of the retiring ocean after a heavy storm. And everywhere covered with a beautiful green turf, and with occasional patches and clusters of trees. The soil in this region is also rich, and capable of making one of the most beautiful and productive countries in the world . . .

Whilst strolling about on the western bank of the river at this place, I found the ancient site of an Indian village, which, from the character of the marks, I am sure was once the residence of the Mandans. I said in a former Letter, when speaking of the Mandans, that within the recollection of some of their oldest men, they lived some sixty or eighty miles down the river from the place of their present residence; and that they then lived in nine villages. On my way down, I became fully convinced of the fact; having landed my canoe, and examined the ground where the foundation of every wigwam can yet be distinctly seen. At that time, they must have been much more numerous than at present, from the many marks they have left, as well as from their own representations.

The Mandans have a peculiar way of building their wigwams, by digging down a couple of feet in the earth, and there fixing the ends of the poles which form the walls of their houses. There are other marks, such as their caches—and also their mode of depositing their dead on scaffolds—and of preserving the skulls in circles on the prairies; which peculiar customs I have before described, and most of which are distinctly to be recognized in each of these places, as well as in several similar remains which I have met with on the banks of the river, between here and the Mandans; which fully convince me, that they have formerly occupied the lower parts of the Missouri, and have gradually made their way quite through the heart of the great Sioux country; and having been well fortified in all their locations, as in their present one, by a regular stockade and ditch; they have been able successfully to resist the continual assaults of the Sioux, that numerous tribe, who have been, and still are, endeavoring to effect their entire destruction. I have examined, at least fifteen or twenty of their ancient locations on the banks of this river, and can easily discover the regular differences in the ages of these antiquities; and around them all I have found numerous bits of their broken pottery, corresponding with that which they are now manufacturing in great abundance; and which is certainly made by no other tribe in these regions. These evidences, and others which I shall not take the time to mention in this place, go a great way in my mind towards strengthening the possibility of their having moved from the Ohio river, and of their being a remnant of the followers of Madoc. I have much further to trace them yet, however, and shall certainly have more to say on so interesting a subject in future.

Almost every mile I have advanced on the banks of this river, I have met evidences and marks of Indians in some form or other; and they have generally been those of the Sioux, who occupy and own the greater part of this immense region of country. In the latter part of my voyage, however, and of which I have been speaking in the former part of this Letter, I met the ancient sites of the O-ma-ha and Ot-to towns, which are easily detected when they are met. In Illustration 31 (letter A), is seen the usual mode of the Omahas, of depositing their dead in the crotches and on the branches of trees, enveloped in skins, and never without a wooden dish hanging by the head of the corpse; probably for the purpose of enabling it to dip up water to quench its thirst on the long and tedious journey, which they generally expect to enter on after death. These corpses are so frequent along the banks of the river, that in some places a dozen or more of them may be seen at one view.

Letter B in the same plate, shews the customs of the Sioux, which are found in endless numbers on the river; and in fact, through every part of this country. The wigwams of these people are only moveable tents, and leave but a temporary mark to be discovered. Their burials, however, are peculiar and lasting remains, which can be long detected. They often deposit their dead on trees, and on scaffolds; but more generally bury in the tops of bluffs, or near their villages; when they often split out staves and drive in the ground around the grave, to protect it from the trespass of dogs or wild animals.

Letter C (same plate), shews the character of Mandan remains, that are met with in numerous places on the river. Their mode of resting their dead upon scaffolds is not so peculiar to them as positively to distinguish them from Sioux, who sometimes bury in the same way; but the excavations for their earth-covered wigwams, which I have said are two feet deep in the ground, with the ends of the decayed timbers remaining in them, are peculiar and conclusive evidence of their being of Mandan construction; and the custom of leaving the skulls bleached upon the ground in circles (as I have formerly described in Illustration 16), instead of burying them as the other tribes do, forms also a strong evidence of the fact that they are Mandan remains.

In most of these sites of their ancient towns, however, I have been unable to find about their burial places, these characteristic deposits of the skulls; from which I conclude, that whenever they deliberately moved to a different region, they buried the skulls out of respect to

Illustration 31. Indian burial customs.

the dead. I found, just back of one of these sites of their ancient towns, however, and at least 500 miles below where they now live, the same arrangement of skulls as that I described in Illustration 16. They had laid so long, however, exposed to the weather, that they were reduced almost to a powder, except the teeth, which mostly seemed polished and sound as ever. It seems that no human hands had dared to meddle with the dead; and that even their enemies had respected them; for every one, and there were at least two hundred in one circle, had mouldered to chalk, in its exact relative position, as they had been placed in a circle. In this case, I am of opinion that the village was besieged by the Sioux, and entirely destroyed; or that the Mandans were driven off without the power to stop and bury the bones of their dead . . .

At this place I was in the country of the Pawnees, a numerous tribe, whose villages are on the Platte river, and of whom I shall say more anon. Major Dougherty has been for many years the agent for this hostile tribe; and by his familiar knowledge of the Indian character, and his strict honesty and integrity, he has been able to effect a friendly intercourse with them, and also to attract the . . . highest confidence . . . of the authorities who sent him there . . .

The mouth of the Platte is a beautiful scene, and no doubt will be the site of a large and flourishing town, soon after Indian titles shall have been extinguished to the lands in these regions, which will be done within a very few years. The Platte is a long and powerful stream, pouring in from the Rocky Mountains and joining with the Missouri at this place . . .

We met immense numbers of buffaloes in the early part of our voyage and used to land our canoe almost every hour in the day; and oftentimes all together approach the unsuspecting herds, through some deep and hidden ravine within a few rods of them and at the word, "pull trigger," each of us bring down our victim.

In one instance, near the mouth of White River, we met the most immense herd crossing the Missouri River—and from an imprudence got our boat into imminent danger amongst them, from which we were highly delighted to make our escape. It was in the midst of the "running season," and we had heard the "roaring" (as it is called) of the herd, when we were several miles from them. When we came in sight, we were actually terrified at the immense numbers that were streaming down the green hills on one side of the river, and galloping up and over the bluffs on the other. The river was filled, and in parts blackened, with their heads and horns, as they were swimming about, following up their objects, and making desperate battle whilst they were swimming.

I deemed it imprudent for our canoe to be dodging amongst them, and ran it ashore for a few hours, where we laid, waiting for the opportunity of seeing the river clear; but we waited in vain. Their numbers, however, got somewhat diminished at last, and we pushed off, and successfully made our way amongst them. From the immense numbers that had passed the river at that place, they had torn down the prairie bank of fifteen feet in height, so as to form a sort of road or landing-place, where they all in succession clambered up. Many in their turmoil had been wafted below this landing, and unable to regain it against the swiftness of the current, had fastened themselves along in crowds, hugging close to the high bank under which they were standing. As we were drifting by these, and supposing ourselves out of danger, I drew up my rifle and shot one of them in the head, which tumbled into the water, and brought with him a hundred others, which plunged in, and in a moment were swimming about our canoe, and placing it in great danger. No attack was made upon us, and in the confusion the poor beasts knew not, perhaps, the enemy that was amongst them; but we were liable to be sunk by them, as they were furiously hooking and climbing on to each other. I rose in my canoe, and by my gestures and hallooing, kept them from coming in contact with us, until we were out of their reach.

This was one of the instances that I formerly spoke of, where thousands and tens of thousands of these animals congregate in the *running season,* and move about from East and West, or wherever accident or circumstances may lead them. In this grand crusade, no one can know the numbers that may have made the ford within a few days; nor in their blinded fury in such scenes, would feeble man be much respected.

During the remainder of that day we paddled onward, and passed many of their carcasses floating on the current, or lodged on the heads of islands and sand-bars. And, in the vicinity of, and not far below the grand turmoil, we passed several that were mired in the quicksand near the shores; some were standing fast and half immersed; whilst others were nearly out of sight, and gasping for the last breath; others were standing with all legs fast, and one half of their bodies above the water, and their heads sunk under it, where they had evidently remained several days; and flocks of ravens and crows were covering their backs, and picking the flesh from their dead bodies.

So much of the Upper Missouri and its modes, at present; though I have much more in store for some future occasion.

Fort Leavenworth, which is on the Lower Missouri, being below the mouth of the Platte, is the nucleus of another neighborhood of Indians, amongst whom I am to commence my labours . . . This Cantonment, which is beautifully situated on the west bank of the Missouri River, and six hundred miles above its mouth, was constructed some years since by General Leavenworth, from whom it has taken its name. Its location is very beautiful, and so is the country around it. It is the concentration point of a number of hostile tribes in the vicinity, and has its influence in restraining their warlike propensities.

There is generally a regiment of men stationed here, for the purpose of holding the Indians in check, and of preserving the peace amongst the hostile tribes . . .

LETTER—NO. 33.

◄————————————————►

Fort Leavenworth, Lower Missouri.

I mentioned in a former epistle, that this is the extreme outpost on the Western Frontier, and built, like several others, in the heart of the Indian country. There is no finer tract of lands in North America, or, perhaps, in the world, than that vast space of prairie country, which lies in the vicinity of this post, embracing it on all sides. This garrison, like many others on the frontiers, is avowedly placed here for the purpose of protecting our frontier inhabitants from the incursions of Indians; and also for the purpose of preserving the peace amongst the different hostile tribes, who seem continually to wage, and glory in, their deadly wars. How far these feeble garrisons, which are generally but half manned, have been, or will be, able to intimidate and controul the warlike ardour of these restless and revengeful spirits; or how far they will be able in desperate necessity, to protect the lives and property of the honest pioneer, is yet to be tested.

They have doubtless been designed with the best views, to effect the most humane objects, though I very much doubt the benefits that are anticipated to flow from them, unless a more efficient number of men are stationed in them than I have generally found; enough to promise protection to the Indian, and then to *ensure* it; instead of promising, and leaving them to seek it in their own way at last, and when they are least prepared to do it.

When I speak of this post as being on the *Lower Missouri*, I do not wish to convey the idea that I am down near the sea-coast, at the mouth of the river, or near it; I only mean that I am on the lower part of the Missouri, yet 600 miles above its junction with the

Mississippi, and near 2000 from the Gulf of Mexico, into which the Mississippi discharges its waters.

In this delightful Cantonment there are generally stationed six or seven companies of infantry, and ten or fifteen officers; several of whom have their wives and daughters with them, forming a very pleasant little community, who are almost continually together in social enjoyment of the peculiar amusements and pleasures of this wild country. Of these pastimes they have many, such as riding on horseback or in carriages over the beautiful green fields of the prairies, picking strawberries and wild plums—deer chasing—grouse shooting—horse-racing, and other amusements of the garrison, in which they are almost constantly engaged; enjoying life to a very high degree.

In these delightful amusements, and with these pleasing companions, I have been for a while participating with great satisfaction; I have joined several times in the deer-hunts, and more frequently in grouse shooting, which constitutes the principal amusement of this place.

This delicious bird, which is found in great abundance in nearly all the North American prairies, and most generally called the Prairie Hen, is, from what I can learn, very much like the English grouse, or heath hen, both in size, in colour, and in habits. They make their appearance in these parts in the months of August and September, from the higher latitudes, where they go in the early part of the summer, to raise their broods. This is the season for the best sport amongst them; and the whole garrison, in fact are almost subsisted on them at this time, owing to the facility with which they are killed.

I was lucky enough the other day, with one of the officers of the garrison, to gain the enviable distinction of having brought in together seventy-five of these fine birds, which we killed in one afternoon; and although I am quite ashamed to confess the manner in which we killed the greater part of them, I am not so professed a sportsman as to induce me to conceal the fact. We had a fine pointer, and had legitimately followed the sportsman's style for a part of the afternoon; but seeing the prairies on fire several miles ahead of us, and the wind driving the fire gradually towards us, we found these poor birds driven before its long line, which seemed to extend from horizon to horizon, and they were flying in swarms or flocks that would at times almost fill the air. They generally flew half a mile or so, and lit down again in the grass, where they would sit until the fire was close upon them, and then they would rise again. We observed by watching their motions, that they lit in great numbers in every solitary tree; and we placed ourselves near each of these trees in turn, and shot them down as they settled in them; sometimes killing five or six at a shot, by getting a range upon them . . .

The prairies burning form some of the most beautiful scenes that are to be witnessed in this country, and also some of the most sublime. Every acre of these vast prairies (being covered for hundreds and hundreds of miles with a crop of grass, which dies and dries in the fall) burns over during the fall or early in the spring, leaving the ground of a black and doleful colour.

There are many modes by which the fire is communicated to them, both by white men and by Indians—*par accident;* and yet many more where it is voluntarily done for the purpose of getting a fresh crop of grass, for the grazing of their horses, and also for easier travelling during the next summer, when there will be no old grass to lie upon the prairies, entangling the feet of man and horse, as they are passing over them.

Over the elevated lands and prairie bluffs, where the grass is thin and short, the fire slowly creeps with a feeble flame, which one can easily step over, where the wild animals often rest in their lairs until the flames almost burn their noses, when they will reluctantly rise, and leap over it, and trot off amongst the cinders, where the fire has past and left the ground as black as jet. These scenes at night become indescribably beautiful, when their flames are seen at many miles distance, creeping over the sides and tops of the bluffs, appearing to be sparkling and brilliant chains of liquid fire (the hills being lost to the view), hanging suspended in graceful festoons from the skies.

But there is yet another character of burning prairies, that requires another Letter, and a different pen to describe—the war, or hell of fires! where the grass is seven or eight feet high, as is often the case for many miles together, on the Missouri bottoms; and the flames are driven forward by the hurricanes, which often sweep over the vast prairies of this denuded country. There are many of these meadows on the Missouri, the Platte, and the Arkansas, of many miles in breadth, which are perfectly level, with a waving grass, so high, that we are obliged to stand erect in our stirrups, in order to look over its waving tops, as we are riding through it. The fire in these, before such a wind, travels at an immense and frightful rate, and often destroys, on their fleetest horses, parties of Indians, who are so unlucky as to be overtaken by it; not that it travels as fast as a horse at full speed, but that the high grass is filled with wild pea-vines and other impediments, which render it necessary for the rider to guide his horse in the zig-zag paths of the deers and buffaloes, retarding his progress, until he is overtaken by the dense column of smoke that is swept before the fire—alarming the horse, which stops and stands terrified and immutable, till the burning grass which is wafted in the wind, falls about him, kindling up in a moment a thousand new fires, which are instantly wrapped in the swelling flood of smoke that is moving on like a black thunder-cloud, rolling on the earth, with its lightning's glare, and its thunder rumbling as it goes . . .

LETTER—NO. 34.

◄——————————————►

Fort Leavenworth, Lower Missouri.

*T*he Indians that may be said to belong to this vicinity, ... and who constantly visit this post, are the Ioways—Konzas —Pawnees—Omahas—Ottoes, and Missouries (primitive), and Delawares—Kickapoos—Potawatomies—Weahs—Peorias—Shawanos, Kaskaskias (semi-civilized remnants of tribes that have been removed to this neighbourhood by the Government, within the few years past). These latter-named tribes are, to a considerable degree, agriculturalists; getting their living principally by ploughing, and raising corn, and cattle and horses. They have been left on the frontier, surrounded by civilized neighbours, where they have at length been induced to sell out their lands, or exchange them for a much larger tract of wild lands in these regions, which the Government has purchased from the wilder tribes.

Of the first names, the Ioways may be said to be the farthest departed from primitive modes, as they are depending chiefy on their corn-fields for subsistence; though their appearance, both in their dwellings and personal looks, dress, modes, &c., is that of the primitive Indian.

The Ioways are a small tribe, of about fourteen hundred persons, living in a snug little village within a few miles of the eastern bank of the Missouri River, a few miles above this place . . .

The Konzas, of 1560 souls, reside at the distance of sixty or eighty miles from this place, on the Konzas River, fifty miles above its union with the Missouri, from the West.

This tribe has undoubtedly sprung from the Osages, as their personal appearance, language and traditions clearly prove. They are living adjoining to the Osages at this time, and although a kindred people, have sometimes deadly warfare with them ... The custom of shaving the head, and ornamenting it with the crest of deer's hair, belongs to this tribe; and also to the Osages, the Pawnees, the Sacs, and Foxes, and Ioways, and to no other tribe that I know of; unless it be in some few instances, where individuals have introduced it into their tribes, merely by way of imitation.

With these tribes, the custom is one uniformly adhered to by every man in the nation; excepting some few instances along the frontier, where efforts are made to imitate white men, by allowing the hair to grow out.

In Illustration 32, is a fair exhibition of this very curious custom— the hair being cut as close to the head as possible, except a tuft the size of the palm of the hand, on the crown of the head, which is left of two inches in length: and in the centre of which is fastened a beautiful crest made of the hair of the deer's tail (dyed red) and horsehair, and oftentimes surmounted with the war-eagle's quill. In the centre of the patch of hair, which I said was left of a couple of inches in length, is preserved a small lock, which is never cut, but cultivated to the greatest length possible, and uniformly kept in braid, and passed through a piece of curiously carved bone; which lies in the centre of the crest, and spreads it out to its uniform shape, which they study with great care to preserve. Through this little braid, and outside of the bone, passes a small wooden or bone key, which holds the crest to the head. This little braid is called in these tribes, the "*scalp-lock*," and is scrupulously preserved in this way, and offered to their enemy if they can get it, as a trophy; which it seems in all tribes they are anxious to yield to their conquerors, in case they are killed in battle; and which it would be considered cowardly and disgraceful for a warrior to shave off, leaving nothing for his enemy to grasp for, when he falls into his hands in the events of battle.

Amongst those tribes who thus shave and ornament their heads, the crest is uniformly blood-red; and the upper part of the head, and generally a considerable part of the face, as red as they can possibly make it with vermillion. I found these people cutting off the hair with small scissors, which they purchase of the Fur Traders; and

Illustration 32. Chesh-oo-hong-ha, Man of Good Sense—a Konzas warrior.

they told me that previous to getting scissors, they cut it away with their knives; and before they got knives, they were in the habit of burning it off with red hot stones, which was a very slow and painful operation.

With the exception of these few, all the other tribes in North America cultivate the hair to the greatest length they possibly can; preserving it to flow over their shoulders and backs in great profusion, and quite unwilling to spare the smallest lock of it for any consideration.

The Pawnees are a very powerful and warlike nation, living on the river Platte, about one hundred miles from its junction with the Missouri; laying claim to, and exercising sway over, the whole country, from its mouth to the base of the Rocky Mountains.

The present number of this tribe is ten or twelve thousand; about one half the number they had in 1832, when that most appalling disease, the small-pox, was accidentally introduced amongst them by the Fur Traders, and whiskey sellers; when ten thousand (or more) of them perished in the course of a few months.

The Omahas, of fifteen hundred; the Ottoes of six hundred; and Missouries of four hundred, who are now living under the protection and surveillance of the Pawnees, and in the immediate vicinity of them, were all powerful tribes, but so reduced by this frightful disease, and at the same time, that they were unable longer to stand against so formidable enemies as they had around them, in the Sioux, Pawnees, Sacs, and Foxes, and at last merged into the Pawnee tribe, under whose wing and protection they now live.

The period of this awful calamity in these regions, was one that will be long felt, and long preserved in the traditions of these people. The great tribe of the Sioux, of whom I have heretofore spoken, suffered severely with the same disease; as well as the Osages and Konzas; and particularly the unfortunate Puncahs, who were almost extinguished by it.

The destructive ravages of this most fatal disease amongst these poor people, who know of no specific for it, is beyond the knowledge, and almost beyond the belief, of the civilized world. Terror and dismay are carried with it; and awful despair, in the midst of which they plunge into the river, when in the highest state of fever, and die in a moment; or dash themselves from precipices; or plunge their knives to their hearts, to rid themselves from the pangs of slow and disgusting death.

Amongst the formidable tribe of Pawnees, the Fur Traders are yet doing some business; but, from what I can learn, the Indians are dealing with some considerable distrust, with a people who introduced so fatal a calamity amongst them, to which one half of their tribe have fallen victims. The Traders made their richest harvest amongst these people, before this disease broke out; and since it subsided, quite a number of their lives have paid the forfeit, according to the Indian laws of retribution.

The Pawnees have ever been looked upon, as a very warlike and hostile tribe; and unusually so, since the calamity which I have mentioned.

Major Dougherty, of whom I have heretofore spoken, has been for several years their agent; and by his unremitted endeavours, with an unequalled familiarity with the Indian character, and unyielding integrity of purpose, has successfully restored and established, a system of good feeling and respect between them and the "pale faces," upon whom they looked, naturally and experimentally, as their destructive enemies.

Of this stern and uncompromising friend of the red man, and of justice, who has taken them close to his heart, and familiarized himself with their faults and their griefs, I take great pleasure in recording here for the perusal of the world, the following extract from one of his true and independent Reports, to the Secretary at War; which sheds honour on his name, and deserves a more public place than the mere official archives of a Government record.

"In comparing this Report with those of the years preceding, you will find there has been little improvement on the part of the Indians, either in literary acquirements or in agricultural knowledge.

"It is my decided opinion, that, so long as the Fur Traders and trappers are permitted to reside among the Indians, all the efforts of the Government to better their condition will be fruitless; or, in a great measure checked by the strong influence of those men over the various tribes.

"Every exertion of the agents, (and other persons, intended to carry into effect the views of Government, and humane societies,) are in such direct opposition to the Trader and his interest, that the agent finds himself continually contending with, and placed in direct and immediate contrariety of interest to the Fur Traders or grossly neglecting his duty by overlooking acts of impropriety; and it is a curious and melancholy fact, that while the General Government is using every means and expense to promote the advancement of those aboriginal people, it is at the same time suffering the Traders to oppose and defeat the very objects of its intentions. So long as the Traders and trappers are permitted in the Indian country, the introduction of spirituous liquors will be inevitable, under any penalty the law may require; and until its prohibition is certain and effectual, every effort of Government, through the most faithful and indefatigable agents, will be useless. It would be, in my humble opinion, better to give up every thing to the Traders, and let them have the sole and entire control of the Indians, than permit them to contend at every point, with the views of the Government; and that contention made manifest, even to the most ignorant Indian.

"While the agent is advising the Indians to give up the chase and settle themselves, with a view to agricultural pursuits, the Traders are urging them on in search of skins.

"Far be it from me to be influenced or guided by improper or personal feeling, in the execution of my duty; but, Sir, I submit my opinion to a candid world, in relation to the subject, and feel fully convinced you will be able to see at once the course which will ever place the Indian Trader, and the present policy of Government, in relation to the Indians, at eternal war.

"The missionaries sent amongst the several tribes are, no doubt, sincere in their intentions. I believe them to be so, from what I have seen; but, unfortunately, they commence their labours where they should end them. They should teach the Indians to work, by establishing schools of that description among them: induce them to live at home, abandon their restless and unsettled life, and live independent of the chase. After they are taught this, their intellectual faculties would be more susceptible of improvement of a moral and religious nature; and their steps towards civilization would become less difficult."

The Pawnees are divided into four bands, or families—designated by the names of Grand Pawnees—Tappage Pawnees—Republican Pawnees, and Wolf Pawnees . . .

The Pawnees live in four villages, some few miles apart, on the banks of the Platte river, having their allies the Omahas and Ottoes so near to them as easily to act in concert, in case of invasion from any other tribe; and from the fact that half or more of them are supplied with guns and ammunition, they are able to withstand the assaults of any tribe that may come upon them . . . All of these tribes, as well as the numerous semi-civilized remnants of tribes, that have been thrown out from the borders of our settlements, have missionary establishments and schools, as well as agricultural efforts amongst them; and will furnish valuable evidence as to the success that those philanthropic and benevolent exertions have met with, contending (as they have had to do) with the contaminating influences of whiskey-sellers, and other mercenary men, catering for their purses and their unholy appetites.

LETTER—NO. 35.

◀——————————————————▶

St. Louis, Missouri.

*M*y little bark has been soaked in the water again, and Ba'tiste and Bogard have paddled, and I have steered and dodged our little craft amongst the snags and sawyers, until at last we landed the humble little thing amongst the huge steamers and floating palaces at the wharf of this bustling and growing city.

And first of all, I must relate the fate of my little boat, which had borne us safe over two thousand miles of the Missouri's turbid and boiling current, with no fault, excepting two or three instances, when the waves became too saucy, she, like the best of boats of her size, went to the bottom, and left us soused, to paddle our way to the shore, and drag out our things and dry them in the sun.

When we landed at the wharf, my luggage was all taken out, and removed to my hotel; and when I returned a few hours afterwards, to look for my little boat, to which I had contracted a peculiar attachment (although I had left it in special charge of a person at work on the wharf); some *mystery* or *medicine* operation had relieved me from any further anxiety or trouble about it—it had gone and never returned, although it had safely passed the countries of mysteries, and had often laid weeks and months at the villages of red men, with no laws to guard it; and where it had also often been taken out of the water by *mystery-men*, and carried up the bank, and turned against my wigwam; and by them again safely carried to the river's edge, and put afloat upon the water, when I was ready to take a seat in it.

St. Louis, which is 1400 miles west of New York, is a flourishing town, of 15,000 inhabitants, and destined to be the great emporium of the West—the greatest inland town in America. Its location is on the Western bank of the Mississippi river, twenty miles below the mouth of the Missouri, and 1400 above the entrance of the Mississippi into the Gulf of Mexico.

This is the great depôt of all the Fur Trading Companies to the Upper Missouri and Rocky Mountains, and their starting-place; and also for the Santa Fe, and other Trading Companies, who reach the Mexican borders overland, to trade for silver bullion, from the extensive mines of that rich country.

I have also made it *my* starting-point, and place of deposit, to which I send from different quarters, my packages of paintings and Indian articles, minerals, fossils, &c., as I collect them in various regions, here to be stored till my return; and where on my *last return*, if I ever make it, I shall hustle them altogether, and remove them to the East.

To this place I had transmitted by steamer and other conveyance, about twenty boxes and packages at different times, as my note-book shewed; and I have, on looking them up and enumerating them, been lucky enough to recover and recognize about fifteen of the twenty, which is a pretty fair proportion for this wild and desperate country, and the very *conscientious hands* they often are doomed to pass through.

Ba'tiste and Bogard (poor fellows) I found, after remaining here a few days, had been about as unceremoniously snatched off, as my little canoe; and Bogard, in particular, as he had made show of a few hundred dollars, which he had saved of his hard earnings in the Rocky Mountains.

He came down with a liberal heart, which he had learned in an Indian life of ten years, with a strong taste, which he had acquired, for whiskey, in a country where it was sold for twenty dollars per gallon; and with an independent feeling, which illy harmonized with rules and regulations of a country of laws; and the consequence soon was, that by the "Hawk and Buzzard" system, and Rocky Mountain liberality, and Rocky Mountain prodigality, the poor fellow was soon "jugged up;" where he could deliberately dream of beavers, and the free and cooling breezes of the mountain air, without the pleasure of setting his trap for the one, or even indulging the hope of ever again having the pleasure of breathing the other.

I had imbibed rather less of these delightful passions in the Indian country, and consequently indulged less in them when I came back; and of course, was rather more fortunate than poor Bogard, whose feelings I soothed as far as it laid in my power, and prepared to "lay my course" to the South, with colours and canvass in readiness for another campaign.

In my sojourn in St. Louis, amongst many other kind and congenial friends whom I met, I have had daily interviews with the venerable Governor Clark, whose whitened locks are still shaken in roars of laughter, and good jests among the numerous citizens, who all love him, and continually rally around him in his hospitable mansion.

Governor Clark, with Captain Lewis, were the first explorers across the Rocky Mountains, and down the Colombia to the Pacific Ocean thirty-two years ago; whose tour has been published in a very interesting work, which has long been before the world. My works and my design have been warmly approved and applauded by this excellent patriarch of the Western World; and kindly recommended by him in such ways as have been of great service to me. Governor Clark is now Superintendant of Indian Affairs for all the Western and North Western regions; and surely, their interests could never have been intrusted to better or abler hands.

LETTER—NO. 36.

◄————————————————►

Pensacola, West Florida.

... ***T***he sudden transition from the ice-bound regions of the North to this mild climate, in the midst of winter, is one of peculiar pleasure. At a half-way of the distance, one's cloak is thrown aside; and arrived on the ever-verdant borders of Florida, the bosom is opened and bared to the soft breeze from the ocean's wave, and the congenial warmth of a summer's sun ...

Florida is, in a great degree, a dark and sterile wilderness, yet with spots of beauty and of loveliness, with charms that cannot be forgotten. Her swamps and everglades, the dens of alligators, and lurking places of the desperate savage, gloom the thoughts of the wary traveller, whose mind is cheered and lit to admiration, when in the solitary pine woods, where he hears nought but the echoing notes of the *sand-hill cranes*, or the howling wolf, he suddenly breaks out into the open savannahs, teeming with their myriads of wild flowers, and palmettos; or where the winding path through which he is wending his lonely way, suddenly brings him out upon the beach, where the rolling sea has thrown up her thousands of hills and mounds of sand as white as the drifted snow, over which her green waves are lashing, and sliding back again to her deep green and agitated bosom (Illustration 33). This sketch was made on *Santa Rosa Island*, within a few miles of Pensacola, of a favourite spot for *tea* (and other convivial) *parties*, which are often held there. The hills of sand are as *purely white as snow*, and fifty or sixty feet in height, and supporting on their tops, and in their sides, clusters of magnolia bushes—or myrtle—of palmetto and heather, all of which are ever-greens, forming the most vivid contrast with the snow-white sand in

Illustration 33. Seminole family drying fish on Santa Rosa Island.

which they are growing. On the beach a family of Seminole Indians are encamped, catching and drying red fish, their chief article of food . . .

Of the few remnants of Indians remaining in this part of the country, I have little to say, at present, that could interest you. The sum total that can be learned or seen of them (like all others that are half civilized) is, that they are to be pitied . . .

Since you last heard from me, I have added on to my former Tour "down the river," the remainder of the Mississippi (or rather Missouri), from St. Louis to New Orleans; and I find that, from its source to the Balize, the distance is 4500 *miles only!* I shall be on the wing again in a few days, for a shake of the hand with the Camanchees, Osages, Pawnees, Kioways, Arapahoes, &c.—some hints of whom I shall certainly give you from their different localities, provided I can keep the hair on my head.

This Tour will lead me up the Arkansas to its source, and into the Rocky Mountains, under the protection of the United States dragoons. You will begin to think ere long, that I shall acquaint myself pretty well with the manners and customs of our country—at least with the *out-land-ish* part of it . . .

LETTER—NO. 37.

◄————————————►

Fort Gibson, Arkansas Territory.

*S*ince the date of my last Letter at Pensacola, in Florida, I travelled to New Orleans, and from thence up the Mississippi several hundred miles, to the mouth of the Arkansas; and up the Arkansas, 700 miles to this place . . . Fort Gibson is the extreme south-western outpost on the United States frontier; beautifully situated on the banks of the river, in the midst of an extensive and lovely prairie; and is at present occupied by the 7th regiment of United States infantry . . .

Being soon to leave this little civilized world for a campaign in the Indian country, I take this opportunity to bequeath a few words before the moment of departure. Having sometime since obtained permission from the Secretary of War to accompany the regiment of the United States dragoons in their summer campaign, I *reported* myself at this place two months ago, where I have been waiting ever since for their organization.—After the many difficulties which they have had to encounter, they have at length all assembled—the grassy plains are resounding with the trampling hoofs of the prancing war-horse—and already the hills are echoing back the notes of the spirit-stirring trumpets, which are sounding for the onset. The *natives* are again "to be astonished," and I shall probably again be a witness to the scene. But whether the approach of eight hundred mounted dragoons amongst the Camanchees and Pawnees, will afford me a better subject for a picture of a *gaping* and *astounded multitude,* than did the first approach of our steam-boat amongst the Mandans, &c., is a question yet to be solved. I am strongly inclined to think that the scene will not be less wild and spirited, and I ardently wish it; for I have become so much Indian of late, that my pencil has lost all appetite for subjects that savour of tameness. I should delight in seeing these red knights of the lance astonished, for it is then that they shew their brightest hues—and I care not how badly we frighten them, provided we hurt them not, nor frighten them out of *sketching distance* . . .

The landscape scenes of these wild and beautiful regions, are, of themselves, a rich reward for the traveller who can place them in his portfolio: and being myself the only one accompanying the dragoons for scientific purposes, there will be an additional pleasure to be derived from those pursuits. The regiment of eight hundred men, with whom I am to travel, will be an effective force, and a perfect protection against any attacks that will ever be made by Indians. It is composed principally of young men of respectable families, who would act, on all occasions, from feelings of pride and honour, in addition to those of the common soldier . . .

Both regiments were drawn up in battle array, in *fatigue dress*, and passing through a number of the manœuvres of battle, of charge and repulse, &c., presenting a novel and thrilling scene in the prairie, to the thousands of Indians and others who had assembled to witness the display. The proud and manly deportment of these young men remind one forcibly of a regiment of Independent Volunteers, and the horses have a most beautiful appearance from the arrangement of colours. Each company of horses has been selected of one colour entire. There is a company of *bays*, a company of *blacks*, one of *whites*, one of *sorrels*, one of *greys*, one of *cream* colour, &c., &c., which render the companies distinct, and the effect exceedingly pleasing. This regiment goes out under the command of Colonel Dodge, and from his well tested qualifications, and from the beautiful equipment of the command, there can be little doubt but that they will do credit to themselves and an honour to their country; so far as honours can be gained and laurels can be plucked from their wild stems in a savage country.

The object of this summer's campaign seems to be to cultivate an acquaintance with the Pawnees and Camanchees. These are two extensive tribes of roaming Indians, who, from their extreme ignorance of us, have not yet recognized the United States in treaty, and have struck frequent blows on our frontiers and plundered our traders who are traversing their country. For this I cannot so much blame them, for the Spaniards are gradually advancing upon them on one side, and the Americans on the other, and fast destroying the furs and game of their country, which God gave them as their only wealth and means of subsistence. This movement of the dragoons *seems* to be one of the most humane in its views, and I heartily hope that it may prove so in the event, as well for our own sakes as for that of the Indian. I can see no reason why we should march upon them with an invading army carrying with it the spirit of chastisement. The object of Government undoubtedly is to effect a friendly meeting with them, that they may see and respect us, and to establish something like a system of mutual rights with them. To penetrate their country with the other view, that of chastising them, even with five times the number that are now going, would be entirely futile, and perhaps *disastrous* in the extreme . . .

In the first place, from the great difficulty of organizing and equipping, these troops are starting too late in the season for their summer's campaign, by two months. The journey which they have to perform is a very long one, and although the first part of it will be picturesque and pleasing, the after part of it will be tiresome and fatiguing in the extreme. As they advance to the West, the grass (and consequently the game) will be gradually diminishing, and water in many parts of the country not to be found.

As the troops will be obliged to subsist themselves a great part of the way, it will be extremely difficult to do it under such circumstances, and at the same time hold themselves in readiness, with half-famished horses and men nearly exhausted, to contend with a numerous enemy who are at home, on the ground on which they were born, with horses fresh and ready for action. It is not probable, however, that the Indians will venture to take advantage of such circumstances; but I am inclined to think, that the expedition will be more likely to fail from another source: it is my opinion that the appearance of so large a military force in their country, will alarm the Indians to that degree, that they will fly with their families to their hiding-places amongst those barren deserts, which they themselves can reach only by great fatigue and extreme privation, and to which our half-exhausted troops cannot possibly follow them. From these haunts their warriors would advance and annoy the regiment as much as they could, by striking at their hunting parties and cutting off their supplies. To attempt to pursue them, if they cannot be called to a council, would be as useless as to follow the wind; for our troops in such a case, are in a country where they are obliged to subsist themselves, and the Indians being on fresh horses, with a supply of provisions, would easily drive all the buffaloes ahead of them; and endeavour, as far as possible, to decoy our troops into the barren parts of the country, where they could not find the means of subsistence.

The plan designed to be pursued, and the only one that can succeed, is to send runners to the different bands, explaining the friendly intentions of our Government, and to invite them to a meeting. For this purpose several Camanchee and Pawnee prisoners have been purchased from the Osages, who may be of great service in bringing about a friendly interview.

I ardently hope that this plan may succeed, for I am anticipating great fatigue and privation in the endeavour to see these wild tribes together; that I may be enabled to lay before the world a just estimate of their manners and customs.

I hope that my suggestions may not be truly prophetic; but I am constrained to say, that I doubt very much whether we shall see anything more of them than their trails, and the sites of their deserted villages . . .

LETTER—NO. 38.

◄————————————————►

Fort Gibson, Arkansas.

*N*early two months have elapsed since I arrived at this post, on my way up the river from the Mississippi, to join the regiment of dragoons on their campaign into the country of the Camanchees and Pawnee Picts [a segment of the Witchitaw Indians]; during which time, I have been industriously at work with my brush and my pen, recording the looks and the deeds of the Osages, who inhabit the country on the North and the West of this.

The Osage, or (as they call themselves) *Wa-saw-see,* are a tribe of about 5200 in numbers, inhabiting and hunting over the head-waters of the Arkansas, and Neosho or Grand Rivers. Their present residence is about 700 miles West of the Mississippi river; in three villages, constituted of wigwams, built of barks and flags or reeds. One of these villages is within forty miles of this Fort; another within sixty, and the third about eighty miles. Their chief place of trade is with the sutlers at this post; and there are constantly more or less of them encamped about the garrison.

The Osages may justly be said to be the tallest race of men in North America, either of red or white skins; there being very few indeed of the men, at their full growth, who are less than six feet in stature, and very many of them six and a half, and others seven feet. They are at the same time well-proportioned in their limbs, and good looking; being rather narrow in the shoulders, and, like most all very tall people, a little inclined to stoop; not throwing the chest out, and the head and shoulders back, quite as much as the Crows and Mandans, and other tribes amongst which I have been familiar. Their movement is graceful and quick;

and in war and the chase, I think they are equal to any of the tribes about them.

This tribe, though living, as they long have, near the borders of the civilized community, have studiously rejected everything of civilized customs: and are uniformly dressed in skins of their own dressing—strictly maintaining their primitive looks and manners, without the slightest appearance of innovations, excepting in the blankets, which have been recently admitted to their use instead of the buffalo robes, which are now getting scarce amongst them.

The Osages are one of the tribes who shave the head, as I have before described when speaking of the Pawnees and Konzas, and they decorate and paint it with great care, and some considerable taste. There is a peculiarity in the heads of these people which is very striking to the eye of a traveller; and which I find is produced by artificial means in infancy. Their children, like those of all the other tribes, are carried on a board, and slung upon the mother's back. The infants are lashed to the boards, with their backs upon them, apparently in a very uncomfortable condition; and with the Osages, the head of the child bound down so tight to the board, as to force in the occipital bone, and create an unnatural deficiency on the back part, and consequently more than a natural elevation of the top of the head. This custom, they told me they practiced, because "it pressed out a bold and manly appearance in front." This I think, from observation, to be rather imaginary than real; as I cannot see that they exhibit any extraordinary development in the front; though they evidently shew a striking deficiency on the back part, and also an unnatural elevation on the top of the head, which is, no doubt, produced by this custom. The difference between this mode and the one practiced by the Flat-head Indians beyond the Rocky Mountains, consists in this, that the Flat-heads press the head *between* two boards; the one pressing the frontal bone down, whilst the other is pressing the occipital up, producing the most frightful deformity; whilst the Osages merely press the occipital in, and that, but to a moderate degree, occasioning but a slight, and in many cases, almost immaterial, departure from the symmetry of nature.

These people, like all those tribes who shave the head, cut and slit their ears very much, and suspend from them great quantities of wampum and tinsel ornaments. Their necks are generally ornamented also with a profusion of wampum and beads; and as they live in a warm climate where there is not so much necessity for warm clothing, as amongst the more Northern tribes, of whom I have been heretofore speaking; their shoulders, arms, and chests are generally naked, and painted in a great variety of picturesque ways, with silver bands on the wrists, and oftentimes a profusion of rings on the fingers.

The head-chief of the Osages at this time, is a young man by the name of Clermont (Illustration 34), the son of a very distinguished chief of that name, who recently died; leaving his son his successor, with the consent of the tribe. I painted the portrait of this chief at full length, in a beautiful dress, his leggings fringed with scalp-locks, and in his hand his favorite and valued war-club.

By his side I have painted also at full length, his wife and child (Illustration 35). She was richly dressed in costly cloths of civilized manufacture, which is almost a solitary instance amongst the Osages, who so studiously reject every luxury and every custom of civilized people; and amongst those, the use of whiskey, which is on all sides tendered to them—but almost uniformly rejected! This is an unusual and unaccountable thing, unless the influence which the missionaries and teachers have exercised over them, has induced them to abandon the pernicious and destructive habit of drinking to excess. From what I can learn, the Osages were once fond of whiskey; and, like all other tribes who have had the opportunity, were in the habit of using it to excess. Several very good and exemplary men have been for years past exerting their greatest efforts, with those of their families, amongst these people; having established schools and agricultural experiments amongst them. And I am fully of the opinion, that this decided anomaly in the Indian country, has resulted from the devoted exertions of these pious and good men . . .

The Osages have been formerly, and until quite recently, a powerful and warlike tribe: carrying their arms fearlessly through all of these realms; and ready to cope with foes of any kind that they were liable to meet. At present, the case is quite different; they have been repeatedly moved and jostled along, from the head waters of

Illustration 34. Clermont, head chief of the Osages.

Illustration 35. Wife and child of Clermont.

the White river, and even from the shores of the Mississippi, to where they now are; and reduced by every war and every move. The small-pox has taken its share of them at two or three different times; and the Konzas, as they are now called, having been a part of the Osages, and receded from them, impaired their strength; and have at last helped to lessen the number of their warriors; so that their decline has been very rapid, bringing them to the mere handful that now exists of them; though still preserving their valour as warriors, which they are continually shewing off as bravely and as profession-ally as they can, with the Pawnees and the Camanchees, with whom they are waging incessant war; although they are the principal sufferers in those scenes which they fearlessly persist in, as if they were actually bent on their self-destruction. Very great efforts have been, and are being made amongst these people to civilize and christianize them; and still I believe with but little success. Agricul-ture they have caught but little of; and of religion and civilization still less. One good result has, however, been produced by these faithful labourers, which is the conversion of these people to temper-ance; which I consider the first important step towards the other results, and which of itself is an achievement that redounds much to the credit and humanity of those, whose lives have been devoted to its accomplishment . . .

LETTER—NO. 39.

◄——————————————►

Mouth of False Washita, Red River.

*U*nder the protection of the United States dragoons, I arrived at this place three days since, on my way again in search of the "Far West." How far I may *this time* follow the flying phantom, is uncertain. I am already again in the land of the *buffaloes* and the *fleet-bounding antelopes;* and I anticipate, with many other beating hearts, rare sport and amusement amongst the wild herds ere long.

We shall start from hence in a few days, and other epistles I may occasionally drop you from *terra incognita,* for such is the great expanse of country which we expect to range over; and names we are to give, and country to explore, as far as we proceed. We are, at this place, on the banks of the Red River, having Texas under our eye on the opposite bank. Our encampment is on the point of land between the Red and False Washita rivers, at their junction; and the country about us is a panorama too beautiful to be painted with a pen: it is, like most of the country in these regions, composed of prairie and timber, alternating in the most delightful shapes and proportions that the eye of a connoisseur could desire. The verdure is every-where of the deepest green, and the plains about us are literally speckled with buffalo. We are distant from Fort Gibson about 200 miles, which distance we accomplished in ten days.

A great part of the way, the country is prairie, gracefully undulating—well watered, and continually beautified by copses and patches of timber. On our way my attention was rivetted to the tops of some of the prairie bluffs, whose summits I approached with inexpressible delight. I rode to the top of one of these noble mounds, in company with my friends ... where we agreed that our *horses* instinctively *looked* and *admired*. They thought not of the rich herbage that was under their feet, but, with deep-drawn sighs, their necks were loftily curved, and their eyes widely stretched over the landscape that was beneath us. From this elevated spot, the horizon was bounded all around us by mountain streaks of blue, softening into azure as they vanished, and the pictured vales that intermidiate lay, were deepening into green as the eye was returning from its roamings. Beneath us, and winding through the waving landscape was seen with peculiar effect, the "bold dragoons," marching in beautiful order forming a train of a mile in length. Baggage waggons and Indians (*engagés*) helped to lengthen the procession. From the point where we stood, the line was seen in miniature; and the undulating hills over which it was bending its way, gave it the appearance of a huge black snake gracefully gliding over a rich carpet of green.

This picturesque country of 200 miles, over which we have passed, belongs to the Creeks and Choctaws, and affords one of the richest and most desirable countries in the world for agricultural pursuits.

Scarcely a day has passed, in which we have not crossed oak ridges, of several miles in breadth, with a sandy soil and scattering timber; where the ground was almost literally covered with vines, producing the greatest profusion of delicious grapes, of five-eighths of an inch in diameter, and hanging in such endless clusters, as justly to entitle this singular and solitary wilderness to the style of a vineyard (and ready for the vintage), for many miles together.

The next hour we would be trailing through broad and verdant valleys of green prairies, into which we had descended; and oftentimes find our progress completely arrested by hundreds of acres of small plum-trees, of four or six feet in height; so closely woven and interlocked together, as entirely to dispute our progress, and sending us several miles around; when every bush that was in sight was so loaded with the weight of its delicious wild fruit, that they were in many instances literally without leaves on their branches, and bent quite to the ground. Amongst these, and in patches, were intervening beds of wild roses, wild currants, and gooseberries. And underneath and about them, and occasionally interlocked with them, huge masses of the prickly pears, and beautiful and tempting wild flowers that sweetened the atmosphere above; whilst an occasional huge yellow rattle-snake, or a copper-head, could be seen gliding over, or basking across their vari-coloured tendrils and leaves.

On the eighth day of our march we met, for the first time, a herd of buffaloes; and being in advance of the command, in company with General Leavenworth, Colonel Dodge, and several other officers; we all had an opportunity of testing the mettle of our horses and *our own tact* at the wild and spirited death. The inspiration of chase took at once, and alike, with the old and the young; a beautiful plain lay before us, and we all gave spur for the onset. General Leavenworth and Colonel Dodge, with their pistols, gallantly and handsomely belaboured a fat cow, and were in together at the death. I was not quite so fortunate in my selection, for the one which I saw fit to gallant over the plain alone, of the same sex, younger and coy, led me a hard chase, and for a long time, disputed my near approach; when, at length, the *full speed* of my horse forced us to close company, and she desperately assaulted his shoulders with her horns. My gun was aimed, but missing its fire, the muzzle entangled in her mane, and was instantly broke in two in my hands, and fell over my shoulder. My pistols were then brought to bear upon her; and though severely wounded, she succeeded in reaching the thicket, and left me without "a deed of chivalry to boast."—Since that day, the Indian hunters in our charge have supplied us abundantly with buffalo meat; and report says, that the country ahead of us will afford us continual sport, and an abundant supply.

We are halting here for a few days to recruit horses and men, after which the line of march will be resumed; and if the Pawnees are as near to us as we have strong reason to believe, from their recent trails and fires, it is probable that within a few days we shall "thrash" them or *"get thrashed;"* unless through their sagacity and fear, they elude our search by flying before us to their hiding-places.

The prevailing policy amongst the officers seems to be, that of flogging them first, and then establishing a treaty of peace. If this plan were *morally right,* I do not think it *practicable;* for, as *enemies,* I do not believe they will stand to meet us; but, as *friends,* I think we *may* bring them to a *talk,* if the proper means are adopted. We are here encamped on the ground on which Judge Martin and servant were butchered, and his son kidnapped by the Pawnees or Camanchees, but a few weeks since; and the moment they discover us in a large body, they will presume that we are relentlessly seeking for revenge, and they will probably be very shy of our approach. We are over the Washita—the "Rubicon is passed." We are invaders of a sacred soil. We are carrying war in our front,—and "we shall soon *see*, what we *shall see*."

The cruel fate of Judge Martin and family has been published in the papers; and it belongs to the regiment of dragoons to demand the surrender of the murderers, and get for the information of the world, some authentic account of the mode in which this horrid outrage was committed.

Judge Martin was a very respectable and independent man, living on the lower part of the Red River, and in the habit of taking his children and a couple of black men-servants with him, and a tent to live in, every summer, into these wild regions; where he pitched it upon the prairie, and spent several months in killing buffaloes and other wild game, for his own private amusement. The news came to Fort Gibson but a few weeks before we started, that he had been set upon by a party of Indians and destroyed. A detachment of troops was speedily sent to the spot, where they found his body horridly mangled, and also of one of his negroes; and it is supposed that his son, a fine boy of nine years of age, has been taken home to their villages by them, where they still retain him, and where it is our hope to recover him.

Great praise is due to General Leavenworth for his early and unremitted efforts to facilitate the movements of the regiment of dragoons, by opening roads from Gibson and Towson to this place. We found encamped two companies of infantry from Fort Towson, who will follow in the rear of the dragoons as far as necessary, transporting with waggons, stores and supplies, and ready, at the same time, to co-operate with the dragoons in case of necessity. General Leavenworth will advance with us from this post, but how far he may proceed is uncertain. We know not exactly the route which we shall take, for circumstances alone must decide that point. We shall probably reach Cantonment Leavenworth in the fall; and one thing is *certain* (in the opinion of one who has already seen something of Indian life and country), we shall meet with many severe privations and reach that place a jaded set of fellows, and as ragged as Jack Falstaff's famous band.

You are no doubt inquiring, who are these Pawnees, Camanchees, and Arapahoes, and why not tell us all about them? Their history, numbers and limits are still in obscurity; nothing definite is yet known of them, but I hope I shall soon be able to give the world a clue to them.

If my life and health are preserved, I anticipate many a pleasing scene for my pencil, as well as incidents worthy of reciting to the world, which I shall occasionally do, as opportunity may occur.

LETTER—NO. 40.

◄——————►

Mouth of False Washita.

... *N*early one half of the command, and included amongst them, several officers, with General Leavenworth, have been thrown upon their backs, with the prevailing epidemic, a slow and distressing bilious fever. The horses of the regiment are also sick, about an equal proportion, and seemingly suffering with the same disease. They are daily dying, and men are calling sick, and General Leavenworth has ordered Col. Dodge to select all the men, and all the horses that are able to proceed, and be off to-morrow at nine o'clock upon the march towards the Camanchees, in hopes thereby to preserve the health of the men, and make the most rapid advance towards the extreme point of destination . . .

I should here remark, that when we started from Fort Gibson, the regiment of dragoons, instead of the eight hundred which it was supposed it would contain, had only organized to the amount of 400 men, which was the number that started from that place; and being at this time half disabled, furnishes but 200 effective men to penetrate the wild and untried regions of the hostile Camanchees . . .

In my last Letter I gave a brief account of a buffalo chase, where General Leavenworth and Col. Dodge took parts, and met with pleasing success. The next day, while on the march, and a mile or so in advance of the regiment, and two days before we reached this place, General Leavenworth, Col. Dodge, Lieut. Wheelock and myself were jogging along, and all in turn complaining of the lameness of our bones from the chase on the former day, when the General, who had long ago had his surfeit of pleasure of this kind on the Upper Missouri, remonstrated against further indulgence, in the following manner: "Well, Colonel, this running for buffaloes is bad business for us—we are getting too old, and should leave such amusements to the young men; I have had enough of this fun in my life, and I am determined not to hazard my limbs or weary my horse any more with it—it is the height of folly for us, but will do well enough for boys." Col. Dodge assented at once to his resolves, and approved them; whilst I, who had tried it in every form (and I had thought, to my heart's content), on the Upper Missouri, joined my assent to the folly of our destroying our horses, which had a long journey to perform, and agreed that I would join no more in the buffalo chase, however near and inviting they might come to me.

In the midst of this conversation, and these mutual declarations (or rather just at the end of them), as we were jogging along in *"Indian file,"* and General Leavenworth taking the lead, and just rising to the top of a little hill over which it seems he had had an instant peep, he dropped himself suddenly upon the side of his horse and wheeled back! and rapidly informed us with an agitated whisper, and an exceeding game contraction of the eye, that a snug little band of buffaloes were quietly grazing just over the knoll in a beautiful meadow for running, and that if I would take to the left! and Lieut. Wheelock to the right! and let him and the Colonel dash right into the midst of them! we could play the devil with them!! one half of this at least was said after he had got upon his feet and taken off his portmanteau and valise, in which we had all followed suit, and were mounting for the start! and I am almost sure nothing else was said, and if it had been I should not have heard it, for I was too far off! and too rapidly dashed over the waving grass! and too eagerly gazing and plying the whip, to hear or to see, anything but the trampling hoofs! and the blackened throng! and the darting steeds! and the flashing of guns! until I had crossed the beautiful lawn! and the limb of a tree, as my horse was darting into the timber, had crossed my horse's back, and had scraped me into the grass, from which I soon raised my head! and all was silent! and all out of sight! save the dragoon regiment, which I could see in distance creeping along on the top of a high hill. I found my legs under me in a few moments, and put them in their accustomed positions, none of which would for some time, answer the usual purpose; but I at last got them to work, and brought "Charley" out of the bushes, where he had "brought up" in the top of a fallen tree, without damage.

No buffalo was harmed in this furious assault, nor horse nor rider. Col. Dodge and Lieut. Wheelock had joined the regiment, and General Leavenworth joined me, with too much game expression *yet* in his eye to allow him more time than to say, "I'll have that calf before I quit!" and away he sailed, "up hill and down dale," in pursuit of a fine calf that had been hidden on the ground during the chase, and was now making its way over the prairies in pursuit of the herd. I rode to the top of a little hill to witness the success of the General's second effort, and after he had come close upon the little affrighted animal, it dodged about in such a manner as evidently to baffle his skill, and perplex his horse, which at last fell in a hole, and both were instantly out of my sight. I ran my horse with all possible speed to the spot, and found him on his hands and knees, endeavouring to get up. I dismounted and raised him on to his feet, when I asked him if he was hurt, to which he replied "no, but I might have been," when he instantly fainted, and I laid him on the grass. I had left my canteen with my portmanteau, and had nothing to administer to him, nor was there water near us. I took my lancet from my pocket and was tying his arm to open a vein, when he recovered, and objected to the operation, assuring me that he was not in the least injured. I caught his horse and soon got him mounted again, when we rode on together, and after two or three hours were enabled to join the regiment.

From that hour to the present, I think I have seen a decided change in the General's face; he has looked pale and feeble, and been continually troubled with a violent cough. I have rode by the side of him from day to day, and he several times told me that he was fearful he was badly hurt. He looks very feeble now, and I very much fear the result of the fever that has set in upon him.

We take up the line of march at bugle-call in the morning . . . I am now to enter upon one of the most interesting parts of the Indian country, inasmuch as it is one of the wildest and most hostile . . .

LETTER—NO. 41.

◄————————►

Great Camanchee Village.

*O*ur course was about due West, on the divide between the
. . . *O* Washita and Red Rivers, with our faces looking towards
the Rocky Mountains. The country over which we passed from day
to day, was inimitably beautiful; being the whole way one continuous
prairie of green fields, with occasional clusters of timber and shrubbery, just enough for the uses of cultivating-man, and for the
pleasure of his eyes to dwell upon. The regiment was rather more
than half on the move, consisting of 250 men, instead of 200 as I
predicted in my Letter from that place. All seemed gay and buoyant
at the fresh start, which all trusted was to liberate us from the fatal
miasma which we conceived was hovering about the mouth of the
False Washita. We advanced on happily, and met with no trouble
until the second night of our encampment, in the midst of which we
were thrown into "pie" (as printers would say,) in an instant of the
most appalling alarm and confusion. We were encamped on a beautiful
prairie, where we were every hour apprehensive of the lurking enemy.
And in the dead of night, when all seemed to be sound asleep and
quiet, the instant sound and flash of a gun within a few paces of
us! and then the most horrid and frightful groans that instantly
followed it, brought us all upon our hands and knees in an instant, and
our affrighted horses (which were breaking their lasos,) in full speed
and fury over our heads, with the frightful and mingled din of snorting, and cries of "Indians! Indians! Pawnees!" &c., which rang from
every part of our little encampment! In a few moments the excitement
was chiefly over, and silence restored; when we could hear the trampling
hoofs of the horses, which were making off in all directions . . .

After an instant preparation for battle, and a little recovery from the fright, which was soon effected by waiting a few moments in vain, for the enemy to come on;—a general explanation took place, which brought all to our legs again, and convinced us that there was no decided obstacle, as yet, to our reaching the Camanchee towns; and after that, "sweet home," and the arms of our wives and dear little children, provided we could ever overtake and recover our horses, which had swept off in fifty directions, and with impetus enough to ensure us employment for a day or two to come.

At the proper moment for it to be made, there was a general enquiry for the cause of this *real misfortune*, when it was ascertained to have originated in the following manner. A "raw recruit," who was standing as one of the sentinels on that night, saw, as he says "he supposed," an Indian creeping out of a bunch of bushes a few paces in front of him, upon whom he levelled his rifle; and as the poor creature did not *"advance* and *give the countersign"* at his call, nor any answer at all, he "let off!" and popped a bullet through the heart of a poor dragoon horse, which had strayed away on the night before, and had faithfully followed our trail all the day, and was now, with a beastly misgiving, coming up, and slowly poking through a little thicket of bushes into camp, to join its comrades, in servitude again!

The sudden shock of a gun, and the most appalling groans of this poor dying animal, in the dead of night, and so close upon the heels of sweet sleep, created a long vibration of nerves, and a day of great perplexity and toil which followed, as we had to retrace our steps twenty miles or more, in pursuit of affrighted horses; of which some fifteen or twenty took up wild and free life upon the prairies, to which they were abandoned, as they could not be found. After a detention of two days in consequence of this disaster, we took up the line of march again, and pursued our course with vigour and success, over a continuation of green fields, enamelled with wild flowers, and pleasingly relieved with patches and groves of timber.

On the fourth day of our march, we discovered many fresh signs of buffaloes; and at last, immense herds of them grazing on the distant hills. Indian trails were daily growing fresh, and their smokes were seen in various directions ahead of us. And on the same day at noon, we discovered a large party at several miles distance, sitting on their horses and looking at us. From the glistening of the blades of their lances, which were blazing as they turned them in the sun, it was at first thought that they were Mexican cavalry, who might have been apprized of our approach into their country, and had advanced to contest the point with us. On drawing a little nearer, however, and scanning them closer with our spy-glasses, they were soon ascertained to be a war-party of Camanchees, on the look out for their enemies.

The regiment was called to a halt, and the requisite preparations made and orders issued, we advanced in a direct line towards them until we had approached to within two or three miles of them, when they suddenly disappeared over the hill, and soon after shewed themselves on another mound farther off and in a different direction. The course of the regiment was then changed, and another advance towards them was commenced, and as before, they disappeared and shewed themselves in another direction. After several such efforts which proved ineffectual, Col. Dodge ordered the command to halt, while he rode forward with a few of his staff, and an ensign carrying a white flag. I joined this advance, and the Indians stood their ground until we had come within half a mile of them, and could distinctly observe all their numbers and movements. We then came to a halt, and the white flag was sent a little in advance, and waved as a signal for them to approach; at which one of their party galloped out in advance of the war-party, on a milk white horse, carrying a piece of white buffalo skin on the point of his long lance in reply to our flag.

This moment was the commencement of one of the most thrilling and beautiful scenes I ever witnessed. All eyes, both from his own party and ours, were fixed upon the manœuvres of this gallant little fellow, and he well knew it.

The distance between the two parties was perhaps half a mile, and that a beautiful and gently sloping prairie; over which he was for the space of a quarter of an hour, reining and spurring his maddened horse, and gradually approaching us by tacking to the right and the left, like a vessel beating against the wind. He at length came prancing and leaping along till he met the flag of the regiment, when he leaned his spear for a moment against it, looking the bearer full in the face, when he wheeled his horse, and dashed up to Col. Dodge (Illustration 36), with his extended hand, which was instantly grasped and shaken. We all had him by the hand in a moment, and the rest of the party seeing him received in this friendly manner, instead of being sacrificed, as they undoubtedly expected, started under "full whip" in a direct line towards us, and in a moment gathered, like a black cloud, around us! The regiment then moved up in regular order, and a general shake of the hand ensued, which was accomplished by each warrior riding along the ranks, and shaking the hand of every one as he passed. This necessary form took up considerable time, and during the whole operation, my eyes were fixed upon the gallant and wonderful appearance of the little fellow who bore us the white flag on the point of his lance. He rode a fine and spirited wild horse, which was as white as the drifted snow, with an exuberant mane, and its long and bushy tail sweeping the ground. In his hand he tightly drew the reins upon a heavy Spanish bit, and at every jump, plunged into the animal's sides, till they were in a gore of blood, a huge pair of spurs, plundered, no doubt, from the Spaniards in their border wars, which are continually waged on the Mexican frontiers. The eyes of this noble little steed seemed to be squeezed out of its head; and its fright, and its agitation had brought out upon its skin a perspiration that was fretted into a white foam and lather. The warrior's quiver was slung on the warrior's back, and his bow grasped in his left hand, ready for instant use, if called for. His shield was on his arm, and across his thigh, in a beautiful cover of buckskin, his gun was slung—and in his right hand his lance of fourteen feet in length.

Thus armed and equipped was this dashing cavalier; and nearly in the same manner, all the rest of the party; and very many of them leading an extra horse, which we soon learned was the favourite war-horse; and from which circumstances altogether, we soon understood that they were a war-party in search of their enemy.

After a shake of the hand, we dismounted, and the pipe was lit, and passed around. And then a "talk" was held, in which we were aided by a Spaniard we luckily had with us, who could converse with one of the Camanchees, who spoke some Spanish.

Illustration 36. Camanchees meeting Colonel Dodge and the Dragoons.

Colonel Dodge explained to them the friendly motives with which we were penetrating their country—that we were sent by the President to reach their villages—to see the chiefs of the Camanchees and Pawnee Picts—to shake hands with them, and to smoke the pipe of peace, and to establish an acquaintance, and consequently a system of trade that would be beneficial to both.

They listened attentively, and perfectly appreciated; and taking Colonel Dodge at his word, relying with confidence in what he told them; they informed us that their great town was within a few days' march, and pointing in the direction—offered to abandon their war-excursion, and turn about and escort us to it, which they did in perfect good faith. We were on the march in the afternoon of that day, and from day to day they busily led us on, over hill and dale, encamping by the side of us at night, and resuming the march in the morning.

During this march, over one of the most lovely and picturesque countries in the world, we had enough continually to amuse and excite us. The whole country seemed at times to be alive with buffaloes, and bands of wild horses.

We had with us about thirty Osage and Cherokee, Seneca and Delaware Indians, employed as guides and hunters for the regiment; and with the war-party of ninety or a hundred Camanchees, we formed a most picturesque appearance while passing over the green fields, and consequently, sad havoc amongst the herds of buffaloes, which we were almost hourly passing. We were now out of the influence and reach of bread stuffs, and subsisted ourselves on buffaloes' meat altogether; and the Indians of the different tribes, emulous to shew their skill in the chase, and prove the mettle of their horses, took infinite pleasure in dashing into every herd that we approached; by which means, the regiment was abundantly supplied from day to day with fresh meat.

In one of those spirited scenes when the regiment were on the march, and the Indians with their bows and arrows were closely plying a band of these affrighted animals, they made a bolt through the line of the dragoons, and a complete breach, through which the whole herd passed, upsetting horses and riders in the most amusing manner, and receiving such shots as came from those guns and pistols that were *aimed*, and not fired off into the empty air.

The buffaloes are very blind animals, and owing, probably in a great measure, to the profuse locks that hang over their eyes, they run chiefly by the nose, and follow in the tracks of each other, seemingly heedless of what is about them; and of course, easily disposed to rush in a mass, and the whole tribe or gang to pass in the tracks of those that have first led the way.

The tract of country over which we passed, between the False Washita and this place, is stocked, not only with buffaloes, but with numerous bands of wild horses, many of which we saw every day. There is no other animal on the prairies so wild and so sagacious as the horse; and none other so difficult to come up with. So remarkably keen is their eye, that they will generally run "at the sight," when they are a mile distant; being, no doubt, able to distinguish the character of the enemy that is approaching when at that distance; and when in motion, will seldom stop short of three or four miles . . . Some were milk white, some jet black—others were sorrel, and bay, and cream colour—many were of an iron grey; and others were pied, containing a variety of colours on the same animal. Their manes were very profuse, and hanging in the wildest confusion over their necks and faces—and their long tails swept the ground . . .

The usual mode of taking the wild horses, is, by throwing the *laso*, whilst pursuing them at full speed, and dropping a noose over their necks, by which their speed is soon checked, and they are "choked down." The laso is a thong of rawhide, some ten or fifteen yards in length, twisted or braided, with a noose fixed at the end of it; which, when the coil of the laso is thrown out, drops with great certainty over the neck of the animal, which is soon conquered.

The Indian, when he starts for a wild horse, mounts one of the fleetest he can get, and coiling his laso on his arm, starts off under the "full whip," till he can enter the band, when he soon gets it over the neck of one of the number; when he instantly dismounts, leaving his own horse, and runs as fast as he can, letting the laso pass out gradually and carefully through his hands, until the horse falls for want of breath, and lies helpless on the ground; at which time the Indian advances slowly towards the horse's head, keeping his laso tight upon its neck, until he fastens a pair of hobbles on the animal's two forefeet, and also loosens the laso (giving the horse chance to breathe), and gives it a noose around the under jaw, by which he gets great power over the affrighted animal, which is rearing and plunging when it gets breath; and by which, as he advances, hand over hand, towards the horse's nose, he is able to hold it down and prevent it from throwing itself over on its back, at the hazard of its limbs. By this means he gradually advances, until he is able to place his hand on the animal's nose, and over its eyes; and at length to breathe in its nostrils, when it soon becomes docile and conquered; so that he has little else to do than to remove the hobbles from its feet, and lead or ride it into camp.

This "breaking down" or taming, however, is not without the most desperate trial on the part of the horse, which rears and plunges in every possible way to effect its escape, until its power is exhausted, and it becomes covered with foam; and at last yields to the power of man, and becomes his willing slave for the rest of its life. By this very rigid treatment, the poor animal seems to be so completely conquered, that it makes no further struggle for its freedom; but submits quietly ever after, and is led or rode away with very little difficulty. Great care is taken, however, in this and in subsequent treatment, not to subdue the spirit of the animal, which is carefully preserved and kept up, although they use them with great severity; being, generally speaking, cruel masters.

The wild horse of these regions is a small, but very powerful animal; with an exceedingly prominent eye, sharp nose, high nostril, small feet and delicate leg; and undoubtedly, have sprung from a stock introduced by the Spaniards, at the time of the invasion of Mexico; which having strayed off upon the prairies, have run wild, and stocked the plains from this to Lake Winnepeg, two or three thousand miles to the North.*

---

*There are many very curious traditions about the first appearance of horses amongst the different tribes, and many of which bear striking proof of the above fact. Most of the tribes have some story about the first appearance of horses; and amongst the Sioux, they have beautifully recorded the fact, by giving it the name of Shonk a-wakon (the medicine-dog).

This useful animal has been of great service to the Indians living on these vast plains, enabling them to take their game more easily, to carry their burthens, &c.,; and no doubt, render them better and handier service than if they were of a larger and heavier breed. Vast numbers of them are also killed for food by the Indians, at seasons when buffaloes and other game are scarce. They subsist themselves both in winter and summer by biting at the grass, which they can always get in sufficient quantities for their food.

Whilst on our march we met with many droves of these beautiful animals, and several times had the opportunity of seeing the Indians pursue them, and take them with the laso. The first successful instance of the kind was effected by one of our guides and hunters, by the name of Beatte, a Frenchman, whose parents had lived nearly their whole lives in the Osage village; and who, himself had been reared from infancy amongst them; and in a continual life of Indian modes and amusements, had acquired all the skill and tact of his Indian teachers, and probably a little more; for he is reputed, without exception, the best hunter in these Western regions.

This instance took place one day whilst the regiment was at its usual halt of an hour, in the middle of the day.

When the bugle sounded for a halt, and all were dismounted, Beatte and several others of the hunters asked permission of Col. Dodge to pursue a drove of horses which were then in sight, at a distance of a mile or more from us. The permission was given, and they started off, and by following a ravine, approached near to the unsuspecting animals, when they broke upon them and pursued them for several miles in full view of the regiment. Several of us had good glasses, with which we could plainly see every movement and every manœuvre. After a race of two or three miles, Beatte was seen with his wild horse down, and the band and the other hunters rapidly leaving him.

Seeing him in this condition, I galloped off to him as rapidly as possible, and had the satisfaction of seeing the whole operation of "breaking down," and bringing in the wild animal . . . When he had conquered the horse in this way, his brother, who was one of the unsuccessful ones in the chase, came riding back, and leading up the horse of Beatte which he had left behind, and after staying with us a few minutes, assisted Beatte in leading his conquered wild horse towards the regiment, where it was satisfactorily examined and commented upon, as it was trembling and covered with white foam, until the bugle sounded the signal for marching, when all mounted; and with the rest, Beatte, astride of his wild horse, which had a buffalo skin girted on its back, and a halter, with a cruel noose around the under jaw. In this manner the command resumed its march, and Beatte astride of his wild horse, on which he rode quietly and without difficulty, until night; the whole thing, the capture, and breaking, all having been accomplished within the space of one hour, our usual and daily halt at midday.

Several others of these animals were caught in a similar manner during our march, by others of our hunters, affording us satisfactory instances of this most extraordinary and almost unaccountable feat.

The horses that were caught were by no means very valuable specimens, being rather of an ordinary quality; and I saw to my perfect satisfaction, that the finest of these droves can never be obtained in this way, as they take the lead at once, when they are pursued, and in a few moments will be seen half a mile or more ahead of the bulk of the drove, which they are leading off. There is not a doubt but there are many very fine and valuable horses amongst these herds; but it is impossible for the Indian or other hunter to take them . . .

After many hard and tedious days of travel, we were at last told by our Camanchee guides that we were near their village; and having led us to the top of a gently rising elevation on the prairie, they pointed to their village at several miles distance, in the midst of one of the most enchanting valleys that human eyes ever looked upon. The general course of the valley is from N.W. to S.E., of several miles in width, with a magnificent range of mountains rising in distance beyond; it being, without doubt, a huge "spur" of the Rocky Mountains, composed entirely of a reddish granite or genis, corresponding with the other links of this stupendous chain. In the midst of this lovely valley, we could just discern amongst the scattering shrubbery that lined the banks of the watercourses, the tops of the Camanchee wigwams, and the smoke curling above them. The valley, for a mile distant about the village, seemed speckled with horses and mules that were grazing in it. The chiefs of the war-party requested the regiment to halt, until they could ride in, and inform their people who were coming. We then dismounted for an hour or so; when we could see them busily running and catching their horses; and at length, several hundreds of their braves and warriors came out at full speed to welcome us, and forming in a line in front of us, as we were again mounted, presented a formidable and pleasing appearance. As they wheeled their horses, they very rapidly formed a line, and "dressed" like well-disciplined cavalry. The regiment was drawn up in three columns, with a line formed in front, by Colonel Dodge and his staff, in which rank my friend Chadwick and I were also paraded; when we had a fine view of the whole manœuvre, which was picturesque and thrilling in the extreme.

In the centre of our advance was stationed a white flag, and the Indians answered to it with one which they sent forward and planted by the side of it.*

The two lines were thus drawn up, face to face, within twenty or thirty yards of each other, as inveterate foes that never had met; and, to the everlasting credit of the Camanchees, whom the world had always looked upon as murderous and hostile, they had all come out in this manner, with their heads uncovered, and without a weapon of any kind, to meet a war-party bristling with arms, and trespassing to the middle of the country. They had every reason to look upon us as their natural enemy, as they have been in the habit of estimating all pale faces; and yet, instead of arms or defences, or even of frowns, they galloped out and looked us in our faces, without an expression of fear or dismay, and evidently with expressions of joy and impatient pleasure, to shake us by the hand, on the bare assertion of Colonel Dodge, which had been made to the chiefs, that "we came to see them on a friendly visit."

*It is a fact which I deem to be worth noting here, that amongst all Indian tribes, that I have yet visited, in their primitive, as well as improved state, the white flag is used as a flag of truce, as it is in the civilized parts of the world, and held to be sacred and inviolable. The chief going to war always carries it in some form or other, generally of a piece of *white skin* or bark, rolled on a small stick, and carried under his dress, or otherwise; and also a red flag, either to be unfurled when occasion requires, the *white flag* as a truce, and the *red* one for battle, or, as they say, "for blood."

After we had sat and gazed at each other in this way for some half an hour or so, the head chief of the band came galloping up to Colonel Dodge, and having shaken him by the hand, he passed on to the other officers in turn, and then rode alongside of the different columns, shaking hands with every dragoon in the regiment; he was followed in this by his principal chiefs and braves, which altogether took up nearly an hour longer, when the Indians retreated slowly towards their village, escorting us to the banks of a fine clear stream, and a good spring of fresh water, half a mile from their village, which they designated as a suitable place for our encampment . . .

The Camanchee horses are generally small, all of them being of the wild breed, and a very tough and serviceable animal; and from what I can learn here of the chiefs, there are yet, farther South, and nearer the Mexican borders, some of the noblest animals in use of the chiefs, yet I do not know that we have any more reason to rely upon this information, than that which had made our horse-jockeys that we have with us, to run almost crazy for the possession of those we were to find at this place. Amongst the immense herds we found grazing here, one-third perhaps are mules, which are much more valuable than the horses.

Of the horses, the officers and men have purchased a number of the best, by giving a very inferior blanket and butcher's knife, costing in all about four dollars! These horses in our cities at the East, independent of the name, putting them upon their merits alone, would be worth from eighty to one hundred dollars each . . .

LETTER—NO. 42.

Great Camanchee Village.

The village of the Camanchees by the side of which we are encamped, is composed of six or eight hundred skin-covered lodges, made of poles and buffalo skins, in the manner precisely as those of the Sioux and other Missouri tribes, of which I have heretofore given some account. This village with its thousands of wild inmates, with horses and dogs, and wild sports and domestic occupations, presents a most curious scene . . . These people, living in a country where buffaloes are abundant, make their wigwams more easily of their skins, than of anything else; and with them find greater facilities of moving about, as circumstances often require; when they drag them upon the poles attached to their horses, and erect them again with little trouble in their new residence. We white men, strolling about amongst their wigwams, are looked upon with as much curiosity as if we had come from the moon; and evidently create a sort of chill in the blood of children and dogs, when we make our appearance . . .

The Camanchees, like the Northern tribes, have many games, and in pleasant weather seem to be continually practicing . . . In their ball-plays, and some other games, they are far behind the Sioux and others of the Northern tribes; but, in racing horses and riding, they are not equalled by any other Indians on the Continent. Racing horses, it would seem, is a constant and almost incessant exercise, and their principal mode of gambling . . . Amongst their feats of riding, there is one that has astonished me more than anything of the kind I have ever seen, or expect to see, in my life:—a stratagem of war, learned and practiced by every young man in the tribe; by

which he is able to drop his body upon the side of his horse and the
instant he is passing, effectually screened from his enemies' weapons
(Illustration 37) as he lays in a horizontal position behind the body of
his horse, with his heel hanging over the horse's back; by which he
has the power of throwing himself up again, and changing to the
other side of the horse if necessary. In this wonderful condition, he
will hang whilst his horse is at fullest speed, carrying with him his
bow and his shield, and also his long lance of fourteen feet in length,
all or either of which he will wield upon his enemy as he passes;
rising and throwing his arrows over the horse's back, or with equal
ease and equal success under the horse's neck.* This astonishing feat
which the young men have been repeatedly playing off to our
surprise as well as amusement, whilst they have been galloping about
in front of our tents, completely puzzled the whole of us; and
appeared to be the result of magic, rather than of skill acquired by
practice. I had several times great curiosity to approach them, to
ascertain by what means their bodies could be suspended in this
manner, where nothing could be seen but the heel hanging over the
horse's back. In these endeavours I was continually frustrated, until
one day I coaxed a young fellow up within a little distance of me, by
offering him a few plugs of tobacco, and he in a moment solved the
difficulty, so far as to render it apparently more feasible than before;
yet leaving it one of the most extraordinary results of practice and
persevering endeavours. I found on examination, that a short hair
halter was passed around under the neck of the horse, and both ends
tightly braided into the mane, on the withers, leaving a loop to hang
under the neck, and against the breast, which, being caught up in
the hand, makes a sling into which the elbow falls, taking the weight
of the body on the middle of the upper arm. Into this loop the rider
drops suddenly and fearlessly, leaving his heel to hang over the back
of the horse, to steady him, and also to restore him when he wishes to
regain his upright position on the horse's back.

*Since writing the above, I have conversed with some of the young men of the
Pawnees, who practise the same feat, and who told me they could throw the arrow
from under the horse's belly, and elevate it upon an enemy with deadly effect!

This feat I did not see performed, but from what I did see, I feel inclined to
believe that these young men were boasting of no more than they were able to perform.

Illustration 37. Camanchee feats of horsemanship.

Besides this wonderful art, these people have several other feats of horsemanship, which they are continually showing off; which are pleasing and extraordinary, and of which they seem very proud. A people who spend so very great a part of their lives, actually on their horses' backs, must needs become exceedingly expert in every thing that pertains to riding—to war, or to the chase; and I am ready, without hesitation, to pronounce the Camanchees the most extraordinary horsemen that I have seen yet in all my travels, and I doubt very much whether any people in the world can surpass them.

The Camanchees are in stature, rather low, and in person, often approaching to corpulency. In their movements, they are heavy and ungraceful; and on their feet, one of the most unattractive and slovenly-looking races of Indians that I have ever seen; but the moment they mount their horses, they seem at once metamorphosed, and surprise the spectator with the ease and elegance of their movements. A Camanchee on his feet is out of his element, and comparatively almost as awkward as a monkey on the ground, without a limb or a branch to cling to; but the moment he lays his hand upon his horse, his *face*, even, becomes handsome, and he gracefully flies away like a different being . . .

The head chief of this village, who is represented to us here, as the head of the nation, is a mild and pleasant looking gentleman, without anything striking or peculiar in his looks (Illustration 38); dressed in a very humble manner, with very few ornaments upon him, and his hair carelessly falling about his face and over his shoulders. The name of this chief is Ee-shah-ko-nee (the bow and quiver). The only ornaments to be seen about him were a couple of beautiful shells worn in his ears, and a boar's tusk attached to his neck, and worn on his breast.

For several days after we arrived at this place, there was a huge mass of flesh, Ta-wah-que-nah (the mountain of rocks), who was put forward as head chief of the tribe; and all honours were being paid to him by the regiment of dragoons, until the above-mentioned chief arrived from the country, where it seems he was leading a war-party; and had been sent for, no doubt, on the occasion. When he arrived, this huge monster, who is the largest and fattest Indian I ever saw, stepped quite into the background, giving way to this

Illustration 38. Ee-shah-ko-nee, Bow and Quiver, first chief.

admitted chief, who seemed to have the confidence and respect of the whole tribe.

This enormous man, whose flesh would undoubtedly weigh three hundred pounds or more, took the most wonderful strides in the exercise of this temporary authority; which, in all probability, he was lawfully exercising in the absence of his superior, as second chief of the tribe . . .

Corpulency is a thing exceedingly rare to be found in any of the tribes, amongst the men, owing, probably, to the exposed and active sort of lives they lead; and that in the absence of all the spices of life, many of which have their effect in producing this disgusting, as well as unhandy and awkward extravagance in civilized society . . .

His-oo-san-ches (the Spaniard, Illustration 38), a gallant little fellow, is represented to us as one of the leading warriors of the tribe; and no doubt is one of the most extraordinary men at present living in these regions. He is half Spanish, and being a half-breed, for whom they generally have the most contemptuous feelings, he has been all his life thrown into the front of battle and danger; at which posts he has signalized himself, and commanded the highest admiration and respect of the tribe, for his daring and and adventurous career. This is the man of whom I have before spoken, who dashed out so boldly from the war-party, and came to us with the white flag raised on the point of his lance, and of whom I have made a sketch in Illustration 36. I have here represented him as he stood for me, with his shield on his arm, with his quiver slung, and his lance of fourteen feet in length in his right hand. This extraordinary little man, whose figure was light, seemed to be all bone and muscle, and exhibited immense power, by the curve of the bones in his legs and his arms. We had many exhibitions of his extraordinary strength, as well as agility; and of his gentlemanly politeness and friendship, we had as frequent evidences . . .

From what I have already seen of the Camanchees, I am fully convinced that they are a numerous and very powerful tribe, and quite equal in numbers and prowess, to the accounts generally given of them.

It is entirely impossible at present to make a correct estimate of their numbers; but taking their own account of villages they point to

Illustration 39. His-oo-san-ches, the Spaniard.

in such numbers, South of the banks of the Red River, as well as those that lie farther West, and undoubtedly North of its banks, they must be a very numerous tribe; and I think I am able to say, from estimates that these chiefs have made me, that they number some 30 or 40,000—being able to shew some 6 or 7000 warriors, well-mounted and well-armed. This estimate I offer not as conclusive, for so little is as yet known of these people, that no estimate can be implicitly relied upon other than that, which, in general terms, pronounces them to be a very numerous and warlike tribe . . .

They speak much of their allies and friends, the Pawnee Picts, living to the West some three or four days' march, whom we are going to visit in a few days, and afterwards return to this village, and then "bend our course" homeward, or, in other words, back to Fort Gibson. Besides the Pawnee Picts, there are the Kiowas and Wicos; small tribes that live in the same vicinity, and also in the same alliance, whom we shall probably see on our march. Every preparation is now making to be off in a few days—and I shall omit further remarks on the Camanchees, until we return, when I shall probably have much more to relate of them and their customs. So many of the men and officers are getting sick, that the little command will be very much crippled, from the necessity we shall be under, of leaving about thirty sick, and about an equal number of well to take care of and protect them; for which purpose, we are constructing a fort, with a sort of breastwork of timbers and bushes, which will be ready in a day or two; and the sound part of the command prepared to start with several Camanchee leaders, who have agreed to pilot the way.

LETTER—NO. 43.

◄————————————►

Great Camanchee Village.

*T*he above Letter it will be seen, was written some time ago, and when all hands (save those who were too sick) were on the start for the Pawnee village. Amongst those exceptions was I, before the hour of starting had arrived; and as the dragoons have made their visit there and returned in a most jaded condition, and I have again got well enough to write, I will render some account of the excursion, which is from the pen and the pencil of my friend Joe, who went with them and took my sketch and note-books in his pocket.

"We were four days travelling over a beautiful country, most of the way prairie, and generally along near the base of a stupendous range of mountains of reddish granite, in many places piled up to an immense height without tree or shrubbery on them; looking as if they had actually dropped from the clouds in such a confused mass, and all lay where they had fallen. Such we found the mountains enclosing the Pawnee village, on the bank of Red River, about ninety miles from the Camanchee town. The dragoon regiment was drawn up within half a mile or so of this village, and encamped in a square, where we remained three days. We found here a very numerous village, containing some five or six hundred wigwams, all made of long prairie grass, thatched over poles which are fastened in the ground and bent in at the top; giving to them, in distance, the appearance of straw beehives, as in Illustration 40, which is an accurate view of it, shewing the Red River in front and the "*mountains of rocks*" behind it.

"To our very great surprise, we have found these people cultivating quite extensive fields of corn (maize), pumpkins, melons, beans

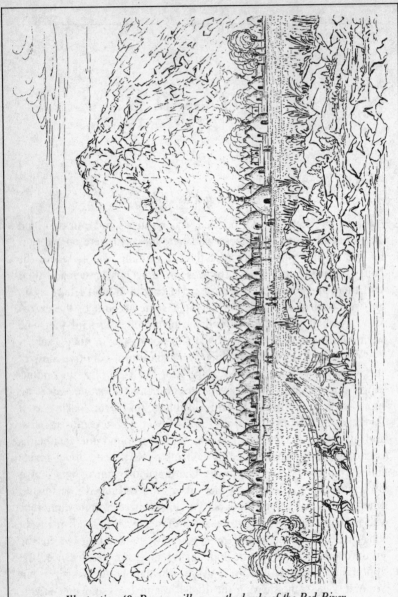

Illustration 40. Pawnee village on the banks of the Red River.

and squashes; so, with these aids, and an abundant supply of buffalo meat, they may be said to be living very well.

"The next day after our arrival here, Colonel Dodge opened a council with the chiefs, in the chief's lodge, where he had the most of his officers around him. He first explained to them the friendly views with which he came to see them; and of the wish of our Government to establish a lasting peace with them, which they seemed at once to appreciate and highly to estimate.

"The head chief of the tribe is a very old man, and he several times replied to Colonel Dodge in a very eloquent manner; assuring him of the friendly feelings of his chiefs and warriors towards the pale faces, in the direction from whence we came.

"After Colonel Dodge had explained in general terms, the objects of our visit, he told them that he should expect from them some account of the foul murder of Judge Martin and his family on the False Washita, which had been perpetrated but a few weeks before, and which the Camanchees had told us was done by the Pawnee Picts. The Colonel told them, also, that he learned from the Camanchees, that they had the little boy, the son of the murdered gentleman, in their possession; and that he should expect them to deliver him up, as an indispensable condition of the friendly arrangement that was now making. They positively denied the fact, and all knowledge of it; firmly assuring us that they knew nothing of the murder, or of the boy. The demand was repeatedly made, and as often denied; until at length a negro-man was discovered, who was living with the Pawnees, who spoke good English; and coming into the council-house, gave information that such a boy had recently been brought into their village, and was now a prisoner amongst them. This excited great surprise and indignation in the council, and Colonel Dodge then informed the chiefs that the council would rest here; and certainly nothing further of a peaceable nature would transpire until the boy was brought in. In this alarming dilemma, all remained in gloomy silence for awhile; when Colonel Dodge further informed the chiefs, that as an evidence of his friendly intentions towards them, he had, on starting, purchased at a very great price, from their enemies the Osages, two Pawnee (and one Kiowa) girls; which had been held by them for some years as prisoners, and which he had brought the whole way home, and had here ready to be delivered to their friends and relations; but whom he certainly would never show, until the little boy was produced. He also made another demand, which was for the restoration of an United States ranger, by the name of Abbé, who had been captured by them during the summer before. They acknowledged the seizure of this man, and all solemnly declared that he had been taken by a party of the Camanchees, over whom they had no controul, and carried beyond the Red River into the Mexican provinces, where he was put to death. They held a long consultation about the boy, and seeing their plans defeated by the evidence of the negro; and also being convinced of the friendly disposition of the Colonel, by bringing home their prisoners from the Osages, they sent out and had the boy brought in, from the middle of a corn-field, where he had been secreted. He is a smart and very intelligent boy of nine years of age, and when he came in, he was entirely naked as they keep their own boys of that age. There was a great excitement in the council when the little fellow was brought in; and as he passed amongst them, he looked around and exclaimed with some surprise, 'What! are there white men here?' to which Colonel Dodge replied, and asked his name; and he promptly answered, 'my name is Matthew Wright Martin.' He was then received into Colonel Dodge's arms; and an order was immediately given for the Pawnee and Kiowa girls to be brought forward; they were in a few minutes brought into the council-house, when they were at once recognized by their friends and relatives, who embraced them with the most extravagant expressions of joy and satisfaction. The heart of the venerable old chief was melted at this evidence of white man's friendship, and he rose upon his feet, and taking Colonel Dodge in his arms, and placing his left cheek against the left cheek of the Colonel, held him for some minutes without saying a word, whilst tears were flowing from his eyes. He then embraced each officer in turn, in the same silent and affectionate manner; which form took half an hour or more, before it was completed.*

*The little boy of whom I have spoken, was brought in the whole distance to Fort Gibson, in the arms of the dragoons, who took turns in carrying him; and after the command arrived there, he was transmitted to the Red River, by an officer, who had the enviable satisfaction of delivering him into the arms of his disconsolate and half-distracted mother.

"From this moment the council, which before had been a very grave and uncertain one, took a pleasing and friendly turn. And this excellent old man ordered the women to supply the dragoons with something to eat, as they were hungry.

"The little encampment, which heretofore was in a woeful condition, having eaten up their last rations twelve hours before, were now gladdened by the approach of a number of women, who brought their 'back loads' of dried buffalo meat and green corn, and threw it down amongst them. This seemed almost like a providential deliverance, for the country between here and the Camanchees, was entirely destitute of game, and our last provisions were consumed.

"The council thus proceeded successfully and pleasantly for several days, whilst the warriors of the Kiowas and Wicos, two adjoining and friendly tribes living further to the West, were arriving; and also a great many from other bands of the Camanchees, who had heard of our arrival; until two thousand or more of these wild and fearless-looking fellows were assembled, and all, from their horses' backs, with weapons in hand, were looking into our pitiful little encampment, of two hundred men, all in a state of dependence and almost literal starvation; and at the same time nearly one half the number too sick to have made a successful resistance if we were to have been attacked."

The command returned to this village after an absence of fifteen days, in a fatigued and destitute condition, with scarcely anything to eat, or chance of getting anything here; in consequence of which, Colonel Dodge almost instantly ordered preparations to be made for a move to the head of the Canadian river, a distance of an hundred or more miles, where the Indians represented to us there would be found immense herds of buffaloes; a place where we could get enough to eat, and by lying by awhile, could restore the sick, who are now occupying a great number of litters. Some days have elapsed, however, and we are not quite ready for the start yet. And during that time, continual parties of the Pawnee Picts and Kioways have come up; and also Camanchees, from other villages, to get a look at us, and many of them are volunteering to go in with us to the frontier . . .

The Pawnee Picts are undoubtedly a numerous and powerful tribe, occupying, with the Kioways and Wicos, the whole country on the head waters of the Red River, and quite into and through the southern part of the Rocky Mountains. The old chief told me by signs, enumerating with his hands and fingers, that they had altogether three thousand warriors; which if true, estimating according to the usual rule, one warrior to four, would make the whole number about twelve thousand; and, allowing a fair per-centage for boasting or bragging, of which they are generally a little guilty in such cases, there would be at a fair calculation from eight to ten thousand. These then, in an established alliance with the great tribe of Camanchees, hunting and feasting together, and ready to join in common defence of their country become a very formidable enemy when attacked on their own ground.

The name of the Pawnee Picts, we find to be in their own language, Tow-ee-ahge, the meaning of which I have not yet learned. I have ascertained also, that these people are in no way related to the Pawnees of the Platte, who reside a thousand miles or more North of them, and know them only as enemies. There is no family or tribal resemblance; nor any in their language or customs. The Pawnees of the Platte shave the head, and the Pawnee Picts abominate the custom; allowing their hair to grow like the Camanchees and other tribes.

The old chief of the Pawnee Picts, of whom I have before spoken, and whose name is We-ta-ra-sha-ro, is undoubtedly a very excellent and kind-hearted old man, of ninety or more years of age, and has consented to accompany us, with a large party of his people, to Fort Gibson; where Colonel Dodge has promised to return him liberal presents from the Government, for the friendship he has evinced on the present occasion.

The second chief of this tribe, Sky-se-ro-ka, we found to be a remarkably clever man, and much approved and valued in his tribe.

The Pawnee Picts, as well as the Camanchees, are generally a very clumsy and ordinary looking set of men, when on their feet; but being fine horsemen, are equally improved in appearance as soon as they mount upon their horses' backs.

Amongst the women of this tribe, there were many that were exceedingly pretty in feature and in form; and also in expression, though their skins are very dark. The dress of the men in this tribe, as amongst the Camanchees, consists generally in leggings of dressed skins, and moccasins; with a flap or breech clout, made also of dressed skins or furs, and often very beautifully ornamented with shells, &c. Above the waist they seldom wear any drapery, owing to the warmth of the climate, which will rarely justify it; and their heads are generally uncovered with a head-dress, like the Northern tribes who live in a colder climate, and actually require them for comfort.

The women of the Camanchees and Pawnee Picts, are always decently and comfortably clad, being covered generally with a gown or slip, that reaches from the chin quite down to the ancles, made of deer or elk skins; often garnished very prettily, and ornamented with long fringes of elk's teeth, which are fastened on them in rows, and more highly valued than any ornament they can put upon them.

In Illustrations 41 and 42, I have given the portraits of two Pawnee girls, Kah-kee-tsee (the thighs), and She-de-a (wild sage), the two Pawnee women who had been held as prisoners by the Osages, and purchased by the Indian Commissioner, the Reverend Mr. Schemmer-hom, and brought home to their own people, and delivered up in the Pawnee town, in the manner that I have just described.

The Kioways are a much finer looking race of men, than either the Camanchees or Pawnees—are tall and erect, with an easy and graceful gait—with long hair, cultivated oftentimes so as to reach nearly to the ground. They have generally the fine and Roman outline of head, that is so frequently found at the North,—and decidedly distinct from that of the Camanchees and Pawnee Picts. These men speak a language distinct from both of the others; and in fact, the Camanchees and Pawnee Picts—and Kioways, and Wicos, are all so distinctly different in their languages, as to appear in that respect as total strangers to each other . . .

All the above chiefs and braves, and many others, forming a very picturesque cavalcade, will move off with us in a day or two, on our way back to Fort Gibson, where it is to be hoped we may arrive more happy than we are in our present jaded and sickly condition.

Illustration 41. Kah-kee-tsee, The Thighs

Illustration 42. She-de-a, Wild Sage

LETTER—NO. 44.

◄————————————►

Camp Canadian, Texas.

Six days of severe travelling have brought us from the Camanchee village to the North bank of the Canadian, where we are snugly encamped on a beautiful plain, and in the midst of countless numbers of buffaloes; and halting a few days to recruit our horses and men, and dry meat to last us the remainder of our journey.

The plains around this, for many miles, seem actually speckled in distance, and in every direction, with herds of grazing buffaloes; and for several days, the officers and men have been indulged in a general licence to gratify their sporting propensities; and a scene of bustle and cruel slaughter it has been, to be sure! From morning till night, the camp had been daily almost deserted; the men have dispersed in little squads in all directions, and are dealing death to these poor creatures to a most cruel and wanton extent, merely for the pleasure of *destroying*, generally without stopping to cut out the meat. During yesterday and this day, several hundreds have undoubtedly been killed, and not so much as the flesh of half a dozen used. Such immense swarms of them are spread over this tract of country; and so divided and terrified have they become, finding their enemies in all directions where they run, that the poor beasts seem completely bewildered—running here and there, and as often as otherwise, come singly advancing to the horsemen, as if to join them for their company, and are easily shot down. In the turmoil and confusion, when their assailants have been pushing them forward, they have galloped through our encampment, jumping over our fires, upsetting pots and kettles, driving horses from their fastenings, and throwing the whole encampment into the greatest instant consternation and alarm. The hunting fever will be satiated in a few days amongst the young men, who are well enough to take parts in the chase; and the bilious fever, it is to be hoped, will be abated in a short time, amongst those who are invalid, and meat enough will be dried to last us to Fort Gibson, when we shall be on the march again, and wending our way towards that garrison.

Many are now sick and unable to ride, and are carried on litters between two horses. Nearly every tent belonging to the officers has been converted to hospitals for the sick; and sighs and groaning are heard in all directions. From the Camanchee village to this place, the country has been entirely prairie; and most of the way high and dry ground, without water, for which we sometimes suffered very much. From day to day we have dragged along exposed to the hot and burning rays of the sun, without a cloud to relieve its intensity, or a bush to shade us, or anything to cast a shadow, except the bodies of our horses. The grass for a great part of the way, was very much dried up, scarcely affording a bite for our horses; and sometimes for the distance of many miles, the only water we could find, was in stagnant pools, lying on the highest ground, in which the buffaloes have been lying and wallowing like hogs in a mud-puddle. We frequently came to these dirty lavers, from which we drove the herds of wallowing buffaloes, and into which our poor and almost dying horses, irresistibly ran and plunged their noses, sucking up the dirty and poisonous draught, until, in some instances, they fell dead in their tracks—the men also (and oftentimes amongst the number, the writer of these lines) sprang from their horses, and laded up and drank to almost fatal excess, the disgusting and tepid draught, and with it filled their canteens, which were slung to their sides, and from which they were sucking the bilious contents during the day.

In our march we found many deep ravines, in the bottoms of which there were the marks of wild and powerful streams; but in this season of drought they were all dried up, except an occasional one, where we found them dashing along in the coolest and clearest manner, and on trial, to our great agony, so *salt* that even our horses could not drink from them; so we had occasionally the tantalizing pleasure of hearing the roar of, and looking into, the clearest and most sparkling streams; and after that the dire necessity of drinking from stagnant pools which lay from month to month exposed to the rays of the sun, till their waters become so poisonous and heavy, from the loss of their vital principle, that they are neither diminished by absorption, or taken into the atmosphere by evaporation.

This poisonous and indigestible water, with the intense rays of the sun in the hottest part of the summer, is the cause of the unexampled sickness of the horses and men. Both appear to be suffering and dying with the same disease, a slow and distressing bilious fever, which seems to terminate in a most frightful and fatal affection of the liver . . .

Since writing the above, an express has arrived from the encampment, which we left at the mouth of False Washita, with the melancholy tidings of the death of General Leavenworth, Lieutenant M'Clure, and ten or fifteen of the men left at that place! This has cast a gloom over our little encampment here, and seems to be received as a fatal foreboding by those who are sick with the same disease; and many of them, poor fellows, with scarce a hope left now for their recovery.

It seems that the General had moved on our trail a few days after we left the Washita, to the "Cross Timbers," a distance of fifty or sixty miles, where his disease at last terminated his existence; and I am inclined to think, as I before mentioned, in consequence of the injury he sustained in a fall from his horse when running a buffalo calf. My reason for believing this, is, that I rode and ate with him every day after the hour of his fall; and from that moment I was quite sure that I saw a different expression in his face, from that which he naturally wore; and when riding by the side of him two or three days after his fall, I observed to him, "General, you have a very bad cough"—"Yes," he replied, "I have killed myself in running that devilish calf; and it was a very lucky thing, Catlin, that you painted the portrait of me before we started, for it is all that my dear wife will ever see of me."

We shall be on the move again in a few days; and I plainly see that I shall be upon a litter, unless my horrid fever leaves me, which is daily taking away my strength, and almost, at times, my senses. Adieu!

LETTER—NO. 45.

◄————————————►

Fort Gibson, Arkansas.

*T*he last Letter was written from my tent, and out upon the wild prairies, when I was shaken and *terrified* by a burning fever, with home and my dear wife and little one, two thousand miles ahead of me, whom I was despairing of ever embracing again. I am now scarcely better off, except that I am in comfortable quarters, with kind attendance, and friends about me. I am yet sick and very feeble, having been for several weeks upon my back since I was brought in from the prairies. I am slowly recovering, and for the first time since I wrote from the Canadian, able to use my pen or my brush.

We drew off from that slaughtering ground a few days after my last Letter was written, with a great number sick, carried upon litters—with horses giving out and dying by the way, which much impeded our progress over the long and tedious route that laid between us and Fort Gibson. Fifteen days, however, of constant toil and fatigue brought us here, but in a most crippled condition. Many of the sick were left by the way with attendants to take care of them, others were buried from their litters on which they breathed their last while travelling, and many others were brought in, to this place, merely to die and get the privilege of a decent burial.

Since the very day of our start into that country, the men have been constantly falling sick, and on their return, of those who are alive, there are not well ones enough to take care of the sick. Many are yet left out upon the prairies, and of those that have been brought in, and quartered in the hospital, with the soldiers of the infantry regiment stationed here, four or five are buried daily; and as an equal number from the 9th regiment are falling by the same disease, I have the mournful sound of "Roslin Castle" with muffled drums, passing six or eight times a-day under my window, to the burying-ground; which is but a little distance in front of my room, where I can lay in my bed and see every poor fellow lowered down into his silent and peaceful habitation. During the day before yesterday, no less than eight solemn processions visited that insatiable ground, and amongst them was carried the corpse of my intimate and much-loved friend Lieutenant West, who was aid-de-camp to General Leavenworth, on this disastrous campaign, and who has left in this place, a worthy and distracted widow, with her little ones to mourn for his untimely end. On the same day was buried also the Prussian Botanist, a most excellent and scientific gentleman, who had obtained an order from the Secretary of War to accompany the expedition for scientific purposes. He had at St. Louis, purchased a very comfortable dearborn wagon, and a snug span of little horses to convey himself and his servant with his collection of plants, over the prairies. In this he travelled in company with the regiment from St. Louis to Fort Gibson, some five or six hundred miles, and from that to the False Washita, and the Cross Timbers and back again. In this Tour he had made an immense, and no doubt, very valuable collection of plants, and at this place had been for some weeks indefatigably engaged in changing and drying them, and at last, fell a victim to the disease of the country, which seemed to have made an easy conquest of him, from the very feeble and enervated state he was evidently in, that of pulmonary consumption. This fine, gentlemanly and urbane, excellent man, to whom I became very much attached, was lodged in a room adjoining to mine, where he died, as he had lived, peaceably and smiling, and that when nobody knew that his life was in immediate danger. The surgeon who was attending me (Dr. Wright) was sitting on my bed-side in his morning-call at my room, when a negro boy, who alone had been left in the room with him, came into my apartment and said Mr. Beyrich was dying—we instantly stepped into his room and found him, not in the *agonies* of death, but quietly breathing his last, without a word or a struggle, as he had laid himself upon his bed with his clothes and his boots on. In this way perished this worthy man, who had no one here of kindred friends to drop tears for him; and on the day previous to his misfortune, died also, and much in the same way, his devoted and faithful servant, a young man, a native of Germany. Their bodies were buried by the side of each other, and a general feeling of deep grief was manifested by the officers and citizens of the post, in the respect that was paid to their remains in the appropriate and decent committal of them to the grave.

After leaving the head waters of the Canadian, my illness continually increased, and losing strength every day, I soon got so reduced that I was necessarily lifted on to and off from, my horse; and at last, so that I could not ride at all. I was then put into a baggage-wagon which was going back empty, except with several soldiers sick, and in this condition rode eight days, most of the time in a delirious state, lying on the hard planks of the wagon, and made still harder by the jarring and jolting, until the skin from my elbows and knees was literally worn through, and I almost *"worn out;"* when we at length reached this post, and I was taken to a bed, in comfortable quarters, where I have had the skillful attendance of my friend and old schoolmate Dr. Wright, under whose hands, thank God, I have been restored, and am now daily recovering my flesh and usual strength.

The experiment has thus been made, of sending an army of men from the North, into this Southern and warm climate, in the hottest months of the year, of July and August; and from this sad experiment I am sure a secret will be learned that will be of value on future occasions.

Of the 450 fine fellows who started from this place four months since, about one-third have already died, and I believe many more there are whose fates are sealed, and will yet fall victims to the deadly diseases contracted in that fatal country. About this post it seems to be almost equally unhealthy, and generally so during this season, all over this region, which is probably owing to an unusual drought which has been visited on the country, and unknown heretofore to the oldest inhabitants.

Since we came in from the prairies, and the sickness has a little abated, we have had a bustling time with the Indians at this place. Colonel Dodge sent *runners* to the chiefs of all the contiguous tribes of Indians, with an invitation to meet the Pawnees, &c. in council, at this place. Seven or eight tribes flocked to us, in great numbers on the first day of the month, when the council commenced; it continued for several days, and gave these semi-civilized sons of the forest a fair opportunity of shaking the hands of their wild and untamed red brethren of the West—of embracing them in their arms, with expressions of friendship, and of smoking the calumet together, as the solemn pledge of lasting peace and friendship.

Colonel Dodge, Major Armstrong (the Indian agent), and General Stokes (the Indian commissioner), presided at this council, and I cannot name a scene more interesting and entertaining than it was; where, for several days in succession, free vent was given to the feelings of men *civilized, half-civilized,* and *wild;* where the three stages of man were fearlessly asserting their rights, their happiness, and friendship for each other. The vain orations of the half-polished (and half-breed) Cherokees and Choctaws, with all their finery and art, found their match in the brief and jarring gutturals of the wild and naked man.

After the council had adjourned, and the fumes of the peace-making calumet had vanished away, and Colonel Dodge had made them additional presents, they soon made preparations for their departure, and on the next day started, with an escort of dragoons, for their own country. This movement is much to be regretted; for it would have been exceedingly gratifying to the people of the East to have seen so wild a group, and it would have been of great service to them to have visited Washington—a journey, though, which they could not be prevailed upon to make . . .

Although the achievement has been a handsome one, of bringing these unknown people to an acquaintance, and a general peace; and at first sight would appear to be of great benefit to them—yet I have my strong doubts, whether it will better their condition, unless with the exercised aid of the strong arm of Government, they can be protected in the rights which by nature, they are entitled to.

There is already in this place a company of eighty men fitted out, who are to start to-morrow, to overtake these Indians a few miles from this place, and accompany them home, with a large stock of goods, with traps for catching beavers, &c., calculating to build a trading-house amongst them, where they will amass, at once, an immense fortune, being the first traders and trappers that have ever been in that part of the country.

I have travelled too much among Indian tribes, and seen too much, not to know the evil consequences of such a system. Goods are sold at such exorbitant prices, that the Indian gets a mere shadow for his peltries, &c. The Indians see no white people but traders and sellers of whiskey; and of course, judge us all by them—they consequently hold us, and always will, in contempt; as inferior to themselves, as they have reason to do—and they neither fear nor respect us. When, on the contrary, if the Government would promptly prohibit such establishments, and invite these Indians to our frontier posts, they would bring in their furs, their robes, horses, mules, &c., to this place, where there is a good market for them all—where they would get the full value of their property—where there are several stores of goods—where there is an honourable competition, and where they would get four or five times as much for their articles of trade, as they would get from a trader in the village, out of the reach of competition, and out of sight of the civilized world.

At the same time, as they would be continually coming where they would see good and polished society, they would be gradually adopting our modes of living—introducing to their country our vegetables, our domestic animals, poultry, &c., and at length, our arts and manufactures; they would see and estimate our military strength, and advantages, and would be led to fear and respect us. In short, it would undoubtedly be the quickest and surest way to a general acquaintance—to friendship and peace, and at last to civilization. If there is a law in existence for such protection of the Indian tribes, which may have been waived in the case of those nations with which we have long traded, it is a great pity that it should not be rigidly enforced in this new and important acquaintance, which we have just made with thirty or forty thousand strangers to the civilized world; yet (as we have learned from their unaffected hospitality when in their villages), with hearts of human mould, *susceptible* of all the noble feelings belonging to civilized man.

This acquaintance has cost the United States a vast sum of money, as well as the lives of several valuable and esteemed officers, and more than 100 of the dragoons; and for the honour of the American name, I think we ought, in forming an acquaintance with these numerous tribes, to adopt and *enforce* some different system from that which has been generally practiced on and beyond our frontiers heretofore . . .

Thus was dragged through and completed this most disastrous campaign; and to Colonel Dodge and Colonel Kearny, who so indefatigably led and encouraged their men through it, too much praise cannot be awarded . . .

When we started, we were fresh and ardent for the incidents that were before us—our little packhorse carried our bedding and culinary articles; amongst which we had a coffee-pot and a frying-pan—coffee in good store, and sugar—and wherever we spread our bear-skin, and kindled our fire in the grass, we were sure to take by ourselves, a delightful repast, and a refreshing sleep. During the march, as we were subject to no military subordination, we galloped about wherever we were disposed, popping away at whatever we chose to spend ammunition upon—and running our noses into every wild nook and crevice, as we saw fit. In this way we travelled happily, until our coffee was gone, and our bread; and even then we were happy upon meat alone, until at last each one in his turn, like every other moving thing about us, both man and beast, were vomiting and fainting, under the poisonous influence of some latent enemy, that was floating in the air, and threatening our destruction. Then came the "tug of war," and instead of catering for our amusements, every one seemed desperately studying the means that were to support him in his feet, and bring him safe home again to the bosoms of his friends. In our start, our feelings were buoyant and light, and we had the luxuries of life—the green prairies, spotted with wild flowers, and the clear blue sky, were an earthly paradise to us, until fatigue and disease, and at last despair, made them tiresome and painful to our jaundiced eyes.

On our way, and while we were in good heart, my friend Joe and I had picked up many minerals and fossils of an interesting nature, which we put in our portmanteaux and carried for weeks, with much pains, and some *pain* also, until the time when our ardour cooled and our spirits lagged, and then we discharged and threw them away; and sometimes we came across specimens again, still more wonderful, which we put in their place, and lugged along till we were tired of *them*, and their weight, and we discharged them as before; so that from our eager desire to procure, we lugged many pounds weight of stones, shells &c. nearly the whole way, and were glad that their mother Earth should receive them again at our hands, which was done long before we got back.

One of the most curious places we met in all our route, was a mountain ridge of fossil shells, from which a great number of the above-mentioned specimens were taken . . . This remarkable ridge is in some parts covered with grass, but generally with mere scattering bunches, for miles together, partially covering this compact mass of shells, forming (in my opinion) one of the greatest geological curiosities now to be seen in this country, as it lies evidently some thousands of feet above the level of the ocean, and seven or eight hundred miles from the nearest point on the sea-coast.

In another section of the country, lying between Fort Gibson and the Washita, we passed over a ridge for several miles, running parallel to this, where much of the way there was no earth or grass under foot, but our horses were travelling on a solid rock, which had on its surface a reddish or oxidized appearance; and on getting from my horse and striking it with my hatchet, I found it to contain sixty or eighty per cent of solid iron, which produced a ringing noise, and a rebounding of the hatchet, as if it were struck upon an anvil.

In other parts, and farther West, between the Camanchee village and the Canadian, we passed over a similiar surface for many miles denuded, with the exception of here and there little bunches of grass and wild sage, a level and exposed surface of solid gypsum, of a dark grey colour; and through it, occasionally, as far as the eye could discover, to the East and the West, streaks of three and five inches wide of snowy gypsum, which was literally as white as the drifted snow.

Of saltpetre and salt, there are also endless supplies; so it will be seen that the mineral resources of this wilderness country are inexhaustible and rich, and that the idle savage who never converts them to his use, must soon yield them to the occupation of enlightened and cultivating man.

In the vicinity of this post there are an immense number of Indians, most of whom have been removed to their present locations by the Government, from their Eastern original positions, within a few years past; and previous to my starting with the dragoon, I had two months at my leisure in this section of the country, which I used in travelling about with my canvass and note-book, and visiting all of them in their villages. I have made many painting amongst them, and have a curious note-book to open at a future day, for which the reader may be prepared. The tribes whom I thus visited, and of whom my note-book will yet speak, are the *Cherokees, Choctaws, Creeks, Seminoles, Chickasaws, Quapaws, Senecas, Delawares,* and several others, whose customs are interesting, and whose history, from their proximity to, and dealings with the civilized community, is one of great interest, and some importance, to the enlightened world. Adieu . . .

Alton, Illinois.

...*A*fter I had gained strength sufficient to warrant it, I made preparations to take informal leave, and wend *my* way also over the prairies to the Missouri, a distance of 500 miles, and most of the way a solitary wilderness. For this purpose I had my horse "Charley" brought up from his pasture, where he had been in good keeping during my illness, and got so fat as to form almost an objectionable contrast to his master, with whom he was to embark on a long and tedious journey again, over the vast and almost boundless prairies.

I had, like the Captain, grown into such a dread of that place, from the scenes of death that were and had been visited upon it, that I resolved to be off as soon as I had strength to get on to my horse, and balance myself upon his back. For this purpose I packed up my canvass and brushes, and other luggage, and sent them down the river to the Mississippi, to be forwarded by steamer, to meet me at St. Louis. So, one fine morning, Charley was brought up and saddled, and a bear-skin and a buffalo robe being spread upon his saddle, and a coffee-pot and tin cup tied to it also—with a few pounds of hard biscuit in my portmanteau—with my fowling-piece in my hand, and my pistols in my belt—with my sketch-book slung on my back, and a small pocket compass in my pocket; I took leave of Fort Gibson, even against the advice of my surgeon and all the officers of the garrison, who gathered around me to bid me farewell. No argument could contend with the fixed resolve in my own mind, that if I could get out upon the prairies, and moving continually to the Northward, I should daily gain strength, and save myself, possibly, from the jaws of that voracious burial-ground that laid in front of my room; where I had for months laid and imagined myself going with other poor fellows, whose mournful dirges were played under my window from day to day. No one can imagine what was the dread I felt for that place; nor the pleasure, which was estatic, when Charley was trembling under me, and I turned him around on the top of a prairie bluff at a mile distance, to take the last look upon it, and thank God, as I did audibly, that I was not to be buried within its enclosure. I said to myself, that "to die on the prairie, and be devoured by wolves; or to fall in combat and be scalped by an Indian, would be far more acceptable than the lingering death that would consign me to the jaws of that insatiable grave," for which, in the fever and weakness of my mind, I had contracted so destructive a terror.

So, alone, without other living being with me than my affectionate horse Charley, I turned my face to the North, and commenced on my long journey, with confidence full and strong, that I should gain strength daily; and no one can ever know the pleasure of that moment, which placed me alone, upon the boundless sea of waving grass, over which my proud horse was prancing, and I with my life in my own hands, commenced to steer my course to the banks of the Missouri.

For the convalescent, rising and escaping from the gloom and horrors of a sick bed, astride of his strong and trembling horse, carrying him fast and safely over green fields spotted and tinted with waving wild flowers; and through the fresh and cool breezes that are rushing about him, as he daily shortens the distance that lies between him and his wife and little ones, there is an exquisite pleasure yet to be learned, by those who never have felt it.

Day by day I thus pranced and galloped along, the whole way through waving grass and green fields, occasionally dismounting and lying in the grass an hour or so, until the grim shaking and chattering of an ague chill had passed off; and through the nights, slept on my bear-skin spread upon the grass, with my saddle for my pillow, and my buffalo robe drawn over me for my covering. My horse Charley was picketed near me at the end of his laso, which gave him room for his grazing; and thus we snored and nodded away the nights, and never were denied the doleful serenades of the gangs of sneaking wolves that were nightly perambulating our little encampment, and stationed at a safe distance from us at sun-rise in the morning—gazing at us, and impatient to pick up the crumbs and bones that were left, when we moved away from our feeble fire that had faintly flickered through the night, and in the absence of timber, had been made of dried buffalo dung . . .

The distance from Fort Gibson to the Missouri, where I struck the river, is about five hundred miles, and most of the way a beautiful prairie, in a wild and uncultivated state without roads and without bridges, over a great part of which I steered my course with my pocket-compass, fording and swimming the streams in the best manner I could; shooting prairie hens, and occasionally catching fish, which I cooked for my meals, and slept upon the ground at night. On my way I visited "Riqua's Village" of Osages, and lodged during the night in the hospitable cabin of my old friend Beatte . . . one of the guides and hunters for the dragoons on their campaign in the Camanchee country. This was the most extraordinary hunter, I think, that I ever have met in all my travels. To "hunt," was a phrase almost foreign to him, however, for when he went out with his rifle, it was "for meat," or "for cattle;" and he never came in without it. He never told how many animals he had seen—how many he had wounded, &c.—but his horse was always loaded with meat, which was thrown down in camp without comment or words spoken . . .

Beatte lived in [a little] village with his aged parents, to whom he introduced me; and with whom, altogether, I spent a very pleasant evening in conversation. They are both French, and have spent the greater part of their lives with the Osages, and seem to be familiar with their whole history. This Beatte was the hunter and guide for a party of rangers (the summer before our campaign), with whom Washington Irving made his excursion to the borders of the Pawnee country; and of whose extraordinary character and powers, Mr. Irving has drawn a very just and glowing account, excepting a "half breed." Beatte had complained of this to me often while out on the prairies; and when I entered his hospitable cabin, he said he was glad to see me, and almost instantly continued, "Now you shall see, Monsieur Catlin, I am not 'half breed,' here I shall introduce you to

my father and my mother, who you see are two very nice and good
old French people."

From this cabin where I fared well and slept soundly, I started in
the morning, after taking with them a good cup of coffee, and went
smoothly on over the prairies on my course . . .

. . . My health improved daily, from the time of my setting out at
Fort Gibson; and I was now moving along cheerfully, and in hopes
soon to reach the end of my toilsome journey. I had yet vast prairies
to pass over, and occasional latent difficulties, which were not
apparent on their smooth and deceiving surfaces. Deep sunken
streams, like ditches, occasionally presented themselves suddenly to
my view, when I was within a few steps of plunging into them from
their perpendicular sides, which were overhung with long wild grass,
and almost obscured from the sight. The bearings of my compass
told me that I must cross them, and the only alternative was to
plunge into them, and get out as well as I could. They were often
muddy, and I could not tell whether they were three or ten feet
deep, until my horse was in them; and sometimes he went down
head foremost, and I with him, to scramble out on the opposite
shore in the best condition we could . . .

The Osage river which is a powerful stream, I struck at a place
which seemed to stagger my courage very much. There had been
heavy rains but a few days before, and this furious stream was rolling
along its wild and turbid waters, with a freshet upon it, that spread
its waters, in many places over its banks, as was the case at the place
where I encountered it. There seemed to be but little choice in
places with this stream, which, with its banks full, was sixty or eighty
yards in width, with a current that was sweeping along at a rapid
rate. I stripped everything from Charley, and tied him with his laso,
until I travelled the shores up and down for some distance, and
collected drift wood enough for a small raft, which I constructed, to
carry my clothes and saddle, and other things, safe over. This being
completed, and my clothes taken off, and they with other things, laid
upon the raft, I took Charley to the bank and drove him in and across,
where he soon reached the opposite shore, and went to feeding on
the bank. Next was to come the *"great white medicine;"* and with
him, saddle, bridle, saddle-bags, sketch-book, gun and pistols, coffee

and coffee-pot, powder, and his clothes, all of which were placed upon the raft, and the raft pushed into the stream, and the "*medicine man*" swimming behind it, and pushing it along before him, until it reached the opposite shore, at least half a mile below! From this, his things were carried to the top of the bank, and in a little time, Charley was caught and dressed, and straddled, and on the way again.

These are a few of the incidents of that journey of 500 miles, which I performed entirely alone, and which at last brought me out at Boonville on the Western bank of the Missouri . . . From Boonville, which is a very pretty little town, building up with the finest style of brick houses, I crossed the river to New Franklin, where I laid by several days, on account of stormy weather; and from thence proceeded with success to the end of my journey [Alton, Illnois], where I now am, under the roof of kind and hospitable friends, with my dear wife, who has patiently waited one year to receive me back, a wreck, as I now am; and who is to start in a few days with me to the coast of Florida, 1400 miles South of this, to spend the winter in patching up my health, and fitting me for future campaigns . . .

LETTER—NO. 47.

◀─────▶

Saint Louis.

*S*upposing that the reader by this time may be somewhat
... tired of following me in my erratic wanderings over these
wild regions, I have resolved to sit down awhile before I go further,
and open to him my *sketch-book,* in which I have made a great many
entries, as I have been dodging about, and which I have not as yet
shewed to him, for want of requisite time and proper opportunity.

In opening this book, the reader will allow me to turn over leaf
after leaf, and describe to him, tribe after tribe, and chief after chief,
of many of those whom I have visited, without the tediousness of
travelling too minutely over the intervening distances; in which I fear
I might lose him as a fellow-traveller, and leave him fagged out by
the way-side, before he would see all that I am anxious to show him.

About a year since I made a visit to the

Kickapoos.

At present but a small tribe, numbering six or 800, the remnant of a
once numerous and warlike tribe. They are residing within the state
of Illinois, near the south end of Lake Michigan, and living in a poor
and miserable condition, although they have one of the finest countries in the world. They have been reduced in numbers by whiskey
and small-pox, and the game being destroyed in their country, and
having little industry to work, they are exceedingly poor and dependent. In fact, there is very little inducement for them to build houses
and cultivate their farms, for they own so large and so fine a tract of
country, which is now completely surrounded by civilized settle-

ments, that they know, from experience, they will soon be obliged to sell out their country for a trifle, and move to the West. This system of moving has already commenced with them, and a considerable party have located on a tract of lands offered to them on the West bank of the Missouri river, a little north of Fort Leavenworth.*

The Kickapoos have long lived in alliance with the Sacs and Foxes, and speak a language so similar that they seem almost to be of one family. The present chief of this tribe, whose name is *Kee-an-ne-kuk* (the foremost man, Illustration 43), usually called the *Shawnee Prophet*, is a very shrewd and talented man. When he sat for his portrait, he took his attitude as seen in the picture, which was that of prayer. And I soon learned that he was a very devoted Christian, regularly holding meetings in his tribe, on the sabbath, preaching to them and exhorting them to a belief in the Christian religion, and to an abandonment of the fatal habit of whiskey-drinking, which he strenuously represented as the bane that was to destroy them all, if they did not entirely cease to use it. I went on the sabbath, to hear this eloquent man preach, when he had his people assembled in the woods; and although I could not understand his language, I was surprised and pleased with the natural ease and emphasis, and gesticulation, which carried their own evidence of the eloquence of his sermon.

I was singularly struck with the noble efforts of this champion of the mere remnant of a poisoned race, so strenuously labouring to rescue the remainder of his people from the deadly bane that has been brought amongst them by enlightened Christians. How far the efforts of this zealous man have succeeded in christianizing, I cannot tell, but it is quite certain that his exemplary and constant endeavours have completely abolished the practice of drinking whiskey in his tribe; which alone is a very praiseworthy achievement, and the first and indispensable step towards all other improvements. I was some time amongst these people, and was exceedingly pleased, and surprised also, to witness their sobriety, and their peaceable conduct; not having seen an instance of drunkenness, or seen or heard of any use made of spirituous liquors whilst I was amongst the tribe.

*Since the above was written, the whole of this tribe have been removed beyond the Missouri, having sold out their lands in the state of Illinois to the government.

Illustration 43. Kee-an-ne-kuk, The Foremost Man, chief of the Kickapoos.

Illustration 44. Ah-ton-we-tuck, Cock Turkey.

Ah-ton-we-tuck (the cock turkey, Illustration 44), is another Kickapoo of some distinction, and a disciple of the Prophet; in the attitude of prayer also, which he is reading off from characters cut upon a stick that he holds in his hands. It was told to me in the tribe by the Traders (though I am afraid to vouch for the whole truth of it), that while a Methodist preacher was soliciting him for permission to preach in his village, the Prophet refused him the privilege, but secretly took him aside and supported him until he learned from him his creed, and his system of teaching it to others; when he discharged him, and commenced preaching amongst his people himself; pretending to have had an interview with some superhuman mission, or inspired personage; ingeniously resolving, that if there was any honour or emolument, or influence to be gained by the promulgation of it, he might as well have it as another person; and with this view he commenced preaching and instituted a prayer, which he ingeniously carved on a maple-stick of an inch and a half in breadth, in characters somewhat resembling Chinese letters. These sticks, with the prayers on them, he has introduced into every family of the tribe, and into the hands of every individual; and as he has necessarily the manufacturing of them all, he sells them at his own price; and has thus added lucre to fame, and in two essential and effective ways, augmented his influence in his tribe. Every man, woman and child in the tribe, so far as I saw them, were in the habit of saying their prayer from this stick when going to bed at night, and also when rising in the morning; which was invariably done by placing the fore-finger of the right hand under the upper character, until they repeat a sentence or two, which it suggests to them; and then slipping it under the next, and the next, and so on, to the bottom of the stick, which altogether required about ten minutes, as it was sung over in a sort of a chaunt, to the end.

Many people have called all this an ingenious piece of hypocrisy on the part of the Prophet, and whether it be so or not, I cannot decide; yet one thing I can vouch to be true, that whether his motives and his life be as pure as he pretends or not, his example has done much towards correcting the habits of his people, and has effectually turned their attention from the destructive habits of dissipation and vice, to temperance and industry, in the pursuits of agriculture and the arts. The world may still be unwilling to allow him much credit for this, but I am ready to award him a great deal, who can by his influence thus far arrest the miseries of dissipation and the horrid deformities of vice, in the descending prospects of a nation who have so long had, and still have, the white-skin teachers of vices and dissipation amongst them . . .

Wee-ahs.

These are also the remnant of a once powerful tribe, and reduced by the same causes, to the number of 200. This tribe formerly lived in the state of Indiana, and have been moved with the Piankeshaws, to a position forty or fifty miles south of Fort Leavenworth.

Go-to-kow-pah-a (he who stands by himself, Illustration 45), and Wa-pon-je-a (the swan), are two of the most distinguished warriors of the tribe, both with intelligent European heads.

Pot-o-wat-o-mies.

The remains of a tribe who were once very numerous and warlike, but reduced by whiskey and small-pox, to their present number, which is not more than 2700. This tribe may be said to be semi-civilized, inasmuch as they have so long lived in contiguity with white people, with whom their blood is considerably mixed, and whose modes and whose manners they have in many respects copied. From a similarity of language as well as of customs and personal appearance, there is no doubt that they have formerly been a part of the great tribe of Chippeways or Ot-ta-was, living neighbors and adjoining to them, on the North. This tribe live within the state of Michigan, and there own a rich and very valuable tract of land; which, like the Kickapoos, they are selling out to the Government, and about to remove to the west bank of the Missouri, where a part of the tribe have already gone and settled, in the vicinity of Fort Leavenworth . . . These people have for some time lived neighbours to, and somewhat under the influence of the Kickapoos; and very many of the tribe have become zealous disciples of the Kickapoo prophet, using his prayers most devoutly . . .

Illustration 45.
Go-to-kow-pah-a, He Who Stands by Himself—a Wee-ah warrior.

Kas-kas-ki-as.

This is the name of a tribe that formerly occupied, and of course owned, a vast tract of country lying on the East of the Mississippi, and between its banks and the Ohio, and now forming a considerable portion of the great and populous state of Illinois. History furnishes us a full and extraordinary account of the once warlike character and numbers of this tribe; and also of the disastrous career that they have led, from their first acquaintance with civilized neighbours; whose rapacious avarice in grasping for their fine lands—with the banes of whiskey and small-pox, added to the unexampled cruelty of neighbouring hostile tribes, who have struck at them in the the days of their adversity, and helped to erase them from existence.

Perhaps there has been no other tribe on the Continent of equal power with the Kas-kas-ki-as, that have so suddenly sank down to complete annihilation and disappeared. The remnant of this tribe have long since merged into the tribe of Peorias of Illinois; and it is doubtful whether one dozen of them are now existing. With the very few remnants of this tribe will die in a few years a beautiful language, entirely distinct from all others about it, unless some enthusiastic person may preserve it from the lips of those few who are yet able to speak it . . .

Pe-o-ri-as.

The name of another tribe inhabiting a part of the state of Illinois; and, like the above tribes, but a remnant and civilized (or *cicatrized*, to speak more correctly). This tribe number about 200, and are, like most of the other remnants of tribes on the frontiers, under contract to move to the West of the Missouri . . .

Pi-an-ke-shaws.

The remnant of another tribe, of the states of Illinois and Indiana, who have also recently sold out their country to Government, and are under contract to move to the East of the Missouri, in the vicinity of Fort Leavenworth . . .

Delawares.

The very sound of this name has carried terror wherever it has been heard in the Indian wilderness; and it has travelled and been known, as well as the people, over a very great part of the Continent. This tribe originally occupied a great part of the Eastern border of Pennsylvania, and great part of the states of New Jersey and Delaware. No other tribe on the Continent has been so much moved and jostled about by civilized invasions; and none have retreated so far, or fought their way so desperately, as they have honourably and bravely contended for every foot of the ground they have passed over. From the banks of the Delaware to the lovely Susquehana, and *my native valley*, and to the base of and over, the Alleghany mountains, to the Ohio river—to the Illinois and the Mississippi, and at last to the West of the Missouri, they have been moved by Treaties after Treaties with the Government, who have now assigned to the mere handful of them that are left, a tract of land, as has been done a dozen times before, in *fee simple, for ever!* In every move the poor fellows have made, they have been thrust against their wills from the graves of their fathers and their children; and planted as they now are, on the borders of new enemies, where their first occupation has been to take up their weapons in self-defence, and fight for the ground they have been planted on. There is no tribe, perhaps, amongst which greater and more continued exertions have been made for their conversion to Christianity; and that ever since the zealous efforts of the Moravian missionaries, who first began with them; nor any, amongst whom those pious and zealous efforts have been squandered more in vain; which has, probably, been owing to the bad faith with which they have so often and so continually been treated by white people, which has excited prejudices that have stood in the way of their mental improvement.

This scattered and reduced tribe, which once contained some 10 or 15,000 numbers at this time but 800; and the greater part of them have been for the fifty or sixty years past, residing in Ohio and Indiana. In these states, their reservations became surrounded by white people, whom they dislike for neighbours, and their lands too valuable for Indians—and the certain consequence has been, that they have sold out and taken lands West of the Mississippi; on to which they have moved, and on which it is, and always will be, almost impossible to find them, owing to their desperate disposition for roaming about, indulging in the chase, and in wars with their enemies.

The wild frontier on which they are now placed, affords them so fine an opportunity to indulge both of these propensities, that they will be continually wandering in little and desperate parties over the vast buffalo plains, and exposed to their enemies, till at last the new country, which is given to them, in "fee simple, for ever," and which is destitute of game, will be deserted, and they, like most of the removed remnants of tribes, will be destroyed; and the faith of the Government will be preserved, which has offered *this* as their *last move*, and these lands as *theirs in fee simple, for ever.*

In my travels on the Upper Missouri, and in the Rocky Mountains, I learned to my utter astonishment, that little parties of these adventurous myrmidons, of only six or eight in numbers, had visited those remote tribes, at 2000 miles distance; and in several instances, after having cajoled a whole tribe—having been feasted in their villages—having solemnized the articles of everlasting peace with them, and received many presents at their hands, and taken affectionate leave, have brought away six or eight scalps with them; and nevertheless, braved their way, and defended themselves as they retreated in safety out of their enemies' country, and through the regions of other hostile tribes, where they managed to receive the same honours, and come off with similar trophies . . .

Mo-hee-con-neuhs, or Mohegans (The Good Canoemen).

There are 400 of this once powerful and still famous tribe, residing near Green Bay, on a rich tract of land given to them by the Government, in the territory of Wisconsin, near Winnebago lake—on which they are living very comfortably; having brought with them from their former country, in the state of Massachusetts, a knowledge of agriculture, which they had there effectually learned and practiced.

This tribe are the remains, and all that are left, of the once powerful and celebrated tribe of Pequots of Massachusetts. History tells us, that in their wars and dissensions with the whites, a considerable portion of the tribe moved off under the command of a rival chief, and established a separate tribe or band, and took the name of Mo-hee-con-neuhs, which they have preserved until the present day; the rest of the tribe having long since been extinct . . .

O-nei-das.

The remnant of a numerous tribe that have been destroyed by wars with the whites—by whiskey and small-pox, numbering at present but five or six hundred, and living in the most miserable poverty, on their reserve in the state of New York, near Utica and the banks of the Mohawk river. This tribe was one of the confederacy, called the Six Nations, and much distinguished in the early history of New York. The present chief is known by the name of *Bread* (Illustration 46). He is a shrewd and talented man, well educated,—speaking good English— is handsome, and a polite and gentlemanly man in his deportment.

Tus-ka-ro-ras.

Another of the tribes in the confederacy of the Six Nations, once numerous, but reduced at present to the number of 500. This little tribe are living on their reserve, a fine tract of land, near Buffalo, in the state of New York, and surrounded by civilized settlements. Many of them are good farmers, raising abundant and fine crops . . .

Sen-e-cas.

One thousand two hundred in numbers at present, living on their reserve, near Buffalo, and within a few miles of Niagara Falls, in the state of New York. This tribe formerly lived on the banks of the Seneca and Cayuga lakes; but, like all the other tribes who had stood in the way of the "march of civilization," have repeatedly bargained away their country, and removed to the West; which easily accounts for the origin of the familiar phrase that is used amongst them, that "they are going to the setting sun."

This tribe, when first known to the civilized world, contained some eight or ten thousand; and from their position in the centre of

Illustration 46. Bread, chief of the O-nei-das.

the state of New York, held an important place in its history. The Senecas were one of the most numerous and effective tribes, constituting the compact called the "Six Nations;" which was a confederacy formed by six tribes, who joined in a league as an effective mode of gaining strength, and preserving themselves by combined efforts which would be sufficiently strong to withstand the assaults of neighbouring tribes, or to resist the incursions of white people in their country. This confederacy consisted of the Senecas, Oneidas, Onondagas, Cayugas, Mohawks, and Tuskaroras; and until the innovations of white people, with their destructive engines of war—with whiskey and small-pox, they held their sway in the country, carrying victory, and consequently terror and dismay, wherever they warred. Their war-parties were fearlessly sent into Connecticut and Massachusetts, to Virginia, and even to the Carolinas, and victory everywhere crowned their efforts. Their combined strength, however, in all its might, poor fellows, was not enough to withstand the siege of their insidious foes—a destroying flood that had risen and advanced, like a flood-tide upon them, and covered their country; has broken up their strong holds, has driven them from land to land; and in their retreat, has drowned the most of them in its waves.

The Senecas are the most numerous remnant of this compact; and have at their head an aged and very distinguished chief, familiarly known throughout the United States, by the name of *Red Jacket* (Illustration 47). I painted this portrait from the life, in the costume in which he is represented; and indulged him also, in the wish he expressed, "that he might be seen standing on the Table Rock, at the Falls of Niagara; about which place he thought his spirit would linger after he was dead" . . .

The fame as well as the face of Red Jacket, is generally familiar to the citizens of the United States and the Canadas; and for the information of those who have not know him, I will briefly say, that he has been for many years the head chief of the scattered remnants of that once powerful compact, the Six Nations; a part of whom reside on their reservations in the vicinity of the Senecas, amounting perhaps in all, to about four thousand, and owning some two hundred thousand acres of fine lands. Of this Confederacy, the Mohawks and Cayugas, chiefly emigrated to Canada, some fifty years

Illustration 47. Red Jacket, chief of the Senecas.

ago, leaving the Senecas, the Tuskaroras, Oneidas, and Onondagas in the state of New York, on fine tracts of lands, completely surrounded with white population; who by industry and enterprize, are making the Indian lands too valuable to be long in their possession, who will no doubt be induced to sell out to the Government, or, in other words to exchange them for lands West of the Mississippi, where it is the avowed intention of the Government to remove all the border tribes.*

Red Jacket has been reputed one of the greatest orators of his day; and, no doubt, more distinguished for his eloquence and his influence in council, than as a warrior, in which character I think history has not said much of him. This may be owing, in a great measure, to the fact that the wars of his nation were chiefly fought before his fighting days; and that the greater part of his life and his talents have been spent with his tribe, during its downfall; where, instead of the horrors of Indian wars, they have had a more fatal and destructive enemy to encounter, in the insidious encroachments of pale faces, which he had been for many years exerting his eloquence and all his talents to resist. Poor old chief—not all the eloquence of Cicero and Demosthenes would be able to avert the calamity, that awaits his declining nation—to resist the despoiling hand of mercenary white man, that opens and spreads liberally, but to entrap the unwary and ignorant within its withering grasp.

This talented old man has for many years past, strenuously remonstrated both to the Governor of New York, and the President of the United States, against the continual encroachments of white people; whom he represented as using every endeavour to wrest from them their lands—to destroy their game, introducing vices of a horrible character, and unknown to his people by nature! and most vehemently of all, has he continually remonstrated against the preaching of missionaries in his tribe; alleging, that the "black coats" (as he calls the clergymen), did more mischief than good in his tribe, by creating doubts and dissensions amongst his people! which are destructive of his peace, and dangerous to the success, and even *existence* of his tribe. Like many other great men who endeavour to

*Since the above was written, the Senecas and all the other remnants of the Six Nations residing in the state of New York, have agreed in Treaties with the United States to remove to tracts of country assigned them, West of the Mississippi, twelve hundred miles from their reservations in the state of New York.

soothe broken and painful feelings, by the kindness of the bottle, he has long since taken up whiskey-drinking to excess; and much of his time, lies drunk in his cabin, or under the corner of a fence, or wherever else its *kindness* urges the necessity of his dropping his helpless body and limbs, to indulge in the delightful *spell*. He is as great a drunkard as some of our most distinguished law-givers and law-makers; and yet *ten times more culpable*, as he has little to do in life, and wields the destinies of a nation in his hands!

There are no better people to be found, than the Seneca Indians—none that I know of that are by Nature more talented and ingenious: nor any that would be found to be better neighbours, if the arts and abuses of white men and whiskey, could be kept away from them. They have mostly laid down their hunting habits, and become efficient farmers, raising fine crops of corn, and a great abundance of hogs, cattle and horses, and other necessaries and luxuries of life.

I-ro-quois.

One of the most numerous and powerful tribes that ever existed in the Northern regions of our country, and now one of the most completely annihilated. This tribe occupied a vast tract of country on the River St. Lawrence, between its banks and Lake Champlain; and at times, by conquest, actually over-run the whole country, from that to the shores of Lakes Erie, Huron, and Michigan. But by their continual wars with the French, English, and Indians, and dissipation and disease, they have been almost entirely annihilated. The few remnants of them have long since merged into other tribes, and been mostly lost sight of.*

*The whole of the Six Nations have been by some writers denominated Iroquois—how correct this may be, I am not quite able to say; one thing is certain, that is, that the Iroquois tribe did not all belong to that Confederacy, their original country was on the shores of the St. Lawrence; and, although one branch of their nation, the Mohawks, formed a part, and the most effective portion of that compact, yet the other members of it spoke different languages; and a great part of the Iroquois moved their settlements further North and East, instead of joining in the continual wars carried on by the Six Nations. It is of this part of the tribe that I am speaking, when I mention them as nearly extinct: and it is from this branch of the family that I got the portrait which I have introduced above.

Illustration 48. Not-o-way, The Thinker—chief of the Iroquois.

Of this tribe I have painted but one, *Not-o-way* (the thinker, Illustration 48). This was an excellent man, and was handsomely dressed for his picture. I had much conversation with him, and became very much attached to him. He seemed to be quite ignorant of the early history of his tribe, as well as of the position and condition of its few scattered remnants, who are yet in existence. He told me, however, that he had always learned that the Iroquois had conquered nearly all the world; but the Great Spirit being offended at the great slaughters by his favourite people, resolved to punish them; and he sent a dreadful disease amongst them, that carried the most of them off, and all the rest that could be found, were killed by their enemies—that though he was an Iroquois, which he was proud to acknowledge to me, as I was to "make him live after he was dead;" he wished it to be generally thought, that he was a Chippeway, that he might live as long as the Great Spirit had wished it when he made him.*

*Since the above Letter was written, all the tribes and remnants of tribes mentioned in it have been removed by the Government, to lands West of the Mississippi and Missouri, given to them, in addition to considerable annuities, in consideration of the immense tracts of country they have left on the frontier, and within the States. The present position of these tribes, and their relative locations to the civilized frontier and the wild, unjostled tribes, can be seen on a map in the beginning of this Volume [U. States' Indian frontier in 1840, p. xxxvi]. There are also other tribes there laid down, who have also been removed by Treaty stipulations, in the same way, which are treated of in subsequent Letters. The Government, under General Jackson, strenuously set forth and carried out, the policy of removing all the semi-civilized and border Indians, to a country West of the Mississippi; and although the project had many violent opponents, yet there were very many strong reasons in favour of it, and the thing *has been at last done;* and a few years will decide, by the best of all arguments, whether the policy was a good one or not. I may have occasion to say more on this subject hereafter; and in the mean time recommend the reader to examine their relative positions, and contemplate their prospects between their mortal foes on the West, and their acquisitive *friends* following them up from the East.

LETTER—NO. 48.

← ———————————— →

St. Louis.

Whilst I am thus taking a hasty glance at the tribes on the Atlantic Coast, on the borders of Mexico, and the confines of Canada, the reader will pardon me for taking him for a few minutes to the mouth of the Columbia, on the Pacific Coast; which place I have not yet quite reached myself, in my wild rambles, but most undoubtedly shall ere long, if my strolling career be not suddenly stopped. I scarcely need tell the reader where the Columbia river is, since its course and its character have been so often, and so well described, by recent travellers through those regions. I can now but glance at this remote country and its customs; and revert to it again after I shall have examined it in its parts, and collected my materials for a fuller account.

Flat Heads.

These are a very numerous people, inhabiting the shores of the Columbia River, and a vast tract of country lying to the South of it, and living in a country which is exceedingly sterile and almost entirely, in many parts, destitute of game for the subsistence of the savage; they are mostly obliged to live on roots, which they dig from the ground, and fish which they take from the streams; the consequences of which are, that they are generally poor and miserably clad; and in no respect equal to the Indians of whom I have heretofore spoken, who live on the East of the Rocky Mountains, in the ranges of the buffaloes; where they are well-fed, and mostly have good horses to ride, and materials in abundance for manufacturing their beautiful and comfortable dresses.

The people generally denominated Flat Heads, are divided into a great many bands, and although they have undoubtedly got their name from the custom of flattening the head; yet there are but very few of those so denominated, who actually practice that extraordinary custom.

The *Nez Percés* who inhabit the upper waters and mountainous parts of the Columbia, are a part of this tribe, though they are seldom known to flatten the head like those lower down, and about the mouth of the river. *Hee-oh'ks-te-kin* (the rabbit skin leggings, Illustration 49), and *H'co-a-h'co-a-h'cotes-min* (no horns on his head, Illustration 50), are young men of this tribe. These two young men, when I painted them, were in beautiful Sioux dresses, which had been presented to them in a talk with the Sioux, who treated them very kindly, while passing through the Sioux country. These two men were part of a delegation that came across the Rocky Mountains to St. Louis, a few years since, to enquire for the truth of a representation which they said some white man had made amongst them, "that our religion was better than theirs, and that they would all be lost if they did not embrace it."

Two old and venerable men of this party died in St. Louis, and I travelled two thousand miles, companion with these two young fellows, towards their own country, and became much pleased with their manners and dispositions.

The last mentioned of the two, died near the mouth of the Yellow Stone river on his way home, with disease which he had contracted in the civilized district; and the other one I have since learned, arrived safely amongst his friends, conveying to them the melancholy intelligence of the deaths of all the rest of his party; but assurances at the same time, from General Clark, and many Reverend gentlemen, that the report which they had heard was well founded; and that missionaries, good and religious men, would soon come amongst them to teach this religion, so that they could all understand and have the benefits of it.

When I first heard the report of the object of this extraordinary mission across the mountains, I could scarcely believe it; but on conversing with General Clark on a future occasion, I was fully convinced of the fact; and I, like thousands of others, have had the

Illustration 49. Hee-oh'ks-te-kin, Rabbit's Skin Leggings.

Illustration 50. H'co-a-h'co-a-h'cotes-min, No Horns on His Head.

satisfaction of witnessing the complete success that has crowned the bold and daring exertions of Mr. Lee and Mr. Spalding, two Reverend gentlemen who have answered in a Christian manner to this unprecedented call; and with their wives have crossed the most rugged wilds and wildernesses of the Rocky Mountains, and triumphantly proved to the world, that the Indians, in their native wilds are a kind and friendly people, and susceptible of mental improvement . . .

The Chinooks

Inhabiting the lower parts of the Columbia, are a small tribe, and correctly come under the name of Flat Heads, as they are almost the only people who strictly adhere to the custom of squeezing and flattening the head . . . In Illustration 51, will be seen the portrait of a Chinook woman, with her child in her arms, her own head flattened, and the infant undergoing the process of flattening; which is done by placing its back on a board, or thick plank, to which it is lashed with thongs, to a position from which it cannot escape, and the back of the head supported by a sort of pillow, made of moss or rabbit skins, with an inclined piece (as is seen in the drawing), resting on the forehead of the child: being every day drawn down a little tighter by means of a cord, which holds it in its place, until it at length touches the nose; thus forming a straight line from the crown of the head to the end of the nose.

This process is seemingly a very cruel one, though I doubt whether it causes much pain; as it is done in earliest infancy, whilst the bones are soft and cartilaginous, and easily pressed into this distorted shape, by forcing the occipital up, and the frontal down; so that the skull at the top in profile, will show a breadth of not more than an inch and a half, or two inches; when in a front view it exhibits a great expansion on the sides, making it at the top, nearly the width of one and a half natural heads.

By this remarkable operation, the brain is singularly changed from its natural shape; but in all probability, not in the least diminished or injured in its natural functions. This belief is drawn from the testimony of many credible witnesses, who have closely scrutinized them; and ascertained that those who have the head

Illustration 51. Chinook woman and child.

flattened, are in no way inferior in intellectual powers to those whose heads are in their natural shapes . . .

This mode of flattening the head is certainly one of the most unaccountable, as well as unmeaning customs, found amongst the North American Indians. What it could have originated in, or for what purpose, other than a mere useless fashion, it could have been invented, no human being can probably ever tell . . .

It is a curious fact, and one that should be mentioned here, that these people have not been alone in this strange custom; but that it existed and was practised precisely the same, until recently, amongst the Choctaws and Chickasaws; who occupied a large part of the states of Mississippi and Alabama, where they have laid their bones, and hundreds of their skulls have been procured, bearing incontrovertible evidence of a similar treatment, with similar results.

The Choctaws who are now living, do not flatten the head; the custom, like that of the *medicine-bag*, and many others, which the Indians have departed from, from the assurances of white people, that they were of no use, and were utterly ridiculous to be followed. Whilst amongst the Choctaws, I could learn little more from the people about such a custom, than that "their old men recollected to have heard it spoken of"—which is much less satisfactory evidence than inquisitive white people get by referring to the grave, which the Indian never meddles with. The distance of the Choctaws from the country of the Chinooks, is certainly between two and three thousand miles; and there being no intervening tribes practising the same custom—and no probability that any two tribes in a state of Nature, would ever hit upon so peculiar an absurdity, we come, whether willingly or not, to the conclusion, that these tribes must at some former period, have lived neighbours to each other, or have been parts of the same family; which time and circumstances have gradually removed to such a very great distance from each other. Nor does this, in my opinion (as many suppose), furnish any very strong evidence in support of the theory, that the different tribes have all sprung from one stock; but carries a strong argument to the other side, by furnishing proof of the very great tenacity these people have for their peculiar customs; many of which are certainly not general, but often carried from one end of the Continent to the other, or from ocean to ocean, by bands or sections of tribes, which often get "run off" by their enemies in wars, or in hunting, as I have before described; where to emigrate to a vast distance is not so unaccountable a thing, but almost the *inevitable result*, of a tribe that have got set in motion, all the way amongst deadly foes, in whose countries it would be fatal to stop.

I am obliged therefore, to believe, that either the Chinooks emigrated from the Atlantic, or that the Choctaws came from the West side of the Rocky Mountains; and I regret exceedingly that I have not been able as yet, to compare the languages of these two tribes, in which I should expect to find some decided resemblance. They might, however, have been near neighbours, and practising a copied custom where there was no resemblance in their language.

Whilst among the Choctaws I wrote down from the lips of one of their chiefs, the following tradition, which seems strongly to favour the supposition that they came from a great distance in the West, and probably from beyond the Rocky Mountains:—*Tradition.* "The Choctaws, a great many winters ago, commenced moving from the country where they then lived, which was a great distance to the West of the great river, and the mountains of snow; and they were a great many years on their way. A great medicine-man led them the whole way, by going before with a red pole, which he stuck in the ground every night where they encamped. This pole was every morning found leaning to the East; and he told them that they must continue to travel to the East, until the pole would stand upright in their encampment, and that there the Great Spirit had directed that they should live. At a place which they named *Nah-ne-wa-ye* (the sloping hill); the pole stood straight up, where they pitched their encampment, which was one mile square, with the men encamped on the outside, and the women and children in the centre; which is the centre of the old Choctaw nation to 'this day.' "

In the vicinity of the mouth of the Columbia, there are, besides the *Chinooks*, the *Klick-a-tacks*, *Cheehaylas*, *Na-as*, and many other tribes . . .

The Indians who inhabit the rugged wildernesses of the Rocky Mountains, are chiefly the Blackfeet and Crows, of whom I have heretofore spoken, and the Shoshonees or Snakes, who are a part of the Camanchees, speaking the same language, and the Shoshokies or root diggers, who inhabit the southern parts of those vast and wild realms, with the Arapohoes and Navahoes, who are neighbours to the Camanchees on the West, having Santa Fe on the South, and the coast of California on the West. Of the Shoshonees and Shoshokies, all travellers who have spoken of them, give them a good character, as a kind and hospitable and harmless people; to which fact I could cite the unquestionable authorities of the excellent Rev. Mr. Parker, who has published his interesting Tour across the Rocky Mountains— Lewis and Clarke—Capt. Bonneville and others; and I allege it to be a truth, that the reason why we find them as they are uniformly described, a kind and inoffensive people, is, that they have not as yet been abused—that they are in their primitive state, as the Great Spirit made and endowed them with good hearts and kind feelings, unalloyed and untainted by the vices of the money-making worlds.

To the same fact, relative to the tribes on the Columbia river, I have been allowed to quote the authority of H. Beaver, a very worthy and kind Reverend Gentleman of England, who has been for several years past living with these people, and writes to me thus:—

"I shall be always ready, with pleasure, to testify my perfect accordance with the sentiments I have heard you express, both in your public lectures, and private conversation, relative to the much-traduced character of our Red brethren, particularly as it relates to their *honesty, hospitality* and *peaceableness,* throughout the length and breadth of the Columbia. Whatever of a contrary disposition has at any time, in those parts, been displayed by them, has, I am persuaded been exotic, and forced on them by the depravity and impositions of the white Traders."

LETTER—NO. 49.

◄──────────►

St. Louis.

*O*f a number of . . . reduced and removed tribes, who have . . . been located West of the Missouri, and North of St. Louis, I have already spoken in a former Letter, and shall yet make brief mention of another, which has been conducted to the same region— and then direct the attention of the reader to those which are settled in the neighbourhood of Fort Gibson, who are the Cherokees— Creeks—Choctaws—Chickasaws—Seminoles, and Euchees.

The people above alluded to are the

Sha-wa-nos.

The history of this once powerful tribe [Shawnees] is so closely and necessarily connected with that of the United States, and the revolutionary war, that it is generally pretty well understood. This tribe formerly inhabited great parts of the state of Pennsylvania, New Jersey, (and for the last sixty years,) a part of the states of Ohio and Indiana, to which they had removed; and now, a considerable portion of them, a tract of country several hundred miles West of the Mississippi, which has been conveyed to them by Government in exchange for their lands in Ohio, from which it is expected the remainder of the tribe will soon move. It has been said that this tribe came formerly from Florida, but I do not believe it. The mere fact, that there is found in East Florida a river by the name of *Su wa-nee*, which bears some resemblance to *Sha-wa-no*, seems, as far as I can learn, to be the principal evidence that has been adduced for the fact. They have evidently been known, and that within the scope of our authenticated history, on the Atlantic coast—on the Delaware and Chesapeak bays. And after that, have fought their way against every sort of trespass and abuse—against the bayonet and disease, through the states of Pennsylvania, Delaware and Ohio, Indiana, Illinois, and Missouri, to their present location near the Kon-zas River, at least 1500 miles from their native country.

This tribe and the Delawares, of whom I have spoken, were neighbours on the Atlantic coast, and alternately allies and enemies, have retrograded and retreated together—have fought their enemies united, and fought each other, until their remnants that have outlived their nation's calamities, have now settled as neighbours together in the Western wilds; where, it is probable, the sweeping hand of death will soon relieve *them* from further necessity of warring or moving; and the *Government,* from the necessity or policy of proposing to them a yet more distant home. In their long and disastrous pilgrimage, both of these tribes laid claim to, and alternately occupied the beautiful and renowned valley of Wy-ô-ming; and after strewing the Susquehana's lovely banks with their bones, and their tumuli, they both yielded at last to the dire necessity, which follows all civilized intercourse with natives, and fled to the Alleghany, and at last to the banks of the Ohio; where necessity soon came again, and again, and again, until the great *"Guardian" of all "red children"* placed them where they now are.

There are of this tribe remaining about 1200; some few of whom are agriculturists, and industrious and temperate, and religious people; but the greater proportion of them are miserably poor and dependent, having scarcely the ambition to labour or to hunt, and a passion for whiskey-drinking, that sinks them into the most abject poverty, as they will give the last thing they possess for a drink of it.

There is not a tribe on the Continent whose history is more interesting than that of the Shawanos, nor any one that has produced more extraordinary men.

The great Tecumseh, whose name and history I can but barely allude to at this time, was the chief of this tribe, and perhaps the most extraordinary Indian of his age . . .

Ten-squa-ta-way (the open door, Illustration 52), called the *"Shawnee Prophet,"* is perhaps one of the most remarkable men, who had flourished on these frontiers for some time past. This man is brother of the famous Tecumseh, and quite equal in his *medicines* or mysteries, to what his brother was in arms; he was blind in his left eye, and in his right hand he was holding his *"medicine fire,"* and his *"sacred string of beans"* in the other. With these mysteries he made his way through most of the North Western tribes, enlisting warriors wherever he went, to assist Tecumseh in effecting his great scheme, of forming a confederacy of all the Indians on the frontier, to drive back the whites and defend the Indians' rights; which he told them could never in any other way be protected. His plan was certainly a correct one, if not a very great one; and his brother, the Prophet, exercised his astonishing influence in raising men for him to fight his battles, and carry out his plans. For this purpose, he started upon an embassy to the various tribes on the Upper Missouri, nearly all of which he visited with astonishing success; exhibiting his mystery fire, and using his sacred string of beans, which every young man who was willing to go to war, was to touch, thereby taking the solemn oath to start when called upon, and not to turn back.

In this most surprising manner, this ingenious man entered the villages of most of his inveterate enemies and of others who never had heard of the name of his tribe; and manœuvred in so successful a way, as to make his medicines a safe passport for him to all of their villages; and also the means of enlisting in the different tribes, some eight or ten thousand warriors, who had solemnly sworn to return with him on his way back; and to assist in the wars that Tecumseh was to wage against the whites on the frontier. I found, on my visit to the Sioux—to the Puncahs, to the Riccarees and the Mandans—that he had been there, and even to the Blackfeet; and everywhere told them of the potency of his mysteries, and assured them, that if they allowed the fire to go out in their wigwams, it would prove fatal to them in every case. He carried with him into every wigwam that he visited, the image of a dead person of the size of life; which was made ingeniously of some light material, and always kept concealed under bandages of thin white muslin cloths and not to be opened; of this he made great mystery, and got his recruits to swear by touching

Illustration 52. Ten-squa-ta-way, The Open Door—the "Shawnee Prophet."

a sacred string of white beans, which he had attached to its neck or some other way secreted about it. In this way, by his extraordinary cunning, he had carried terror into the country as far as he went; and had actually enlisted some eight or ten thousand men, who were sworn to follow him home; and in a few days would have been on their way with him, had not a couple of his political enemies in his own tribe, followed on his track, even to those remote tribes, and defeated his plans, by pronouncing him an imposter; and all of his forms and plans an imposition upon them, which they would be fools to listen to. In this manner, this great recruiting officer was defeated in his plans, for raising an army of men to fight his brother's battles; and to save his life, he discharged his medicines as suddenly as possible, and secretly travelled his way home, over those vast regions, to his own tribe, where the death of Tecumseh, and the opposition of enemies, killed all his splendid prospects, and doomed him to live the rest of his days in silence, and a sort of disgrace; like all men in Indian communities who pretend to *great medicine*, in any way, and fail; as they all think such failure an evidence of the displeasure of the Great Spirit, who always judges right.

This, no doubt, has been a very shrewd and influential man, but circumstances have destroyed him, as they have many other great men before him; and he now lives respected, but silent and melancholy in his tribe. I conversed with him a great deal about his brother Tecumseh, of whom he spoke frankly, and seemingly with great pleasure; but of himself and his own great schemes, he would say nothing. He told me that Tecumseh's plans were to embody all the Indian tribes in a grand confederacy, from the province of Mexico, to the Great Lakes, to unite their forces in an army that would be able to meet and drive back the white people, who were continually advancing on the Indian tribes, and forcing them from their lands towards the Rocky Mountains—that Tecumseh was a great general, and that nothing but his premature death defeated his grand plan.

The Shawanos, like most of the other remnants of tribes, in whose countries the game has been destroyed, and by the use of whiskey, have been reduced to poverty and absolute want, have become, to a certain degree, agriculturists; raising corn and beans, potatoes, hogs, horses, &c., so as to be enabled, if they could possess anywhere on earth, a country which they could have a certainty of holding in perpetuity, as their own, to plant and raise their own crops, and necessaries of life from the ground.

The Government have effected with these people, as with most of the other dispersed tribes, an arrangement by which they are to remove West of the Mississippi, to lands assigned them; on which they are solemnly promised a home *for ever*; the uncertain definition of which important word, time and circumstances alone will determine . . .

The Cher-o-kees.

Living in the vicinity of, and about Fort Gibson, on the Arkansas, and 700 miles west of the Mississippi river, are a third part or more of the once very numerous and powerful tribe who inhabited and still inhabit, a considerable part of the state of Georgia, and under a Treaty made with the United States Government, have been removed to those regions, where they are settled on a fine tract of country; and having advanced somewhat in the arts and agriculture before they started, are now found to be mostly living well, cultivating their fields of corn and other crops, which they raise with great success.

Under a serious difficulty existing between these people (whom their former solemn Treaties with the United States Government, were acknowledged a free and independent nation, with powers to make and enforce their own laws), and the state of Georgia, which could not admit such a Government within her sovereignty, it was thought most expedient by the Government of the United States, to propose to them, for the fourth or fifth time, to enter into Treaty stipulations again to move; and by so doing to settle the difficult question with the state of Georgia, and at the same time, to place them in peaceable possession of a large tract of fine country, where they would for ever be free from the continual trespasses and abuses which it was supposed they would be subjected to, if they were to remain in the state of Georgia, under the present difficulties and the high excited feelings which were then existing in the minds of many people along their borders.

John Ross, a civilized and highly educated and accomplished gentleman, who is the head-chief of the tribe, and several of his leading subordinate chiefs, have sternly and steadily rejected the proposition of such a Treaty; and are yet, with a great majority of the nation remaining on their own ground in the state of Georgia, although some six or 7000 of the tribe have several years since removed to the Arkansas, under the guidance and controul of an aged and dignified chief by the name of *Jol-lee*.

This man, like most of the chiefs, as well as a very great proportion of the Cherokee population, has a mixture of white and red blood in his veins, of which, in this instance, the first seems decidedly to predominate . . .

I have travelled pretty generally through the several different locations of this interesting tribe, both in the Western and Eastern divisions, and have found them, as well as the Choctaws and Creeks, their neighbours, very far advanced in the arts; affording to the world the most satisfactory evidences that are to be found in America, of the fact, that the Indian was not made to shun and evade good example, and necessarily to live and die a brute, as many speculating men would needs record them and treat them, until they are robbed and trampled into the dust; that no living evidences might give the lie to their theories, or draw the cloak from their cruel and horrible iniquities.

As I have repeatedly said to my readers, in the course of my former epistles, that the greater part of my time would be devoted to the condition and customs of the tribes that might be found in their primitive state, they will feel disposed to pardon me for barely introducing the Cherokees, and several others of these very interesting tribes, and leaving them and their customs and histories (which are of themselves enough for volumes), to the reader, who is, perhaps, nearly as familiar, as I am myself, with the full and fair accounts of these people, who have had their historians and biographers.

The history of the Cherokees and other numerous remnants of tribes, who are the exhabitants for the finest and most valued portions of the United States, is a subject of great interest and importance, and has already been woven into the most valued histories of the country, as well as forming material parts of the archives of the Government, which is my excuse for barely introducing the reader to them, and beckoning him off again to the native and untrodden wilds, to teach him something new and unrecorded. Yet I leave the subject, as I left the people (to whom I became attached, for their kindness and friendship), with a heavy heart, wishing them success and the blessing of the Great Spirit, who alone can avert the *doom* that would almost seem to be fixed for their unfortunate race.

The Cherokees amount in all to about 22,000, 16,000 of whom are yet living in Georgia, under the Government of their chief, John Ross, whose name I have before mentioned; with this excellent man, who has been for many years devotedly opposed to the Treaty stipulations for moving from their country, I have been familiarly acquainted; and, notwithstanding the bitter invective and animadversions that have been by his political enemies heaped upon him, I feel authorized, and bound, to testify to the unassuming and gentlemanly urbanity of his manners as well as to the rigid temperance of his habits, and the purity of his language, in which I never knew him to transgress for a moment, in public or private interviews.

At this time, the most strenuous endeavours are making on the part of the Government and the state of Georgia, for the completion of an arrangement for the removal of the whole of this tribe, as well as of the Choctaws and Seminoles; and I have not a doubt of their final success, which seems, from all former experience, to attend every project of the kind made by the Government to their red children* . . .

Besides the Cherokees in Georgia, and those that I have spoken of in the neighbourhood of Fort Gibson, there is another band or

*Since writing the above, the Government have succeeded in removing the remainder of the Cherokees beyond the Mississippi, where they have taken up their residence along side of their old friends, who emigrated several years since under *Jol-lee*, as I have before mentioned. In the few years past, the Government has also succeeded in stipulating with, and removing West of the Mississippi, nearly every remnant of tribes spoken of in this and the two last Letters, so that there are at this time but a few hundreds of the red men East of the Mississippi; and it is probable, that a few months more will effect the removal of the remainder of them. See their present locations West of the Mississippi on the map at the beginning of this Volume [U. States Indian frontier in 1840, p. xxxvi].

family of the same tribe, of several hundreds, living on the banks of the Canadian river, an hundred or more miles South West of Fort Gibson, under the government of a distinguished chief by the name of *Tuch-ee* (familiarly called by the white people, "*Dutch*"). This is one of the most extraordinary men that lives on the frontiers at the present day, both for his remarkable history, and for his fine and manly figure, and character of face.

This man was in the employment of the Government as a guide and hunter for the regiment of dragoons, on their expedition to the Camanchees, where I had him for a constant companion for several months, and opportunities in abundance, for studying his true character, and of witnessing his wonderful exploits in the different varieties of the chase. The history of this man's life has been very curious and surprising; and I sincerely hope that some one, with more leisure and more talent than myself, will take it up, and do it justice. I promise that the life of this man furnishes the best materials for a popular tale, that are now to be procured on the Western frontier.

He is familiarly known, and much of his life, to all the officers who have been stationed at Fort Gibson, or at any of the posts in that region of country.

Some twenty years or more since, becoming fatigued and incensed with civilized encroachments, that were continually making on the borders of the Cherokee country in Georgia, where he then resided, and probably, foreseeing the disastrous results they were to lead to, he beat up for volunteers to emigrate to the West, where he had designed to go, and colonize in a wild country beyond the reach and contamination of civilized innovations; and succeeded in getting several hundred men, women, and children, whom he led over the banks of the Mississippi, and settled upon the head waters of White River, where they lived until the appearance of white faces, which began to peep through the forests at them, when they made another move of 600 miles to the banks of the Canadian, where they now reside; and where, by the system of desperate warfare, which he has carried on against the Osages and the Camanchees, he has successfully cleared away from a large tract of fine country, all the enemies that could contend for it, and now holds it, with his little band of myrmidons, as their own undisputed soil, where they are living comfortably by raising from the soil fine crops of corn and potatoes, and other necessaries of life; whilst they indulge whenever they please, in the pleasures of the chase amongst the herds of buffaloes, or in the natural propensity for ornamenting their dresses and their war-clubs with the scalp-locks of their enemies.

The Creeks (or Mus-ko-gees).

Of 20,000 in numbers, have, until quite recently, occupied an immense tract of country in the states of Mississippi and Alabama; but by a similiar arrangement (and for a similiar purpose) with the Government, have exchanged their possessions there for a country, adjoining to the Cherokees, on the South side of the Arkansas, to which they have already all removed, and on which, like the Cherokees, they are laying out fine farms, and building good houses, in which they live; in many instances, surrounded by immense fields of corn and wheat. There is scarcely a finer country on earth than that now owned by the Creeks; and in North America, certainly no Indian tribe more advanced in the arts and agriculture than they are. It is no uncommon thing to see a Creek with twenty or thirty slaves at work on his plantation, having brought them from a slave-holding country, from which, in their long journey, and exposure to white man's ingenuity, I venture to say, that most of them got rid of one-half of them, whilst on their long and disastrous crusade.

The Creeks, as well as the Cherokees and Choctaws, have good schools and churches established amongst them, conducted by excellent and pious men, from whose example they are drawing great and lasting benefits . . .

The Choctaws.

Of fifteen thousand, are another tribe, removed from the Northern parts of Alabama, and Mississippi, within the few years past, and now occupying a large and rich tract of country, south of the Arkansas and the Canadian rivers; adjoining to the country of the Creeks and the Cherokees, equally civilized, and living much in the same manner . . .

These people seem, even in their troubles, to be happy; and have, like all the other remnants of tribes, preserved with great tenacity their different games, which it would seem they are everlastingly practicing for want of other occupations or amusements in life. Whilst I was staying at the Choctaw agency in the midst of their nation, it seemed to be a sort of season of amusements, a kind of holiday; when the whole tribe almost, were assembled around the establishment, and from day to day we were entertained with some games or feats that were exceedingly amusing: horse-racing, dancing, wrestling, foot-racing, and ball-playing, were amongst the most exciting; and of all the catalogue, the most beautiful, was decidedly that of ball-playing. This wonderful game, which is the favourite one among all the tribes, and with these Southern tribes played exactly the same, can never be appreciated by those who are not happy enough to see it.

It is no uncommon occurrence for six or eight hundred or a thousand of these young men, to engage in a game of ball, with five or six times that number of spectators, of men, women, and children, surrounding the ground, and looking on. And I pronounce such a scene, with its hundreds of Nature's most beautiful models, denuded, and painted of various colours, running and leaping into the air, in all the most extravagant and varied forms, in the desperate struggles for the ball, a school for the painter or sculptor, equal to any of those which ever inspired the hand of the artist in the Olympian games or the Roman forum.

I have made it an uniform rule, whilst in the Indian country, to attend every ball-play I could hear of, if I could do it by riding a distance of twenty of thirty miles; and my usual custom has been on such occasions, to straddle the back of my horse, and look on to the best advantage. In this way I have sat, and oftentimes reclined, and almost dropped from my horse's back, with irresistible laughter at the succession of droll tricks, and kicks and scuffles which ensue, in the almost superhuman struggles for the ball. These plays generally commence at nine o'clock, or near it, in the morning; and I have more than once balanced myself on my pony, from that time till near sundown, without more than one minute of intermission at a time, before the game has been decided . . .

While at the Choctaw agency it was announced, that there was to be a great play on a certain day, within a few miles, on which occasion I attended, and made the three sketches which are hereto annexed; and also the following entry in my note-book, which I literally copy out:

Monday afternoon at three, o'clock, I rode out with Lieutenants S. and M., to a very pretty prairie, about six miles distant, to the ball-play-ground of the Choctaws, where we found several thousand Indians encamped. There were two points of timber about half a mile apart, in which the two parties for the play, with their respective families and friends, were encamped; and lying between them, the prairie on which the game was to be played. My companions and myself, although we had been apprised, that to see the whole of a ball-play, we must remain on the ground all the night previous, had brought nothing to sleep upon, resolving to keep our eyes open, and see what transpired through the night. During the afternoon, we loitered about amongst the different tents and shantees of the two encampments, and afterward, at sundown, witnessed the ceremony of measuring out the ground, and erecting the "byes" or goals which were to guide the play. Each party had their goal made with two upright posts, about 25 feet high and six feet apart, set firm in the ground, with a pole across at the top. These goals were about forty or fifty rods apart; and at a point just half way between, was another small stake, driven down, where the ball was to be thrown up at the firing of a gun, to be struggled for by the players. All this preparation was made by some old men, who were, it seems, selected to be the judges of the play, who drew a line from one bye to the other; to which directly came from the woods, on both sides, a great concourse of women and old men, boys and girls, and dogs and horses, where bets were to be made on the play. The betting was all done across this line, and seemed to be chiefly left to the women, who seemed to have martialled out a little of everything that their houses and their fields possessed. Goods and chattels—knives—dresses—blankets—pots and kettles—dogs and horses, and guns; and all were placed in the possession of *stake-holders*, who sat by them, and watched them on the ground all night, preparatory to the play.

The sticks with which this tribe play, are bent into an oblong hoop at the end, with a sort of slight web of small thongs tied across, to prevent the ball from passing through. The players hold one of these in each hand, and by leaping into the air, they catch the ball between the two nettings and throw it, without being allowed to strike it, or catch it in their hands.

The mode in which these sticks are constructed and used, will be seen in the portrait of *Tullock-chish-ko* (he who drinks the juice of the stone), the most distinguished ball-player of the Choctaw nation (Illustration 53), represented in his ball-play dress, with his ball-sticks in his hands. In every ball-play of these people, it is a rule of the play, that no man shall wear moccasins on his feet, or any other dress than his breech-cloth around his waist, with a beautiful bead belt, and a "tail," made of white horsehair or quills, and a "mane" on the neck, of horsehair dyed of various colours.

This game has been arranged and "made up," three or four months before the parties met to play it, and in the following manner:— The two champions who led the two parties, and had the alternate choosing of the players through the whole tribe, sent runners, with the ball-sticks most fantastically ornamented with ribbons and red paint, to be touched by each one of the chosen players; who thereby agreed to be on the spot at the appointed time and ready for the play. The ground having been all prepared and preliminaries of the game all settled, and the bettings all made, the goods all "staked," night came on without the appearance of any players on the ground. But soon after dark, a procession of lighted flambeaux was seen coming from each encampment, to the ground where the players assembled around their respective byes; and at the beat of the drums and chaunts of the women, each party of players commenced the "ball-play dance." Each party danced for a quarter of an hour around their respective byes, in their ball-play dress; rattling their ball-sticks together in the most violent manner, and all singing as loud as they could raise their voices; whilst the women of each party, who had their goods at stake, formed into two rows on the line between the two parties of players, and danced also, in an uniform step, and all their voices joined in chaunts to the Great Spirit; in which they were soliciting his favour in deciding the game

Illustration 53. Tullock-chish-ko, He Who Drinks the Juice of the Stone.

to their advantage; and also encouraging the players to exert every power they possessed, in the struggle that was to ensue. In the mean time, four old *medicine-men*, who were to have the starting of the ball, and who were to be judges of the play, were seated at the point where the ball was to be started: and busily smoking to the Great Spirit for their success in judging rightly, and impartially, between the parties in so important an affair.

This dance was one of the most picturesque scenes imaginable, and was repeated at intervals of every half hour during the night, and exactly in the same manner; so that the players were certainly awake all the night, and arranged in their appropriate dress, prepared for the play which was to commence at nine o'clock the next morning. In the morning, at the hour, the two parties and all their friends, were drawn out and over the ground; when at length the game commenced, by the judges throwing up the ball at the firing of a gun; when an instant struggle ensued between the players, who were some six or seven hundred in numbers, and where mutually endeavoring to catch the ball in their sticks, and throw it home and between their respective stakes; which, whenever successfully done, counts one for game. In this game every player were dressed alike, that is, *divested* of all dress, except the girdle and the tail, which I have before described; and in these desperate struggles for the ball, when it is *up* (Illustration 54, where hundreds are running together and leaping, actually over each other's heads, and darting between their adversaries' legs, tripping and throwing, and foiling each other in every possible manner, and every voice raised to the highest key, in shrill yelps and barks)! there are rapid successions of feats, and of incidents, that astonish and amuse far beyond the conception of any one who has not had the singular good luck to witness them. In these struggles, every mode is used that can be devised, to oppose the progress of the foremost, who is likely to get the ball; and these obstructions often meet desperate individual resistance, which terminates in a violent scuffle, and sometimes in fisticuffs; when their sticks are dropped, and the parties are unmolested, whilst they are settling it between themselves; unless it be by a general *stampedo*, to which they are subject who are down, if the ball happens to pass in their direction. Every weapon, by a rule of all ball-plays, is laid by

Illustration 54. Ball-play of the Choctaw.

in their respective encampments, and no man allowed to go for one; so that the sudden broils that take place on the ground, are presumed to be as suddenly settled without any probability of much personal injury; and no one is allowed to interfere in any way with the contentious individuals.

There are times, when the ball gets to the ground, and such a confused mass rushing together around it, and knocking their sticks together, without the possibility of any one getting or seeing it, for the dust that they raise, that the spectator loses his strength, and everything else but senses; when the condensed mass of ball-sticks, and shins, and bloody noses, is carried around the different parts of the ground, for a quarter of an hour at a time, without any one of the mass being able to see the ball; and which they are often thus scuffling for, several minutes after it had been thrown off, and played over another part of the ground.

For each time that the ball was passed between the stakes of either party, one was counted for their game, and a halt of about one minute; when it was again started by the judges of the play, and a similar struggle ensued; and so on until the successful party arrived to 100, which was the limit of the game, and accomplished at an hour's sun, when they took the stakes; and then, by a previous agreement, produced a number of jugs of whiskey, which gave all a wholesome drink, and sent them all off merry and in good humour, but not drunk.

After this exciting day, the concourse was assembled in the vicinity of the agency house, where we had a great variety of dances and other amusements; the most of which I have described on former occasions. One, however, was new to me, and I must say a few words of it: this was the *Eagle Dance*, a very pretty scene, which is got up by their young men, in honour of that bird, for which they seem to have a religious regard. This picturesque dance was given by twelve or sixteen men, whose bodies were chiefly naked and painted white, with white clay, and each one holding in his hand the tail of the eagle, while his head was also decorated with an eagle's quill. Spears were stuck in the ground, around which the dance was performed by four men at a time, who had simultaneously, at the beat of the drum, jumped up from the ground where they had all sat in rows of four, one row immediately behind the other, and ready to take the place of the first four when they left the ground fatigued, which they did by hopping or jumping around behind the rest, and taking their seats, ready to come up again in their turn, after each of the other sets had been through the same forms . . .

The Deluge. "Our people have always had a tradition of the Deluge, which happened in this way:—there was total darkness for a great time over the whole of the earth; the Choctaw doctors or mystery-men looked out for daylight for a long time, until at last they despaired of ever seeing it, and the whole nation were very unhappy. At last a light was discovered in the North, and there was great rejoicing, until it was found to be great mountains of water rolling on, which destroyed them all, except a few families who had expected it and built a great raft, on which they were saved."

Future State. "Our people all believe that the spirit lives in a future state—that it has a great distance to travel after death towards the West—that it has to cross a dreadful deep and rapid stream, which is hemmed in on both sides by high and rugged hills—over this stream, from hill to hill, there lies a long and slippery pine-log, with the bark peeled off, over which the dead have to pass to the delightful hunting-grounds. On the other side of the stream there are six persons of the good hunting-grounds, with rocks in their hands, which they throw at them all when they are on the middle of the log. The good walk on safely, to the good hunting-grounds, where there is one continual day—where the trees are always green—where the sky has no clouds—where there are continual fine and cooling breezes—where there is one continual scene of feasting, dancing and rejoicing—where there is no pain or trouble, and people never grow old, but for ever live young and enjoy the youthful pleasures.

"The wicked see the stones coming, and try to dodge, by which they fall from the log, and go down thousands of feet to the water, which is dashing over the rocks, and is stinking with dead fish, and animals, where they are carried around and brought continually back to the same place in whirlpools—where the trees are all dead, and the waters are full of toads and lizards, and snakes—where the dead are always hungry, and have nothing to eat—are always sick, and never die—where the sun never shines, and where the wicked are continally climbing up by thousands on the sides of a high rock from which they can overlook the beautiful country of the good hunting-grounds, the place of the happy, but never can reach it."

Origin of the *Craw-fish band*. "Our people have amongst them a band which is called, the *Craw-fish band*. They formerly, but at a very remote period, lived under ground, and used to come up out of the mud—they were a species of craw-fish; and they went on their hands and feet, and lived in a large eave deep under ground, where there was no light for several miles. They spoke no language at all, nor could they understand any. The entrance to their cave was through the mud—and they used to run down through that, and into their cave; and thus, the Choctaws were for a long time unable to molest them. The Choctaws used to lay and wait for them to come out into the sun, where they would try to talk to them, and cultivate an acquaintance.

"One day, a parcel of them were run upon so suddenly by the Choctaws, that they had no time to go through the mud into their cave, but were driven into it by another entrance, which they had through the rocks. The Choctaws then tried a long time to smoke them out, and at last succeeded—they treated them kindly—taught them the Choctaw language—taught them to walk on two legs— made them cut off their toe nails, and pluck the hair from the bodies, after which they adopted them into their nation—and the remainder of them are living under ground to this day."

LETTER—NO. 50.

◄——————————————►

Fort Snelling, Fall of St. Anthony.

*T*he Upper Missisippi, like the Upper Missouri, must be ap-
. . . proached to be appreciated; for all that can be seen on the
Missisippi below St. Louis, or for several hundred miles above it,
gives no hint or clue to the magnificence of the scenes which are
continually opening to the view of the traveller, and riveting him to
the deck of the steamer, through sunshine, lightning or rain, from
the mouth of the Ouisconsin to the Fall of St. Anthony.

The traveller in ascending the river, will see but little of picturesque
beauty in the landscape, until he reaches Rock Island; and from
that point he will find it growing gradually more interesting, until
he reaches Prairie du Chien; and from that place until he arrives at
Lake Pepin, every reach and turn in the river presents to his eye
a more immense and magnificent scene of grandeur and beauty. From
day to day, the eye is riveted in listless, tireless admiration, upon
the thousand bluffs which tower in majesty above the river on either
side, and alternate as the river bends, in countless fascinating forms.

The whole face of the country is covered with a luxuriant growth
of grass, whether there is timber or not; and the magnificent bluffs,
studding the sides of the river, and rising in the forms of immense
cones, domes and ramparts, give peculiar pleasure, from the deep
and soft green in which they are clad up their broad sides, and to
their extreme tops, with a carpet of grass, with spots and clusters of
timber of a deeper green; and apparently in many places, arranged
in orchards and pleasure-grounds by the hands of art . . .

Dubuque's Grave is a place of great notoriety on this river, in
consequence of its having been the residence and mining place of the

first lead mining pioneer of these regions, by the name of Dubuque, who held his title under a grant from the Mexican Government (I think), and settled by the side of his huge bluff, on the pinnacle of which he erected the tomb to receive his own body, and placed over it a cross with his own inscription on it. After his death, his body was placed within the tomb, at his request, lying in state (and uncovered except with his winding-sheet), upon a large flat stone, where it was exposed to the view, as his bones now are, to the gaze, of every traveller who takes the pains to ascend this beautiful, grassy and lily-covered mound to the top, and peep through the gratings of two little windows, which had admitted the eyes, but stopped the sacrilegious *hands* of thousands who have taken a walk to it.

At the foot of this bluff, there is now an extensive smelting furnace, where vast quantities of lead are melted from the ores which are dug out of the hills in all directions about it.

The Fall of St. Anthony (Illustration 55), which is 900 miles above St. Louis, is the natural curiosity of this country, and nine miles above the mouth of St. Peters, from whence I am at this time writing. At this place, on the point of land between the Mississippi and the St. Peters rivers, the United States' Government have erected a strong Fort, which has taken the name of Fort Snelling, from the name of a distinguished and most excellent officer of that name, who superintended the building of it. The site of this Fort is one of the most judicious that could have been selected in the country, both for health and defence; and being on an elevation of 100 feet or more about the water, has an exceedingly bold and picturesque effect, as seen in Illustration 56.

This Fort is generally occupied by a regiment of men placed here to keep the peace amongst the Sioux and Chippeways, who occupy the country about it, and also for the purpose of protecting the citizens on the frontier.

The Fall of St. Anthony is about nine miles above this Fort, and the junction of the two rivers; and, although a picturesque and spirited scene, is but a pigmy in size to Niagara, and other cataracts in our country—the actual perpendicular fall being but eighteen feet, though of half a mile or so in extent, which is the width of the river; with brisk and leaping rapids above and below, giving life and spirit to the scene.

Illustration 55. The Fall of St. Anthony.

Illustration 56. Fort Snelling.

The Sioux who live in the vicinity of the Fall, and occupy all the country about here, west of the Mississippi, are a part of the great tribe on the Upper Missouri; and the same in most of their customs, yet very dissimilar in personal appearance, from the changes which civilized examples have wrought upon them. I mentioned in a former Letter, that the country of the Sioux, extended from the base of the Rocky Mountains to the banks of the Mississippi; and for the whole of that way, it is more or less settled by this immense tribe, bounding the East side of their country by the Mississippi River.

The Sioux in these parts, who are out of reach of the beavers and buffaloes, are poor and very meanly clad, compared to those on the Missouri, where they are in the midst of those and other wild animals, whose skins supply them with pictureque and comfortable dresses. The same deterioration also in seen in the morals and constitutions of these, as amongst all other Indians, who live along the frontiers, in the vicinity of our settlements, where whiskey is sold to them, and the small-pox and other diseases are introduced to shorten their lives.

The principal bands of the Sioux that visit this place, and who live in the vicinity of it, are those known as the Black Dog's band—Red Wing's band, and Wa-be-sha's band; each band known in common parlance, by the name of its chief, as I have mentioned. The Black Dog's band reside but a few miles above Fort Snelling, on the banks of the St. Peters, and number some five or six hundred. The Red Wing's band are at the head of Lake Pepin, sixty miles below this place on the West side of the river. And Wa-be-sha's band and village are some sixty or more miles below Lake Pepin on the West side of the river, on a beautiful prairie, known (and ever will be) by the name of "Wa-be-sha's prairie." Each of these bands, and several others that live in this section of country, exhibit considerable industry in their agricultural pursuits, raising very handsome corn-fields, laying up their food, thus procured, for their subsistence during the long and tedious winters.

The greater part of the inhabitants of these bands are assembled here at this time, affording us, who are visitors here, a fine and wild scene of dances, amusements, &c. They seem to take great pleasure in "showing off" in these scenes, to the amusement of the many fashionable visitors, both ladies and gentlemen, who are in the habit of reaching this post, as steamers are arriving at this place every week in the summer from St. Louis.

Many of the customs of these people create great surprise in the minds of the travellers of the East, who here have the first satisfactory opportunity of seeing them; and none, I observe, has created more surprise, and pleasure also, particularly amongst the ladies, than the mode of carrying their infants, slung on their backs, in their beautifully ornamented cradles . . .

LETTER—NO. 51.

◄————————————►

Fort Snelling, Fall of St. Anthony.

The fourth of July was hailed and celebrated by us at this place, in an unusual, and not uninteresting manner. With the presence of several hundreds of the wildest of the Chippeways, and as many hundreds of the Sioux; we were prepared with material in abundance for the novel—for the wild and grotesque—as well as for the grave and ludicrous. Major Talliafferro, the Indian agent, to aid my views in procuring sketches of manners and customs, represented to them that I was a great *medicine-man*, who had visited, and witnessed the sports of, a vast many Indians of different tribes, and had come to see whether the Sioux and Chippeways were equal in a ball-play, &c. to their neighbours; and that if they would come in on the *next* day (fourth of July), and give us a ball-play, and some of their dances, in their best style, he would have the *big gun* fired twenty-one times (customary salute for that day), which they easily construed into a high compliment to themselves. This, with still stronger inducements, a barrel of flour—a quantity of pork and tobacco, which I gave them, brought the scene about on the day of independence, as follows:—About eleven o'clock (the usual time for Indians to make their appearance on any great occasion), the young men, who were enlisted for ball-play, made their appearance on the ground with ball-sticks in hand—with no other dress on than the flap, and attached to a girdle or ornamental sash, a tail, extending nearly to the ground, made of the choicest arrangement of quills and feathers, or of the hair of white horses' tails. After an excited and warmly contested play of two hours, they adjourned to a place in front of the agent's office, where they entertained us for two or three hours longer, with a continued variety of their most fanciful and picturesque dances. They gave us the *beggar's dance*—the *buffalo-dance*—the *bear-dance*—the *eagle-dance*—and *dance of the braves*. This last is peculiarly beautiful, and exciting to the feelings in the highest degree.

At intervals they stop, and one of them steps in the ring, and vociferates as loud as possible, with the most significant gesticulations, the feats of bravery which he has performed during his life—he boasts of the scalps he has taken—of the enemies he has vanquished, and at the same time carries his body through all the motions and gestures, which have been used during these scenes when they were transacted. At the end of his boasting, all assent to the truth of his story, and give in their approbation by the guttural "*waugh!*" and the dance again commences. At the next interval, another makes his boasts, and another, and another, and so on . . . My wife, who was travelling this part of the country with me, was a spectator of these scenes, as well as the ladies and officers of the garrison, whose polite hospitality we are at this time enjoying.

Several days after this, the plains of St. Peters and St. Anthony, rang with the continual sounds of drums and rattles, in time with the thrilling yells of the dance, until it had doubly ceased to be novelty. General Patterson, of Philadelphia, and his family arrived about this time, however, and a dance was got up for their amusement; and it proved to be one of an unusual kind, and interesting to all. Considerable preparation was made for the occasion, and the Indians informed me, that if they could get a couple of dogs that were of no use about the garrison, they would give us their favourite, the "*dog dance.*" The two dogs were soon produced by the officers, and in presence of the whole assemblage of spectators, they butchered them and placed their two hearts and livers entire and uncooked, on a couple of crotches about as high as a man's face. These were then cut into strips, about an inch in width, and left hanging in this condition, with the blood and smoke upon them. A spirited dance then ensued; and in a confused manner, every one sung forth his own deeds of bravery in ejaculatory gutturals, which were almost deafening; and they danced up, two at a time to the stakes, and after spitting several times upon the liver and hearts, catched a piece in their mouths, bit it off, and swallowed it. This was all done without losing the step (which was in time to their music), or interrupting the times of their voices.

Each and every one of them in this wise bit off and swallowed a piece of the livers, until they were demolished; with the exception of the two last pieces hanging on the stakes, which a couple of them carried in their mouths, and communicated to the mouths of the two musicians who swallowed them. This is one of the most valued dances amongst the Sioux, though by no means the most beautiful or most pleasing. The beggar's dance, the discovery dance, and the eagle dance, are far more graceful and agreeable. The *dog dance* is one of *distinction*, inasmuch as it can only be danced by those who have taken scalps from the enemy's heads, and come forward boasting, that they killed their enemy in battle, and swallowed a piece of his heart in the same manner.

As the Sioux own and occupy all the country on the West bank of the river in this vicinity; so do the Chippeways claim all lying East, from the mouth of the Chippeway River, at the outlet of Lake Pepin, to the source of the Mississippi; and within the month past, there have been one thousand or more of them encamped here, on business with the Indian agent and Sioux, with whom they have recently had some difficulty. These two hostile foes, who have, time out of mind, been continual at war, are now encamped here, on different sides of the Fort; and all difficulties having been arranged by their agent, in whose presence they have been making their speeches, for these two weeks past, have been indulging in every sort of their amusements, uniting in their dances, ball-plays and other games; and feasting and smoking together, only to raise the war-cry and the tomahawk again, when they get upon their hunting grounds.

Major Talliafferro is the Government agent for the Sioux at this place, and furnishes the only instance probably, of a public servant on these frontiers, who had performed the duties of his office, strictly and faithfully, as well as kindly, for fifteen years. The Indians think much of him, and call him Great Father, to whose advice they listen with the greatest attention. . . .

After the business and amusements of this great Treaty between the Chippeways and Sioux were all over, the Chippeways struck their tents by taking them down and rolling up their bark coverings, which, with their bark canoes seen in the picture, turned up amongst their wigwams, were carried to the water's edge; and all things being packed in, men, women, dogs, and all, were swiftly propelled by paddles to the Fall of St. Anthony, where we had repaired to witness their mode of passing the cataract, by "*making* (as it is called) *the portage*," which we found to be a very curious scene; and was done by running all their canoes into an eddy below the Fall, and as near as they could get by paddling; when all were landed, and every thing taken out of the canoes, and with them carried by the women, around the Fall, and half a mile or so above, where the canoes were put into the water again; and goods and chattels being loaded in, and all hands seated, the paddles were again put to work, and the light and bounding crafts upon their voyage.

The bark canoe of the Chippeways is, perhaps, the most beautiful and light model of all the water crafts that ever were invented. They are generally made complete with the rind of one birch tree, and so ingeniously shaped and sewed together, with roots of the tamarack, which they call *wat-tap*, that they are water-tight, and ride upon the water, as light as a cork. They gracefully lean and dodge about, under the skillful balance of an Indian, or the ugliest squaw; but like everything wild, are timid and treacherous under the guidance of white man; and, if he be not an experienced equilibrist, he is sure to get two or three times soused, in his first endeavours at familiar acquaintance with them . . .

. . . The skin canoes of the Mandans, (of the Upper Missouri) . . . are made almost round like a tub, by straining a buffalo's skin over a frame of wicker work, made of willow or other boughs. The woman in paddling these awkward tubs, stands in the bow, and makes the stroke with the paddle, by reaching it forward in the water and drawing it to her, by which means she pulls the canoe along with some considerable speed. These very curious and rudely constructed canoes, are made in the form of the *Welsh coracle;* and, if I mistake not, propelled in the same manner, which is a very curious circumstance; inasmuch as they are found in the heart of the great wilderness of America, when all the other surrounding tribes construct their canoes in decidedly different forms, and of different materials.

. . . Sioux and Chippeway *snow shoes* . . . are used in the deep snows of the winter, under the Indians' feet, to buoy him up as he runs in pursuit of his game. The hoops or frames of these are made of elastic wood, and the webbing, of strings of rawhide, which form such a resistance to the snow, as to carry them over without sinking into it; and enabling them to come up with their game, which is wallowing through the drifts, and easily overtaken . . . The *snow-shoe dance* . . . is exceedingly picturesque, being danced with the snow shoes under the feet, at the falling of the first snow in the beginning of winter: when they sing a song of thanksgiving to the Great Spirit for sending them a return of snow, when they can run on their snow shoes in their valued hunts, and easily take the game for their food.

LETTER—NO. 52.

◄————————————————►

Camp Des Moines.

*P*rairie du Chien [near the water of the Ouisconsin River,
... *and 600 miles above St. Louis] is the concentrating place
of the Winnebagoes and Menomonies, who inhabit the waters of the
Ouisconsin and Fox Rivers, and the chief part of the country lying
East of the Mississippi, and West of Green Bay.

The *Winnebagoes* are the remnant of a once powerful and warlike
tribe, but are now left in a country where they have neither beasts or
men to war with; and are in a most miserable and impoverished
condition. The numbers of this tribe do not exceed four thousand;
and the most of them have sold even their guns and ammunition for
whiskey. Like the Sioux and Menomonies that come in to this post,
they have several times suffered severely with the small-pox, which
has in fact destroyed the greater proportion of them ... The
Menomonies, like the Winnebagoes, are the remnant of a much
more numerous and independent tribe, but have been reduced and
enervated by the use of whiskey and the ravages of the small-pox,
and number of this time, something like three thousand, living
chiefly on the banks of Fox River, and the Western shore of Green
Bay.

... I lingered along the shores of this magnificent river then, in
my fragile bark, to Prairie du Chien—Dubuque—Galena, to Rock
Island, and lastly to this place [Camp Des Moines]. During such a
Tour between the almost endless banks, carpeted with green, with
one of the richest countries in the world, extending back in every
direction, the mind of a contemplative man is continually building
for posterity splendid seats, cities, towers and villas, which a few

years of rolling time will bring about, with new institutions, new states, and almost empires; for it would seem that this vast region of rich soil and green fields was almost enough for a world of itself . . .

A visit of a few days to Dubuque will be worth the while of every traveller; and for the speculator and man of enterprise, it affords the finest field now open in our country. It is a small town of 200 houses, built entirely within the last two years, on one of the most delightful sites on the river, and in the heart of the richest and most productive parts of the mining regions; having this advantage over most other mining countries, that immediately over the richest (and in fact all) of the lead mines; the land on the surface produces the finest corn, and all other vegetables that may be put into it. This is certainly the richest section of country on the Continent, and those who live a few years to witness the result, will be ready to sanction my assertion, that it is to be the *mint of our country*.

From Dubuque, I descended the river on a steamer, with my bark canoe laid on its deck, and my wife was my companion, to Camp Des Moines, from whence I am now writing.

After arriving at this place, which is the wintering post of Colonel Kearney, with his three companies of dragoons, I seated my wife and two gentlemen of my intimate acquaintance, in my bark canoe, and paddled them through the Des Moine's Rapids, a distance of fourteen miles, which we performed in a very short time and at the foot of the Rapids, placed my wife on the steamer for St. Louis, in company with friends, when I had some weeks to return on my track, and revert back again to the wild and romantic life that I occasionally loved to lead. I returned to Camp Des Moines, and in a few days joined General Street, the Indian Agent, in a Tour to Ke-o-kuck's village of Sacs and Foxes.

Colonel Kearney gave us a corporal's command of eight men, with horses, &c. for the journey; and we reached the village in two days' travel, about sixty miles up the Des Moines. The whole country that we passed over was like a garden, wanting only cultivation, being mostly prairie, and we found their village beautifully situated on a large prairie, on the bank of the Des Moines River. They seemed to be well supplied with the necessaries of life, and with some of its luxuries. I found Ke-o-kuck to be a chief of fine and portly figure, with a good countenance, and great dignity and grace in his manners.

General Street had some documents from Washington, to read to him, which he and his chiefs listened to with great patience; after which he placed before us good brandy and good wine, and invited us to drink, and to lodge with him; he then called up five of his *runners* or *criers,* communicated to them in a low, but emphatic tone, the substance of the talk from the agent, and of the letters read to him, and they started at full gallop—one of them proclaiming it through his village, and the others sent express to their other villages, comprising the whole nation. Ke-o-kuck came in with us, with about twenty of his principal men—he brought in all his costly wardrobe, that I might select for his portrait such as suited me best; but at once named (of his own accord) the one that was purely Indian. In that he paraded for several days, and in it I painted him at full length. He is a man of a great deal of pride, and makes truly a splendid appearance on his black horse. He owns the finest horse in the country, and is excessively vain on his appearance when mounted, and arrayed, himself and horse, in all their gear and trappings. He expressed a wish to see himself represented on horseback, and I painted him in that plight. He rode and nettled his prancing steed in front of my door, until its sides were in a gore of blood. I succeeded to *his* satisfaction, and his vanity is increased, no doubt, by seeing himself immortalized in that way. After finishing him, I painted his favourite wife (the favoured one of seven), his favourite boy, and eight or ten of his principal men and women; after which, he and all his men shook hands with me, wishing me well, and leaving, as tokens of regard, the most valued article of his dress, and a beautiful string of wampum, which he took from his wife's neck.

They then departed for their village in good spirits, to prepare for their *fall hunt* . . .

◀ ─────────────────────────────── ▶

Red Pipe Stone Quarry, Côteau Des Prairies.

... *T*here have been two companies of United States dragoons, ordered and marched to Green Bay, where I saw them; and three companies of infantry from Prairie du Chien to Fort Winnebago, in anticipation of difficulties; but in all probability, without any real cause or necessity, for the Winnebago chief answered the officer, who asked him if they wanted to fight, "that they *could* not, had they been so disposed; for," said he, "we have no guns, no ammunition, nor anything to eat; and, what is worst of all, one half of our men are dying with the small-pox. If you will give us guns and ammunition, and pork, and flour, and feed and take care of our squaws and children, we will fight you; nevertheless, we will *try* to fight if you wants us to, as it is."

There is, to appearance (and there is no doubt of the truth of it), the most humble poverty and absolute necessity for peace among these people at present, that can possibly be imagined. And, amidst their poverty and wretchedness, the only war that suggests itself to the eye of the traveller through their country, is the *war of sympathy and pity*, which wages in the breast of a feeling, thinking man.

The small-pox, whose ravages have now pretty nearly subsided, has taken off a great many of the Winnebagoes and Sioux. The famous Wa-be-sha, of the Sioux, and more than half of his band, have fallen victims to it within a few weeks, and the remainder of them, blackened with its frightful distortions, look as if they had just emerged from the sulphurous regions below. At Prairie du Chien, a considerable number of the half-breeds, and French also, suffered death by this baneful disease; and at that place I learned one fact, which may be of service of science, which was this: that in all cases of vaccination, which had been given several years ago, it was an efficient protection; but in those cases where the vaccine had been recent (and there were many of them), it had not the effect to protect, and in almost every instance of such, death ensued.

At the Sault de St. Marys on Lake Superior, I saw a considerable number of Chippeways, living entirely on fish, which they catch with great ease at that place.

I need not detain the reader a moment with a description of St. Marys, or of the inimitable summer's paradise, which can always be seen at Mackinaw; and which, like the other, has been an hundred times described. I shall probably have the chance of seeing about 3,000 Chippeways at the latter place on my return home, who are to receive their annuities at that time through the hands of Mr. Schoolcraft, their agent . . .*

. . . The Chippeways living in the vicinity of the Sault, live entirely on fish; and it is almost literally true also, that the French and English, and Americans, who reside about there live on fish, which are caught in the greatest abundance in the rapids at that place, and are, perhaps, one of the greatest luxuries of the world. The *white fish*, which is in appearance much like a salmon, though smaller, is the luxury I am speaking of, and is caught in immense quantities by the scoop-nets of the Indians and Frenchmen, amongst the foaming and dashing water of the rapids, where it gains strength and flavour not to be found in the same fish in any other place. This unequalled fishery has long been one of vast importance to the immense numbers of Indians, who have always assembled about it; but of late, has been found by *money-making men*, to be too valuable a spot for the exclusive occupancy of the savage, like hundreds of others, and has at last been filled up with adventurers, who have dipped *their* nets till the poor Indian is styled an intruder; and his timid bark is seen dodging about in the coves for a scanty subsistence, whilst he scans and envies insatiable white man filling his barrels and boats, and sending them to market to be converted into money.

. . . A great concourse of Indians had assembled to witness an

*Henry Schoolcraft. See p. xvi.

Indian regatta or *canoe race*, which went off with great excitement, firing of guns, yelping, &c. The Indians in this vicinity are all Chippeways, and their canoes all made of birch bark and chiefly of one model; they are exceedingly light, as I have before described, and propelled with wonderful velocity. . . .

From Mackinaw I proceeded to Green Bay, which is a flourishing beginning of a town, in the heart of a rich country, and the head-quarters of land speculators. From thence, I embarked in a large bark canoe, with five French voyageurs at the oars . . . bound for Fort Winnebago and the Mississippi . . . Our fragile bark brought us in good time to Fort Winnebago, with impressions engraven on our hearts which can never be erased, of this sweet and beautiful little river . . . At this post, after remaining a day, our other companions took a different route, leaving Mr. Wood and myself to cater anew, and to buy a light bark canoe for our voyage down the Ouisconsin, to Prairie du Chien; in which we embarked the next day, while paddles in hand, and hearts as light as the zephyrs, amid which we propelled our little canoe. Three days' paddling, embracing two nights' encampment, brought us to the end of our voyage. We entered the mighty Mississippi, and mutually acknowledged ourselves paid for our labours, by the inimitable scenes of beauty and romance, through which we had passed, and on which our untiring eyes had been riveted during the whole way.

The Ouisconsin, which the French most appropriately denominate "La belle rivière," may certainly vie with any other on the Continent or in the world, for its beautifully skirted banks and prairie bluffs. It may justly be said to be equal to the Mississippi about the Prairie du Chien in point of sweetness and beauty, but not on quite so grand a scale.

My excellent and esteemed fellow-traveller, like a true Englishman, has untiringly stuck by me through all difficulties, passing the countries above-mentioned, and also the Upper Mississippi, the St. Peters, and the overland route to our present encampment on this splendid plateau of the Western world.

. . . This tract of country as well as that along the St. Peters river, is mostly covered with the richest soil, and furnishes an abundance of good water, which flows from a thousand living springs. For many miles we had the Côteau in view in the distance before us, which looked like a blue cloud settling down in the horizon; and we were scarcely sensible of the fact, when we had arrived at its base, from the graceful and almost imperceptible swells with which it commences its elevation above the country around it. Over these swells or terraces, gently rising one above the other, we travelled for the distance of forty or fifty miles, when we at length reached the summit; and from the base of this mound, to its top, a distance of forty or fifty miles, there was not a tree or bush to be seen in any direction, and the ground everywhere was covered with a green turf of grass, about five or six inches high; and we were assured by our Indian guide, that it descended to the West, towards the Missouri, with a similar inclination, and for an equal distance, divested of every thing save the grass that grows, and the animals that walk upon it.

On the very top of this mound or ridge, we found the far-famed quarry or fountain of the Red Pipe, which is truly an anomaly in nature. The principal and most striking feature of this place, is a perpendicular wall of close-grained, compact quartz, of twenty-five and thirty feet in elevation, running nearly North and South with its face to the West, exhibiting a front of nearly two miles in length, when it disappears at both ends by running under the prairie, which becomes there a little more elevated, and probably covers it for many miles, both to the North and the South. The depression of the brow of the ridge at this place has been caused by the wash of a little stream, produced by several springs on the top, a little back from the wall; which has gradually carried away the super-incumbent earth, and having bared the wall for the distance of two miles, this now left to glide for some distance over a perfectly level surface of quartz rock; and then to leap from the top of the wall into a deep basin below, and from thence seek its course to the Missouri, forming the extreme source of a noted and powerful tributary, called the "Big Sioux."

This beautiful wall is horizontal, and stratified in several distinct layers of light grey, and rose or flesh-coloured quartz; and for most of the way, both on the front of the wall, and for acres of its horizontal surface, highly polished or glazed, as if by ignition.

At the base of this wall there is a level prairie, of half a mile in width, running parallel to it; in any and all parts of which, the Indians procure the red stone for their pipes, by digging through the soil and several slaty layers of the red stone, to the depth of four or five feet.* From the very numerous marks of ancient and modern diggings or excavations, it would appear that this place has been for many centuries resorted to for the red stone; and from the great number of graves and remains of ancient fortifications in its vicinity, it would seem, as well as from their actual traditions, that the Indian tribes have long held this place in high superstitious estimation; and also that it has been the resort of different tribes, who have made their regular pilgrimages here to renew their pipes.

The red pipe stone, I consider, will take its place amongst minerals, as an interesting subject of itself; and the "Côteau des Prairies" will become hereafter an important theme for geologists; not only from the fact that this is the only known locality of that mineral, but from other phenomena relating to it. The single fact of such a table of quartz, in horizontal strata, resting on this elevated plateau, is of itself (in my opinion) a very interesting subject for investigation; and one which calls upon the scientific world for a correct theory with regard to the time when, and the manner in which, this formation was produced. That it is of a secondary character, and of a sedimentary deposit, seems evident; and that it has withstood the force of the diluvial current, while the great valley of the Missouri, from this very wall of rocks to the Rocky Mountains, has been excavated, and its debris carried to the ocean, there is also not a shadow of doubt; which opinion I confidently advance on the authority of the following remarkable facts:

At the base of the wall, and within a few rods of it, and on the very ground where the Indians dig for the red stone, rests a group of five stupendous boulders of gneiss, leaning against each other; the smallest of which is twelve or fifteen feet, and the largest twenty-five feet in diameter, altogether weighing, unquestionably, several hundred tons. These blocks are composed chiefly of felspar and mica, of an exceedingly coarse grain (the felspar often occurring in crystals of an inch in diameter). The surface of these boulders is in every part

---

*From the very many excavations recently and anciently made, I could discover that these layers varied very much, in their thickness in different parts; and that in some places they were overlaid with four or five feet of rock, similar to, and in fact a part of, the lower stratum of the wall.

covered with a grey moss, which gives them an extremely ancient and venerable appearance, and their sides and angles are rounded by attrition, to the shape and character of most other erratic stones, which are found throughout the country. It is under these blocks that the two holes, or ovens are seen, in which, according to the Indian superstition, the two old women, the guardian spirits of the place, reside; of whom I have before spoken.

That these five immense blocks, of precisely the same character, and differing materially from all other specimens of boulders which I have seen in the great vallies of the Mississippi and Missouri, should have been hurled same hundreds of miles from their native bed, and lodged in so singular a group on this elevated ridge, is truly matter of surprise for the scientific world, as well as for the poor Indian, whose superstitious veneration of them is such, that not a spear of grass is broken or bent by his feet, within three or four rods of them, where he stops, and in humble supplication, by throwing plugs of tobacco to them, solicits permission to dig and carry away the red stone for his pipes. The surface of these boulders are in every part entire and unscratched by anything; wearing the moss everywhere unbroken, except where I applied the hammer, to obtain some small specimens, which I shall bring away with me.

The fact alone, that these blocks differ in character from all other specimens which I have seen in my travels, amongst the thousands of boulders which are strewed over the great valley of the Missouri and Mississippi, from the Yellow Stone almost to the Gulf of Mexico, raises in my mind an unanswerable question, as regards the location of their native bed, and the means by which they have reached their isolated position; like five brothers, leaning against and supporting each other, without the existence of another boulder within many miles of them. There are thousands and tens of thousands of boulders scattered over the prairies, at the base of the Côteau, on either side; and so throughout the valley of the St. Peters and Mississippi, which are also subjects of very great interest and importance to science, inasmuch as they present to the world, a vast variety of characters; and each one, though strayed away from its original position, bears incontestible proof of the character of its native bed. The tract of country lying between the St. Peters river and the Côteau, over which we passed, presents innumberable specimens of this kind; and near the base of the Côteau they are strewed over the prairie in countless numbers, presenting almost an incredible variety of rich and beautiful colours; and undoubtedly traceable, (if they can be traced), to separate and distinct beds.

Amongst these beautiful groups, it was sometimes a very easy matter to sit on my horse and count within my sight, some twenty or thirty different varieties, of quartz and granite, it rounded boulders, of every hue and colour, from snow white to intense red, and yellow, and blue, and almost to a jet black; each one well characterized and evidently from a distinct quarry. With the beautiful hues and almost endless characters of these blocks, I became completely surprised and charmed; and I resolved to procure specimens of every variety, which I did with success, by dismounting from my horse, and breaking small bits from them with my hammer; until I had something like an hundred different varieties, containing all the tints and colours of a painter's palette. These, I at length threw away, as I had on several former occasions, other minerals and fossils, which I had collected and lugged along from day to day, and sometimes from week to week.

Whether these varieties of quartz and granite can all be traced to their native beds, or whether they all have origins at this time exposed above the earth's surface, are equally matters of much doubt in my mind. I believe that the geologist may take the different varieties, which he may gather at the base of the Côteau in one hour, and travel the Continent of North America all over without being enabled to put them all in place; coming at last to the unavoidable conclusion, that numerous chains or beds of primitive rocks have reared their heads on this Continent, the summits of which have been swept away by the force of diluvial currents, and their fragments jostled together and strewed about, like foreigners in a strange land, over the great vallies of the Mississippi and Missouri, where they will ever remain, and be gazed upon by the traveller, as the only remaining evidence of their native beds, which has again submerged or been covered with diluvial deposits.

There seems not to be, either on the Côteau or in the great vallies on either side, so far as I have travelled, any slaty or other formation exposed above the surface on which grooves or scratches can be seen, to establish the direction of the diluvial currents in those regions; yet I think the fact is pretty clearly established by the general shapes of the vallies, and the courses of the mountain ridges which wall them in on their sides.

The Côteau des Prairies is the dividing ridge between the St. Peters and Missouri rivers; its southern termination or slope is about in the latitude of the Fall of St. Anthony, and it stands equi-distant between the two rivers; its general course bearing two or three degrees West of North for the distance of two or three hundred miles, when it gradually slopes again to the North, throwing out from its base the head-waters and tributaries of the St. Peters on the East. The Red River, and other streams, which empty into Hudson's Bay, on the North; La Riviere Jaque and several other tributaries to the Missouri, on the West; and the Red Cedar, the Ioway and the Des Moines, on the South.

This wonderful feature, which is several hundred miles in length, and varying from fifty to a hundred in width, is, perhaps, the noblest mound of its kind in the world; it gradually and gracefully rises on each side, by swell after swell, without tree, or bush or rock (save what are to be seen in the vicinity of the Pipe Stone Quarry), and everywhere covered with green grass, affording the traveller, from its highest elevations, the most unbounded and sublime views of— nothing at all—save the blue and boundless ocean of prairies that lie beneath and all around him, vanishing into azure in the distance without a speck or spot to break their softness.

The direction of this ridge, I consider, pretty clearly establishes the course of the diluvial current in this region, and the erratic stones which are distributed along its base, I attribute to an origin several hundred miles North West from the Côteau. I have not myself traced the Côteau to its highest points, nor to its Northern extremity; but it has been a subject, on which I have closely questioned a number of traders, who have traversed every miles of it with their carts, and from thence to Lake Winnepeg on the North, who uniformly tell me, that there is no range of primitive rocks to be crossed in travelling the whole distance, which is one connected and continuous prairie.

The top and sides of the Côteau are everywhere strewed over the surface with granitic sand and pebbles, which, together with the fact of the five boulders resting at the Pipe Stone Quarry, shew clearly that every part of the ridge has been subject to the action of these currents, which could not have run counter to it, without having disfigured or deranged its beautiful symmetry.

The glazed or polished surface of the quartz rocks at the Pipe Stone Quarry, I consider a very interesting subject, and one which will excite hereafter a variety of theories, as to the manner in which it has been produced, and the causes which have led to such singular results. The quartz is of a close grain, and exceedingly hard, eliciting the most brilliant spark from steel; and in most places, where exposed to the sun and the air, has a high polish on its surface, entirely beyond any results which could have been produced by diluvial action, being perfectly glazed as if by ignition. I was not sufficiently particular in my examinations to ascertain whether any parts of the surface of these rocks under the ground, and not exposed to the action of the air, were thus affected, which would afford an important argument in forming a correct theory with regard to it; and it may also be a fact of similar importance, that this polish does not extend over the whole wall or area; but is distributed over it in parts and sections, often disappearing suddenly, and reappearing again, even where the character and exposure of the rock is the same and unbroken. In general, the parts and points most projecting and exposed, bear the highest polish, which would naturally be the case whether it was produced by ignition, or by the action of the air and sun. It would seem almost an impossibility, that the air passing these projections for a series of centuries, could have produced so high a polish on so hard a substance; and it seems equally unaccountable, that this effect could have been produced in the other way, in the total absence of all igneous matter.

I have broken off specimens and brought them home, which certainly bear a high as polish and lustre on the surface, as a piece of melted glass; and then as these rocks have undoubtedly been formed where they now lie, it must be admitted, that this strange effect on their surface has been produced either by the action of the air and sun, or by igneous influence; and if by the latter course, there is no other conclusion we can come to, than that these results are volcanic; that this wall has once formed the side of a crater, and that the Pipe Stone, laying in horizontal strata, is formed of the lava which has issued from it. I am strongly inclined to believe, however, that the former supposition is the correct one; and that the Pipe Stone, which differs from all known specimens of lava, is a new variety of *steatite*, and will be found to be a subject of great interest and one worthy of a careful analysis.

After having glutted our curiosity at the fountain of the Red Pipe, our horses brought us to the base of the Côteau, and then over the extended plain that lies between that and the Traverse de Sioux, on the St. Peters with about five days' travel. This place is great (not in history, for there is none of it, but) in traditions, and stories, of which this Western world is full and rich.

"Here (according to their traditions), happened the mysterious birth of the red pipe, which has blown its fumes of peace and war to the remotest corners of the Continent; which has visited every warrior, and passed through its reddened stem the irrevocable oath of war and desolation. And here also, the peace-breathing calumet was born, and fringed with the eagle's quills, which has shed its thrilling fumes over the land, and soothed the fury of the relentless savage.

"The Great Spirit at an ancient period, here called the Indian nations together, and standing on the precipice of the red pipe stone rock, broke from its wall a piece, and made a huge pipe by turning it in his hand, which he smoked over them, and to the North, the South, the East, and the West, and told them that this stone was red—that it was their flesh—that they must use it for their pipes of peace—that it belonged to them all, and that the war-club and scalping knife must not be raised on its ground. At the last whiff of his pipe his head went into a great cloud, and the whole surface of the rock for several miles was melted and glazed; two great ovens were opened beneath, and two women (guardian spirits of the place), entered them in a blaze of fire; and they are heard there yet (Tso-mec-cos-tee, and Tso-me-cos-te-won-dee), answering to the invocations of the high priest or medicine-men, who consult them when they are visitors to this sacred place."

Near this spot, also, on a high mound, is the *"Thunder's nest" (nid-du-Tonnere)*, where "a very small bird sits upon her eggs during fair weather, and the skies are rent with bolts of thunder at the

. approach of a storm, which is occasioned by the hatching of her brood!

"This bird is eternal, and incapable of reproducing her own species: she has often been seen by the medicine-men, and is about as large as the end of the little finger! Her mate is a serpent, whose fiery tongue destroys the young ones as they are hatched, and the fiery noise darts through the skies" . . .

With my excellent companion, I am encamped on, and writing from, the very rock where "the Great Spirit stood when he consecrated the *pipe of peace*, by moulding it from the rock, and smoking it over the congregated nations that were assembled about him" . . . The rock . . . is the summit of a precipice thirty feet high, extending two miles in length and much of the way polished, as if a liquid glazing had been poured over its surface. Not far from us, in the solid rock, are the deep impressed "footsteps of the Great Spirit (in the form of a track of a large bird), where he formerly stood when the blood of the buffaloes that he was devouring, ran into the rocks and turned them red." At a few yards from us, leaps a beautiful little stream, from the top of the precipice, into a deep basin below. Here, amid rocks of the loveliest hues, but wildest contour, is seen the poor Indian performing ablution; and at a little distance beyond, on the plain, at the base of five huge granite boulders, he is humbly propitiating the guardian spirits of the place, by sacrifices of tobacco, entreating for permission to take away a small piece of the red stone for a pipe.

On our way to this place, my English companion and myself were arrested by a rascally band of the Sioux, and held in *durance vile*, for having dared to approach the sacred *fountain of the pipe!* While we had halted at the trading-hut of "Le Blanc," at a place called *Traverse des Sioux*, on the St. Peters river, and about 150 miles from the Red Pipe, a murky cloud of dark-visaged warriors and braves commenced gathering around the house, closing and cramming all its avenues, when one began his agitated and insulting harangue to us, announcing to us in the preamble, that we were prisoners, and could not go ahead. About twenty of them spoke in turn; and we were doomed to sit nearly the whole afternoon, without being allowed to speak a word in our behalf, until they had all got through. We were compelled to keep our seats like culprits, and hold our tongues, till all had brandished their fists in our faces, and vented all the threats and invective which could flow from Indian malice, grounded on the presumption that we had come to trespass on their dearest privilege—their religion.

Te-o-kun-hko (the swift man), first rose and said—

"My friends, I am not a chief, but the son of a chief—I am the son of my father—he is a chief—and when he is gone away, it is my duty to speak for him—he is not here—but what I say is the talk of his mouth. We have been told that you are going to the Pipe Stone Quarry. We come now to ask for what purpose you are going, and what business you have to go there." ('How! how!' vociferated all of them, thereby approving what was said, giving assent by the word *how*, which is their word for yes).

"Brothers—I am a brave, but not a chief—my arrow stands in the top of the leaping-rock; all can see it, and all know that Te-o-kun-hko's foot has been there. ('How! how!')

"Brothers—We look at you and we see that you are Che-mo-ke-mon capitains (white men officers): we know that you have been sent by your Government, to see what that place is worth, and we think the white people want to buy it. ('How, how').

"Brothers—We have seen always that the white people, when they see anything in our country that they want, send officers to value it, and then if they can't buy it, they will get it some other way ('How! how!')

"Brothers—I speak strong, my heart is strong, and I speak fast; this red pipe was given to the red men by the Great Spirit—it is a part of our flesh, and therefore is great *medicine*. ('How! how!')

"Brothers—We know that the whites are like a great cloud that rises in the East, and will cover the whole country. We know that they will have all our lands; but, if ever they get our Red Pipe Quarry they will have to pay very dear for it. ('How! how! how!')

"Brothers—We know that no white man has ever been to the Pipe Stone Quarry, and our chiefs have often decided in council that no white man shall ever go to it. ('How! how!')

"Brothers—You have heard what I have to say, and you can go no further, but you must turn about and go back. ('How! how! how!')

"*Brothers*—You see that the sweat runs from my face, for I am troubled."

Then I commenced to reply in the following manner:—

"My friends, I am sorry that you have mistaken us so much, and the object of our visit to your country. We are not officers—we are not sent by any one—we are two poor men travelling to see the Sioux and shake hands with them, and examine what is curious or interesting in their country. This man who is with me is my friend; he is a *Sa-ga-nosh* (an Englishman).

('How! how! how!')

(All rising and shaking hands with him, and a number of them taking out and showing British medals which were carried in their bosoms.)

"We have heard that the Red Pipe Quarry was a great curiosity, and we have started to go to it, and we will not be stopped." (Here I was interrupted by a grim and black-visaged fellow, who shook his long shaggy locks as he rose, with his sunken eyes fixed in direst hatred on me, and his fist brandished within an inch of my face.)

"*Pale faces!* you cannot speak till we have all done; you are our *prisoners*—our young men (our soldiers) are about the house, and you must listen to what we have to say. What has been said to you is true, you must go back. ('How! how!')

"We heard the word *Saganosh*, and it makes our hearts glad; we shook hand with our brother—his father is our father—he is our Great Father—he lives across the big lake—his son is here, and we are glad—we wear our Great Father the sag-a-nosh on our bosoms, and we keep his face bright—we shake hands, but no white man has been to the red pipe and none shall go. ('How!')

"You see (holding a red pipe to the side of his naked arm) that this pipe is a part of our flesh. The red men are a part of the red stone. ('How, how!')

"If the white men take away a piece of the red pipe stone, it is a hole made in our flesh, and the blood will always run. We cannot stop the blood from running. ('How, how!')

"The Great Spirit has told us that the red stone is only to be used for pipes, and through them we are to smoke to him. ('How!')

"Why do the white men want to get there? You have no good object in view; we know you have none, and the sooner you go back, the better." ('How, how!")

Muz-za (the iron) spoke next.

"My friends, we do not wish to harm you; you have heard the words of our chief men, and you now see that you must go back. ('How, how!')

"*Tchan-dee-pah-sha-kah-free* (the red pipe stone) was given to us by the Great Spirit, and no one need ask the price of it, for it is *medicine*. ('How, how!')

"My friends, I believe what you have told us; I think your intentions are good; but our chiefs have always told us, that no white man was allowed to go there—and you cannot go." ("How, how!") . . .

Another.—"My friends, you see I am a young man; you see on my war-club two scalps from my enemies' heads; my hands have been dipped in blood, but I am a good man. I am a friend to the whites, to the traders; and they are your friends. I bring them 3000 muskrat skins every year, which I catch in my own traps. ('How, how!')

"We love to go to the Pipe Stone, and get a piece for our pipes; but we ask the Great Spirit first. If the white men go to it, they will take it out, and not fill up the holes again, and the Great Spirit will be offended." ("How, how, how!")

Another.—"My friends, listen to me! what I am to say will be the truth. ('How!')

"I brought a large piece of the pipe stone, and gave it to a white man to make a pipe; he was our trader, and I wished him to have a good pipe. The next time I went to his store, I was unhappy when I saw that stone made into a dish! ('Eugh!')

"This is the way the white men would use the red pipe stone, if they could get it. Such conduct would offend the Great Spirit, and make a red man's heart sick. ('How, how!')

"*Brothers*, we do not wish to harm you—if you turn about and go back, you will be well, both you and your *horses*—you cannot go forward. ('How, how!')

"We know that if you go to the pipe stone, the Great Spirit looks upon you—the white people do not think of that. ('How, how!')

"I have no more to say."

These, and a dozen other speeches to the same effect, having been pronounced, I replied in the following manner:

"*My friends,* you have entirely mistaken us; we are no officers, nor are we sent by any one—the white men do not want the red pipe—it is not worth their carrying home so far, if you were to give it all to them. Another thing, they don't use pipes—they don't know how to smoke them.

'How, how!'

"*My friends,* I think as you do, that the Great Spirit has given that place to the red men for their pipes.

'How, how, how!'

"I give you great credit for the course you are taking to preserve and protect it; and I will do as much as any man to keep white men from taking it away from you.

'How, how!'

"But we have started to go and see it; and we cannot think of being stopped."

Another rose (interrupting me):—

"White men! your words are very smooth; you have some object in view or you would not be so determined to go—you have no good design, and the quicker you turn back the better; there is no use of talking any more about it—if you think best to go, try it; that's all I have to say." ("How, how!")

During this scene, the son of Monsr. Le Blanc was standing by, and seeing this man threatening me so hard by putting his fist near my face; he several times stepped up to him, and told him to stand back at a respectful distance, or that he would knock him down. After their speaking was done, I made a few remarks, stating that we should go ahead, which we did the next morning, by saddling our horses and riding off through the midst of them . . .

Le Blanc told us, that these were the most disorderly and treacherous part of the Sioux nation, that they had repeatedly threatened his life, and that he expected they would take it. He advised us to go back as they ordered; but we heeded not his advice.

On our way we were notified at several of their villages which we passed, that we must go back; but we proceeded on, and over a beautiful prairie country, of one hundred miles or more, when our Indian guide brought us to the trading-house of an old acquaintance of mine, Monsieur La Fromboise, who lives very comfortably, and in the employment of the American Fur Company, near the base of the Côteau, and forty or fifty miles from the Pipe Stone Quarry . . .

There was some allowance to be made, and some excuse, surely, for the rashness of these poor fellows, and we felt disposed to pity, rather than resent, though their *unpardonable stubborness* excited us almost to desperation. Their superstition was sensibly touched, for we were persisting, in the most peremptory terms, in the determination to visit this, their greatest medicine (mystery) place; where, it seems, they had often resolved no white man should ever be allowed to go. They took us to be "officers sent by Government to see what this place was worth," &c. As "this red stone was a part of their flesh," it would be sacrilegious for white man to touch or take it away"—"a hole would be made in their flesh, and the blood could never be made to stop running." My companion and myself were here in a *fix*, one that demanded the use of every energy we had about us; astounded at so unexpected a rebuff, and more than ever excited to go ahead, and see what was to be seen at this strange place; in this emergency, we mutually agreed to go forward, even if it should be at the hazard of our lives; we heard all they had to say, and then made our own speeches—and at length had our horses brought, which we mounted and rode off without further molestation; and having arrived upon this interesting ground, have found it quite equal in interest and beauty to our sanguine expectations, abundantly repaying us for all our trouble in travelling to it.

I had long ago heard many curious descriptions of this spot given by the Indians, and had contracted the most impatient desire to visit it. It will be seen by some of the traditions inserted in this Letter, from my notes taken on the Upper Missouri four years since, that those tribes have visited this place freely in former times; and that it has once been held and owned in common, as neutral ground, amongst the different tribes who met here to renew their pipes, under some superstition which stayed the tomahawk of natural foes, always raised in deadly hate and vengeance in other places. It will be seen also, that within a few years past (and that, probably, by the instigation of the whites, who have told them that by keeping off other tribes and manufacturing the pipes themselves, and trading them to other adjoining nations, they can acquire much influence and wealth), the Sioux have laid entire claim to this quarry; and as it is in the centre of their country, and they are more powerful than any other tribes, they are able successfully to prevent any access to it.

That this place should have been visited for centuries past by all the neighbouring tribes, who have hidden the war-club as they approached it, and stayed the cruelties of the scalping-knife, under the fear of the vengeance of the Great Spirit, who overlooks it, will not seem strange or unnatural, when their religion and superstitions are known.

Here are to be seen (and will continue to be seen for ages to come), the *totems* and *arms* of the different tribes, who have visited this place for ages past, deeply engraved on the quartz rocks, where they are to be recognized in a moment (and not to be denied) by the passing traveller, who has been among these tribes, and acquired even but a partial knowledge of them and their respective modes.* The thousands of inscriptions and paintings on the rocks at this place, as well as the ancient diggings for the pipe-stone, will afford amusement for the world who will visit it, without furnishing the least data, I should think, of the time at which these excavations commenced, or of the period at which the Sioux assumed the exclusive right to it.

Among the many traditions which I have drawn personally from the different tribes, and which go to support the opinion above

* I am aware that this interesting fact may be opposed by subsequent travellers, who will find nobody but the Sioux upon this ground, who now claim exclusive right to it; and for the satisfaction of those who doubt, I refer them to Lewis and Clark's Tour thirty-three years since, before the influence of Traders had deranged the system and truth of things, in these regions. I have often conversed with General Clark, of St. Louis, on this subject, and he told me explicitly, and authorized me to say it to the world, that every tribe on the Missouri told him they had been to this place, and that the Great Spirit kept the peace amongst his red children on that ground, where they had smoked with their enemies.

advanced, is the following one, which was related to me by a distinguished Knisteneaux, on the Upper Missouri, four years since, on occasion of presenting to me a handsome red stone pipe. After telling me that he had been to this place—and after describing it in all its features, he proceeded to say:—

"That in the time of a great freshet, which took place many centuries ago, and destroyed all the nations of the earth, all the tribes of the red men assembled on the Côteau du Prairie, to get out of the way of the waters. After they had all gathered here from all parts, the water continued to rise, until at length it covered them all in a mass, and their flesh was converted into red pipe stone. Therefore it has always been considered neutral ground—it belonged to all tribes alike, and all were allowed to get it and smoke it together.

"While they were all drowning in a mass, a young woman, K-wap-tah-w (a virgin), caught hold of the foot of a very large bird that was flying over, and was carried to the top of a high cliff, not far off, that was above the water. Here she had twins, and their father was the war-eagle, and her children have since peopled the earth.

"The pipe stone, which is the flesh of their ancestors, is smoked by them as the symbol of peace, and the eagle's quill decorates the head of the brave."

Tradition of the Sioux.—"Before the creation of man, the Great Spirit (whose tracks are yet to be seen on the stones, at the Red Pipe, in form of the tracks of a large bird) used to slay the buffaloes and eat them on the ledge of the Red Rocks, on the top of the Côteau des Prairies, and their blood running on to the rocks, turned them red. One day when a large snake had crawled into the nest of the bird to eat his eggs, one of the eggs hatched out in a clap of thunder, and the Great Spirit catching hold of a piece of the pipe stone to throw at the snake, moulded it into a man. This man's feet grew fast in the ground where he stood for many ages, like a great tree, and therefore he grew very old; he was older than an hundred men at the present day; and at last another tree grew up by the side of him, when a large snake ate them both off at the roots, and they wandered off together; from these have sprung all the people that now inhabit the earth."

... Theories respecting their origin, creation of the world, &c, &c., are by no means uniform throughout the different tribes, nor even through an individual tribe . . . Very many of these theories are but the vagaries, or the ingenious systems of their medicine or mystery-men, conjured up and taught to their own respective parts of a tribe, for the purpose of gaining an extraordinary influence over the minds and actions of the remainder of the tribe, whose superstitious minds, under the supernatural controul and dread of these self-made magicians, are held in a state of mysterious vassalage.

Amongst the Sioux of the Mississippi, and who live in the region of the Red Pipe Stone Quarry, I found the following and not less strange tradition on the same subject. "Many ages after the red men were made, when all the different tribes were at war, the Great Spirit sent runners and called them all together at the 'Red Pipe.'—He stood on the top of the rocks, and the red people were assembled in infinite numbers on the plains below. He took out of the rock a piece of the red stone, and made a large pipe; he smoked it over them all; told them that it was part of their flesh; that though they were at war, they must meet at this place as friends; that it belonged to them all; that they must make their calumets from it and smoke them to him whenever they wished to appease him or get his good-will—the smoke from his big pipe rolled over them all, and he disappeared in its cloud; at the last whiff of his pipe a blaze of fire rolled over the rocks, and melted their surface—at that moment two squaws went in a blaze of fire under the two medicine rocks, where they remain to this day, and must be consulted and propitiated whenever the pipe stone is to be taken away."

The following speech of a Mandan, which was made to me in the Mandan village four years since, after I had painted his picture, I have copied from my note-book as corroborative of the same facts:

"My brother—You have made my picture and I like it much. My friends tell me they can see the eyes move, and it must be very good—it must be partly alive. I am glad it is done—though many of my people are afraid. I am a young man, but my heart is strong. I have jumped on to the medicine-rock—I have placed my arrow on it and no Mandan can take it away.* The red stone is slippery, but my

---

*The medicine (or leaping) rock is a part of the precipice which has become severed from the main part, standing about seven or eight feet from the wall, just equal in height, and about seven feet in diameter.

foot was true—it did not slip. My brother, this pipe which I give to you, I brought from a high mountain, it is toward the rising sun—many were the pipes that we brought from there—and we brought them away in peace. We left our *totems* or marks on the rocks—we cut them deep in the stones, and they are there now. The Great Spirit told all nations to meet there in peace, and all nations hid the war-club and the tomahawk. The *Dah-co-tahs*, who are our enemies, are very strong—they have taken up the tomahawk, and the blood of our warriors has run on the rocks. My friend, we want to visit our medicines—our pipes are old and worn out. My friend, I wish you to speak to our Great Father about this."

The chief of the Puncahs, on the Upper Missouri, also made the following allusion to this place, in a speech which he made to me on the occasion of presenting me a very handsome pipe about four years since:—

"My friend, this pipe, which I wish you to accept, was dug from the ground, and cut and polished as you now see it, by my hands. I wish you to keep it, and when you smoke through it, recollect that this red stone is a part of our flesh. This is one of the last things we can ever give away. Our enemies the Sioux, have raised the red flag of blood over the Pipe Stone Quarry, and our medicines there are trodden under foot by them. The Sioux are many, and we cannot go to the mountain of the red pipe. We have seen all nations smoking together at that place—but, my brother, it is not so now."

It stands like an immense column of thirty-five feet high, and highly polished on its top and sides. It requires a daring effort to leap on to its top from the main wall, and back again, and many a heart has sighed for the honour of the feat without daring to make the attempt. Some few have tried it with success, and left their arrows standing in its crevice, several of which are seen there at this time; others have leapt the chasm and fallen from the slippery surface on which they could not hold, and suffered instant death upon the craggy rocks below. Every young man in the nation is ambitious to perform this feat; and those who have successfully done it are allowed to boast of it all their lives. In the sketch already exhibited, there will be seen, a view of the "leaping rock;" and in the middle of the picture, a mound, of a conical form, of ten feet height, which was erected over the body of a distinguished young man who was killed by making this daring effort, about two years before I was there, and whose sad fate was related to me by a Sioux chief, who was father of the young man, and was visiting the Red Pipe Stone Quarry, with thirty others of his tribe, when we were there, and cried over the grave, as he related the story to Mr. Wood and myself, of his son's death.

Rock Island, Upper Mississippi.

We had heard that the whole nation of Sacs and Foxes ... were to meet Governor Dodge here in treaty at this time, and nerve was given liberally to our paddles, which had brought us from Traverse de Sioux, on the St. Peters river; and we reached here luckily in time to see the parades and forms of a savage community, transferring the rights and immunities of their natural soil, to the insatiable grasp of pale faced voracity ... we found the river, the shores, and the plains contiguous, alive and vivid with plumes, with spears, and war-clubs of the yelling red men.

We are now six hundred miles below the Fall of St. Anthony, where steamers daily pass; and we feel, of course, at home. I spoke of the *Treaty*. We were just in time, and beheld its conclusion. It was signed yesterday; and this day, of course, is one of revel and amusements—shows of war-parades and dances. The whole of the Sacs and Foxes are gathered here, and their appearance is very thrilling, and at the same time pleasing. These people have sold so much of their land lately, that they have the luxuries of life to a considerable degree, and may be considered rich; consequently they look elated and happy, carrying themselves much above the humbled manner of most of the semi-civilized tribes, whose heads are hanging and drooping in poverty and despair.

In a former epistle, I mentioned the interview which I had with Kee-o-kuk, and the leading men and women of his tribe, when I painted a number of their portraits and amusements as follow:

Kee-o-kuk (the running fox, Illustration 57), is the present chief of the tribe, a dignified and proud man, with a good share of talent,

Illustration 57. Kee-o-kuk, The Running Fox.

and vanity enough to force into action all the wit and judgment he possesses, in order to command the attention and respect of the world. At the close of the "Black Hawk War," in 1833, which had been waged with disastrous effects along the frontier, by a Sac chief of that name; *Kee-o-kuk* was acknowledged chief of the Sacs and Foxes by General Scott, who held a Treaty with them at Rock Island. His appointment as chief, was in consequence of the friendly position he had taken during the war, holding two-thirds of the warriors neutral, which was no doubt the cause of the sudden and successful termination of the war, and the means of saving much bloodshed. Black Hawk and his two sons, as well as his principal advisers and warriors, were brought into St. Louis in chains, and *Kee-o-kuk* appointed chief with the assent of the tribe. In his portrait I have represented him in the costume, precisely, in which he was dressed when he stood for it, with his shield on his arm, and his staff (insignia of office) in his left hand. There is no Indian chief on the frontier better known at this time, or more highly appreciated for his eloquence, as a public speaker, than Kee-o-kuk; as he has repeatedly visited Washington and others of our Atlantic towns, and made his speeches before thousands, when he has been contending for his people's rights, in their stipulations with the United States Government, for the sale of their lands . . .

The Sacs and Foxes, who were once two separate tribes, but with a language very similar, have, at some period not very remote, united into one, and are now an inseparable people, and go by the familiar appellation of the amalgam name of "Sacs and Foxes."

These people . . . shave and ornament their heads, like the Osages and Pawnees, of whom I have spoken heretofore; and are amongst the number of tribes who have relinquished their immense tracts of lands, and recently retired West of the Mississippi river. Their numbers at present are not more than five or six thousand, yet they are a warlike and powerful tribe . . .

The dances and other amusements amongst this tribe are exceedingly spirited and pleasing; and I have made sketches of a number of them, which I briefly introduce here, and leave them for further comments at a future time, provided I ever get leisure and space to enable me to do it.

The *slave-dance* is a picturesque scene, and the custom in which it is founded a very curious one. This tribe has a society which they call the *"slaves,"* composed of a number of the young men of the best families in the tribe, who volunteer to be slaves for the term of two years, and subject to perform any menial service that the chief may order, no matter how humiliating or how degrading it may be; by which, after serving their two years, they are exempt for the rest of their lives, on war-parties or other excursions, or wherever they may be—from all labour or degrading occupations, such as cooking, making fires, &c. &c.

These young men elect one from their numbers to be their master, and all agree to obey his command whatever it may be, and which is given to him by one of the chiefs of the tribe. On a certain day or season of the year, they have to themselves a great feast, and preparatory to it the above-mentioned dance.

Smoking horses is another of the peculiar and very curious customs of this tribe. When General Street and I arrived at Kee-o-kuk's village, we were just in time to see this amusing scene, on the prairie a little back of his village. The Foxes, who were making up a war-party to go against the Sioux, and had not suitable horses enough by twenty, had sent word to the Sacs, the day before (according to an ancient custom), that they were coming on that day, at a certain hour, to "smoke" that number of horses, and they must not fail to have them ready. On that day, and at the hour, the twenty young men who were beggars for horses, were on the spot, and seated themselves on the ground in a circle, where they went to smoking. The villagers flocked around them in a dense crowd, and soon after appeared on the prairie, at half a mile distance, an equal number of young men of the Sac tribe, who had agreed, each to give a horse, and who were then galloping them about at full speed; and, gradually, as they went around in a circuit, coming in nearer to the centre, until the were at last close around the ring of young fellows seated on the ground. Whilst dashing about thus, each one, with a heavy whip in his hand, as he came within reach of the group on the ground, selected the one to whom he decided to present his horse, and as he passed him, gave him the most tremendous cut with his lash, over his naked shoulders; and as he darted around again he plied the whip as before and again and again, with a violent "crack!" until the blood could be seen trickling down over his naked shoulders, upon which he instantly dismounted, and placed the bridle and whip in his hands, saying, "here, you are a beggar—I present you a horse, but you will carry my mark on your back." In this manner, they were all in a little time "*whipped up*," and each had a good horse to ride home, and into battle. His necessity was such, that he could afford to take the stripes and the scars as the price of the horse, and the giver could afford to make the present for the satisfaction of putting his mark upon the other, and of boasting of his liberality, which he has always a right to do, when going into the dance, or on other important occasions.

The *Begging Dance* is a frequent amusement, and one that has been practised with some considerable success at this time, whilst there have been so many distinguished and liberal visitors here. It is got up by a number of desperate and long-winded fellows, who will dance and yell their visitors into liberality; or, if necessary, laugh them into it, by their strange antics, singing a song of importunity, and extending their hands for presents, which they allege are to gladden the hearts of the poor, and ensure a blessing to the giver.

The Sacs and Foxes, like all other Indians, are fond of living along the banks of rivers and streams; and like all others, are expert swimmers and skilful canoemen.

Their canoes, like those of the Sioux and many other tribes, are dug out from a log, and generally made extremely light; and they dart them through the coves and along the shores of the rivers, with astonishing quickness. I was often amused at their freaks in their canoes, whilst travelling; and I was induced to make a sketch of one which I frequently witnessed, that of sailing with the aid of their blankets, which the men carry; and when the wind is fair, stand in the bow of the canoe and hold by two corners, with the other two under the foot or tied to the leg; while the woman sit in the other end of the canoe, and steer it with their paddles.

The *Discovery Dance* has been given here, amongst various others, and pleased the bystanders very much; it was exceedingly droll and picturesque, and acted out with a great deal of pantomimic effect—without music, or any other noise than the patting of their feet, which all came simultaneously on the ground, in perfect time, whilst they were dancing forward two or four at a time, in a skulking posture, overlooking the country, and professing to announce the approach of animals or enemies which they have discovered, by giving the signals back to the leader of the dance.

Dance to the Berdashe is a very funny and amusing scene, which happens once a year or oftener, as they choose, when a feast is given to the "Berdashe," as he is called in French, (or *I-coo-coo-a*, in their own language), who is a man dressed in woman's clothes, as he is known to be all his life, and for extraordinary privileges which he is known to possess, he is driven to the most servile and degrading duties, which he is not allowed to escape; and he being the only one of the tribe submitting to this disgraceful degradation is looked upon as *medicine* and sacred, and a feast is given to him annually . . . As there are but a precious few in the tribe who have legitimately gained this singular privilege, or willing to make a public confession of it, it will be seen that the society consists of quite a limited number of "odd fellows."

This is one of the most unaccountable and disgusting customs, that I have ever met in the Indian country, and so far as I have been able to learn, belongs only to the Sioux and Sacs and Foxes— perhaps it is practised by other tribes, but I did not meet with it; and for further account of it I am constrained to refer the reader to the country where it is practiced, and where I should wish that it might be extinguished before it be more fully recorded.

Dance to the *Medicine of the Brave*. This is a custom well worth recording, for the beautiful moral which is contained in it. In this plate is represented a party of Sac warriors who have returned victorious from battle, with scalps they have taken from their enemies, but having lost one of their party, they appear and dance in front of his wigwam, fifteen days in succession, about an hour on each day, when the widow hangs his *medicine-bag* on a green bush which she erects before her door, under which she sits and cries, whilst the warriors dance and brandish the scalps they have taken, and at the same time recount the deeds of bravery of their deceased comrade in arms, whilst they are throwing presents to the widow to heal her grief and afford her the means of a living.

The Sacs and Foxes are already drawing an annuity of 27,000 dollars, for thirty years to come, in cash; and by the present Treaty just concluded, that amount will be enlarged to 37,000 dollars per annum. This Treaty with the Sacs and Foxes, held at Rock Island, was for the purchase of a tract of land of 256,000 acres, lying on the Ioway river, West of the Mississippi, a reserve which was made in the tract of land conveyed to the Government by Treaty after the Sac war, and known as the "Black Hawk purchase." The Treaty has been completed by Governor Dodge, by stipulating on the part of Government to pay them seventy-five cents per acre for the reserve, (amounting to 192,000 dollars), in the manner and form following:—

Thirty thousand dollars to be paid in specie in June next, at the Treaty-ground; and ten thousand dollars annually, for ten years to come, at the same place, and in the same manner; and the remaining sixty-two thousand, in the payment of their debts, and some little donations to widows and half-breed children. The American Fur Company was their principal creditor, whose account for goods advanced on credit, they admitted, to the amount of nearly fifty thousand dollars. It was stipulated by an article in the Treaty that one half of these demands should be paid in cash as soon as the Treaty should be ratified—and that five thousand dollars should be appropriated annually, for their liquidation, until they were paid off.

It was proposed by Kee-o-kuk in his speech (and it is a fact worthy of being known, for such has been the proposition in every Indian Treaty that I ever attended), that the first preparatory stipulation on the part of Government, should be to pay the requisite sum of money to satisfy all their creditors, who were then present, and whose accounts were handed in, acknowledged and admitted.

The price paid for this tract of land is a liberal one, comparatively speaking, for the usual price heretofore paid for Indian lands, has been one and a half or three quarter cents, (instead of seventy-five cents) per acre, for land which Government has since sold out for ten shillings.

Even one dollar per acre would not have been too much to have paid for this tract, for every acre of it can be sold in one year, for ten shillings per acre, to actual settlers, so desirable and so fertile is the tract of country purchased. These very people sold to Government a great part of the rich states of Illinois and Missouri, at the low rates above-mentioned; and this small tract being the last that they can ever part with, without throwing themselves back upon their natural enemies, it was no more than right that Government should deal with them, as they have done, liberally.

As an evidence of the immediate value of that tract of land to Government, and, as a striking instance of the overwhelming torrent of emigration to the "Far West," I will relate the following occurrence which took place at the close of the Treaty:—After the Treaty was signed and witnessed, Governor Dodge addressed a few very judicious and admonitory sentences to the chiefs and braves, which he finished by requesting them to move their families, and all their property from this tract, within one month, which time he would allow them, to make room for the whites.

Considerable excitement was created among the chiefs and braves, by this suggestion, and a hearty laugh ensued, the cause of which was soon after explained by one of them in the following manner:—

"My father, we have to laugh—we require no time to move—we have all left the lands already, and sold our wigwams to Chemokemons (white men)—some for one hundred, and some for two hundred dollars, before we came to this Treaty. There are already four hundred Chemokemons on the land, and several hundred more on their way moving in; and three days before we came away, one Chemokemon sold his wigwam to another Chemokemon for two thousand dollars, to build a great town."

In this wise is this fair land filling up, one hundred miles or more West of the Mississippi—not with barbarians, but with people from the East, enlightened and intelligent—with industry and perseverance that will soon rear from the soil all the luxuries, and add to the surface, all the taste and comforts of Eastern refinement.

The Treaty itself, in all its forms, was a scene of interest, and *Kee-o-kuk* was the principal speaker on the occasion, being recognized as the head chief of the tribe. He is a very subtle and dignified man, and well fitted to wield the destinies of his nation. The poor dethroned monarch, old Black Hawk, was present, and looked an object of pity. With an old frock coat and brown hat on, and a cane in his hand, he stood the whole time outside of the group, and in dumb and dismal silence, with his sons by the side of him, and also his *quondam* aide-de-camp, Nah-pope, and the prophet. They were not allowed to speak, nor even to sign the Treaty. *Nah-pope* rose, however, and commenced a very earnest speech on the subject of *temperance*! but Governor Dodge ordered him to sit down, (as being out of order), which probably saved him from a much more *peremptory command* from *Kee-o-kuk,* who was rising at that moment, with looks on his face that the Devil himself might have shrunk from . . .

◄————————————————►

Fort Moultrie, South Carolina.

*S*ince the date of my last Letter, I have been a wanderer as usual, and am now at least 2000 miles from the place where it was dated. At this place are held 250 of the Seminolees and Euchees, prisoners of war, who are to be kept here awhile longer, and transferred to the country assigned them, 700 miles West of the Mississippi, and 1400 from this. The famous Os-ce-o-la is amongst the prisoners; and also *Mick-e-no-pah*, the head chief of the tribe, and *Cloud, King Phillip*, and several others of the distinguished men of the nation, who have celebrated themselves in the war that is now waging with the United States' Government.

There is scarcely any need of my undertaking in an epistle of this kind, to give a full account of this tribe, of their early history—of their former or present location—or of their present condition, and the disastrous war they are now waging with the Unites States' Government, who have held an invading army in their country for four or five years, endeavouring to dispossess them and compel them to remove to the West, in compliance with Treaty stipulations. These are subjects generally understood already (being matters of history), and I leave them to the hands of those who will do them more complete justice than I could think of doing at this time, with the little space that I could allow them; in the confident hope that justice may be meted out to them, at least by the historian, if it should not be by their great Guardian, who takes it upon herself, as with all the tribes, affectionately to *call* them her *"red children."*

For those who know nothing of the Seminolees, it may be proper for me here just to remark, that they are a tribe of three or four thousand; occupying the peninsula of Florida—and speaking the language of the Creeks, of whom I have heretofore spoken, and who were once a part of the same tribe.

The word Seminolee is a Creek word, signifying runaways; a name which was given to a part of the Creek nation, who emigrated in a body to a country farther South, where they have lived to the present day; and continually extended their dominions by overrunning the once numerous tribe that occupied the Southern extremity of the Florida Cape, called the Euchees; whom they have at last nearly annihilated, and taken the mere remnant of them in, as a part of their tribe. With this tribe the Government have been engaged in deadly and disastrous warfare for four or five years; endeavouring to remove them from their lands, in compliance with a Treaty stipulation, which the Government claims to have been justly made, and which the Seminolees aver, was not. Many millions of money, and some hundreds of lives of officers and men have already been expended in the attempt to dislodge them; and much more will doubtless be yet spent before they can be removed from their almost impenetrable swamps and hiding-places, to which they can, for years to come, retreat; and from which they will be enabled, and no doubt disposed, in their exasperated state, to make continual sallies upon the unsuspecting and defenceless inhabitants of the country; carrying their relentless feelings to be reeked in cruel vengeance on the unoffending and innocent.

The prisoners who are held here, to the number of 250, men, women, and children, have been captured during the recent part of this warfare, and amongst them the distinguished personages whom I named a few moments since; of these, the most conspicuous at this time is Os-ce-o-la (Illustration 58), commonly called Powell, as he is generally supposed to be a half-breed, the son of a white man (by that name), and a Creek woman.

I have painted him precisely in the costume, in which he stood for his picture, even to a string and a trinket. He wore three ostrich feathers in his head, and a turban made of a vari-coloured cotton shawl—and his dress was chiefly of calicos, with a handsome bead sash or belt around his waist, and his rifle in his hand.

This young man is, no doubt, an extraordinary character, as he has been for some years reputed, and doubtless looked upon by the

Illustration 58. Osceola, Black Drink.

Seminolees as the master spirit and leader of the tribe, although he is not a chief. From his boyhood, he had led an energetic and desperate sort of life, which had secured for him a conspicuous position in society; and when the desperate circumstances of war were agitating his country, he at once took a conspicuous and decided part; and in some way whether he deserved it or not, acquired an influence and a name that soon sounded to the remotest parts of the United States, and amongst the Indian tribes, to the Rocky Mountains.

This gallant fellow, who was, undoubtedly, *captured* a few months since, with several of his chiefs and warriors, was at first brought in, to Fort Mellon in Florida, and afterwards sent to this place for safe-keeping, where he is grieving with a broken spirit, and ready to die, cursing white man, no doubt, to the end of his breath.

The surgeon of the post, Dr. Weedon, who has charge of him, and has been with him ever since he was taken prisoner, has told me from day to day, that he will not live many weeks; and I have my doubts whether he will, from the rapid decline I have observed in his face and his flesh since I arrived here.

During the time that I have been here, I have occupied a large room in the officers' quarters, by the politeness of Captain Morrison, who has command of the post, and charge of the prisoners; and on every evening, after painting all day at their portraits, I have had Os-ce-o-la, Mick-e-no-pa, Cloud, Co-a-had-jo, King Phillip, and others in my room, until a late hour at night, where they have taken great pains to give me an account of the war, and the mode in which they were captured, of which they complain bitterly.

I am fully convinced from all that I have seen, and learned from the lips of Osceola, and from the chiefs who are around him, that he is a most extraordinary man, and one entitled to a better fate.

In stature he is about at mediocrity, with an elastic and graceful movement; in his face he is good looking, with rather an effeminate smile; but of so peculiar a character, that the world may be ransacked over without finding another just like it. In his manners, and all his movements in company, he is polite and gentlemanly, though all his conversation is entirely in his own tongue; and his general appearance and actions, those of a full-blooded and wild Indian . . .

Mick-e-no-pah (Illustration 59), is the head chief of the tribe, and a

Illustration 59. Mick-e-no-pah.

very lusty and dignified man. He took great pleasure in being present every day in my room, whilst I was painting the others; but positively refused to be painted, until he found that a bottle of whiskey, and another of wine, which I kept on my mantelpiece, by permission of my kind friend Captain Morrison, were only to deal out their occasional kindnesses to those who sat for their portraits; when he at length agreed to be painted, "if I could make a fair likeness of his *legs*," which he had very tastefully dressed in a handsome pair of red leggings, and upon which I at once began, (as he sat cross-legged), by painting *them* on the lower part of the canvass, leaving room for his body and head above; all of which, through the irresistible influence of a few kindnesses from my bottle of wine, I soon had fastened to the canvass, where they will firmly stand I trust, for some hundreds of years.

Since I finished my portrait of Os-ce-o-la, and since writing the first part of this Letter, he has been extremely sick, and lies so yet, with an alarming attack of his quinsey or putrid sore throat, which will probably end his career in a few days. Two or three times the

---

*From accounts which left Fort Moultrie a few days after I returned home, it seems, that this ill-fated warrior died, a prisoner, the next morning after I left him. And the following very interesting account of his last moments was furnished me by Dr. Weedon, the surgeon who was by him, with the officers of the garrison, at Os-ce-o-la's request.

"About half an hour before he died, he seemed to be sensible that he was dying; and although he could not speak, he signified by signs that he wished me to send for the chiefs and for the officers of the post, whom I called in. He made signs to his wives (of whom he had two, and also two fine little children by his side,) to go and bring his full dress, which he wore in time of war; which having been brought in, he rose up in his bed, which was on the floor, and put on his shirt, his leggings and moccasins—girded on his war-belt—his bullet-pouch and powder-horn, and laid his

surgeon has sent for the officers of the Garrison and myself, to come and see him *"dying"*—we were with him that night before last till the middle of the night, every moment expecting his death; but he had improved during the last twenty-four hours, and there is some slight prospect of his recovery. The steamer starts to-morrow morning for New York, and I must use the opportunity; so I shall from necessity, leave the subject of Os-ce-o-la and the Seminolees for future consideration. Adieu.*

---

knife by the side of him on the floor. He then called for his red paint, and his looking-glass, which was held before him, when he deliberately painted one half of his face, his neck and his throat—his wrists—the backs of his hands, and the handle of his knife, red with vermilion; a custom practised when the irrevocable oath of war and destruction is taken. His knife he then placed in its sheath, under his belt; and he carefully arranged his turban on his head, and his three ostrich plumes that he was in the habit of wearing in it. Being thus prepared in full dress, he laid down a few minutes to recover strength sufficient, when he rose up as before, and with most benignant and pleasing smiles, extended his hand to me and to all of the officers and chiefs that were around him; and shook hands with us all in dead silence; and also with his wives and his little children; he made a signal for them to lower him down upon his bed, which was done, and he then slowly drew from his war-belt, his scalping-knife, which he firmly grasped in his right hand, laying it across the other, on his breast, and in a moment smiled away his last breath, without a struggle or a groan."

LETTER—NO. 58.

←————————→

North Western Frontier.

*H*aving finished my travels in the "Far West" for awhile, and being detained a little time, sans occupation, in my nineteenth or twentieth transit of what, in common parlance is denominated the Frontier; I have seated myself down to give some further account of it, and of the doings and habits of people, both red and white, who live upon it.

The Frontier may properly be denominated the fleeting and unsettled line extending from the Gulf of Mexico to the Lake of the Woods, a distance of three thousand miles; which indefinitely separates civilized from Indian population—a moving barrier, where the unrestrained and natural propensities of two people are concentrated, in an atmosphere of lawless iniquity, that offends Heaven, and holds in mutual ignorance of each other, the honourable and virtuous portions of two people, which seem destined never to meet.

From what has been said in the foregoing epistles, the reader will agree that I have pretty closely adhered to my promise made in the commencement of them; that I should confine my remarks chiefy to people I have visited, and customs that I have *seen*, rather than by taking up his time with matter that might be gleaned from books. He will also agree, that I have principally devoted my pages, as I promised, to an account of the condition and customs of those Indians whom I have found entirely beyond the Frontier, acting and living as Nature taught them to live and act, without the examples, and consequently without the taints of civilized encroachments . . .

I have seen a vast many of these wild people in my travels, it will be admitted by all. And I have had toils and difficulties, and dangers to encounter in paying them my visits; yet I have had my pleasures as I went along, in shaking their friendly hands, that never had felt the contaminating touch of *money*, or the withering embrace of pockets; I have shared the comforts of their hospitable wigwams, and always have been preserved unharmed in their country. And if I have spoken, or am to speak of them, with a seeming bias, the reader will know what allowance to make for me, who am standing as the champion of a people, who have treated me kindly, of whom I feel bound to speak well; and who have no means of speaking for themselves . . .

The peculiar condition in which we are obliged to contemplate these most unfortunate people at this time—hastening to destruction and extinction, as they evidently are, lays an uncompromising claim upon the sympathies of the civilized world, and gives a deep interest and value to such records as are truly made—setting up, and perpetuating from the life, their true native character and customs.

If the great family of North American Indians were all dying by a scourge or epidemic of the country, it would be natural, and a virtue, to weep for them; but merely to sympathize with them (and but partially to do that) when they are dying at our hands, and rendering their glebe to our possession, would be to subvert the simplest law of Nature, and turn civilized man, with all his boasted virtues, back to worse than savage barbarism . . .

Long and cruel experience has well proved that it is impossible for enlightened Governments or money-making individuals to deal with these credulous and unsophisticated people, without the sin of injustice; but the humble biographer or historian, who goes amongst them from a different motive, *may* come out of their country with his hands and his conscience clean, and himself an anomaly, a white man dealing with Indians, and meting out justice to them; which I hope it may be my good province to do with my pen and my brush, with which, at least, I will have the singular and valuable satisfaction of having done them no harm . . .

Of the *general appearance* of the North American Indians, much might be yet said, that would be new and instructive. In *stature,* as I have already said, there are some of the tribes that are considerably above the ordinary height of man, and others that are evidently below it; allowing their average to be about equal to that of their fellow-men in the civilized world. In girth they are less, and lighter in their limbs, and almost entirely free from corpulency or useless flesh. Their bones are lighter, their skulls are thinner, and their muscles less hard than those of their civilized neighbours, excepting in the legs and feet, where they are brought into more continual action by their violent exercise on foot and on horseback, which swells the muscles and gives them great strength in those limbs, which is often quite as conspicuous as the extraordinary development of muscles in the shoulders and arms of our labouring men.

Although the Indians are generally narrow in the shoulders, and less powerful with the arms, yet it does not always happen by any means, that they are so effeminate as they look, and so widely inferior in brachial strength, as the spectator is apt to believe, from the smooth and rounded appearance of their limbs. The contrast between one of our labouring men when he denudes his limbs, and the figure of a naked Indian is to be sure very striking, and entirely too much so, for the actual difference in the power of the two persons. There are several reasons for this which account for so disproportionate a contrast, and should be named.

The labouring man, who is using his limbs the greater part of his life in lifting heavy weights, &c. sweats them with the weight of clothes which he has on him, which softens the integuments and the flesh, leaving the muscles to stand out in more conspicuous relief when they are exposed; whilst the Indian, who exercises his limbs for the most of his life, denuded and exposed to the air, gets over his muscles a thicker and more compact layer of integuments which hide them from the view, leaving the casual spectator, who sees them only at rest, to suppose them too decidedly inferior to those which are found amongst people of his own colour. Of muscular strength in the legs, I have met many of the most extraordinary instances in the Indian country, that ever I have seen in my life; and I have watched and studied such for hours together, with utter surprise and admiration, in the violent exertions of their dances, where they leap and jump with every nerve strung, and every muscle swelled, till their legs will often look like a bundle of ropes, rather than a mass of human flesh. And from all that I have seen, I am inclined to say, that whatever differences there may be between the North American

Indians and their civilized neighbours in the above respects, they are decidedly the results of different habits of life and modes of education rather than of any difference in constitution. And I would also venture the assertion, that he who would see the Indian in a condition to judge of his muscles, must see him in motion; and he who would get a perfect study for an Hercules or an Atlas, should take a stone-mason for the upper part of his figure, and a Camanchee or a Blackfoot Indian from the waist downwards to the feet.

There is a general and striking character in the facial outline of the North American Indians, which is bold and free, and would seem at once to stamp them as distinct from natives or other parts of the world. Their noses are generally prominent and aquiline—and the whole face, if divested of paint and of copper-colour, would seem to approach to the bold and European character. Many travellers have thought that their eyes were smaller than those of Europeans; and there is good cause for one to believe so, if he judges from first impressions, without taking pains to inquire into the truth and causes of things. I have been struck, as most travellers, no doubt have, with the want of expansion and apparent smallness of the Indians' eyes, which I have found upon examination, to be principally the effect of continual exposure to the rays of the sun and the wind, without the shields that are used by the civilized world; and also when in-doors, and free from those causes, subjected generally to one more distressing, and calculated to produce similar results, the smoke that almost continually hangs about their wigwams, which necessarily contracts the lids of the eyes, forbidding that full flame and expansion of the eye, that the cool and clear shades of our civilized domiciles are calculated to promote.

The teeth of the Indians are generally regular and sound, and wonderfully preserved to old age, owing, no doubt, to the fact that they live without the spices of life—without saccharine and without salt, which are equally destructive to teeth, in civilized communities. Their teeth, though sound, are not white, having a yellowish cast; but for the same reason that a negro's teeth are "like ivory," they look white—set as they are in bronze, as any one with a *tolerable* set of teeth can easily test, by painting his face the colour of an Indian, and grinning for a moment in his looking-glass.

Beards they generally have not—esteeming them great vulgarities, and using every possible means to eradicate them whenever they are so unfortunate as to be annoyed with them. Different writers have been very much at variance on this subject ever since the first accounts given of these people; and there seems still an unsatisfied curiosity on the subject, which I would be glad to say that I could put entirely at rest.

From the best information that I could obtain amongst forty-eight tribes that I have visited, I feel authorized to say, that, amongst the wild tribes, where they have made no efforts to imitate white men, at least, the proportion of eighteen out of twenty, by nature are entirely without the appearance of a beard; and of the very few who have them by nature, nineteen out of twenty eradicate it by plucking it out several times in succession, precisely at the age of puberty, when its growth is successfully arrested; and occasionally one may be seen who has omitted to destroy it at that time, and subjects his chin to the repeated pains of its extractions, which he is performing with a pair of clamshells or other tweezers, nearly every day of his life—and occasionally again, but still more rarely, one is found, who from carelessness or inclination has omitted both of these, and is allowing it to grow to the length of an inch or two on his chin, in which case it is generally very soft, and exceedingly sparse. Wherever there is a cross of the blood with the European or African, which is frequently the case along the Frontier, a proportionate beard is the result; and it is allowed to grow, or is plucked out with much toil, and with great pain.

There has been much speculation, and great variety of opinions, as to the results of the intercourse between the European and African population with the Indians on the borders; and I would not undertake to decide so difficult a question, though I cannot help but express my opinion, which is made up from the vast many instances that I have seen, that generally speaking, these half-breed specimens are in both instances a decided deterioration from the two stocks, from which they have sprung; which I grant may be the consequence that generally flows from illicit intercourse, and from the inferior rank in which they are held by both, (which is mostly confined to the lowest and most degraded portions of society), rather than from any constitutional object, necessarily growing out of the amalgamation.

The finest built and most powerful men that I have ever yet seen have been some of the last-mentioned, the negro and the North American Indian mixed, of equal blood. These instances are rare to be sure, yet are occasionally to be found amongst the Seminolees and Cherokees, and also amongst the Camanchees, even, and the Caddoes; and I account for it in this way: From the slave-holding States to the heart of the country of a wild tribe of Indians, through almost boundless and impassable wilds and swamps, for hundreds of miles, it requires a negro of extraordinary leg and courage and persever-ance, to travel; absconding from his master's fields, to throw himself into a tribe of wild and hostile Indians, for the enjoyment of his liberty; of which there are occasional instances, and when they succeed, they are admired by the savage; and as they come with a good share of the tricks and arts of civilization, they are at once looked upon by the tribe, as extraordinary and important person-ages; and generally marry the daughters of chiefs, thus uniting theirs with the best blood in the nation, which produces these remarkably fine and powerful men that I have spoken of above.

Although the Indians of North America, where dissipation and disease have not got amongst them, undoubtedly are a longer lived and healthier race, and capable of enduring far more bodily priva-tion and pain, than civilized people can; yet I do not believe that the differences are constitutional, or anything more than the results of different circumstances, and a different education. As an evidence in support of this assertion, I will allude to the hundreds of men whom I have seen, and travelled with, who have been for several years together in the Rocky Mountains, in the employment of the Fur Companies; where they have lived exactly upon the Indian system, continually exposed to the open air, and the weather, and, to all the disappointments and privations peculiar to that mode of life; and I am bound to say, that I never saw a more hardy and healthy race of men in my life, whilst they remain in the country; nor any who fall to pieces quicker when they get back to confined and dissipated life, which they easily fall into, when they return to their own country.

The Indian women who are obliged to lead lives of severe toil and drudgery, become exceedingly healthy and robust, giving easy birth and strong constitutions to their children; which, in a measure, may account for the simplicity and fewness of their diseases, which in infancy and childhood are very seldom known to destroy life.

If there were anything like an equal proportion of deaths amongst the Indian children, that is found in the civilized portions of the world, the Indian country would long since have been depopulated, on account of the decided disproportion of children they produce. It is a very rare occurrence for an Indian woman to be *"blessed"* with more than four or five children during her life; and generally speaking, they seem contented with two or three; when in civilized communities it is no uncommon thing for a woman to be the mother of ten or twelve, and sometimes to bear two or even three at a time; of which I never recollect to have met an instance during all my extensive travels in the Indian country, though it is possible that I might occasionally have passed them.

For so striking a dissimilarity as there evidently is between these people, and those living according to the more artificial modes of life, in a subject, seemingly alike natural to both, the reader will perhaps expect me to furnish some rational and decisive causes. Several very plausible reasons have been advanced for such a deficiency on the part of the Indians, by authors who have written on the subject, but whose opinions I should be very slow to adopt; inasmuch as they have been based upon the Indian's inferiority, (as the same authors have taken great pains to prove in most other respects,) to their pale-faced neighbours.

I know of but one decided cause for this difference, which I would venture to advance, and which I confidently believe to be the principal obstacle to a more rapid increase of their families; which is the very great length of time that the woman submit to lactation, generally carrying their children at the breast to the age of two, and sometimes three, and even four years!

The astonishing ease and success with which the Indian women pass through the most painful and most trying of all human difficulties, which fall exclusively to the lot of the gentler sex; is quite equal, I have found from continued enquiry, to the representations that have often been made to the world by other travellers, who have gone before me. Many people have thought this a wise provision of Nature, in framing the constitutions of these people, to suit the exigencies of their exposed lives, where they are beyond the pale of skilful surgeons, and the nice little comforts that visit the sick beds in the enlightened world; but I never have been willing to give to Nature quite so much credit, for stepping aside of her own rule, which I believe to be about half way between—from which I am inclined to think that the refinements of art, and its spices, have led the civilized world into the pains, and perils of one unnatural extreme; whilst the extraordinary fatigue and exposure, and habits of Indian life, have greatly released them from natural pains on the other. With this view of the case, I fully believe that Nature has dealt everywhere impartially; and that, if from their childhood, our mothers had, like the Indian women, carried loads like beasts of burthen—and those over the longest journeys, and highest mountains—had swam the broadest rivers—and galloped about for months and even years of their lives, *astride* of their horse's backs; we should have taxed them as lightly in stepping into the world, as an Indian pappoose does its mother, who ties her horse under the shade of a tree for half an hour, and before night, overtakes her travelling companions with her infant in her arms, which has often been the case.

As to the probable origin of the North American Indians, which is one of the first questions that suggests itself to the enquiring mind, and will be perhaps, the last to be settled; I shall have little to say in this place . . . For a professed philanthropist, I should deem it cruel and hypocritical to waste time and space in the discussion of a subject, ever so interesting, (though unimportant), when the present condition and prospects of these people are calling so loudly upon the world for justice, and for mercy; and when their evanescent existence and customs are turning, as it were, on a wheel before us, but soon to be lost; whilst the mystery of their origin can as well be fathomed at a future day as now, and recorded with their exit . . .

It seems natural to enquire at once who these people are, and from whence they came; but this question is natural, only because we are out of nature. To an Indian, such a question would seem absurd—he would stand aghast and astounded at the *anomaly* before *him*—himself upon his own ground, "where the Great Spirit made him"—hunting in his own forests; if an exotic, with a "pale face," and from across the ocean, should stand before him, to ask him where he came from, and how he got there . . .

I never yet have been made to see the *necessity* of showing how these people *came here,* or that they *came here* at all; which might easily have been done, by the way of Behring's Straits from the North of Asia . . . For myself, I am quite satisfied with the fact, which is a thing certain, and to be relied on, that this Continent was found peopled in every part, by savages; and so, nearly every Island in the South Seas, at the distance of several thousand miles from either Continent . . .

I believe, with many others, that the North American Indians are a mixed people—that they have Jewish blood in their veins, though I would not assert, as some have undertaken to prove, *"that they are Jews,"* or that they are *"the ten lost tribes of Israel."* From the character and conformation of the heads, I am compelled to look upon them as an amalgam race, but still savages; and from many of their customs, which seem to me, to be peculiarly Jewish, as well as from the character of their heads, I am forced to believe that some part of those ancient tribes, who have been dispersed by Christians in so many ways, and in so many different eras, have found their way to this country, where they have entered amongst the native stock, and have lived and intermarried with the Indians, until their identity has been swallowed up and lost in the greater numbers of their new acquaintance, save the bold and decided character which they have bequeathed to the Indian races; and such of their customs as the Indians were pleased to adopt, and which they have preserved to the present day.

I am induced to believe thus from the very many customs which I have witnessed amongst them, that appear to be decidedly Jewish; and many of them so peculiarly so, that it would seem almost impossible, or at all events, exceedingly improbable, that two people in a state of nature should have hit upon them, and practiced them exactly alike . . .

I am compelled to believe that the Continent of America, and each of the other Continents, have had their aboriginal stocks, peculiar in colour and in character—and that each of these native stocks had undergone repeated mutations (at periods, of which history had kept no records), by erratic colonies from abroad, that have been engrafted upon them—mingling with them, and materially affecting their original character. By this process, I believe that the North American Indians, even where we find them in their wildest condition, are several degrees removed from their original character; and that one of their principal alloys has been a part of those dispersed people, who have mingled their blood and their customs with them, and even in their new disguise, seem destined to be followed up with oppression and endless persecution . . .

Many writers are of opinion, that the natives of America are all from one stock, and their languages from one root—that that stock is exotic, and that that language was introduced with it. And the reason assigned for this theory is, that amongst the various tribes, there is a reigning similarity in looks—and in their languages a striking resemblance to each other.

Now, if all the world were to argue in this way, I should reason just in the other; and pronounce this, though evidence to a certain degree, to be very far from conclusive, inasmuch as it is far easier and more natural for distinct tribes, or languages, grouped and used together, to *assimilate* than to *dissimilate;* as the pebbles on a sea-shore, that are washed about and jostled together, lose their angles, and incline at last to one rounded and uniform shape. So that if there had been, *ab origine*, a variety of different stocks in America, with different complexions, with different characters and customs, and of different statures, and speaking entirely different tongues; where they have been for a series of centuries living neighbours to each other, moving about and intermarrying; I think we might reasonably look for quite as great a similarity in their personal appearance and languages, as we now find; when, on the other hand, if we are to suppose that they were all from one foreign stock, with but one language, it is a difficult thing to conceive how or in what space of time, or for what purpose, they could have formed so many tongues, and so widely different, as those that are now spoken on the Continent.

It is evident I think, that if an island or continent had been peopled with black, white and red; a succession of revolving centuries of intercourse amongst these different colours would have had a tendency to bring them to one standard complexion, when no computable space of time, nor any conceivable circumstances could restore them again; re-producing all, or either of the distinct colours, from the compound.

That *customs* should be found similar, or many of them exactly the same, on the most opposite parts of the Continent, is still less surprising; for these will travel more rapidly, being more easily taught at Treaties and festivals between hostile bands, or disseminated by individuals travelling through neighbouring tribes, whilst languages and blood require more time for their admixture.

That the languages of the North American Indians, should be found to be so numerous at this day, and so very many of them radically different, is a subject of great surprise, and unaccountable, whether these people are derived from one individual stock, or from one hundred, or one thousand.

Though languages like colour and like customs, are calculated to assimilate, under the circumstances above named; yet it is evident that, (if derived from a variety of sources), they have been unaccountably kept more distinct than the others; and if from one root, have still more unaccountably dissimilated and divided into at least one hundred and fifty, two-thirds of which, I venture to say, are entirely and radically distinct; whilst amongst the people who speak them, there is a reigning similarity in looks, features and in customs, which would go very far to pronounce them one family, by nature or by convention.

I do not believe, with some very learned and distinguished writers, that the languages of the North American Indians can be traced to one root or to three or four, or any number of distinct idioms; nor do I believe all, or any one of them, will ever be fairly traced to a foreign origin . . . Amongst the tribes that I have visited, I consider that thirty, out of the forty-eight, are distinct and radically different in their languages, and eighteen are dialects of some three or four. It is a very simple thing for the off-hand theorists of the scientific world, who do not go near these people, to arrange and classify them; and a very clever thing to *simplify* the subject, and bring it, like everything else, under three or four heads, and to solve, and *re*solve it, by as many simple rules . . .

From what has been said in the foregoing Letters, it will have been seen that there are three divisions under which the North

American Indians may be justly considered; those who are dead—those who are dying, and those who are yet living and flourishing in their primitive condition ... The present condition of these once numerous people, contrasted with what it was, and what it is soon to be, is a subject of curious interest, as well as some importance, to the civilized world ... This very numerous and respectable part of the human family, which occupied the different parts of North America, at the time of its first settlement by the Anglo-Americans, contained more than fourteen millions, who have been reduced since that time, and undoubtedly in consequences of that settlement, to something less than two millions! ... The rapid declension of these people ... must at that rate be going on at this day, and sooner or later, lead to the most melancholy result of their final extinction ...

... As they stand at this day, there may be four or five hundred thousand in their primitive state; and a million and a half, that may be said to be semi-civilized, contending with the sophistry of white men, amongst whom they are timidly and unsuccessfully endeavouring to hold up their heads, and aping their modes; whilst they are swallowing their poisons, and yielding their lands and their lives, to the superior act and cunning of their merciless cajolers. In such parts of their community, their customs are uninteresting; being but poor and ridiculous imitations of those that are *bad enough,* those practised by their first treachers ...

For their Government, which is purely such as has been dictated to them by Nature and necessity alone, they are indebted to now foreign, native or civilized nation. For their religion, which is simply Theism, they are indebted to the Great Spirit, and not to the Christian world. For their modes of war, they owe nothing to enlightened nations—using only those weapons, and those modes which are prompted by nature, and within the means of their rude manufactures.

If, therefore, we do not find in their systems of polity and jurisprudence, the efficacy and justice that are dispensed in civilized institutions—if we do not find in their religion the light and the grace that flow from Christian faith—if in wars they are less honourable, and wage them upon a system of *"murderous stratagem,"* it is the duty of the enlightened world, who administer justice in a better way—who worship in a more acceptable form—and who war on a more *honourable* scale, to make great allowance for their ignorance, and yield to their credit, the fact, that if their systems are less wise, they are often more free from injustice—from hypocrisy and from carnage.

Their Governments, if they have any (for I am almost disposed to question the propriety of applying the term), are generally alike; each tribe having at its head, a chief (and most generally a war and civil chief), whom it would seem, alternately hold the ascendency, as the circumstances of peace or war may demand their respective services. These chiefs, whose titles are generally hereditary, hold their offices only as long as their ages will enable them to perform the duties of them by taking the lead in war-parties, &c., after which they devolve upon the next incumbent, who is the eldest son of the chief, provided he is decided by the other chiefs to be as worthy of it as any other young man in the tribe—in default of which, a chief is elected from amongst the sub-chiefs; so that the office is *hereditary on condition*, and *elective* in *emergency*.

The chief has no controul over the life or limbs, or liberty of his subjects, nor other power whatever, excepting that of *influence* which he gains by his virtues, and his exploits in war, and which induces his warriors and braves to follow him, as he leads them to battle—or to listen to him when he speaks and advises in council. In fact, he is no more than a *leader*, whom every young warrior may follow, or turn about and go back from, as he pleases, if he is willing to meet the disgrace that awaits him, who deserts his chief in the hour of danger.

It may be a difficult question to decide, whether their Government savours most of a democracy or an aristocracy; it is in some respects purely democratic—and in others aristocratic. The influence of names and families is strictly kept up, and their qualities and relative distinctions preserved in heraldric family Arms; yet entirely severed, and free from influences of wealth, which is seldom amassed by any persons in Indian communities; and most sure to slip from the hands of chiefs, or others high in office, who are looked upon to be liberal and charitable; and oftentimes, for the sake of popularity, render themselves the poorest, and most meanly dressed and equipped of any in the tribe.

These people have no written laws, nor others, save the penalties affixed to certain crimes, by long-standing custom, or by the decisions of the chiefs in council, who form a sort of Court and Congress too, for the investigation of crimes, and transaction of the public business. For the sessions of these dignitaries, each tribe has, in the middle of their village, a Government or council-house, where the chiefs often try and convict, for capital offences—leaving the punishment to be inflicted by the nearest of kin, to whom all eyes of the nation are turned, and who has no means of evading it without suffering disgrace in his tribe. For his purpose, the custom, which is the common law of the land, allows him to use any means whatever, that he may deem necessary to bring the thing effectually about; and he is allowed to *waylay* and shoot down the criminal—so that punishment is *certain* and *cruel*, and as effective from the hands of a feeble, as from those of a stout man, and entirely beyond the hope that often arises from the "glorious uncertainty of the law."

As I have in a former place said, cruelty is one of the leading traits of the Indian's character; and a little familiarity with their modes of life and government will soon convince the reader, that *certainty* and *cruelty* in punishments are requisite (where individuals undertake to inflict the penalties of the laws), in order to secure the lives and property of individuals in society.

In the treatment of their prisoners also, in many tribes, they are in the habit of inflicting the most appalling tortures, for which the enlightened world are apt to condemn them as cruel and unfeeling in the extreme; without stopping to learn that in every one of these instances, these cruelties are practiced by way of retaliation, by individuals or families of the tribe, whose relatives have been previously dealt with in a similar way by their enemies, and whose *manes* they deem it their duty to appease by this horrid and cruel mode of retaliation.

And in justice to the savage, the reader should yet know, that amongst these tribes that torture their prisoners, these cruelties are practised but upon the few whose lives are required to atone for those who have been similarly dealt with by their enemies, and that the *remainder are adopted into the tribe,* by marrying the widows whose husbands have fallen in battle, in which capacity they are received and respected like others of the tribe, and enjoy equal rights and immunities. And before we condemn them too far, we should yet pause and enquire whether in the enlightened world we are not guilty of equal cruelties—whether in the ravages and carnage of war, and treatment of prisoners, we practise any virtue superior to this; and whether the annals of history which are familiar to all, do not furnish abundant proof of equal cruelty to prisoners of war, as well as in many instances, to the members of our own respective communities. It is a remarkable fact and one well recorded in history, as it deserves to be, to the honour of the savage, that no instance has been known of violence to their captive females, a virtue yet to be learned in civilized warfare.

If their punishments are certain and cruel, they have the merit of being *few*, and those confined chiefly to their enemies. It is natural to be cruel to enemies; and in this, I do not see that the improvements of the enlightened and Christian world have yet elevated them so very much above the savage. To their friends, there are no people on earth that are more kind; and cruelties and punishments (except for capital offences) are amongst themselves, entirely dispensed with. No man in their communities is subject to any restraints upon his liberty, or to any coporal or degrading punishment; each one valuing his limbs, and his liberty to use them as his inviolable right, which no power in the tribe can deprive him of; whilst each one holds the chief as amenable to him as the most humble individual in the tribe.

On an occasion when I had interrogated a Sioux chief, on the Upper Missouri, about their Government—their punishments and tortures of prisoners, for which I had freely condemned them for the cruelty of the practice, he took occasion when I had got through, to ask *me* some questions relative to modes in the *civilized world,* which, with his comments upon them, were nearly as follow; and struck me, as I think they must every one, with great force.

"Among white people, nobody ever take your wife—take your children—take your mother, cut off nose—cut eyes out—burn to death?" No! "Then *you* no cut off nose—*you* no cut out eyes—*you* no burn to death—very good."

He also told me he had often heard that white people hung their criminals by the neck and choked them to death like dogs, and those their own people; to which I answered, "yes." He then told me he had learned that they shut each other up in prisons, where they keep them a great part of their lives *because they can't pay money!* I replied in the affirmative to this, which occasioned great surprise and excessive laughter, even amongst the women. He told me that he had been to our Fort, at Council Bluffs, where we had a great many warriors and braves, and he saw three of them taken out on the prairies and tied to a post and whipped almost to death, and he had been told that they submit to all this to get a little money, "yes." He said he had been told, that when all the white people were born, their white *medicine-men* had to stand by and look on—that in the Indian country the women would not allow that—they would be ashamed—that he had been along the Frontier, and a good deal amongst the white people, and he had seen them whip their little children—a thing that is very cruel—he had heard also, from several white *medicine-men*, that the Great Spirit of the white people was the child of a white woman, and that he was at last put to death by the white people! This seemed to be a thing that he had not been able to comprehend, and he concluded by saying, "the Indians' Great Spirit got no mother—the Indians no kill him, he never die." He put me a chapter of other questions, as to the trespasses of the white people on their lands—their continual corruption of the morals of their women—and digging open the Indians' graves to get their bones, &c. To all of which I was compelled to reply in the affirmative, and quite glad to close my note-book, and quietly to escape from the throng that had collected around me, and saying (though to myself and silently), that these and an hundred other vices belong to the civilized world, and are practiced upon (but certainly, in no instance, reciprocated by) the "cruel and relentless savage."

Of their modes of war, of which, a great deal has been written by other travellers—I could say much, but in the present place, must be brief. All wars, offensive or defensive, are decided on by the chiefs and doctors in council, where majority decides all questions. After their resolve, the chief conducts and leads—his pipe with the reddened stem is sent through the tribe by his *runners,* and every man who consents to go to war, draws the smoke once through its stem; he is then a *volunteer,* like all of their soldiers in war, and bound by no compulsive power, expect that of pride, and dread of the disgrace of turning back. After the soldiers are enlisted, the war-dance is performed in presence of the whole tribe: when each warrior in the warrior's dress, with weapons in hand, dances up separately, and striking the reddened post, thereby takes the solemn oath not to desert his party.

The chief leads in full dress to make himself as conspicuous a mark as possible for his enemy; whilst his men are chiefly denuded, and their limbs and faces covered with red earth or vermilion, and oftentimes with charcoal and grease, so as completely to disguise them, even from the knowledge of many of their intimate friends.

At the close of hostilities, the two parties are often brought together by a flag of truce, where they sit in Treaty, and solemnize by smoking through the calumet or pipe of peace, as I have before described; and after that, their warriors and braves step forward, with the pipe of peace in the left hand, and the war-club in the right, and dance around in a circle—going through many curious and exceedingly picturesque evolutions in the "*pipe of peace dance.*"

To each other I have found these people kind and honourable, and endowed with every feeling of parental, of filial, and conjugal affection, that is met in more enlightened communities. I have found them moral and religious: and I am bound to give them great credit for their zeal, which is often exhibited in their modes of worship, however insufficient they may seem to us, or may be in the estimation of the Great Spirit.

I have heard it said by some very good men, and some who have even been preaching the Christian religion amongst them, that they have no religion—that all their zeal in their worship of the Great Spirit was but the foolish excess of ignorant superstition—that their humble devotions and supplications to the Sun and the Moon, where many of them suppose that the Great Spirit resides, were but the absurd rantings of idolatry. To such opinions as these I never yet gave answer, nor drew other instant inferences from them, than, that from the bottom of my heart, I pitied the persons who gave them.

I fearlessly assert to the world, (and I defy contradiction,) that the North American Indian is everywhere, in his native state, a highly moral and religious being, endowed by his Maker, with an intuitive knowledge of some great Author of his being, and the Universe; in dread of whose displeasure he constantly lives, with the apprehension before him, of a future state, where he expects to be rewarded or punished according to the merits he has gained or forfeited in this world.

I have made this a subject of unceasing enquiry during all my travels, and from every individual Indian with whom I have conversed on the subject, from the highest to the lowest and most pitiably ignorant, I have received evidence enough, as well as from their numerous and humble modes or worship, to convince the mind, and elicit the confessions of, any man whose gods are not beaver and muskrats' skins—or whose ambition is not to be deemeed an apostle, or himself, their only redeemer.

Morality and virtue, I venture to say, the civilized world need not undertake to teach them; and to support me in this, I refer the reader to the interesting narrative of the Rev. Mr. Parker, amongst the tribes through and beyond the Rocky Mountains; to the narratives of Captain Bonneville, through the same regions; and also to the reports of the Reverend Messrs. Spalding and Lee, who have crossed the Mountains, and planted their little colony amongst them. And I am also allowed to refer to the account given by the Rev. Mr. Beaver, of the tribes in the vicinity of the Columbia and the Pacific Coast.

Of their extraordinary modes and sincerity of worship, I speak with equal confidence; and although I am compelled to pity them for their ignorance, I am bound to say that I never saw any other people of any colour, who spend *so much of their lives* in humbling themselves before, and worshipping the Great Spirit, as some of these tribes do, nor any whom I would not as soon suspect of insincerity and hypocrisy.

Self-denial, which is comparatively a word of no meaning in the enlightened world; and self-torture and almost self-immolation, are continual modes of appealing to the Great Spirit for his countenance and forgiveness; and these, not in studied figures of rhetoric, resounding in halls and synagogues, to fill and astonish the ears of the multitude; but humbly cried forth from starved stomachs and parched throats, from some lone and favourite haunts, where the poor penitents crawl and lay with their faces in the dirt from day to day, and day to day, sobbing forth their humble confession of their sins, and their earnest implorations for divine forgiveness and mercy.

I have seen man thus prostrating himself before his Maker, and worshipping as Nature taught him; and I have seen mercenary white man with his bottle and its associate vices, *unteaching* them; and after that, good and benevolent and pious men, devotedly wearing out their valuable lives, all but in vain, endeavouring to break down confirmed habits of cultivated vice and dissipation, and to engraft upon them the blessings of Christianity and civilization. I have visited most of the stations, and am acquainted with many of the excellent missionaries, who, with their families falling by the diseases of the country about them, are zealously labouring to benefit these benighted people: but I have, with thousands and millions of others, to deplore the ill success with which their painful and faithful labours have generally been attended.

This failure I attribute not to the want of capacity on the part of the savage, nor for lack of zeal and Christian endeavours of those who have been sent, and to whom the eyes of the sympathizing part of the world have been anxiously turned, in hopes of a more encouraging account. The misfortune has been, in my opinion, that these efforts have mostly been made in the wrong place—along the Frontier, where (though they have stood most in need of Christian advice and example) they have been the least ready to hear it or to benefit from its introduction; where whiskey has been sold for twenty, or thirty, or fifty years, and every sort of fraud and abuse that could be engendered and visited upon them, and amongst their families, by ingenious, *money-making* white man; rearing up under a burning sense of injustice, the most deadly and thwarting prejudices, which, and which alone, in my opinion, have stood in the way of the introduction of Christianity—of agriculture, and everything which virtuous society has attempted to teach them; which they meet and suspect, and reject as some new trick or enterprize of white man, which is to redound to his advantage rather than for their own benefit.

The pious missionary finds himself here, I would venture to say, in an indescribable vicinity of mixed vices and stupid ignorance, that disgust and discourage him; and just at the moment when his new theory, which has been at first received as a mystery to them, is about to be successfully revealed and explained, the whiskey bottle is handed again from the bushes; and the poor Indian (whose perplexed mind is just ready to catch the brilliant illumination of Christianity), grasps it, and, like too many people in the enlightened world, quiets his excited feelings with its soothing draught, embracing most affectionately the friend that brings him the most sudden relief; and is contented to fall back, and linger—and die in the moral darkness that is about him . . .

I have always been, and still am, an advocate for missionary efforts amongst these people, but I never have had much faith in the success of any unless they could be made amongst the tribes in their primitive state; where, if the strong arm of the Government could be extended out to protect them, I believe that with the example of good and pious men, teaching them at the same time, agriculture and the useful arts, much could be done with these interesting and talented people, for the successful improvement of their moral and physical condition.

I have ever thought, and still think, that the Indian's mind is a beautiful blank, on which anything might be written, if the right mode were taken to do it.

Could the enlightened and virtuous society of the East, have been brought in contact with him as his first neighbours, and his eyes been first opened to improvements and habits worthy of his imitation; and could religion have been taught him without the interference of the counteracting vices by which he is surrounded, the best efforts of the world would not have been thrown away upon him, nor posterity been left to say, in future ages, when he and his race shall have been swept from the face of the earth, that he was destined by Heaven to be unconverted and uncivilized.

The Indian's calamity is surely far this side of his origin—his misfortune had been in his education. Ever since our first acquaintance with these people on the Altantic shores, have we regularly advanced upon them; and far a-head of good and moral society have their first teachers travelled (and are yet travelling), with vices and iniquities so horrible as to blind their eyes for ever to the light and loveliness of virture, when she is presented to them.

It is in the bewildering maze of this moving atmosphere that he, in his native simplicity, finds himself lost amidst the ingenuity and sophistry of his new acquaintance. He stands amazed at the arts and improvements of civilized life—his proud spirit which before was founded on his ignorance, droops, and he sinks down discouraged, into melancholy and despair; and at that moment grasps the bottle (which is ever ready), to soothe his anguished feelings to the grave. It is in this deplorable condition that the civilized world, in their approach, have ever found him; and here in his inevitable misery, that the charity of the world has been lavished upon him, and religion has exhausted its best efforts almost in vain.

Notwithstanding his destructive ordeal, through which all the border tribes have had to pass, and of whom I have spoken but in general terms, there are striking and noble exceptions on the Frontiers, of individuals, and in some instances, of the remaining remnants of tribes, who have followed the advice and example of their Christian teachers; who have entirely discarded their habits of dissipation, and successfully outlived the dismal wreck of their tribe—having embraced, and are now preaching, the Christian religion; and proving by the brightest example, that they are well worthy of the sincere and well-applied friendship of the enlightened world, rather than their enmity and persecution.

By nature they are decent and modest, unassuming and inoffensive—and all history (which I could quote to the end of a volume), proves them to have been found friendly and hospitable, on the first approach of white people to their villages on all parts of the American Continent—and from what I have *seen*, (which I offer as proof, rather than what I have *read*,) I am willing and proud to add, for the ages who are only to read of these people, my testimony to that which was given by the immortal Columbus, who wrote back to his Royal Master and Mistress, from his first position on the new Continent, "I swear to your majesties, that there is not a better people in the world than these; more affectionate, affable, or mild. They love their neighbours as themselves, and they always speak smilingly."

They are ingenious and talented, as many of their curious manufactures will prove, which are seen by thousands in my Collection.

In the *mechanic arts* they have advanced but little, probably because they have had but little use for them and have had no teachers to bring them out. In the *fine arts*, they are perhaps still more rude, and their productions are very few. Their materials and implements that they work with, are exceedingly rare and simple; and their principal efforts at pictorial effects, are found on their buffalo robes; of which I have given some account in former Letters, and of which I shall herein furnish some additional information.

I have been unable to find anything like a *system* of hieroglyphic writing amongst them; yet, their *picture writings* on the rocks, and on their robes, approach somewhat towards it. Of the former, I have seen a vast many in the course of my travels; and I have satisfied myself that they are generally the *totems* (symbolic names) merely, of Indians who have visited those places, and from a similiar feeling of vanity that everywhere belongs to man much alike, have been in the habit of recording their names or symbols, such as birds, beasts, or reptiles; by which each family, and each individual, is generally known, as white men are in the habit of recording their names at watering places, &c.

Many of these have recently been ascribed to the North-men, who probably discovered this country at an early period, and have been extinguished by the savage tribes. I might have subscribed to such a theory, had I not at the Red Pipe Stone Quarry, where there are a vast number of these inscriptions cut in the solid rock, and at other places also, seen the Indian at work, recording this totem amongst those of more ancient dates; which convinced me that they had been progressively made, at different ages, and without any system that could be called hieroglyphic writing.

The paintings on their robes are in many cases exceedingly curious, and generally represent the exploits of their military lives, which they are proud of recording in this way and exhibiting on their backs as they walk . . .

He who will sit and contemplate that vast Frontier, where, by the past policy of the Government, one hundred and twenty thousand of these poor people, (who had just got initiated into the mysteries and modes of civilized life, surrounded by examples of industry and agriculture which they were beginning to adopt), have been removed several hundred miles to the West, to meet a second siege of the whiskey-sellers and traders in the wilderness, to whose enormous exactions their semi-civilized habits and appetites have subjected them, will assuredly pity them. Where they have to quit their acquired luxuries, or pay ten times their accustomed prices for them—and to scuffle for a few years upon the plains, with the wild tribes, and with white men also, for the flesh and the skins of the last of the buffaloes; where their carnage, but not their *appetites*, must stop in a few years, and with the ghastliness of hunger and despair, they will find themselves gazing at each other up on the vacant waste, which will afford them nothing but the empty air, and the desperate resolve to flee to the woods and fastnesses of the Rocky Mountains; whilst more lucky white man will return to his comfortable home, with no misfortune, save that of *deep remorse* and a *guilty conscience*. Such a reader will find enough to claim his pity and engage his whole soul's indignation, at the wholesale and retail system of injustice, which has been, from the very first landing of our forefathers, (and is equally at the present day, being) visited upon these poor, and naturally unoffending, untrespassing people.

In alluding to the cruel policy of removing the different tribes to their new country, West of the Mississippi, I would not do it without the highest respect to the motives of the Government ... but when I go, as I have done, through every one of those tribes removed, who had learned at home to use the ploughshare, and also contracted a passion, and a taste of civilized manufactures; and after that, removed twelve and fourteen hundred miles West, to a wild and lawless region, where their wants are to be supplied by the traders, at eight or ten times the prices they have been in the habit of paying; where whiskey can easily be sold to them in a boundless and lawless forest, without the restraints that can be successfully put upon the sellers of it in their civilized neighbourhoods; and where also they are allured from the use of the ploughs, by the herds of buffaloes and other wild animals on the plains; I am compelled to state, as my irresistible conviction, that I believe the system one well calculated to benefit the interests of the voracious land-speculators and Indian Traders; the first of whom are ready to grasp at their lands, as soon as they are vacated—and the others, at the *annuities* of one hundred and twenty thousand extravagant customers. I believe the system is calculated to aid these, and perhaps to facilitate the growth and the wealth of the civilized border; but I believe, like everything else that tends to white man's aggrandizement, and the increase of his wealth, it will have as rapid a tendency to the poverty and destruction of the poor *red men;* who, unfortunately, *almost* seem *doomed*, never in any way to be associated in interest with their pale-faced neighbours.

The system of trade, and the small-pox, have been the great and wholesale destroyers of these poor people, from the Atlantic Coast to where they are now found. And no one but God, knows where the voracity of the one is to stop, short of the acquisition of everything that is desirable to money-making man in the Indian's country; or when the mortal destruction of the other is to be arrested, whilst there is untried flesh for it to act upon, either within or beyond the Rocky Mountains.

From the first settlements on the Atlantic Coast, to where it is now carried on at the base of the Rocky Mountains, there has been but one system of trade and money-making, by hundreds and thousands of white men, who are desperately bent upon making their fortunes in this trade, with the unsophisticated children of the forest; and generally they have succeeded in the achievement of their object.

The Governments of the United States, and Great Britain, have always held out every encouragement to the Fur Traders, whose traffic has uniformly been looked upon as beneficial, and a source of wealth to nations; though surely, they never could have considered such intercourse as advantageous to the savage.

Besides the many thousands who are daily and hourly selling whiskey and rum, and useless gewgaws, to the Indians on the United States, the Canada, the Texian and Mexican borders, there are, of hardy adventurers, in the Rocky Mountains and beyond, or near them, and out of all limits of laws, one thousand armed men in the annual employ of the United States' Fur Companies—and equal number in the employment of the British Factories, and twice that number in the Russian and Mexican possessions; all of whom pervade the countries of the wildest tribes they can reach, with guns and gunpowder in their hands, and other instruments of death, unthought of by the simple savage, calculated to terrify and coerce him to favourable terms in his trade: and in all instances they assume the right, (and prove it if necessary, by the superiority of their weapons), of hunting and trapping the streams and lakes of their countries.

These traders, in addition to the terror, and sometimes death, that they carry into these remote realms, at the muzzles of their guns, as well as by whiskey and the small-pox, are continually arming tribe after tribe with fire-arms; who are able thereby, to bring their unsuspecting enemies into unequal combats, where they are slain by thousands, and who have no way to heal the awful wound but by arming themselves in turn; and in a similar manner reeking their vengeance upon *their* defenceless enemies on the West. In this wholesale way, and by whiskey and disease, tribe after tribe sink their heads and lose their better, proudest half, before the next and succeeding waves of civilization flow on, to see or learn anything definite of them.

Without entering at this time, into any detailed history of this immense system, or denunciation of any of the men or their motives, who are engaged in it, I would barely observe, that, from the very nature of their traffic, where their goods are to be carried several thousands of miles, on the most rapid and dangerous streams, over mountains and other almost discouraging obstacles; and that at the continual hazard to their lives, from accident and diseases of the countries, the poor Indians are obliged to pay such enormous prices for their goods, that the balance of trade is so decidedly against them, as soon to lead them to poverty; and, unfortunately for them, they mostly contract a taste for whiskey and rum, which are not only ruinous in their prices, but in their effects destructive to life—destroying the Indians, much more rapidly than an equal indulgence will destroy the civilized constitution.

In the Indian communities, where there is no law of the land or custom denominating it a vice to drink whiskey, and to get drunk; and where the poor Indian meets whiskey tendered to him by white men, whom he considers wiser than himself, and to whom he naturally looks for example; he thinks it no harm to drink to excess, and will lie drunk as long as he can raise the means to pay for it. And after his first means, in his wild state, are exhausted, he becomes a beggar for whiskey, and begs until he disgusts, when the honest pioneer becomes his neighbour; and then, and not before, gets the name of the "poor, degraded, naked, and drunken Indian," to whom the epithets are well and truly applied.

On this great system of carrying the Fur Trade into the Rocky Mountains and other parts of the wilderness country, where whiskey is sold at the rate of twenty and thirty dollars per gallon, and most other articles of trade at a similar rate; I know of no better comment, nor any more excusable, than the quotation of a few passages from a very popular work, which is being read with great avidity, from the pen of a gentleman whose name gives currency to any book, and whose fine taste, pleasure to all who read. The work I refer to, "The Rocky Mountains, or Adventures in the Far West; by W. Irving," is a very interesting one; and its incidents, no doubt, are given with great candour, by the excellent officer, Captain Bonneville, who spent five years in the region of the Rocky Mountains, on a furlough; endeavouring, in competition with others, to add to his fortune, by pushing the Fur Trade to some of the wildest tribes in those remote regions.

"The worthy Captain (says the Author) started into the country with 110 men; whose very appearance and equipment exhibited a piebald mixture—half-civilized and half-savage, &c." And he also preludes his work by saying, that it was revised by himself from Captain Bonneville's own notes, which can, no doubt, be relied on.

This medley group, it seems, traversed the country to the Rocky Mountains, where, amongst the Nez Percés and Flatheads, he says, "They were friendly in their dispositions, and honest to the most scrupulous degree in their intercourse with the white men. And of the same people, the Captain continues—Simply to call these people religious, would convey but a faint idea of the deep hue of piety and devotion which pervades the whole of their conduct. Their honesty is immaculate; and their purity of purpose, and their observance of the rites of their religion, are most uniform and remarkable. They are, certainly, more like a nation of saints than a horde of savages."

Afterwards, of the *"Root-Diggers,"* in the vicinity of the Great Salt Lake, who are a band of the Snake tribe, (and of whom he speaks thus:—"In fact, they are a simple, timid, inoffensive race, and scarce provided with any weapons, except for the chase"); he says that, "one morning, one of his trappers, of a violent and savage character, discovering that his traps had been carried off in the night, took a horrid oath that he would kill the first Indian he should meet, innocent or guilty. As he was returning with his comrades to camp, he beheld two unfortunate Root-Diggers seated on the river bank fishing—advancing upon them, he levelled his rifle, shot one upon the spot, and flung his bleeding body into the stream."

A short time afterwards, when his party of trappers "were about to cross Ogden's river, a great number of Shoshokies or Root-Diggers were posted on the opposite bank, when they *imagined* they were there with hostile intent; they advanced upon them, levelled their rifles, and killed twenty-five of them on the spot. The rest fled to a short distance, then halted and turned about, howling and whining like wolves, and uttering most piteous wailings. The trappers chased them in every direction; the poor wretches made no defence, but fled with terror; neither does it appear from the accounts of the boasted victors, that a weapon had been wielded, or a weapon launched by the Indians throughout the affair."

After this affair, this "piebald" band of trappers wandered off to Monterey, on the coast of California, and on their return on horseback through an immense tract of the Root-Diggers' country, he gives the further following accounts of their transactions:—

"In the course of their journey through the country of the poor Root-Diggers, there seems to have been an emulation between them, which could inflict the greatest outrages upon the natives. The trappers still considered them in the light of dangerous foes; and the Mexicans, very probably, charged them with the sin of horse-stealing; we have no other mode of accounting for the infamous barbarities, of which, according to their own story, they were guilty—hunting the poor Indians like wild beasts, and killing them without mercy— chasing their unfortunate victims at full speed; noosing them around the neck with their lasos, and then dragging them to death."

It is due to Captain Bonneville, that the world should know that these cruel (not "*savage*") atrocities were committed by his men, when they were on a Tour to explore the shores of the Great Salt Lake, and many hundreds of miles from him, and beyond this controul; and that in his work, both the Captain and the writer of the book have expressed in a proper way, their abhorrence of such fiendish transactions.

A part of the same "piebald mixture" of trappers, who were encamped in the Riccaree country, and trapping the beavers out of their streams, when, finding that the Riccarees had stolen a number of their horses one night, in the morning made prisoners of two of the Riccarees, who loitered into their camp, and probably without knowledge of the offence committed, when they were bound hand and foot as hostages, until every one of the horses should be returned.

"The mountaineers declared, that unless the horses were relinquished, the prisoners should be burned to death. To give force to their threat, a pyre of logs and faggots was heaped up and kindled into a blaze. The Riccarees released one horse, and then another; but finding that nothing but the relinquishment of all their spoils would purchase the lives of their captives, they abandoned them to their fate, moving off with many parting words and howlings, when the prisoners were dragged to the blazing pyre, and burnt to death in sight of their retreating comrades.

"Such are the savage cruelties that white men learn to practice, who mingle in savage life; and such are the acts that lead to terrible recrimination on the part of the Indians. Should we hear of any atrocities committed by the Riccarees upon captive white men; let this signal and recent provocation be born in mind. Individual cases of the kind dwell in the recollections of whole tribes—and it is a point of honour and conscience to revenge them."

To quote the author further—"The facts disclosed in the present work, clearly manifest the policy of establishing military posts, and a mounted force to protect our Traders in their journeys across the great Western wilds; and of pushing the outposts into the heart of the singular wilderness we have laid open, so as to maintain some degree of sway over the country, and to put an end to the kind of 'black mail,' levied on all occasions, by the savage 'chivalry of the mountains' "!

. . . From the above facts, as well as from others enumerated in the foregoing epistles, the discerning reader will easily see how prejudices are raised in the minds of the savage, and why so many murders of white people are heard of on the Frontier, which are uniformly attributed to the wanton cruelty and rapacity of the savage—which we denominate "Indian murders," and "ruthless barbarities," before we can condescend to go to the poor savage, and ask him for a reason, which there is no doubt he could generally furnish us.

From these, and hundreds of others that might be named, and equally barbarous, it can easily be seen, that white men may well feel a dread at every step they take in Indian realms, after atrocities like these, that call so loudly and so justly for revenge, in a country where there are no laws to punish; but where the cruel savage takes vengeance in his own way—and white men fall, in the Indian's estimation, not as *murdered*, but *executed*, under the common law of their land.

Of the hundreds and thousands of such *murders*, as they are denominated by white men, who are the only ones to tell of them in the civilized world; it should also be kept in mind by the reader, who passes his sentence on them, that they are all committed on Indian ground—that the Indian hunts not, nor traps anywhere on white man's soil, nor asks him for his lands—or molests the sacred graves where they have deposited the bones of their fathers, their wives and their little children.

I have said that the principal means of the destruction of these people, were the system of trade, and the introduction of small-pox, the infallible plague that is consequent, sooner or later, upon the introduction of trade and whiskey-selling to every tribe ... Each one has had this exotic disease in their turn—and in a few months have lost one half or more of their numbers ... from living evidences, and distinct traditions, this appalling disease has several times, before our days, run like a wave through the Western tribes, over the Rocky Mountains, and to the Pacific Ocean—thinning the ranks of the poor Indians to an extent which no knowledge, save that of the overlooking eye of the Almighty, can justly comprehend.

... So long as the past and present system of trade and whiskey-selling is tolerated amongst them, there is little hope for their improvement, nor any chance for more than a temporary existence. I have closely studied the Indian character in its native state, and also in its secondary form along our Frontiers; civilized, as it is often (but incorrectly) called. I have seen it in every phase, and although there are many noble instances to the contrary, and with many of whom I am personally acquainted; yet the greater part of those who have lingered along the Frontiers, and been kicked about like dogs, by white men, and beaten into a sort of civilization, are very far from being what I would be glad to see them, and proud to call them, civilized by the aids and examples of good and moral people ...

Such are the results to which the present system of civilization brings that small part of these poor unfortunate people, who outlive the first calamities of their country and in this degraded and pitiable condition, the most of them end their days in poverty and wretchedness, without the power of rising above it. Standing on the soil which they have occupied from their childhood, and inherited from their fathers; with the dread of "pale faces," and the deadly prejudices that have been reared in their breasts against them, for the destructive influences which they have introduced into their country, which have thrown the greater part of their friends and connexions into the grave, and are now promising the remainder of them no better prospect than the dreary one of living a few years longer, and then to sink into the ground themselves; surrendering their lands and their fair hunting grounds to the enjoyment of their enemies, and their bones to be dug up and strewed about the fields . . .

For the Christian and philanthropist, in any part of the world, there is enough, I am sure, in the character, condition, and history of these unfortunate people, to engage his sympathies—for the Nation, there is an unrequited account of sin and injustice that sooner or later will call for *national retribution*—and for the American citizens, who live, every where proud of their growing wealth and their luxuries, over the bones of these poor fellows, who have surrendered their hunting-grounds and their lives, to the enjoyment of their cruel dispossessors, there is a lingering terror yet, I fear, for the reflecting minds, whose mortal bodies must soon take their humble places with their red, but injured brethren, under the same glebe; to appear and stand, at last, with guilt's shivering conviction, amidst the myriad ranks of accusing spirits, that are to rise in their own fields, at the final day of resurrection!

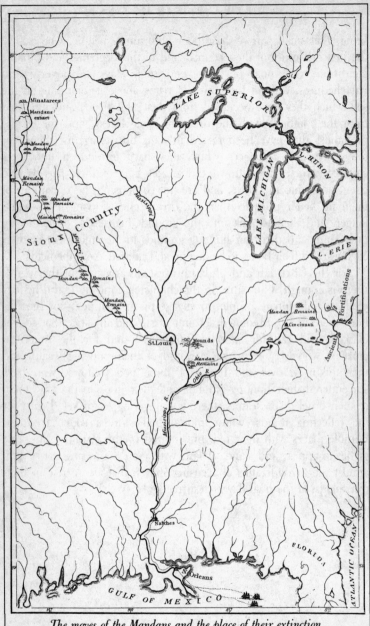

The moves of the Mandans and the place of their extinction.

APPENDIX

◀———▶

Extinction of the Mandans.

*F*rom the accounts brought to New York in the fall of 1838, by
Messrs. M'Kenzie, Mitchell, and others, from the Upper Missouri, and with whom I conversed on the subject, it seems that in
the summer of that year the small-pox was accidentally introduced
amongst the Mandans, by the Fur Traders; and that in the course of
two months they all perished, except some thirty or forty, who were
taken as slaves by the Riccarees; an enemy living two hundred miles
below them, and who moved up and took possession of their village
soon after their calamity, taking up their residence in it, it being a
better built village than their own; and from the lips of one of the
Traders who had more recently arrived from there, I had the following account of the remaining few, in whose destruction was the
final termination of this interesting and once numerous tribe.

The Riccarees, he said, had taken possession of the village after
the disease had subsided, and after living some months in it, were
attacked by a large party of their enemies, the Sioux, and whilst
fighting desperately in resistance, in which the Mandan prisoners
had taken an active part, the latter had concerted a plan for their
own destruction, which was effected by their simultaneously running
through the piquets on to the prairie, calling out to the Sioux (both
men and women) to kill them, "that they were Riccaree dogs, that
their friends were all dead, and they did not wish to live,"—that they
here wielded their weapons as desperately as they could, to excite the
fury of their enemy, and that they were thus cut to pieces and
destroyed.

The accounts given by two or three white men, who were amongst the Mandans during the ravages of this frightful disease, are most appalling and actually too heart-rending and disgusting to be recorded. The disease was introduced into the country by the Fur Company's steamer from St. Louis; which had two of their crew sick with the disease when it approached the Upper Missouri, and imprudently stopped to trade at the Mandan village, which was on the bank of the river, where the chiefs and others were allowed to come on board, by which means the disease got ashore.

I am constrained to believe, that the gentlemen in charge of the steamer did not believe it to be the small-pox; for if they had known it to be such, I cannot conceive of such imprudence, as regarded their own interests in the country, as well as the fate of these poor people, by allowing their boat to advance into the country under such circumstances.

It seems that the Mandans were surrounded by several war-parties of their more powerful enemies the Sioux, at that unlucky time, and they could not therefore disperse upon the plains, by which many of them could have been saved; and they were necessarily enclosed within the piquets of their village, where the disease in a few days became so very malignant that death ensued in a few hours after its attacks; and so slight were their hopes when they were attacked, that nearly half of them destroyed themselves with their knives, with their guns, and by dashing their brains out by leaping head-foremost from a thirty foot ledge of rocks in front of their village. The first symptom of the disease was a rapid swelling of the body, and so very virulent had it become, that very many died in two or three hours after their attack, and that in many cases without the appearance of the disease upon the skin. Utter dismay seemed to possess all classes and all ages, and they gave themselves up in despair, as entirely lost. There was but one continual crying and howling and praying to the Great Spirit for his protection during the nights and days; and there being but few living, and those in too appalling despair, nobody thought of burying the dead, whose bodies, whole families together, were left in horrid and loathsome piles in their own wigwams, with a few buffalo robes, &c. thrown over them, there to decay, and be devoured by their own dogs. That such a proportion of their community as that above-mentioned, should have perished in so short a time, seems yet to the reader, an unaccountable thing; but in addition to the causes just mentioned, it must be borne in mind that this frightful disease is everywhere far more fatal amongst the native than in civilized population, which may be owing to some extraordinary constitutional susceptibility; or, I think more probably, to the exposed lives they live, leading more directly to fatal consequences. In this, as in most of their diseases, they ignorantly and imprudently plunge into the coldest water, whilst in the highest state of fever, and often die before they have the power to get out.

Some have attributed the unexampled fatality of this disease amongst the Indians to the fact of their living entirely on animal food; but so important a subject for investigation I must leave for sounder judgments than mine to decide. They are a people whose constitutions and habits of life enable them most certainly to meet most of its ills with less dread, and with decidedly greater success, than they are met in civilized communities; and I would not dare to decide that their simple meat diet was the cause of their fatal exposure to one frightful disease, when I am decidedly of opinion that it has been the cause of their exemption and protection from another, almost equally destructive, and, like the former, of civilized introduction.

During the season of the ravages of the Asiatic cholera which swept over the greater part of the western country, and the Indian frontier, I was a traveller through those regions, and was able to witness its effects; and I learned from what I saw, as well as from what I have heard in other parts since that time, that it travelled to and over the frontiers, carrying dismay and death amongst the tribes on the borders in many cases, so far as they had adopted the civilized modes of life, with its dissipations, using vegetable food and salt; but wherever it came to the tribes living exclusively on meat, and that without the use of salt, its progress was suddenly stopped. I mention this as a subject which I looked upon as important to science, and therefore one on which I made many careful enquiries; and so far as I have learned along that part of the frontier over which I have since passed, I have to my satisfaction ascertained that such became the utmost limits of this fatal disease in its travel to the West, unless where it might have followed some of the routes of the

Fur Traders, who, of course, have introduced the modes of civilized life.

From the Trader who was present at the destruction of the Mandans I had many most wonderful incidents of this dreadful scene, but I dread to recite them. Amongst them, however, there is one that I must briefly describe, relative to the death of that noble *gentleman* of whom I have already said so much, and to whom I became so much attached, *Mah-to-toh-pa*, or "the Four Bears." This fine fellow sat in his wigwam and watched every one of his family die about him, his wives and his little children, after he had recovered from the disease himself; when he walked out, around the village, and wept over the final destruction of his tribe; his braves and warriors, whose sinewy arms alone he could depend on for a continuance of their existence, all laid low; when he came back to his lodge, where he covered his whole family in a pile, with a number of robes, and wrapping another around himself, went out upon a hill at a little distance, where he laid several days, despite all the solicitations of the Traders, resolved to *starve* himself to death. He remained there till the sixth day, when he had just strength to creep back to the village, when he entered the horrid gloom of his own wigwam, and laying his body along-side of the group of his family, drew his robe over him and died on the ninth day of his fatal abstinence.

So have perished the friendly and hospitable Mandans, from the best accounts I could get; and although it may be *possible* that some few individuals may yet be remaining, I think it is not probable; and one thing is certain, even if such be the case, that, as a nation, the Mandans are extinct, having no longer an existence.

There is yet a melancholy part of the tale to be told, relating to the ravages of this frightful disease in that country on the same occasion, as it spread to other contiguous tribes, to the Minatarrees, the Knisteneaux, the Blackfeet, the Chayennes and Crows; amongst whom 25,000 perished in the course of four or five months, which most appalling facts I got from Major Pilcher, now Superintendent of Indian affairs at St. Louis, from Mr. M'Kenzie, and others.

It may be naturally asked here, by the reader, whether the Government of the United States have taken any measures to prevent the ravages of this fatal disease amongst these exposed tribes; to which I answer, that repeated efforts have been made, and so far generally, as the tribes have ever had the disease, (or, at all events, within the recollections of those who are now living in the tribes,) the Government agents have succeeded in introducing vaccination as a protection; but amongst those tribes in their wild state, and where they have not suffered with the disease, very little success has been met with in the attempt to protect them, on account of their superstitions, which have generally resisted all attempts to introduce vaccination. Whilst I was on the Upper Missouri, several surgeons were sent into the country with the Indian agents, where I several times saw the attempts made without success. They have perfect confidence in the skill of their own physicians, until the disease has made one slaughter in their tribe, and then, having seen white men amongst them protected by it, they were disposed to receive it, before which they cannot believe that so minute a puncture in the arm is going to protect them from so fatal a disease; and as they see white men so earnestly urging it, they decide that it must be some new mode or trick of pale faces, by which they are to gain some new advantage over them, and they stubbornly and successfully resist it.

The Welsh Colony,

Which I barely spoke of in [Letters 21 and 22], which sailed under the direction of Prince Madoc, or Madawc, from North Wales, in the early part of the fourteenth century in ten ships, according to numerous and accredited authors, and never returned to their own country, have been supposed to have landed somewhere on the coast of North or South America; and from the best authorities, (which I will suppose everybody has read, rather than quote them at this time,) I believe it has been pretty clearly proved that they landed either on the coast of Florida, or about the mouth of the Mississippi, and according to the history and poetry of their country, settled somewhere in the interior of North America, where they are yet remaining, intermixed with some of the savage tribes.

In [the letters] just referred to, I barely suggested, that the Mandans, whom I found with so many peculiarities in looks and customs, which I have already described, might possibly be the remains of this lost colony, amalgamated with a tribe, or part of a tribe, of the natives, which would account for the unusual appearances of this tribe of Indians, and also for the changed character and customs of the Welsh colonists, provided these be the remains of them.

Since these notes were written, as will have been seen by my subsequent Letters, and particularly [on pages 273–274], I have descended the Missouri river from the Mandan village to St. Louis, a distance of 1800 miles, and have taken pains to examine its shores; and from the repeated remains of the ancient locations of the Mandans, which I met with on the banks of that river, I am fully convinced that I have traced them down nearly to the mouth of the Ohio river; and from exactly similar appearances, which I recollect to have seen several years since in several places in the interior of the state of Ohio, I am fully convinced that they have formerly occupied that part of the country, and have, from some cause or other, been put in motion, and continued to make their repeated moves until they arrived at the place of their residence at the time of their extinction, on the Upper Missouri.

In the annexed chart of the Missouri and Ohio rivers, will be seen laid down the different positions of the ancient marks of their towns which I have examined; and also, nearly (though not exactly) the positions of the very numerous civilized fortifications which are now remaining on the Ohio and Muskingum rivers, in the vicinity of which I believe the Mandans once lived.

These ancient fortifications, which are very numerous in that vicinity, some of which enclose a great many acres, and being built on the banks of the rivers, with walls in some places twenty or thirty feet in height, with covered ways to the water, evince a knowledge of the science of fortifications, apparently not a century behind that of the present day, were evidently never built by any nation of savages in America, and present to us incontestable proof of the former existence of a people very far advanced in the arts of civilization, who have, from some cause or other, disappeared, and left these imperishable proofs of their former existence.

Now I am inclined to believe that the ten ships of Madoc, or a part of them at least, entered the Mississippi river at the Balize, and made their way up the Mississippi, or that they landed somewhere on the Florida coast, and that their brave and persevering colonists made their way through the interior, to a position on the Ohio river, where they cultivated their fields, and established in one of the finest countries on earth, a flourishing colony; but were at length set upon by the savages, whom, perhaps, they provoked to warfare, being trespassers on their hunting-grounds, and by whom, in overpowering hordes, they were beseiged, until it was necessary to erect these fortifications for their defence, into which they were at last driven by a confederacy of tribes, and there held till their ammunition and provisions gave out, and they in the end have all perished, except, perhaps, that portion of them who might have formed alliance by marriage with the Indians, and their offspring, who would have been half-breeds, and of course attached to the Indians' side; whose lives have been spared in the general massacre; and at length, being despised, as all half-breeds of enemies are, have gathered themselves into a band, and severing from their parent tribe, have moved off, and increased in numbers and strength, as they have advanced up the Missouri river to the place where they have been known for many years past by the name of the *Mandans*, a corruption or abbreviation, perhaps, of *"Madawgwys,"* the name applied by the Welsh to the followers of Madawc.

If this be a startling theory for the world, they will be the more sure to read the following brief reasons which I bring in support of my opinion; and if they do not support me, they will at least be worth knowing, and may, at the same time, be the means of eliciting further and more successful enquiry.

As I have said [on pages 273–276], and in other places, the marks of the Mandan villages are known by the excavations of two feet or more in depth, and thirty or forty feet in diameter, of a circular form, made in the ground for the foundations of their wigwams, which leave a decided remain for centuries, and one that is easily detected the moment that it is met with. After leaving the Mandan village, I found the marks of their former residence about sixty miles below where they were then living, and from which they removed (from their own account) about sixty or eighty years since; and from the appearance of the number of their lodges, I should think, that at that recent date there must have been three times the number that were living when I was amongst them. Near the mouth of the big Shienne river, 200 miles below their last location, I found still more ancient remains, and in as many as six or seven other places between that and the mouth of the Ohio, as I have designated on the chart, and each one, as I visited them, appearing more and more ancient, convincing me that these people, wherever they might have come from, have gradually made their moves up the banks of the Missouri, to the place where I visited them.

For the most part of this distance they have been in the heart of the great Sioux country, and being looked upon by the Sioux as trespassers, have been continually warred upon by this numerous tribe, who have endeavoured to extinguish them, as they have been endeavouring to do ever since our first acquaintance with them; but who, being always fortified by a strong piquet, or stockade, have successfully withstood the assaults of their enemies, and preserved the remnant of their tribe. Through this sort of gauntlet they have run, in passing through the countries of these warlike and hostile tribes.

It may be objected to this, perhaps, that the Riccarees and Minatarees build their wigwams in the same way; but this proves nothing, for the Minatarees are Crows, from the north-west; and by their own showing, fled to the Mandans for protection, and forming their villages by the side of them, built their wigwams in the same manner.

The Riccarees have been a very small tribe, far inferior to the Mandans; and by the traditions of the Mandans, as well as from the evidence of the first explorers, Lewis and Clarke, and others, have lived, until quite lately, on terms of intimacy with the Mandans, whose villages they have successively occupied as the Mandans have moved and vacated them, as they now are doing, since disease has swept the whole of the Mandans away.

Whether my derivation of the word *Mandan* from *Madawgwys* be correct or not, I will pass it over to the world at present merely as *presumptive* proof, for want of better, which, perhaps, this enquiry may elicit; and, at the same time, I offer the Welsh word *Mandon*, (the woodroof, a species of madder used as a red dye,) as the name that might possibly have been applied by their Welsh neighbours to these people, on account of their very ingenious mode of giving the beautiful red and other dyes to the porcupine quills with which they garnish their dresses.

In their own language they called themselves *See-pohs-ka-nu-mah-ka-kee*, (the people of the pheasants,) which was probably the name of the primitive stock, before they were mixed with any other people; and to have got such a name, it is natural to suppose that they must have come from a country where *pheasants* existed, which cannot be found short of reaching the timbered country at the base of the Rocky Mountains, some six or eight hundred miles West of the Mandans, or the forests of Indiana and Ohio, some hundreds of miles to the South and East of where they last lived.

The above facts, together with the other one which they repeatedly related to me, and which I have before alluded to, that they had often been to the hill of the *Red Pipe Stone*, and that they once lived near it, carry conclusive evidence, I think, that they have formerly occupied a country much farther to the South; and that they have repeatedly changed their locations, until they reached the spot of their last residence, where they have met with their final misfortune. And as evidence in support of my opinion that they came from the banks of the Ohio, and have brought with them some of the customs of the civilized people who erected those ancient fortifications, I am able to say, that the numerous specimens of pottery which have been taken from the graves and tumuli about those ancient works, (many of which may be seen now, in the Cincinnati Museum, and some of which, my own donations, and which have so much surprised the enquiring world,) were to be seen in great numbers in the use of the Mandans; and scarcely a day in the summer, when the visitor to their village would not see the women at work with their hands and fingers, moulding them from black clay, into vases, cups, pitchers, and pots, and baking them in their little kilns in the sides of the hill, or under the bank of the river.

In addition to this art, which I am sure belongs to no other tribe on the Continent, these people have also, as a secret with themselves, the extraordinary art of manufacturing a very beautiful and lasting kind of blue glass beads, which they wear on their necks in great quantities, and decidedly value above all others that are brought amongst them by the Fur Traders.

This secret is not only one that the Traders did not introduce amongst them, but one that they cannot learn from them; and at the same time, beyond a doubt, an art that has been introduced amongst them by some civilized people, as it is as yet unknown to other Indian tribes in that vicinity, or elsewhere. Of this interesting fact, Lewis and Clarke have given an account thirty-three years ago, at a time when no Traders, or other white people, had been amongst the Mandans, to have taught them so curious an art.

The Mandan canoes which are altogether different from those of all other tribes, are exactly the Welsh *coracle*, made of *raw-hides*, the skins of buffaloes, stretched underneath a frame made of willow or other boughs, and shaped nearly round, like a tub; which the woman carries on her head from her wigwam to the water's edge, and having stepped into it, stands in front, and propels it by dipping her paddle *forward*, and *drawing it to her*, instead of paddling by the side . . .

How far these extraordinary facts may go in the estimation of the reader, with numerous others which I have mentioned, whilst speaking of the Mandans, of their various complexions, colours of hair, and blue and grey eyes, towards establishing my opinion as a sound theory, I cannot say; but this much I can safely aver, that at the moment that I first saw these people, I was so struck with the peculiarity of their appearance, that I was under the instant conviction that they were an amalgam of a native, with some civilized race; and from what I have seen of them, and of the remains on the Missouri and Ohio rivers, I feel fully convinced that these people have emigrated from the latter stream; and that they have, in the manner that I have already stated, with many of their customs, been preserved from the *almost total* destruction of the bold colonists of Madawc, who, I believe, settled upon and occupied for a century or so, the rich and fertile banks of the Ohio. In adducing the proof for the support of this theory, if I have failed to complete it, I have the satisfaction that I have not taken up much of the reader's time, and I can therefore claim his attention a few moments longer, whilst I refer him to a brief vocabulary of the Mandan langauge in the following pages, where he may compare it with that of the Welsh; and better, perhaps, than I can, decide whether there is any affinity existing between the two; and if he finds it, it will bring me a friendly aid in support of the position I have taken.

From the comparison, that I have been able to make, I think I am authorized to say, that in the following list of words, which form a part of that vocabulary, there is a striking similarity, and quite sufficient to excite surprise in the minds of the attentive reader, if it could be proved that those resemblances were but the results of accident between two foreign and distinct idioms.

English.	Mandan.	Welsh.	Pronounced.
I	Me	Mi	Me
You	Ne	Chwi	Chwe
He	E	A	A
She	Ea	E	A
It	Ount	Hwynt	Hooynt
We	Noo	Ni	Ne
They	Eonah	Hwna *mas.*	Hoona
		Hona *fem.*	Hona
Those ones	Yrhai	Hyna	
No, or, there is not	Megosh	Nagoes	Nagosh
No		Nage	
		Nag	
		Na	
Head	Pan	Pen	Pan
The Great Spirit	Maho peneta	Mawr penaethir*	Maoor panaether
		Ysprid mawr†	Uspryd maoor

*To act as a great chief—head or principal—sovereign or supreme.
†The Great Spirit.

INDEX

◀━━━━━━━▶

NOTE: The names of Indian tribes are spelled as in the original text. Place names also conform to Catlin's spellings but their modern versions are included in brackets.

Abbé (U.S. ranger), 338
Abysinian [Abyssinian] chiefs, 102
Africans, 460
Aged people, 213–15
Agriculture
  and Cherokees, 392
  and Creeks, 396
  and Ioways, 284
  and Mandans, 124, 137, 138, 143, 182
  and Minatarees, 190–92
  and Mo-hee-con-neuhs, 369
  and Pawnee Picts, 335, 337
  and Senecas, 375
  and Shawanos, 388, 391–92
  and Sioux, 410
Ah-ton-we-tuck (the cock turkey), *363*, 364
Alabama, 384, 396
Alleghany [Allegheny] mountains, 4, 368
Alleghany [Allegheny] river, 388
Alton, Ill., 359
America, aboriginal stocks of, 464–65
  See also United States; United States Government
American Fur Company, 9, 51, 136, 203, 206, 241, 435, 446
Americans, 33, 421, 485
Amusements. *See* Games
Anglo-Americans, 467
Anishinasi, the. *See* Ojibbeways, the

Antelope, 15, 69, 307
Antelope, the. *See* Ko-ka
Arapahoes, the, 296, 311, 386
Arikaras, the. *See* Riccarees, the
Arkansas, the (river), 283, 296, 297, 301, 392, 393, 396
Armstrong, Major, 350
Asia
  North of, 464
  Steppes of, 70
Assinneboins, the, 17, 20, 42, 63–64, 202
  customs of, 99
  games of, 55
  as hunters, 55
  language of, 55
  numbers of, 52
  personal appearance of, 55
Atlantic coast, 4, 61, 62, 378, 385, 388, 475, 479
  states on, 61
  towns on, 442
Atlantic Ocean, 97, 262
Atlas (Greek legendary figure), 459
Atrocities, 483–84

Badgers, 180
Bad River. *See* Teton river
Bad Spirits, 38
  See also Evil Spirit
Balize, the, 296
Bathing, of Mandans, 93–94, 186